Studies in Economic Transition

This series brings together theoretical and empirical studies on the transformation of economic systems and their economic development. The transition from planned to market economies is one of the main areas of applied theory because in this field the most dramatic examples of change and economic dynamics can be found. It is aimed to contribute to the understanding of specific major economic changes as well as to advance the theory of economic development. The implications of economic policy will be a major point of focus.

More information about this series at
http://www.palgrave.com/gp/series/14147

Michael Landesmann • István P. Székely
Editors

Does EU Membership Facilitate Convergence? The Experience of the EU's Eastern Enlargement - Volume II

Channels of Interaction

palgrave
macmillan

Editors
Michael Landesmann
Vienna Institute for International
Economic Studies (WIIW)
Vienna, Austria

István P. Székely
DG ECFIN, European Commission
Brussels, Belgium

Corvinus University of Budapest
Budapest, Hungary

ISSN 2662-6675 ISSN 2662-6683 (electronic)
Studies in Economic Transition
ISBN 978-3-030-57701-8 ISBN 978-3-030-57702-5 (eBook)
https://doi.org/10.1007/978-3-030-57702-5

This Palgrave Macmillan imprint is published by the registered company Springer Nature Switzerland AG.
The registered company address is: Gewerbestrasse 11, 6330 Cham, Switzerland

Praise for *Does EU Membership Facilitate Convergence? The Experience of the EU's Eastern Enlargement - Volume II*

"The volume is an excellent account of how the EU convergence machine worked for the CEEC. Questions arise: will it continue? why has it stalled with some "older" EU members?"

—Marek Belka, *member of the European Parliament, former Prime Minister and Finance Minister of Poland*

"To create greater convergence, we need more integration". This message, conveyed recently by a distinguished European statesman, perfectly reflects the key hypothesis this book discusses. By relevant and balanced synthesis of theory, empirical findings and country experiences, the book provides comprehensive and multi-dimensional insight into all important aspects of the linkages between integration and convergence, a rich material of a value-added to scholars, policymakers and corporate managers. Researchers will particularly value the model-based framework that builds on the various channels through which EU membership influences convergence. For policymakers such as myself, this book serves as a reminder of unique changes and reforms we witnessed and contributed to in the recent past but, more importantly, as an inspiration on how to face and address current challenges, from climate change, ageing to migration."

—Boris Vujčić, Governor, *Croatian National Bank*

"This two-volume study is a truly major contribution to our understanding of key issues related to the convergence of the New Member States of the European Union (EU11) to the frontier. The editors, Michael Landesmann and István P. Székely, and authors are among the most experienced analysts in this area and their contributions constitute a veritable tour de force. The focus on economic, institutional and social aspects of convergence, together with their interaction, is very appropriate and provides a rich set of insights into the past evolution and likely future trends. The two volumes are important by providing an in-depth analysis of the convergence of EU11, but their relevance is much broader, including the importance of what I would call the terminal conditions – the possibility of entering the EU – a factor with great effects that cannot be analyzed in the context of other emerging market economies. The authors identify the weakness of institutions as a major potential limitation on the speed of EU 11 convergence in the future. The EU 11 countries have performed remarkably well and I am hopeful, together with the authors of these two volumes, that these countries will tackle successfully their present and future challenges. The two volumes are a must read for everyone interested in EU11 and emerging market economies in general."

—Jan Svejnar, *James T. Shotwell Professor of Global Political Economy and Founding Director of the Center on Global Economic Governance at Columbia University's School of International and Public Affairs*

"This two volume collection is a treasure chest of timely information on the accession to the Economic Union (EU) of former Warsaw-Pact nations. Volume I presents overall analysis of convergence and extensive background information on the new members. Volume II contains careful analyses of four major linkages among new and old EU members, namely trade, finance, migration, and institutional reform, with a focus on the impacts of interdependencies across countries and their role in convergence. The authors of the individual chapters are well-known scholars in transition economics and in-country specialists in the topics. Experts in the field, the editors have compiled scholarship that is invaluable to anyone, researcher and student alike, who is interested in the future prospects for the newly constituted EU. This two-volume book is a must for academic libraries and the bookshelves of researchers. Students will find much useful information to supplement course materials."

—John Bonin, *Chester D. Hubbard Professor of Economics and Social Science at Wesleyan University*

"Economic convergence in Central and Eastern Europe is an absolutely central question for public policy in national but also EU context. This volume provides sound analysis about the long-term trends, especially for the period following the first EU enlargement in 2004. Readers must be pleased to see that the attention of the editors and authors expanded beyond macroeconomics, finance and trade to sensitive issues like migration, corruption and climate as well."

—László Andor, *Former European Commissioner*

"What was the impact of the Eastern Enlargement of the European Union regarding the convergence of new and existing members? This is a splendid collection of essays that cover an rich body of national experiences and offer detailed analysis about the main channels through which accession affected convergence. It is required reading for scholars and policy-makers interested in globalization, integration, and transition."

—Nauro F. Campos, *Professor of Economics, University College London, and Director, UCL Centre for Comparative Economics*

"From this an informative and interesting volume, readers may learn more than they may have wanted to learn, about the process of convergence of the 11 "transition economies" that became EU members in past years. The main message in the book, perhaps a not surprising one, is that, joining the EU gave the EU11 access to a large market and to a lot of foreign investment. These contributed to their economic "growth". Unfortunately, as the first development economists learned 70 years ago, and as many modern economists forgot, economic growth is not the same thing as developments. Development depends on the existence of institutions that distribute widely the benefits of economic growth. The creation of these institutions is more difficult than the generation of growth because it depends on established local cultural traits. In the EU11 countries, institutional or social development has lagged behind their growth. This is likely to create potential future problems."

—Vito Tanzi, *former Director of the Fiscal Affairs Department of the IMF*

Contents

Notes on Contributors

Agnieszka Chłoń-Domińczak is an associate professor and Director of the Institute of Statistics and Demography in the SGH Warsaw School of Economics. In the past, she was the Deputy Minister of Labour and Social Policy overseeing the social insurance system and a member of the 1999 pension reform team in Poland. She is an author of many publications in the field of pensions, social protection, labour markets and education.

Ştefan Ciobanu heads the Fiscal Governance Unit (in charge of national fiscal frameworks) in the European Commission's DG ECFIN. Before joining the Commission in 2011, he worked in the Romanian public administration on EU affairs and management of EU funds. Stefan holds a BA in international business administration from the Academy of Economic Studies and an MA in European public administration from the National University of Political Studies and Public Administration (both in Bucharest).

Fabrizio Coricelli Is a professor in the Department of Political and International Science at the University of Siena and emeritus professor at the Paris School of Economics. He is a research fellow at the Centre for Economic Policy Research (CEPR). He holds a PhD from the University of Pennsylvania. He has previously worked at the International Monetary Fund, the World Bank, the EBRD and the European Commission. His research interest is in international economics, economic integration and the link between institutions and economic growth.

Adam Czelleng is a Director at GKI Economic Research, where he has led various research and consultancy projects for international institutions, financial institutions, multinational and Hungarian companies, public institutions and local governments. Previously, he worked for three years in investment banking. He participated in a working group of the Hungarian Academy of Sciences and was guest lecturer at various Hungarian universities.

Marco Frigerio is a research fellow of Banking and Finance in the Department of Economics, Management and Quantitative methods of the University of Milan. In 2006 he graduated in Economics from the University of Siena. He holds a PhD in Economics, Markets, Institutions from the IMT Lucca Institute for Advanced Studies. His research interests are in financial economics, monetary economics, international finance and development banks.

Miklós Hajdu graduated from Eötvös Loránd University in 2014. He holds a master degree in survey statistics. He joined the team of the Corruption Research Center Budapest (CRCB) in 2015. His main research interests are the methodological problems of data collection and analysis. He is also interested in research on corruption, hidden economy, rent seeking and quality of government. He is working as an assistant lecturer at the Corvinus University of Budapest (CUB) teaching quantitative methods.

Leire Ormaetxea Igarzabal obtained her MSc in Economics and Politics from the University of Freiburg im Breisgau (Germany), where she also worked as a teaching assistant for Advanced Macroeconomics. After a traineeship at the European Fiscal Board, in 2017 she joined the fiscal governance team at the European Commission's DG ECFIN. She is part of the team that manages DG ECFIN's Fiscal Governance Database, and recently she has started working on subnational fiscal rules.

László Jankovics received his PhD in Economics from the University of Debrecen, Hungary, in 2007. In 2006, he joined the European Commission's DG ECFIN as an economic and fiscal analyst, where the functioning of independent fiscal institutions has recently become his main dossier. In 2009 and 2010, he served as director for fiscal analysis at the Office of the Hungarian Fiscal Council. He is the author of several publications on fiscal governance and economic policy issues.

Jorge Durán Laguna is a senior economist at the European Commission since 2009, first at the Directorate-General of Enterprise and Industry and since 2013 in Economic and Financial Affairs. He holds a PhD in Economics from Universidad Carlos III de Madrid. He was a professor at several universities in Spain, Belgium and Mexico. He was a Marie Curie Fellow in CEPREMAP, France, in 2001–02.

Michael Landesmann is a senior research associate, former Scientific Director (1996–2016), of the Vienna Institute for International Economic Studies (WIIW), and Professor of Economics at the Johannes Kepler University, Austria. He has a DPhil from Oxford University and taught and researched at Cambridge University's Department of Applied Economics and Jesus College, Cambridge. He held many visiting professorships including the Pierre Keller and Schumpeter professorships at Harvard University.

Werner Roeger is the former head of the unit "Models and Databases" in the Directorate General for Economics and Finance at the European Commission in Brussels. He received his PhD from the University of Freiburg (Germany) and worked at the Institute for Applied Economic Research in the University of Tübingen before joining the European Commission in 1988. In 2001 he was a visiting professor at Humboldt University in Berlin. His research interests focus on quantitative analysis of fiscal and structural policies as well as the analysis of external and internal imbalances.

Septimiu Szabo is an economist at the European Commission with a background in economics, public finance and regional development. Previously he worked as a public manager in the Romanian government dealing with public finance, programme management and international affairs. He holds a PhD in Economics from Bucharest University of Economic Studies and is a former Fulbright Fellow.

István P. Székely is a principal advisor in the Directorate General for Economic and Financial Affairs at the European Commission and honorary professor at Corvinus University of Budapest. He has a PhD in economics from the University of Cambridge. Before joining the European Commission in 2007, he worked at the International Monetary Fund and the National Bank of Hungary as a general manager and advisor to the governor. His research focuses on financial market and macroeconomic policy issues and on Central and Eastern European economies.

István János Tóth is a senior research fellow at the Centre for Economic and Regional Studies (CERS) and managing director of Corruption Research Center Budapest (CRCB). He obtained his PhD from the Hungarian Academy of Sciences in 1998. His main research interests are the problems of corruption, economic institutions and good governance. He worked as an expert for the World Bank, EBRD, OECD and European Commission.

János Varga is an economist at the European Commission, DG Economic and Financial Affairs, where he is a member of the macroeconomic modelling team. He obtained his postgraduate research degree in economics from the Central European University in Budapest. Prior to joining the European Commission, he worked as a research assistant at Collegium Budapest—Institute for Advanced Studies and Harvard University. His research focuses on structural reforms, climate change and cohesion policy assessment.

Jan in 't Veld is an economist and the Head of Sector at the European Commission, DG Economic and Financial Affairs. He holds degrees from the Free University in Amsterdam, the London School of Economics and obtained his PhD in Economics from Birkbeck College (University of London). Before joining the European Commission, he worked at the National Institute of Economic and Social Research (NIESR) in London. His research interests are in the areas of macromodelling, fiscal policy and structural reforms.

Andras Vertes is an expert in economic research, focus on macroeconomic analysis, in Hungary. Since 1998, he has been the Chairman of the Board of GKI Economic Research, the biggest independent economic research institute in Central Europe. Previously, he was the head of Department at the National Planning Office and chief executive officer at GKI Economic research. He is the Deputy Chairman of the Business Hungary Association and Vice-Chair of the Business at OECD Economic Policy Committee.

Hermine Vidovic is senior economist at the Vienna Institute for International Economic Studies, wiiw, where her research focuses on labour markets, social policy and migration. She has been working on several studies for DG Employment, the ILO, ETF and Austrian authorities. She is the lead author of the Western Balkans Labor Market Trends report, which is conducted in cooperation with the World Bank. Vidovic obtained her MA degree in Economics from the Vienna University of Economics and Business Administration.

Lúcio Vinhas de Souza is an advisor in the Directorate General for Economic and Financial Affairs at the European Commission. Previously, he headed the economics team at EPSC at the European Commission and served as managing director and chief economist at Moody's in New York. In the past, he also worked at the World Bank, DG ECFIN, the Kiel Institute for World Economics and the United Nations Secretariat in New York. He holds a PhD in economics from the Erasmus University Rotterdam and master and bachelor degrees in economics from the New University of Lisbon.

List of Figures

List of Charts

List of Tables

CHAPTER 1

Introduction: The Working of the Channels of Interaction Between the EU and the EU11 Member States

Michael Landesmann and István P. Székely

Starting on 1 May 2004, 11 countries in Central-Eastern and South-Eastern Europe and in the Baltics (EU11) joined the European Union (EU) in three consecutive waves.[1] Half a generation later, and a full

The views expressed are solely those of the authors and do not necessarily represent the official views of the European Commission.

[1] We will refer to the region as CESE and the 11 countries as EU11 and to the process as the eastern enlargement of the EU throughout the two volumes.

M. Landesmann
Vienna Institute for International Economic Studies (WIIW), Vienna, Austria
e-mail: landesmann@wiiw.ac.at

I. P. Székely (✉)
DG ECFIN, European Commission, Brussels, Belgium

Corvinus University of Budapest, Budapest, Hungary
e-mail: istvan-pal.szekely@ec.europa.eu

M. Landesmann, I. P. Székely (eds.), *Does EU Membership Facilitate Convergence? The Experience of the EU's Eastern Enlargement - Volume II*, Studies in Economic Transition,
https://doi.org/10.1007/978-3-030-57702-5_1

generation after the start of transition in the region, we thought it would be opportune to look into the convergence experience of these countries. The two volumes of this book offer a collection of contributions on this matter.

Volume I sets out the analytical framework for analysis and focuses on the country experiences, that is, it looks at the various issues involved and the way they emerged and interacted with each other in these countries.

This volume, Volume II, looks into the channels of interaction between the EU and EU11 countries. That is, the contributions in this volume focus on the different channels relevant for convergence processes for all the countries or a subset of them.

A unique characteristic of the convergence process in this part of Europe relative to other European countries and middle-income countries in other parts of the world is EU membership. Thus, like in Volume I, the focus is on this and the authors ask the following basic research questions: What impact did the EU have on the convergence process in EU11? What difference did it make, relative to other converging economies, that these countries were part of a closely knit supranational organization?

1.1 The Channels of Interaction

Chapter 2 in Volume I sets out a framework to analyse convergence in a country, or a group of countries, which belongs to the EU. This framework identifies the channels through which EU membership influences economic, institutional and social convergence in a member state: the trade, investment, finance, mobility and institutional channels. The first four of these channels are related to the four freedoms in the EU, albeit structured somewhat differently, the free movement of goods, services, capital and people. The institutional channel captures the way the EU shapes national institutions, as defined by Douglas North, that is, laws, rules, norms and institutions. The channels also interact, strengthen or weaken each other. These interactions are very important as they can change the nature of the process over time and can make it state dependent.

The EU is not the only supranational institution that affects the development of EU11 and their peer groups of converging middle-income countries in other parts of the world. There are several international organizations that impact on and facilitate the channels this framework identifies, such as the WTO, which was created to facilitate and regulate the trade channel at the global level. There are also other regional supranational organizations that promote regional integration in other parts of the world, such as ASEAN. However, the EU represents a much deeper integration of its member states. Thus, its impact is much more direct and much stronger than that of other such organizations.

Regarding the role of the four channels identified above, the overall analysis in Volume I suggests that the trade and investment channels worked well and provided a strong growth impetus to EU11. Regarding foreign trade, within this rather short period, EU11 countries became the most open economies in the world. This was a unique development in the world; very few other countries outside Europe followed a similar trend, and trade openness in the world economy as a whole did not significantly change much during this period. Chapter 2 in this volume offers a model-based analysis of the contribution of the single market of the EU to growth and economic development in the EU. This analysis supports the findings of the overall analysis mentioned above. Without a single market for trade, EU countries would have lower income levels. In fact, the gain the single market offers is bigger for EU11 than the rest of the EU, because these countries on average are more open than the rest of the EU.

Chapter 3 analyses foreign direct investment (FDI) flows in EU11, that is the working of the private part of the investment channel. This analysis too supports the overall analysis in Volume I mentioned above. The stock of inward FDI relative to GDP in EU11 rapidly reached the levels observed in countries that had been open market economies for a much longer period of time. While FDI became a main driving force in many successful middle-income countries too, the development in EU11 was closely linked to EU membership. A large part of inward FDI came from other EU countries, and a significant portion was related to global value chains set up by EU countries in industries that went through such development also at the global level, such as car production.

The analyses presented in these chapters also support the general finding in the literature regarding the strong interaction between the trade and investment channels. Close trade integration, the single market of the EU, induces major FDI flows, which in turn create further trade flows. Institutional convergence further amplifies this positive interaction by creating a legally safe environment for FDI.

Chapters 4 and 5 investigate the public part of the investment channel by analysing the impact of EU funds on economic development in EU11. Using dynamic stochastic general equilibrium models, they find that EU funds made a major contribution to accelerating growth and during the crisis stabilized the external and fiscal balances of EU11 countries. While a large contribution of FDI to growth is a global phenomenon, such a strong role of the public part of the investment channel is a unique characteristic of the convergence process of EU11. Official financing for other middle-income countries, particularly the grant component of it, is much less and of narrower focus, and it is phased out at a much lower income level.

Chapters 6 and 7 focus on the finance channel, which played a mixed role in the convergence process. As the analysis in Chap. 6 shows, the eastern enlargement took place during a period of rapid increase in cross-border financial flows in the world and in the EU. A large part of the globally significant surplus savings of some of the EU countries found its way into the rest of the EU, mostly through the financial system in the Southern European countries, and more or less equally distributed between FDI and financial flows in the EU11. As a result, credit to the private sector relative to the GDP reached historical heights in both groups. However, the crisis that started in 2008–09 quickly reversed this trend, in fact fully erased the former gain in Southern Europe. However, in EU11, a significant part of the increase in the degree of financial intermediation has been preserved, and despite the ups and downs, this brought them in line with the levels observed in other middle-income countries. Given their very low starting point in this area, a legacy of their central planning past, this is a major development.

The analysis of firm-level data in Chap. 7 offers an explanation for these developments, both in EU11 and in Southern Europe. It finds that while intra-sectoral misallocation of capital through corporate lending in the banking sector was present in Southern Europe, this was not the case in EU11. Put simply, the expansion of corporate lending was largely healthy in EU11, and thus was preserved even after the crisis. Misallocation among sectors, most importantly an inordinate growth in lending to the real estate and construction sectors, and to households in the form of mortgage loans, was a general phenomenon in both groups, and globally. Hence the strong re-adjustment in both groups.

The migration channel also shaped the convergence process in EU11 in important ways. As the analysis in Chap. 8 shows, cross-border migration increased significantly after EU accession, albeit from rather low levels by international comparison and to greatly varying extents in individual EU11 countries. While evidence in the literature suggests that the overall welfare impact of increased mobility in EU11 was positive for the EU as a whole, the gains were distributed unequally. The mobility impacts on the

EU11 countries were considerably higher in relative (and absolute) terms than for the other EU countries, but with mixed short-term and longer-term results. Thus the 'migration rent' is distributed between the migrants themselves and the countries of destination, and in the countries' origin there can be positive short-term (reduced unemployment rates, remittances) but also substantial negative longer-term impacts (such as on the age structure, labour force and skill shortages). Further there are differential impacts on low-skill and high-skill people in EU11 and in the rest of the EU (often in opposite directions).

The impact on the sections of the low-skill labour force in the receiving countries, which might have suffered a rather small (but significant) loss, deserves special attention. In the light of Brexit, this is an important lesson, which suggests that it is crucial to understand how these channels work and interact, and to complement their working with public policies that mitigate negative side effects. The gains are plenty to pay for this, albeit they may not emerge in the same fiscal constituency where the need arises, so internal and cross-border fiscal transfers might be needed. Such transfers are never easy to implement politically.

The analysis also shows strong interaction between the investment (FDI) and migration channels. An increase in FDI tended to go together with a moderation in net outward migration, and vice versa. As FDI was highly concentrated in certain geographical areas of EU11 countries, mostly in capitals and in regions close to those companies in EU15, mostly in Germany, which created global value chains. FDI also induced internal migration inside EU11 countries, mostly of young low-/medium-skill people.

The overall assessment of the convergence experience of EU11 countries suggests that the institutional channel has not worked well in the EU. The rapid economic convergence was not matched by a comparable institutional convergence in EU11. In fact, most of the institutional convergence took place before EU accession.

The remaining chapters of this volume (Chaps. 9, 10, 11 and 12) look into different aspects of institutional convergence in EU11 and the working of the institutional channel in the EU.

Corruption is a mechanism of central importance that can undermine improvements in institutional quality, which in turn weakens the trade, investment and financial channels, and thus slows economic convergence. Moreover, it also reduces the capacity of a country to turn economic convergence into social convergence. An area where the role of corruption is particularly important is public procurement, the focus of Chap. 9. A large part of EU funding reaches the economy through public procurement. Corruption in this part can significantly reduce allocative efficiency and the efficiency with which the selected projects are implemented. Moreover, particularly in net contributor countries, it weakens public and political support to sizable EU funding for lower-income members (regions). Such funding, as we mentioned above, is a unique characteristic of the convergence process in EU11, which has the potential to significantly accelerate economic convergence. As the transaction-level econometric analysis in Chap. 9 shows, the level of corruption control varied significantly among EU11 countries, and over time, and it was an important element of the deterioration in institutional quality in Southern Europe.

Climate change, the focus of Chap. 10, is among the biggest challenges mankind faces at this stage. In total, 93% of European Union citizens see climate change as a serious problem. The EU has been at the forefront of the fight against climate change. As one of its actions, the newly elected European Parliament declared a climate and environment emergency in November 2019, and the newly elected European Commission proposed a European Green Deal in December.

As a legacy of their shared Soviet-type centrally planned past, EU11 countries started the economic transition with highly energy- and carbon-intensive economies. As the analysis in Chap. 10 shows, since then, they embarked on a unique path of rapid decarbonization of their economies. No other group of medium-income countries has managed to follow such a path so far. Their energy intensity declined rapidly in the early phase of transition as the oversized heavy industry collapsed and remained on a relatively fast declining trend afterwards as they restructured their economies. The reduction in carbon-intensity of energy use was more gradual but continuous, as there were more hurdles to transforming their energy systems (Fig. 1.1).

EU membership played an important role in bringing about these positive developments, directly and indirectly. Plant-level empirical analysis shows that power plants in EU11, after controlling for all relevant factors, emitted less CO_2 than other plants in the Central-Eastern and South-Eastern Europe (CESE) region, the longer the membership in the EU the stronger this impact. FDI played an important role in allowing EU11 countries to rapidly re-industrialize their economies and benefit from trade globalization and FDI without reversing the declining trend of CO_2 intensity. As mentioned above one of the key findings of these volumes is

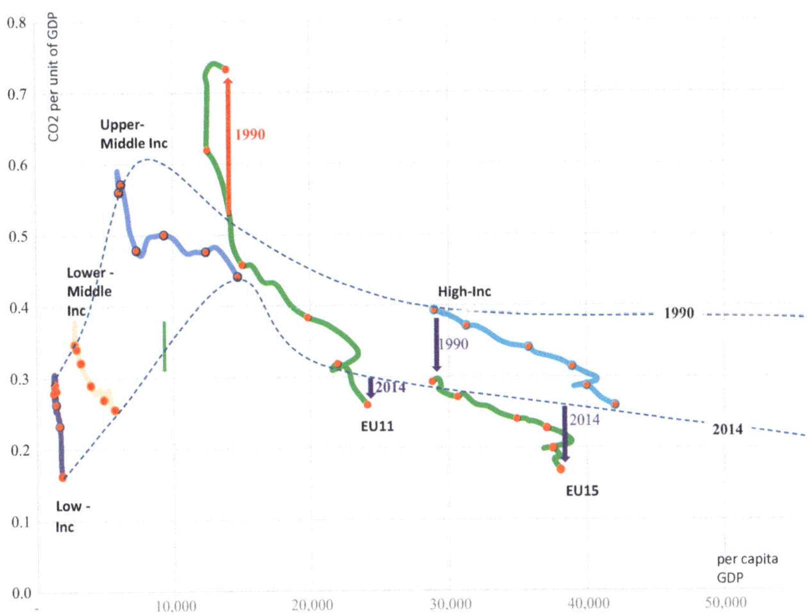

Fig. 1.1 Carbon emission Kuznets curves 1990–2014. (Source: Székely 2021)

that the speed of institutional convergence did not keep up with the pace of economic convergence and even regressed at times after EU accession. However, in this area the opposite was true. EU membership helped EU11 countries to quickly catch up with high-income countries regarding the CO_2 intensity of their economies.

Another unique characteristic of the convergence process in EU11 is the strong impact of EU membership on their fiscal institutions, a manifestation of the institutional channel. Chapter 11 focuses on this aspect. This is a rather recent development, which emerged as a reaction of the EU to the European sovereign debt crisis. It is evident that the institutional channel remains important after EU accession. As a result, EU11 countries are equipped with fiscal institutions that are typically observable in highly developed countries. Given the findings in the literature that good-quality fiscal institutions tend to enhance growth potential in the medium to long run, this is a potentially growth-enhancing development. Only potentially, because institutions do not always work in the way that is most helpful to economic and social convergence, a phenomenon Székely and Ward-Warmedinger (2018) call *behavioural reversal.* They analyse several concrete examples of this, some in this very area, resulting in counter-cyclical fiscal policies particularly during strong upturns.

The pension system is a central part of the fiscal system, with direct relevance to the relationship between economic and social convergence. EU legislation has little direct impact on the design of the pension systems in member states. Nevertheless, as the discussion in Chap. 12 shows, the institutional channel still works through other forms in this area. Most evidently, through the European Semester, in which countries were given numerous country-specific recommendations regarding pension system design, mostly to enhance their sustainability and to improve labour market participation, both being critical given the rapid population ageing in the EU. Reform reversals in this area in EU11 are prominent examples of reversals that were observable in the region.

1.2 Looking Forward: Will Rapid Economic Convergence in EU11 Continue?

While most of the analyses focus on the historical experience of EU11, the main messages of these two volumes concern the future of the region. The weakness of the institutional channel is clearly a major potential limitation on the speed of convergence in the future. While this is an important finding for EU11, it fits with the main findings of the traditional convergence/development literature. Social cohesion and climate change are however newly emerging areas of development that can put severe limitations on the pace of convergence in the future, hence the separate discussion on these aspects above. Weakening social cohesion not only reduces the growth potential of a country by limiting labour force participation and human capital utilization and accumulation, but can also lead to weakening institutions and to reform reversals. This is the political economy of convergence, which is as important as the economics of the process. Deteriorating the environment, and particularly aggravating climate change, will no doubt also limit the development of high-income countries at or close to the frontier and the convergence of others to the frontier. Any hindrances to the development of the global frontier also make convergence a much more vulnerable process, increasing inter alia the likelihood of geo-political tensions.

As the experience of Southern European EU members shows, and as the vast literature on the middle-income trap points out, getting closer to the frontier changes the nature of the economic convergence process. The relative importance of different factors changes rapidly. While this is well described in the literature in general and historically, there is yet little research available on the impact of the current wave of rapid and disruptive technological change and on the reforms that are necessary to break through the middle-income threshold inside the EU. Volume I fills some of this gap by drilling into the key factors that will determine future convergence in EU11, allocative efficiency and innovation.

1.3 The Corona Crisis and the Future of Convergence in the European Union

Since the submission of the manuscript to the publisher a rather dramatic break in global developments has taken place: the outbreak of a severe health crisis in the form of the Covid-19 virus epidemic. For months, Europe became the epicentre of a worldwide health crisis, having the highest infection and deaths rates in the world.

Most EU11 countries did relatively well during the epidemic to maintain relatively low infection and death rates. Studies show that this was due to early and rigorous lockdown policies. However, the early economic impact with sharply declining production and GDP levels was rather similar to that experienced in most Western European countries. The most vulnerable countries were those that depended most on trade, in particular those that hosted cross-border production networks, and those that depended strongly on tourism (see Grieveson, 2020).

What is the likely impact in the future? In the immediate future, these countries face similar problems as other European countries. Public spending will be crucial to compensate for the hesitant resumption of consumption and private investment after a relaxation of the lockdown. Public debt will increase sharply as GDP declines and fiscal stimulus kicks in. While this is likely to be a general trend in Europe, there are important specific factors that will shape macroeconomic developments in the region.

Like other severely affected countries, EU11 countries will receive massive financial support from the EU. At the time of writing, the next financial framework (MFF) for the years 2021–27 is still being negotiated. Nevertheless, it is likely that due to the corona-crisis, the EU budget will be significantly strengthened, through the Next Generation EU facility, and front-loaded and targeted towards countering the effects of the crisis, while maintaining longer-term priorities by investing in a green, digital and resilient Europe. Moreover, CEE countries will be able to benefit from the various new schemes that the EU has been setting up as a collective response to the economic crisis, such as SURE, a new instrument for temporary Support to mitigate Unemployment Risks in an Emergency, or the Pan-European Guarantee Fund set up by the European Investment Bank (EIB) to support SMEs. Financial support from the EU will take away some of the pressure on their national budgets and will allow them to spread their additional borrowing over a long period.

In the countries where public debt was relatively high prior to the pandemic, such as Croatia, Hungary and Slovenia, 'fiscal space' available to governments to give a stimulus to the economy from their own budgets is somewhat smaller than in other EU11 countries. Thus, their structural deficit is likely to deteriorate less and/or for shorter period. Consequently, the increase in the public debt ratio is not likely to be sizable in these countries either, albeit their policy responses may be somewhat hindered by this limitation. Therefore, albeit for different reasons, debt sustainability is unlikely to be a major issue in the region. The first post-pandemic economic forecast of the European Commission confirms these trends.

Developments regarding international trade and external finance in the region will also be somewhat different from general trends in Europe and globally. The dependence of EU11 countries on foreign capital fell quite dramatically because of the improvements in their current accounts position following the financial crisis. Hence, they are less affected by short-term capital outflows than emerging economies globally.

However, the situation in this regard is different in the South East European (SEE) countries (particularly in the West Balkan) which had sizable trade deficits prior to the pandemic, in large part covered by remittances. As people from these countries who work abroad are going to face very harsh labour market situations, and as many of them have already returned home, remittance flows are likely to subside for an extended period. Foreign direct investment will also ebb for a while, as international companies will be hesitant to expand (or even maintain) their operations abroad.

On the other hand, EU11, and perhaps even more so SEE countries that attracted FDI later, are likely to benefit from the newly emerging trend of 'regionalist' production networks. If this trend gets stronger, those in closer geographic and legal/institutional proximity to highly developed countries will gain from the retrenchment of global production networks.

Apart from these factors directly linked to the impact of the Coronavirus crisis, the longer-term development of EU11 and associated Eastern European economies will continue to be shaped by the general factors that are extensively analysed in these two volumes. Amongst these, we would single out demographic trends, differences in institutional and political-economic developments in the region and the evolution of the European Union as a whole. Moreover, global developments will also influence the region, such as the increasing US-China rivalry, challenges to the international trading system, the climate crisis and migration challenges.

1.4 Structure of Volumes

The two volumes of this book are both stand-alone collections of novel contributions to the literature on the convergence process in Europe. They can be fully enjoyed separately. In order to help the reader to understand the logic of grouping together the chapters in these two volumes, and to encourage venturing into the other volume, we provide below a brief description of the areas the volumes cover and how they are organized.

Contributions in Volume I spell out the framework for analysing the impact of EU membership on convergence and analyse the main trends for the EU11 as a whole, they also look at the future challenges EU11 will face to maintain rapid economic convergence and analyse regional dynamics in EU11. This is followed by a set of country studies looking into the convergence process in individual countries or groups of EU11 countries. The volume concludes with a joint analysis of European countries that are not members of the EU.

In Volume II, we look into various aspects of the working of the individual channels. In Chap. 2, Roeger and in 't Veld (2021) look into the working of the trade channel and analyse the economic impact of Single Market membership on EU11 economies using a version of the QUEST model, a dynamic stochastic general equilibrium (DSGE) model. In Chap. 3, Szabo and Durán Laguna (2021) analyse FDI flows into EU11, the private part of the investment channel. In Chaps. 4 and 5, the focus is on the public part of the investment channel and on the impact of EU Funds on the economies of EU11; both analyses use a DSGE model. Vértes and Czelleng (2021) focus on the Visegrád 4 countries and on a shorter period, but also consider fiscal and external stabilization during the crisis. Varga and in 't Veld (2021) cover two programming periods and focus on the impact on growth. They use a very detailed framework that can model explicitly a large variety of intervention areas. Chapters 6 and 7 focus on the finance channel. In Chap. 6, Vinhas de Souza (2021) briefly describes the historical process of financial liberalization and integration in EU11 since the 1990s. It investigates the hypothesis that the type of financial integration chosen played an important role in determining whether liberalization could deliver the welfare enhancing outcomes. In Chap. 7, Coricelli and Frigerio (2021) analyse the finance channel. In Chap. 8, Landesmann and Vidovic (2021) focus on the labour market and the working of the migration channel. Chapters 9, 10, 11 and 12 look into different aspects of the working of the institutional channel. In Chap. 9, Tóth and Hajdu (2021) zoom in on a crucial element of the functioning of the institutional channel, corruption. Using transaction-level big data for public procurement, they analyse trends in control of corruption in EU11 and in Southern European countries. In Chap. 10, Székely (2021) investigates the trends in the CO_2 intensity of EU11 countries during convergence and impact of EU in this regard. In Chap. 11, Jankovics et al. (2021) discuss the impact of EU on the development of national fiscal governance, fiscal institutions and rules in EU11. In Chap. 12, Chłoń-Domińczak (2021) also focuses on fiscal institutions and looks into the way pension systems developed in the region.

Acknowledgements We would like to thank the institutions and people who helped and supported these two volumes and the underlying collaborative project on the 15th anniversary of the eastern enlargement of the EU. DG ECFIN of the European Commission launched a Theme for Team project on this topic, which initiated the work underlying the contributions of authors from DG ECFIN, Chaps. 2 and 4 in Volume I and Chaps. 2, 3, 5, 10 and 11 in Volume II. Moreover, as part of the T4T project, DG ECFIN financed contract studies that formed the basis for Chap. 9 in Volume I and Chaps. 4, 9 and 12 in Volume II. We are grateful to Marc Puig and Melanie Ward Warmedinger for their contribution to organizing this project and to Peter Koh for copy editing several chapters of the volume.

As part of the project, DG ECFIN, EPSC and WIIW jointly organized a two-day international conference in Vienna and Bratislava on 8–9 April 2019, which focused on the policy issues involved. The materials of this conference can be found at https://ec.europa.eu/info/conference-15th-anniversary-2004-eu-enlargement-looking-back-looking-forward_en. DG ECFIN provided finance, and the participants of the T4T in DG ECFIN contributed in a major way to the organization of the international conference. We are particularly thankful to Marc Puig for helping to organize this conference. We are also grateful to EPSC, particularly Lucio Vinhas de Souza, the head of EPSC's economics team, Vladimir C. Isaila and Matthias Busse for their major contribution to putting together the programme of this conference and organizing this conference. We are also thankful to WIIW, particularly to Elisabeth Hagen, for the great help with the organization of this conference and for the active participation of WIIW staff in the conference. We are also grateful for the contribution of WIIW staff to these two volumes, Chap. 9 in Volume I and Chap. 8 in Volume II.

Related to this conference, WIIW published the *Faces of Convergence*, an open access e-book that carries the personal testimonies of many of the authors of this volume, as well as many other people who made major contribution to the transition process in their own countries and/or across the region (Székely, 2019). This book can be freely downloaded at https://wiiw.ac.at/faces-of-convergence-p-4908.html. We are grateful to Mario Holzner for his support to and help with this publication. We are also grateful to Gábor Székely for designing and producing the electronic version of this publication, to Peter Koh, Ayesha Landesmann and Melanie Ward Wardeminger for their help with editing.

Finally, we are particularly grateful to Marco Buti and Maarten Verwey from the European Commission for their support to the entire project.

References

Chłoń-Domińczak, A. (2021). *Towards Sustainable and Adequate Pension Systems: Old-Age Pension Reforms After Economic Transition and EU Accession in Central-Eastern and South-Eastern Europe.* In: Landesmann and Székely (2021).

Coricelli, F., & Frigerio, M. (2021). *15 years from the Eastern Enlargement: Financial Integration and Economic Convergence in Europe.* In: Landesmann and Székely (2021).

Czelleng, A., & Vértes, A. (2021). *The Impact of EU Cohesion Funds on Macroeconomic Development in the Visegrad Countries After the 2008–2009 Financial Crisis.* In: Landesmann and Székely (2021).

Durán, J., & Szabo, S. (2021). *FDI as Vector of Convergence in the CESEE Countries.* In: Landesmann and Székely (2021).

Grieveson, R. (2020). Regional Overview. In *Looking for Shelter from the Storm: Economic forecasts for Eastern Europe 2020–21; WIIW Monthly Report 5/2020.* Vienna: The Vienna Institute for International Economic Studies.

Jankovics, L., Igarzabal, L. O., & Ciobanu, Ş. (2021). *The Impact of the EU on National Fiscal Governance Systems.* In: Landesmann and Székely (2021).

Landesmann, M., & Székely, I. P. (Eds.). (2021). *Does EU Membership Facilitate Convergence? The Experience of the EU's Eastern Enlargement.* London: Palgrave Macmillan.

Landesmann, M., & Vidovic, H. (2021). *Labour Markets, Demography, Migration and Skills*. In: Landesmann and Székely (2021).

Roeger, W., & in 't Veld, J. (2021). *The Economic Impact of Single Market Membership on the EU Enlargement Countries*. In: Landesmann and Székely (2021).

Székely, I. P. (ed.), (2019). *Faces of Convergence*, WIIW, Vienna. Open-access e-book.

Székely, I. P. (2021). *Climate Change and EU Membership: The Journey of Central and Eastern Europe Towards a Carbon-Free World*. In: Landesmann and Székely (2021).

Székely, I. P., & Ward-Warmedinger, M. (2018). Reform Reversals: Areas, Circumstances and Motivations. *Comparative Economic Studies, 60*(4), 559–582.

Tóth, I. J., & Hajdu, M. (2021). Corruption, Institutions and Convergence. In: Landesmann and Székely (2021).

Varga, J., & in 't Veld, J. (2021). *The Impact of the EU Cohesion Policy Spending: A Model-Based Assessment*. In: Landesmann and Székely (2021).

Vinhas de Souza, L. (2021). *Models of Financial Integration: The Experience of the Baltics and Central Eastern Europe*. In: Landesmann and Székely (2021).

PART I

Trade and Investment Channels

CHAPTER 2

The Economic Impact of Single Market Membership on the EU Enlargement Countries

Werner Roeger and Jan in 't Veld

2.1 Introduction

When the 11 Baltics, Central and South Eastern European countries (EU11) joined the European Union, they became part of the European Single Market, the most successful project of regional integration in the world, covering a territory of more than 500 million inhabitants, and accounting for one-fifth of global economic output. Although the ultimate objective of one territory without any internal borders or other regulatory obstacles has not been reached yet, the Single Market has removed

W. Roeger
DIW, Berlin, Germany

VIVES, KU Leuven, Leuven, Belgium
e-mail: Werner.Roeger@ec.europa.eu

J. in 't Veld (✉)
DG ECFIN, European Commission, Brussels, Belgium
e-mail: Jan.Intveld@ec.europa.eu

M. Landesmann, I. P. Székely (eds.), *Does EU Membership Facilitate Convergence? The Experience of the EU's Eastern Enlargement - Volume II*, Studies in Economic Transition,
https://doi.org/10.1007/978-3-030-57702-5_2

internal tariffs and significantly reduced other barriers to trade, promoting the free movement of goods and services. Membership of the Single Market raised their integration with the rest of the EU, stimulated competition and trade, improved efficiency, raised quality and reduced prices. It boosted trade with the old member states of the EU15 as well as among each other. It also had a large impact on incomes and welfare.

Recent studies have estimated the impact the Single Market programme has had on the EU economies. Mayer et al. (2019) assess a non-Single Market counterfactual and estimate an average impact on EU GDP of 5.5%, with larger effects for the more open EU11 countries. Felbermayr et al. (2018) in a similar exercise estimate an average EU effect of about 4%, but also with much large effects for EU11. These effects are referred to as welfare effects, but are typically measured in terms of consumption effects. Using a structural macromodel, and including competition effects, In 't Veld (2019) finds larger effects for the EU on average, around 9%. All these studies find that in particular the EU11 members benefited enormously from the Single Market. This chapter elaborates on this and discusses in greater detail the effects of the Single Market using a structural macromodel to assess the impact on trade and on competition.

There have been a number of ex ante evaluations of Eastern enlargement (see Baldwin 1995; Baldwin et al. 1997). Depending on assumptions made the projected GDP effects of accession to the internal market range from 1.5% to 18%. The large positive GDP effects are generated under the assumption that accession lowers the risk premium for investing in EU11 countries. Caliendo et al. (2019) provide an ex post evaluation of both the impact of trade integration and migration using a computable general equilibrium model. They find welfare effects from trade integration (measured in consumption equivalents) of 0.81% for the new member states and 0.18% for EU15. However, these calculations are conducted under the assumption of inelastic domestic labour supply (only migration is allowed) and zero effect on investment. In contrast to this chapter we allow elastic labour supply, but we disregard an endogenous migration response. We also allow for a trade-induced investment response and finally we allow for productivity effects.

One of the most striking stylised facts for EU11 countries is their strong convergence to income levels in the old member states (EU15). Growth has on average been at least 2 pps higher than in the EU15 with both higher investment shares and higher total factor productivity (TFP) growth. They are also much more open than the old member states, with an average import share now in excess of 55% of GDP, and have become increasingly closer integrated both with EU15 countries and with each other. This suggests that they should indeed benefit more from membership of the Single Market, a result borne out by our model simulations which show large trade and strong investment effects.

It is important to stress that we are not simulating a dismantling of the Single Market and the EU11 leaving. We are focusing here on how much the EU11 members benefit from the Single Market compared to the EA and EU averages. We are building a counterfactual case in which the Single Market does not exist for any of the EU countries, and then compare how EU11 countries are affected relative to the EU15. A scenario in which the EU11 alone were to leave the EU Single Market would be different, with potentially lower negative trade demand effects but larger trade diversion effects. One would then have to make assumptions on alternative trade agreements, and consider the possibility of voluntary 'regulatory alignment' between the EU11 and the remaining EU15. That would be highly speculative and it is not something we can do here. Instead, by looking at a counterfactual of no Single Market, we can show the stronger impact of membership on the EU11 because of their greater degree of openness.

This chapter is structured as follows. The next section summarises the main macroeconomic trends in the EU11 countries since accession. This is followed by a model-based analysis of the impact of the elimination of tariffs and non-tariff barriers in the Single Market on bilateral trade flows and GDP and investment. The final section concludes.

2.2 Some Macroeconomic Trends

The EU11 countries are strongly converging towards income levels in EU15.[1] In the early 2000s potential GDP growth accelerated (see Fig. 2.1a) with a peak growth rate of more than 4.5% in 2007. Associated with the great recession potential growth came down strongly but there remains a stable growth differential of 2% with respect to EU15 countries. Both high investment rates (see Fig. 2.1b) and high rates of technical

[1] The EU11 includes Estonia, Latvia, Lithuania, Slovenia, Slovakia, Czechia, Hungary, Poland (all joined in 2004), Bulgaria, Romania (joined in 2007) and Croatia (joined in 2013). Cyprus and Malta also joined in 2004 but are excluded from the EU11 aggregate of formerly communist countries. The EU15 includes the old member states (Belgium, Germany, Ireland, Greece, Spain, France, Italy, Luxembourg, Netherlands, Austria, Portugal and Finland).

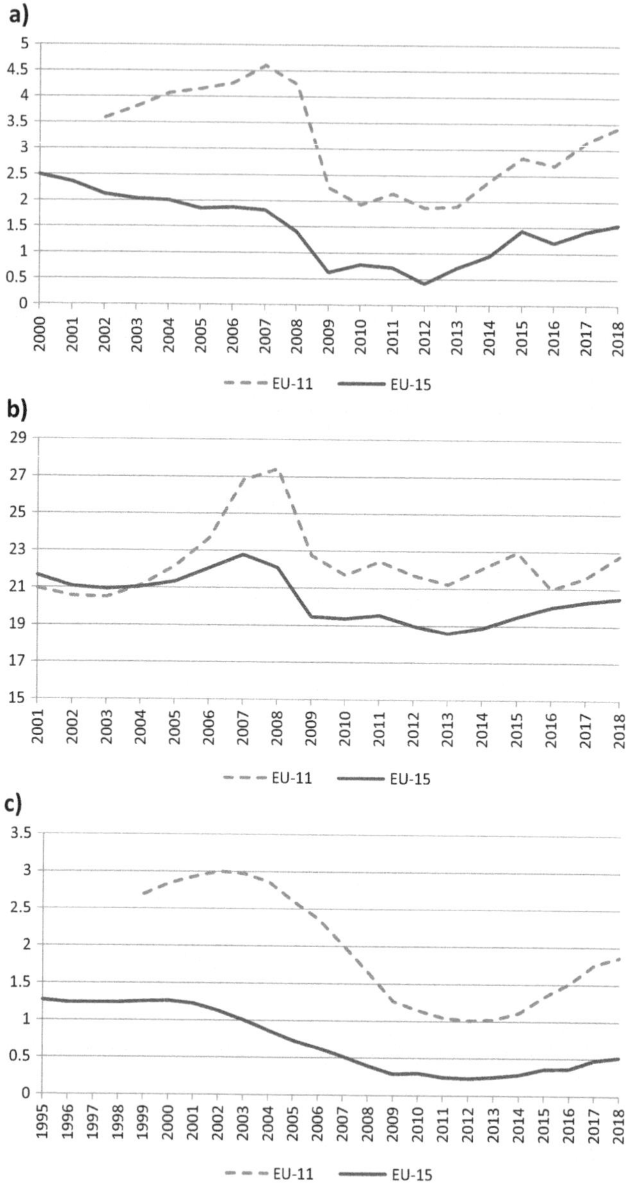

Fig. 2.1 (**a**) GDP: Potential growth rate EU11 and EU15. (Source: Ameco). (**b**) Investment to potential output ratio EU11 versus EU15. (**c**) Trend TFP Growth EU11 and EU15. Note: Ratio of gross fixed capital formation at 2010 prices over potential output at 2010 reference levels. (Source: Ameco). (**c**) Trend TFP Growth EU11 and EU15. (Source: Ameco)

progress, as measured by the total factor productivity trend (see Fig. 2.1c), explain persistent differences in trend growth between EU11 and EU15. Interestingly, corporate investment rates (see Fig. 2.1b) diverged from EU15 levels around the time of the accession, while TFP growth rates were higher already before accession (Fig. 2.1c).

EU11 countries are on average more open to trade compared to EU15 and have increased their export and import shares more strongly over the last 15 years (See Figs. 2.2a–b). By 2018, their average openness was close to 60% of GDP. They also trade relatively more with EU countries (Figs. 2.3a–b), which is because they are strongly integrated into the EU value chain. These features suggest that they should benefit more from accession to the internal market.

2.3 A Model-Based Counterfactual Analysis

This section describes a model-based assessment of the impact of the Single Market on the EU11 Member States. We assess the impact using a structural macroeconomic model, building a counterfactual scenario by raising tariffs and non-tariff barriers to intra-EU trade that would apply if trade would revert back to WTO rules. We quantify the macroeconomic benefits of the Single Market in goods and services by the reductions in bilateral trade and GDP in such a counterfactual scenario. These simulations are based on estimates of the reduction in trade costs that the Single Market has established and it is assumed in the counterfactual that trade reverts to WTO rules, and Most Favoured Nation (MFN) rates are applied as tariffs on goods. For non-tariff barriers (NTBs), which apply to trade in goods and services, estimates are based on those calculated for trade between the EU and the United States. As acknowledged in the introduction, this assumption that trade barriers would be similar to those between the EU and the United States is an extreme assumption, but serves the purpose of a counterfactual of no Single Market.

The model used in this exercise is a multi-country version of the QUEST model. QUEST is a structural macroeconomic model, derived from micro-principals of dynamic intertemporal optimisation. It distinguishes between a tradable and non-tradable sector, both importing intermediate goods and services, and explicitly models bilateral trade

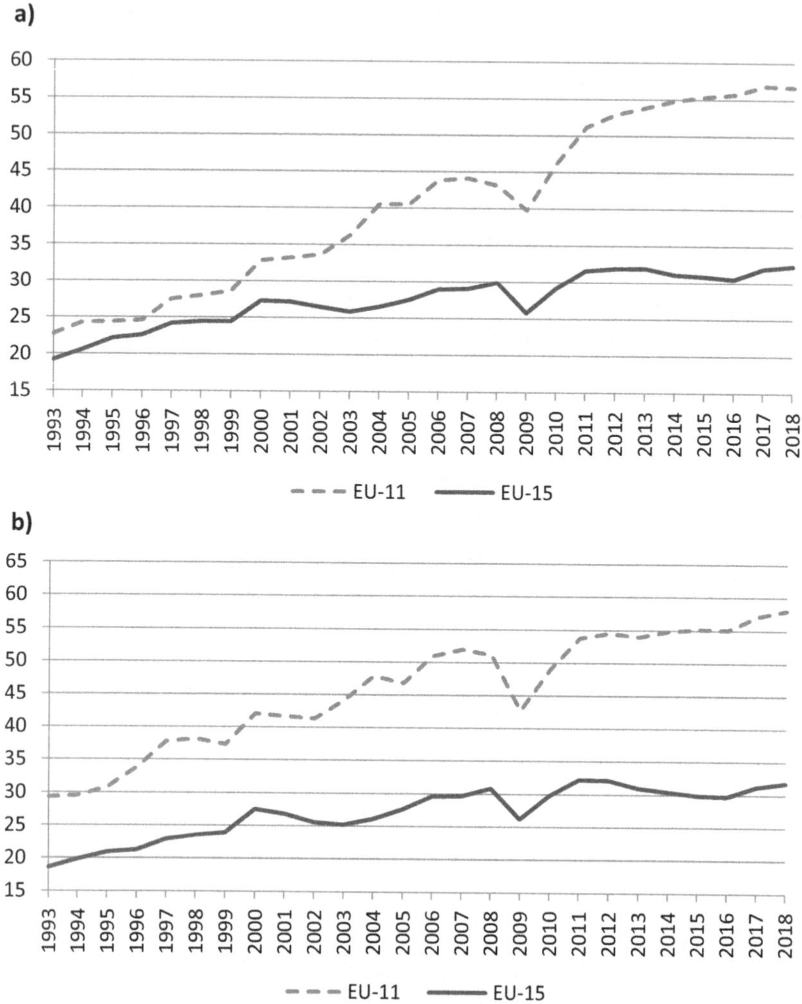

Fig. 2.2 (**a**) Total exports as percentage of GDP: EU11 and EU15. Note: Ratio of exports of goods and services over GDP. (Source: Ameco); (**b**) Total imports as percentage of GDP EU11 and EU15. Note: Ratio of imports of goods and services over GDP. (Source: Ameco)

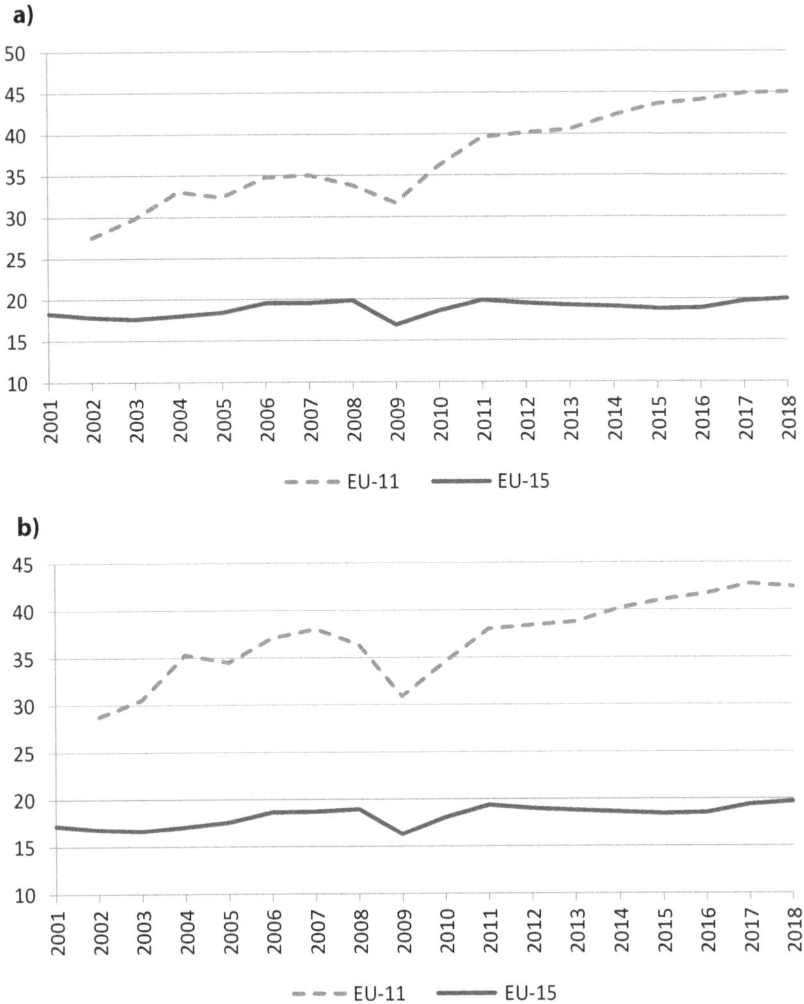

Fig. 2.3 (**a**) Intra-EU exports (goods) percentage of GDP EU11 and EU15. Note: Exports of goods to other EU28 member states. (Source: Ameco); (**b**) Intra-EU imports (goods) per centage of GDP EU11 and EU15. Note: Imports of goods to other EU28 member states. (Source: Ameco)

flows.[2] Although it lacks the sectoral details found in typical trade computable general equilibrium (CGE) models, and can therefore not assess the impact on specific sectors, the modelling of trade in intermediate inputs captures linkages through cross-border value chains. This is important, as trade in intermediates amplifies the effects of trade barriers. The model can also assess the wider macroeconomic consequences of trade barriers on the major EU economies, on output and its components. The model version used here includes each of the 28 EU member states as well as the United States and a block representing the rest of the world. Aggregates are reported for the EU and the euro area (EA), and for each of the EU11 countries.

This assessment of the impact of the Single Market is restricted to trade in goods and services, while the Single Market involves four freedoms—the free movement of goods, services, capital and people. The benefits and costs of the freedom of movement are much debated, both for recipient countries and for the EU11 countries that have in some cases seen a significant outflow of (skilled) people. While migration may have been beneficial for the people involved, for many of the EU11 countries emigration flows have further worsened already detrimental demographic trends, with an additional negative effect from a 'braindrain' of skilled workers. Our focus on goods and services can be justified as this was the emphasis of the Single Market Programme (SMP) in 1992. But it must be stressed that the Single Market is not complete yet and further initiatives have focused on deepening the Single Market. For instance additional legislation has been introduced to strengthen the Single Market in services, transport and the digital Single Market. It should also be noted that this analysis excludes the effects of membership of the customs union (Free-Trade Agreements (FTAs) with third countries), euro membership and Schengen. The implicit assumption in the counterfactual is no Single Market in goods and services, but, for example for continued membership of the euro, this is to identify the macroeconomic benefits of the Single Market alone.

There are two other caveats to be mentioned. Firstly, the counterfactual scenarios simulated here are stylised in the sense that new trading conditions are introduced as a sudden shock. This is why we only report long-run effects of a reintroduction of trade barriers on the economies of the

[2] The non-tradable sector includes sectors such as public administration, human health and education, as well as other sectors with a low export share, like real estate activities, and electricity, gas, water supply. Other services are treated as tradable See Burgert et al. (2020).

member states. Secondly, the analysis is restricted to the 28 member states of the EU, while 31 countries participate in the Single Market, including Norway, Iceland and Lichtenstein. By not including these three members, the results may underestimate the impact for some close trading partners of these countries.

Table 2.1 shows how MFN rates vary per sector. They are typically highest for 'textiles' and 'transport equipment', and lowest for 'paper and pulp' and 'mining'. In aggregate, these tariffs amount to approximately 3½% for goods. For individual countries tariffs are weighted by sector import shares. Trade in goods amount to approximately 70% of all trade in goods and services, and in the model the tariff shock is adjusted accordingly.

Non-tariff barriers (NTBs), such as differences between regulatory regimes or product standards, represent a greater impediment to trade than tariffs. Following the elimination of tariffs on goods and services, much of the work on strengthening the Single Market has been related to reducing remaining NTBs, particularly for trade in services. For our

Table 2.1 MFN tariffs

Goods	*MFN Tariff*
Transport equipment	*8.09*
Chemicals and chemical products	*2.71*
Electrical and optical equipment	*1.97*
Food, beverages and tobacco	*7.26*
Coke, Refined petroleum and nuclear fuel	*2.69*
Basic metals and fabricated metal	*2.05*
Machinery, Nec*	*2.05*
Mining and quarrying	*0.00*
Textiles and textile products; leather, leather and footwear	*9.58*
Rubber and plastics	*5.35*
Manufacturing, Nec; recycling	*1.71*
Pulp, paper, printing and publishing	*0.04*
Agriculture, hunting, forestry and fishing	*5.90*
Other non-metallic mineral	*3.78*
Wood and products of wood and cork	*2.35*
EU sector weighted average MFN tariff	*3.5*

Source: Berden et al. (2009), Berden and Francois (2015), Dhingra et al. (2017), own calculations based on WIOD (Timmer et al. 2015)

*Not Elsewhere Classified

counterfactual we base our shocks on available estimates of NTBs that apply to trade between the EU and the United States, as published in studies assessing the potential impact of Transatlantic Trade and Investment Partnership (TTIP) (Berden et al. 2009). By using these estimates we assume that trade between EU member atates without a Single Market would be subject to similar conditions as now apply between the EU and the United States.

The authors calculate detailed tariff equivalents of NTBs, using econometric techniques and business surveys. These are estimated to be highest for 'food, beverages and tobacco', and lowest for 'construction' and other services (Table 2.2). Not all NTBs are 'actionable' or 'reducible' by trade agreements or other policy actions (e.g. 110/240 voltage differences between the United States and the EU, or translation costs for manuals, cannot be eliminated by a trade agreement). A 'reducible' share is therefore also estimated by sector and taken into account when calculating the change in the tariff-equivalent of NTBs that would apply with or without a trade agreement. Conversely, when simulating a reversal of the Single Market, we also take the reducible share of NTBs and use this to calculate individual country NTBs (weighted by import sector shares). On average

Table 2.2 Non-tariff barriers (NTBs) used in counterfactual

Sector	*NTB cost EU/United States (tariff equivalent)*	*Reducible share of NTB*
Transport equipment	22.1	0.53
Chemicals and chemical products	23.9	0.63
Post and telecommunications	11.7	0.70
Electrical and optical equipment	6.5	0.41
Financial intermediation	11.3	0.49
Food, beverages and tobacco	56.8	0.53
Construction	4.6	0.38
Renting of machinery & equip and other business activities	14.9	0.51
Services Nec (*)	4.4	0.37
Basic metals and fabricated metal	11.9	0.62
Textiles and textile products; leather, leather and footwear	19.2	0.50
Wood and products of wood and cork	11.3	0.60
Reducible sector-weighted average	*10.3*	

Source: Berden et al. (2009), Berden and Francois (2015), Dhingra et al. (2017), WIOD (Timmer et al. (2015))

the tariff equivalent cost of NTBs amount to 10.3 percentage points (GDP-weighted EU average).

In the model, the costs of NTBs come on top of the MFN tariff and add to the overall increase in trade costs. Tariffs and NTBs are applied to trade in final goods and to trade in intermediate inputs. NTBs are more distortive than MFN tariffs, and unlike tariffs, which are a revenue for the government and which can be recycled by reducing other distortionary taxes, NTBs have no economic gains (although they could of course have health and safety and environmental benefits).

2.3.1 *Effects of Trade Barriers*

Adding the MFN tariffs and NTBs as additional costs to the bilateral trade between EU member states, we can simulate a counterfactual scenario with the model. The results are reported in Table 2.3. The increase in trade costs of around 13% on average reduces intra-EU trade, replacing it by internal domestic trade and diverts some trade to non-EU countries (increase in extra-EU trade). Intra-EU imports decline by about 20–30% in the long run, while total imports fall by about 20% on average. The fall in imports is larger than that in exports as there is a large decline in domestic demand in the EU.

Table 2.3 Long-run macroeconomic impact of trade barriers

	GDP	*Consumption*	*Investment*	*Exports*	*Imports*	*Imports intra-EU*	*Capital*	*Employment*
EE	-12.6	-24.4	-23.3	-16.2	-22.6	-25.1	-18.8	-2.1
CY	-7.8	-14.7	-16.6	-11.6	-19.7	-25.8	-13.0	-1.1
LV	-11.1	-21.5	-20.0	-14.8	-22.5	-28.6	-15.9	-1.5
LT	-9.6	-20.5	-19.5	-12.2	-19.1	-25.2	-15.7	-1.6
MT	-12.1	-22.3	-24.1	-13.4	-19.1	-20.0	-20.1	-1.7
SI	-12.8	-26.0	-23.6	-17.1	-26.1	-28.0	-19.1	-2.0
SK	-16.2	-30.3	-28.9	-20.7	-27.5	-28.6	-23.7	-3.4
EA19	-6.8	-13.6	-13.7	-12.5	-20.5		-10.7	-1.0
BG	-10.2	-20.6	-18.4	-13.7	-20.6	-23.6	-14.8	-1.7
CZ	-14.9	-29.1	-25.5	-20.2	-28.7	-29.1	-20.5	-3.0
HR	-7.1	-14.8	-14.2	-11.4	-20.7	-23.0	-11.0	-0.9
HU	-13.7	-26.9	-25.3	-18.1	-25.2	-25.6	-20.7	-2.8
PL	-8.0	-16.4	-15.6	-13.3	-22.2	-24.2	-12.3	-1.3
RO	-6.8	-14.9	-12.9	-11.9	-21.3	-23.1	-10.0	-0.9
EU28	-6.6	-13.2	-13.1	-12.1	-19.9		-10.2	-1.0

There are various channels in which tariffs and non-tariff barriers affect output and welfare. Roughly speaking one distinguishes direct trade effects for consumers and supply effects, which have indirect effects on consumption via changes in real income. A tariff/NTB adversely affects consumption via an increase in import prices. This is especially negative in the case of NTBs, while in the case of tariffs consumer can partially be compensated if tariff revenues are recycled in the form of lower taxes. But more importantly than the direct effects on consumption are various indirect supply effects. With elastic labour supply an increase of consumer prices leads to a reduction of labour supply for the same nominal wage or an increase in the nominal wage for the same amount of labour offered. This reduces employment and real consumption wage income. To the extent in which domestic firms are using imported investment goods, an increase of tariffs raises the rental cost of capital which lowers the optimal capital output ratio. This has a direct negative income effect via a reduction of productivity and an indirect effect on wage income via a reduction in the demand for labour. Similarly, an increase in the price of intermediate imports, that is an interruption of EU wide supply chains, also lowers productivity of capital and labour and leads to inward shifts in the demand for labour and for capital. While the direct consumption effect of a tariff only operates via tradable consumption, the supply channel of a tariff reduces supply in both the tradable and non-tradable sectors. In the QUEST model, the adverse productivity effects are increased by the presence of scale effects, because of overhead labour and fixed capital.

Government spending, both government consumption and (productive) government investment, is kept constant in real terms in this scenario, to avoid additional fiscal contraction effects (see discussion below). Nevertheless, government finances deteriorate as prices rise for imported government spending, and as lower domestic demand reduces tax revenues and raises social expenditure. This more than offsets the extra revenue coming in from tariffs and the increase in the government deficit forces an increase in taxes. Higher taxes have a further negative impact on consumption.

Overall GDP is about 7% lower in the Euro Area. However, the effects are significantly larger in EU11 countries, which are smaller but also more open, and especially they trade more with EU countries as shown by a higher share of intra trade. In addition, accession to the internal market also means opening trade among EU11 countries. For Poland, output is 8% lower, for Hungary almost 14%, for Slovakia 16%. The integration effects are large, with intra-EU trade flows down by between 23% and 28%. Lower GDP in the counterfactual is mostly a productivity effect, which is largely the result of lower investment. Employment falls by 1% on average in the EU, much less than the more than 6% decline in GDP, while the capital stock falls by 10%. Note that the decline in productivity is mostly the direct result of the model hypothesis that links wages to productivity, which in this case leads to a decline in wage growth that stabilises employment, up to the decline due to the terms of trade effect described above.

The scenario described here assumes that real government consumption and investment remain fixed. If fiscal expenditure was instead kept constant as a share of GDP, real spending would decline in line with GDP and have additional negative output effects. But as (nominal) government consumption and investment fall in line with (nominal) GDP, there is also a smaller deterioration in the government budget position. As a result the tax increase needed to stabilise the debt-to-GDP ratio is smaller, which leads to a less negative impact on private consumption and a smaller negative employment effect. But the first effect dominates as government investment is productivity enhancing, and the overall GDP effect would be more negative in such a scenario. Another sensitivity analysis focuses on the trade elasticity. There is some uncertainty about the value of this elasticity of substitution between imported goods, with trade models typically using a larger elasticity. For example the preferred value reported in Head and Mayer (2014) is around -5. The macro studies on which macromodels base their trade elasticities find generally much lower values, as these also capture a (lower) sensitivity to exchange rate changes. In the simulations used here, we have set the trade elasticity already higher than the standard setting, at -3. When we raise the elasticity in the model to -5, the trade effects become significantly larger, with lower imports and exports, and intra-EU imports falling between 25% and 35%. The magnitude of the real GDP effects is slightly lower, by up a tenth, when substitution is higher.

2.3.2 *Effects of Lower Competition*

The scenario described above, based on higher trade barriers in the EU, shows a significant negative effect on productivity. But it does not capture the impact the Single Market has had on competition. Greater trade openness has increased competition and lowered prices, and the re-establishment of trade barriers is likely to reduce competitive pressures. This would allow firms to raise the mark-ups of their prices over their marginal costs, and have a negative impact on output.

One study that examines the impact of the Single Market on mark-ups is Badinger (2007). This chapter uses a panel approach, covering ten EU member states over the period 1981–99, to test whether the EU's Single Market Programme has led to a reduction in firms' mark-ups over marginal costs. Mark-up reductions are found for aggregate manufacturing, but mark-ups have gone up in most service industries since the early 1990s, which confirms in his view the weak state of the Single Market for services and suggests that anti-competitive defence strategies have emerged in EU service industries. The relative reduction in mark-ups reported in this chapter in manufacturing is 26%.

We apply this in our model to the mark-up in the manufacturing share of the tradable goods sector. In our view the observed increase in mark-ups in service industries is more difficult to link directly to the Single Market, and there is some evidence that there too mark-ups have come down in more recent years. In the second counterfactual simulation we assume only a change in mark-ups in manufacturing and no change in the services sector.

Table 2.4 reports the results for this scenario. An increase in mark-ups in manufacturing leads to a reduction in GDP of about 2% on average. It lowers profits and has a negative impact on demand for capital and reduces investment. It also lowers consumption. Note that there is also a further reduction in trade, with intra-EU trade flows falling by about 5%.

2.3.3 Total Effects of the Single Market

In order to come to a total estimate of the effects of the Single Market we combine the two counterfactual scenarios described above and simulate the combined impact of higher trade barriers and higher mark-ups. Table 2.5 shows macroeconomic effects for individual countries. Overall the impact is roughly linear and the sum of the two scenarios described above.

The increase in trade costs and lower competition raises prices and reduces economic activity. Lower demand for labour reduces real wages, while lower investment leads to lower capital accumulation. This reduces output. Intra-EU trade flows fall between 25% and 35%, as a direct result of higher trade barriers and indirectly due to less competition. Overall trade openness is also strongly reduced, with exports falling by 15% and

Table 2.4 Long-run macroeconomic impact of less competition

	GDP	*Consumption*	*Investment*	*Exports*	*Imports*	*Imports intra-EU*	*Capital*	*Employment*
EE	-2.3	-2.0	-4.9	-3.9	-3.4	-4.6	-3.4	0.0
CY	-1.7	-1.5	-4.1	-3.3	-2.7	-4.6	-2.7	0.0
LV	-2.2	-1.9	-4.6	-3.7	-3.0	-4.7	-3.1	0.0
LT	-1.7	-1.2	-3.8	-3.0	-2.5	-4.3	-2.6	0.0
MT	-1.3	-0.7	-3.2	-3.1	-2.5	-4.9	-2.0	0.1
SI	-2.4	-2.6	-5.1	-3.8	-3.7	-4.8	-3.6	-0.1
SK	-2.9	-2.7	-6.0	-4.8	-4.3	-5.2	-4.3	-0.1
EA19	-2.2	-2.1	-4.8	-3.7	-3.1		-3.3	0.0
BG	-2.4	-2.1	-4.9	-3.8	-3.1	-4.8	-3.5	-0.1
CZ	-3.3	-3.5	-6.5	-4.9	-4.5	-5.4	-4.7	-0.2
HR	-2.0	-2.1	-4.3	-3.2	-3.0	-4.3	-3.0	0.0
HU	-2.7	-2.4	-5.7	-4.4	-3.9	-5.1	-4.0	0.0
PL	-2.6	-2.6	-5.4	-4.1	-3.6	-4.8	-3.9	-0.1
RO	-2.5	-2.7	-5.0	-3.6	-3.4	-4.4	-3.6	-0.1
EU28	-2.1	-2.0	-4.6	-3.6	-3.1		-3.2	0.0

imports by 22%, more due to the additional impact of lower domestic demand.

Lower demand leads to lower tax revenues, and this more than offsets the extra revenue from tariffs. The increase in the government deficit forces an increase in taxes in order to stabilise government debt, and this has an additional negative impact on consumption.[3] There is a strong heterogeneity across countries. Overall GDP is about 9% lower in the EU. The effects are larger in EU11 countries, for the Baltics between 11% and 15%, for Poland 10.6%, Hungary 16.5%, Czech Republic 18.5% and for Slovakia 19.3%. Again, lower GDP in the member states is mostly a productivity effect, coming from lower capital accumulation.

2.4 Concluding Remarks

This chapter has assessed the impact of Single Market membership for the EU11 economies. The Single Market, though incomplete, has boosted trade flows within the EU through the elimination of trade tariffs and reduction in non-tariff barriers, and so raised output and domestic

[3] Note that government consumption and (productive) government investment are kept fixed in real terms in this scenario, to avoid additional fiscal contraction effects.

Table 2.5 Simulated long-run effects of counterfactual non-Single Market

	GDP	*Consumption*	*Investment*	*Exports*	*Imports*	*Imports intra-EU*	*Capital*	*Employment*
EE	-14.9	-26.2	-27.1	-19.6	-25.3	-28.7	-21.5	-2.3
CY	-9.5	-16.0	-20.0	-14.6	-21.8	-29.5	-15.3	-1.1
LV	-13.3	-23.2	-23.6	-18.0	-24.8	-32.3	-18.4	-1.7
LT	-11.2	-21.5	-22.4	-14.8	-21.0	-28.7	-17.8	-1.6
MT	-13.3	-22.8	-26.4	-16.0	-21.1	-24.2	-21.5	-1.7
SI	-15.3	-28.5	-27.7	-20.6	-28.9	-31.8	-22.1	-2.4
SK	-19.3	-33.0	-33.4	-24.9	-30.9	-32.8	-27.0	-4.0
EA19	-9.0	-15.6	-17.9	-15.8	-23.0		-13.6	-1.1
BG	-12.6	-22.5	-22.4	-17.1	-23.0	-27.5	-17.7	-1.9
CZ	-18.5	-32.7	-30.7	-24.7	-32.3	-33.6	-24.4	-3.8
HR	-9.1	-16.9	-18.0	-14.4	-23.1	-26.6	-13.7	-1.0
HU	-16.5	-29.2	-29.7	-22.0	-28.2	-29.8	-23.9	-3.2
PL	-10.6	-18.9	-20.4	-16.9	-25.1	-28.1	-15.7	-1.5
RO	-9.2	-17.5	-17.3	-15.1	-24.0	-26.8	-13.3	-1.2
EU28	-8.7	-15.1	-17.2	-15.3	-22.3		-13.0	-1.1

demand. The opening-up of domestic economies has also increased competition, reduced mark-ups and lowered prices. The combined impact of these two channels is found to have raised trade flows, investment and GDP in the long run.

This simulated impact is within the admittedly large range suggested by Baldwin et al. (1997). It is significantly higher than the welfare effect of 0.8% estimated by Caliendo et al. (2019) but their calculations are conducted under the assumption of inelastic domestic labour supply (only migration is allowed) and zero effect on investment. In contrast, our estimates allow for elastic labour supply, but we disregard an endogenous migration response. We also allow for a trade-induced investment response, which we find to be significant, and we allow for productivity effects.

The focus here has been on only two of the four freedoms of the Single Market, namely free movement of goods and services. Missing from our analysis are the effects of free movement labour (migration). But in addition, besides the scale and competition effects that we do capture, there is a third channel through which trade can impact on productivity and that is linked to innovation. Higher trade openness increases market access and can induce more innovation and stimulate cross-border spillovers from innovation. There is no consensus on this, with conflicting evidence that increased import competition from China (Autor et al. 2016) might have actually reduced innovation and had a negative impact on economic growth in the longer run, although Bloom et al. (2016) find a positive impact of Chinese competition on innovation activities for a panel of European firms.

There is also a general recognition that the Single Market is incomplete and the European Commission has published its assessment on how the Single Market can be deepened (European Commission, 2018). This includes dealing with persistent challenges in products and services markets, but also further progress towards a digital Single Market, capital markets union and banking union. This chapter has only given a snapshot of the macroeconomic benefits of the Single Market in goods and services, and this is only one part of the overall benefits of the European Union.

Acknowledgements We would like to thank François Blondeau for statistical assistance. The views expressed in this chapter are those of the author and should not be attributed to the European Commission.

References

Autor, D., Dorn, D., Hanson, G., Pisano, G., & Shu, P. (2016). *Foreign Competition and Domestic Innovation: Evidence from US Patents* (NBER Working Papers 22879).

Badinger, H. (2007). Has the EU's Single Market Programme Fostered Competition? Testing for a Decrease in Mark-up Ratios in EU Industries. *Oxford Bulletin of Economics and Statistics, 69*(4), 497–519.

Baldwin, R. (1995). The Eastern Enlargement of the European Union. *European Economic Review, 39*, 474–481.

Baldwin, R., Francois, J., & Portes, R. (1997). The Costs and Benefits of Eastern Enlargement: The Impact on the EU and Central Europe. *Economic Policy, 12*, 125–176.

Berden K., & Francois, J. (2015). *Quantifying Non-Tariff Measures for TTIP*. CEPS Special Report no 116.

Berden, K. G., Francois, J., Tamminen, S., Thelle, M., & Wymenga, P. (2009). *Non-Tariff Measures in EU-US Trade and Investment – An Economic Analysis*. Ecorys Report Prepared for the European Commission, Reference OJ 2007/ S180-219493.

Bloom, N., Draca, M., & Reenen, J. (2016). Trade Induced Technical Change? The Impact of Chinese Imports on Innovation, IT and Productivity. *Review of Economic Studies, 83*(1), 87–117.

Burgert, M., Roeger, W, Varga, J., In 't Veld, J.,Vogel, L. (2020). A Global Economy Version of QUEST: Simulation Properties, ECFIN Discussion Paper 126, June 2020.

Caliendo, L., Opromolla, L. D., Parro, F., & Sforza, A. (2019). Goods and Factor Market Integration: A Quantitative Assessment of the EU Enlargement. *NBER Working Papers 23695*, National Bureau of Economic Research, Inc.

Dhingra, S., Huang, H., Ottaviano, G., Pessoa, J. P., Sampson, T., & Van Reenen, J. (2017). Trade After Brexit. *Economic Policy, 92*, 651–705.

European Commission. (2018). *The Single Market in a Changing World*. COM 772. Downloadable from: https://ec.europa.eu/docsroom/documents/ 32662

Felbermayr, G., Groschl, J., & Heiland, I. (2018). *Undoing Europe in a New Quantitative Trade Model* (Ifo Working Papers 250-2018).

Head, K., & Mayer, T. (2014). Gravity Equations: Workhorse, Toolkit, and Cookbook. In G. Gopinath, E. Helpman, & K. Rogoff (Eds.), *Handbook of International Economics* (Vol. 4, pp. 131–196). Amsterdam: Elsevier.

In 't Veld, J. (2019). The Economic Benefits of the EU Single Market in Goods and Services. *Journal of Policy Modeling*, 41, Issue 5, 803–818.

Mayer, T., Vicard, V., & Zignago, S. (2019). The Cost on Non-Europe, Revisited. *Economic Policy*, Vol 34, 98, April 2019, 145–199.
Timmer, M. P., Dietzenbacher, E., Los, B., Stehrer, R., & de Vries, G. J. (2015). An Illustrated User Guide to the World Input–Output Database: The Case of Global Automotive Production. *Review of International Economics*, *23*, 575–605.

CHAPTER 3

FDI as Force of Convergence in the CESEE Countries

Septimiu Szabo and Jorge Durán Laguna

3.1 Internationalisation in the Early 1990s

The transition from a planned economy to a market economy entailed a deep internationalisation of the CESEE countries. Economic and political integration in the Western block—EU and NATO—required them to modernise and liberalise their economic structures. This started during the 1990s when most of these countries signed trade and association agreements with the EU[1] and began developing a modern regulatory environment, in line with EU laws and regulations. Opening to trade and international investment triggered a remarkable development process and played a key role in the economic take-off. Legal and regulatory improvements in autarchy can promote growth but force development to rely on domestic demand, local savings and local equipment. When regulatory

[1] Poland and Hungary were the first countries to sign the Association Agreements in 1994. Croatia signed it in 2005.

S. Szabo • J. D. Laguna (✉)
DG ECFIN, European Commission, Brussels, Belgium
e-mail: Septimiu.SZABO@ec.europa.eu; Jorge.DURAN-LAGUNA@ec.europa.eu

M. Landesmann, I. P. Székely (eds.), *Does EU Membership Facilitate Convergence? The Experience of the EU's Eastern Enlargement - Volume II*, Studies in Economic Transition,
https://doi.org/10.1007/978-3-030-57702-5_3

changes are combined with trade and foreign capital, particularly FDI, the effect is magnified as growth also starts being propelled by global forces.

When democratisation started, the economic and institutional structures in the CESEE countries were very different from those in Western Europe. The traditional trade links collapsed and there was a need to dismantle the large, inefficient and uncompetitive industries from the Soviet era. The collapse of the economies was in most cases traumatic and entailed large losses in income and employment. Furthermore, political instability and hyperinflation in some countries had a profound negative impact.[2] This hard transition left these countries with very low levels of initial income and subject to very high levels of uncertainty at the institutional, political and economic level. Perceptions of high geopolitical risks and high inflation held back domestic and foreign direct investment and delayed the recovery.

On the positive side, progress in negotiations to join NATO and the EU sent a strong signal of commitment to democracy, market economy and international trade. Alongside a tight and credible monetary policy, this reduced inflation pressures and helped stabilise the political landscape in most countries. At the turn of the century, the legal and regulatory systems had undergone an important modernisation process by incorporating most of the EU legislation. All these developments helped lower risk perceptions leading to more stability and made the countries more attractive for investment. FDI surged and spurred economic growth, productivity started catching up fast with the EU average and living conditions improved significantly.

3.2 The FDI and Trade Boom in the Pre-accession Phase

At the turn of the century, the combination of geopolitical stability, access to foreign markets and opening to foreign capital speeded up the convergence process with the West. For example, the investment rate increased from 19% to 28% in the Baltics, Romania and Bulgaria, compared to the 15% EU average.[3] Less uncertainty, a better regulatory framework and some large privatisations attracted massive investments from abroad, most

[2] At various times in the 1990s, inflation in Romania or Bulgaria reached more than 300% but Slovenia, Poland or Czechia also witnessed rates of 30% to 50% in the early 1990s.

[3] See Annex A with some basic charts. The Baltics are Estonia, Latvia and Lithuania; Visegrád is the Czech Republic, Slovakia, Poland and Hungary; the South is Bulgaria, Romania, Slovenia and Croatia.

notably in the financial and trade sectors. The ability to tap external markets and funding allowed for an unconstrained catching-up and an accelerated integration in international markets.

GDP in the CESEE countries reached almost $1.4 trillion[4] in 2017 (in nominal values), representing around 8% of the GDP of EU. GDP per capita is only one-third of the EU15 average, despite a lot of catch-up in the last 25 years. In 1992, GDP was barely $250 billion, behind, for example, Australia, Mexico, Korea or EFTA. Twenty-five years later, the CESEE countries combined managed to overtake all these blocs, growing in nominal terms by roughly 470%. Similar growth patterns as in CESEE are noticed in other development regions and countries such Malaysia (+430%), Central and Caribbean America (+470%), the Andean Community (+440%) or in the ASEAN (+470%). On the other hand, EU15 countries had a cumulative growth of less than 100% in the past 25 years. Following the current trend, it can be possible for the CESEE countries to reach the nominal GDP of EU3 (Spain, Portugal and Greece) in the next five to ten years, despite starting from only 30% of the EU3 level in 1992.

Between 2000 and 2007, real exports per capita increased by a factor of 2.5 in the Baltics and the Visegrád region compared to only 1.35 in EU15. This export boom stemmed from the ability to produce goods and services to the standards of international markets and integration into the global value chains. In addition, joining the EU entailed the prospects of accessing the Single Market, an important condition for non-EU firms looking to gain a market share in the EU. Today, the Baltics are exporting in real terms almost five times as much as in 2000, whereas the Visegrád countries, Romania or Bulgaria have multiplied their exports by a factor of 2.5. During the same period, the EU15 did not even double its exports. This increase in trade was not only within the Single Market but with other non-EU countries as well.

This significant increase in trade openness was facilitated to a large degree by the inflow of FDI. These countries had an important increase in FDI stock from barely $10 billion in 1992 to almost $800 bn today. It has to be acknowledged, however, that foreign investment in this region was minimal before 1990, since most countries were functioning as closed economies. Czechoslovakia ($1.3 bn in 1988) and Yugoslavia ($1.6 bn in

[4] For consistency with UN data, we use US Dollars when comparing the CESEE countries with the rest of the world. We use euro when comparing the countries at the EU level.

1988) were the first countries in the region to open their economies to foreign investors. In 1992, two thirds of the FDI stock in CESEE was generated by Czechoslovakia ($3.3 bn) and Hungary ($3.4 bn). Apart from Slovenia ($1.8 bn) and Poland ($1.4 bn), the stock of the other countries in the region was below $200 m. By 1997, the stock increased five-fold, and by 2002, just before enlargement, it grew by a factor of 16. The largest nominal increase took place between 2002 and 2007 when the stock increased with almost $400 bn. The 2004 and 2007 enlargement waves encouraged foreign investors to bring in equity to these countries as labour costs were significantly lower and the EU legal protection of their investments was ensured. Since 2007, the stock growth stabilised, growing by only 25%. The cumulative stock of the CESEE countries in 2017 was similar to countries or regions like Brazil, the Eurasian Economic Union, Australia, Africa, EU3 or ASEAN (excluding Singapore).

As a share of GDP, the FDI stock grew from 4% in 1992 to 53% in 2017, one of the strongest increases seen in recent history. Most of the growth took place between 1992 and 2007 when the increase was around 45 percentage points (pps). Between 2007 and 2012, the stock to GDP in the CESEE countries was actually higher than in the EU. Among the regional blocks having a similar population (around 100 million people), only Egypt (56%) and Vietnam (58%) have higher shares. Rather surprisingly, the share of FDI stock in GDP in the EU periphery countries[5] is significantly higher (63%), having increased by 26 pps since 2012. During the same period, the share in the CESEE countries remained unchanged, suggesting some investors may have moved their attention to the periphery of the EU. This may mirror the 2002–2007 period when the share in the CESEE countries increased by 17 pps, significantly above the 5 pps growth in EU3, as investors moved from southern Europe to the newer member states in Central and Eastern Europe. The FDI stock per capita, however, gives a different picture. At $7500, the CESEE countries still lag behind the EU average ($18,000) but are significantly above most other regional blocs.

The stock of FDI in the EU from within the Single Market is around 65%, with the rest coming primarily from the USA, Switzerland and Bermuda. However, the figure is much higher in the CESEE countries, showing a higher dependency on the Single Market than in older member

[5] Albania, Bosnia-Herzegovina, Georgia, Moldova, Montenegro, North Macedonia, Serbia, Ukraine.

states. The share reaches at least 80% in most CESEE countries, going up to 93% in the case of Slovakia. This reflects the integration of the new member states in the regional value chains. Non-EU FDI is the highest in Latvia at 27%, mostly due to Russian investments. Looking at the (immediate) partner countries, the Netherlands is the biggest investor in 6 out of the 11 countries, followed by Germany and Austria.[6] Sweden is the biggest investor in the Baltics, while Czechia is a large investor in Slovakia.

In 2017, Poland (€180 bn) and Czechia (€116 bn) had the largest FDI stocks among the CESEE countries, while Latvia (€13 bn), Lithuania (€14 bn) and Slovenia (€13 bn) had the lowest ones. Poland has the largest stock in most economic sectors as well as in the economy as a whole. Only in the hotels and restaurants sector is it overtaken by Croatia, as the tourism industry is much larger there. Czechia comes second and although it has a smaller economy, its nominal stock is similar to that of Poland in car manufacturing and financial services. Romania comes in third, with particularly large foreign investments in energy and construction. At the other end, Slovenia, Latvia and Lithuania are the smallest contributors, as their stock in any sector does not contribute with more than 4% to the total CESEE stock. Looking more closely at sectors, data suggest that apart from the Baltics and Bulgaria, the share of manufacturing in total FDI stock is significantly larger than the EU average (13%). The Visegrád countries, Slovenia and Romania all have shares above 30%. On the other hand, apart from Estonia (79%), all countries have a lower share for services compared to the EU average. Romania is the lowest in this regard, with only 47% of total stock.

While at the EU level half of the FDI stock is generated via Special-Purpose Entities (SPEs),[7] amongst the CESEE countries, this phenomenon is only prevalent in Hungary, where out of the €226 bn inward stock, €150 bn are channelled using these SPEs. A similar figure is seen for the outward stock, suggesting large quantities of funds are only channelled through Hungary, leaving the actual investment in the country

[6] The Netherlands appears often among top investors because of their intermediate role: many investment projects are channelled via special purpose vehicles and entities for fiscal and regulatory reasons (see, e.g. Weyzig 2013).

[7] An SPE is legal entity with no or few non-financial assets and employees, little or no production or operations and sometimes no physical presence beyond a 'brass plate' confirming its place of registration. Half of EU's FDI is channelled via SPEs, particularly in Netherlands, Luxembourg and Malta.

significantly lower. A limited amount of FDI channelled via SPEs is also visible in Poland and Estonia, but the quantities are rather negligible.

In 2016, at the regional (NUTS 2) level (see Annex C), the largest stock of FDI relative to GDP is found in the capital regions of the Visegrád countries, namely Prague (164%), Bratislava (130%) and Warsaw (101%). Excluding the capital regions, the largest levels are found in the Hungarian Western Danube (95%) and Central Transdanubia (67%) and in the Czech Moravian-Silesia (46%). On the other side, the lowest are found in three Polish regions—Podlaskie (6%), Lublin (8%) and Warmian-Masurian (9%), the Romanian North West (9%) and Eastern Slovenia (13%). In nominal terms, the highest stock is found in Masovian Region (Warsaw), followed by Prague, Central Hungary (Budapest), the Silesian Region and Bucharest-Ilfov, all with more than €40 billion. The Polish regions of Podlaskie and Warminsko-Mazurskie and the Bulgarian Northwestern region[8] have a stock below €1 bn.

According to the Coface ranking of the largest companies operating in Central and Eastern Europe, 9 of the largest 15 companies were foreign-owned in 2017. These include Skoda Auto (Czechia), Jeronimo Martins (Poland), Audi Hungary, VW Slovakia, Alpiq Energy (Czechia), Hyundai Motors (Czechia), Kia Motors (Slovakia) and Dacia (Romania). The other six companies in the top-15 not considered foreign-owned operate in Poland (five) and Hungary (one). In this regard, the discrepancy between Poland and Romania, the two largest countries in the region, is noticeable. While in Poland only three of the largest 10 companies were foreign-owned, Romania had no domestic companies in the rankings. Similarly, while most top-10 Slovenian are domestic, most Slovak and Czech companies are foreign-owned. In Hungary, two out of the top three companies are domestic but all the rest in the top ten are foreign-owned.

In general, the CESEE countries are recipients of FDI. While the total stock of inward FDI in CESEE is around 10% of the total EU stock (excluding SPEs), the total stock of outward FDI generated by these 11 countries amounts to only 1.2% of the EU total. Estonia (26%), Hungary (21%) and Slovenia (14%) are the most active in this regard, having a more significant share of outward stock to GDP.[9] On the other hand, Romania

[8] Figures for Bulgarian regions only include non-financial FDI.

[9] However, some of the data may be misleading. A case in point is Estonia where outward FDI in the financial sector is driven by local branches of Swedish banks operating in the region (see, e.g. Durán 2019).

(0.4%), Slovakia (3%) and Bulgaria (4%) have very low levels. Similar to inward FDI, most outward FDI is mostly done in other EU countries, particularly in the Netherlands, Luxembourg and Cyprus (countries that have a significant amount of FDI channelled via SPEs). The Baltics also focus on Russia while Slovenia and Croatia focus a lot on the non-EU countries of the former Yugoslavia. Hungary has a particular interest in Israel. At the EU level, similar to the inward FDI, most outward FDI goes to (or via) the USA, Switzerland and Bermuda.

3.3 The Benefits of EU Membership for FDI

As argued above, first the prospects of joining the EU, and later actual membership, played a key role in attracting FDI in the CESEE countries. Foreign investors became very interested in these countries due to their proximity to the West, the adoption of the EU legislation and the fact that their goods, services and capital could move freely within the union. While the access to the Single Market and the Customs Union may be the most obvious advantages, investors may also be interested in the fact that some of the CESEE countries have also become part of the euro area and/or the Schengen area.

3.3.1 Benefits of the Single Market

The most obvious advantage of membership is full access to the Single Market, without the tariffs and barriers imposed to non-EU members and with more legal certainty than any kind of trade agreement. The Single Market is not only about trade, but also about the Four Freedoms: movement of goods, services, people and capital. All the four are very important for foreign investors. Goods can be easily traded across borders, businesses can be set up anywhere in the union and workers can be employed from any member state. Finally, capital can flow freely throughout the union, allowing investors a significant flexibility in deciding where to put their money. In this regard, Single Market rules allow to tax dividends in the country of origin of a company.

Joining the Single Market comes along with adoption of the EU legislation with implications that range from the functioning of the judicial sector, to public procurement rules and regulatory quality. For the CESEE countries, this regulatory framework started applying even before the proper accession, going back to the signing of the Association Agreements.

Joining the EU also entitled these countries to benefit from pre-accession Structural Funds, which helped them to modernise infrastructures in preparation for membership. Large flows of EU funds continue even today to support their economic development and further convergence towards the West.

3.3.2 *Benefits of the Customs Union*

Being part of the EU Customs Union is of paramount importance for foreign investors that focus their business on cross-border trade. Being part of this union allows the countries to trade without tariffs and non-tariff barriers to trade with the old member states. It also allows them to be part of major free trade deals with benefits they could have not obtained if they negotiated individually from outside the Customs Union. The Customs Union also allowed the CESEE countries to become more integrated in the global value chains, as the customs checks at their borders were eliminated. All these benefits have significantly increased the potential for FDI within but also outside the EU. On the other side, it also stopped these countries from giving preferential tariffs and it put constraints on providing subsidies to declining industries.

3.3.3 *Benefits of the Schengen Agreement*

Particularly in the case of the trade of goods, the fact that there are no border checks within the Schengen area can provide an important incentive for investors. A recent study from the European Parliament (2016) suggested that a full and permanent suspension of Schengen could lead to a loss of 0.14% of GDP for the EU as a whole, amounting to around €230 billion over ten years. The Schengen agreement has also been beneficial for labour mobility, particularly in areas where cross-border mobility is important (i.e. Vienna and Bratislava).

3.3.4 *Benefits of Euro Adoption*

Already years before enlargement, most CESEE countries committed to low and stable inflation, many with a view to joining the euro. Joining the common currency eliminated exchange rate risk and lowers transaction costs, a significant benefit for countries relying heavily on trade and foreign funding. Eliminating exchange rate risks also reduced risk premia and, thus, funding costs, particularly in smaller countries with potentially more volatile currencies. Joining the euro also meant adopting the second largest reserve currency and the second most traded currency in the world.

3.4 Productivity Growth in the FDI-Intensive Economic Sectors

The share of FDI stock in sectoral gross value added (GVA) shows a mixed picture across sectors.[10] Somewhat contrary to common belief, in the manufacturing sector the share of FDI in 2015 was higher in the EU (91%) than in the CESEE countries (74%). That is, however, not the case for car manufacturing where the share of FDI (110%) is almost triple the EU level (45%). In the other manufacturing subsectors, however, the share of FDI is around 30 percentage points below the EU level. These figures show that when excluding the car industry, manufacturing in this region is not that FDI-intensive. FDI in energy, transport and financial services is higher in the EU, while FDI in real estate, construction, hotels and restaurants and ICT is higher in the CESEE countries. In wholesale and retail trade it is rather similar to the EU average. The difference is particularly striking in financial services where due to the inclusion of SPE-generated FDI, the share of FDI stock in GVA reached 1226% in EU, compared to 'only' 287% in the CESEE countries.

In most of the sectors, the increase in the share of FDI stock in GVA between 2004 and 2015 was not very high (between +5 and +20 pps). Only in ICT (+27 pps), real estate (+46 pps) and financial services (+99 pps) the growth was more significant as, after accession, most foreign investors focused on services. The share in the car industry increased by around 12 pps and in other sectors by 7 pps, suggesting that the sector was already consolidated by the time of accession. There are, however, large sectoral differences between the CESEE countries. The largest difference is seen in the financial sector where the share of FDI stock in GVA varies from 140% in Romania to 655% in Estonia. All three Baltic countries have a very high share of FDI in this sector. Large variations are also seen in real estate (from 30% in Slovenia to 178% in Estonia), car manufacturing (from 25% in Croatia to 134% in Poland) and wholesale/retail

[10] Due to data availability, all data in this section include FDI generated via SPEs.

(from 26% in Lithuania to 115% in Estonia). Estonia is somewhat of an outlier, having disproportionally higher figures compared to the other countries in finance, real estate, transport and wholesale/retail.

3.4.1 Productivity Developments in the CESEE Countries

Excluding the information and communications sector (ICT) sector, in all the analysed sectors gross value added per hour of employee increased more in the CESEE countries than in EU. The largest increase was in the car manufacturing sector where it grew by 80% between 2004 and 2015. Still, the level achieved in 2015 is just about half the EU as a whole had in 2004 and more than half lower than the EU level in 2015. The gap in productivity shrank by 2–5 pps in most sectors but remains consistently high. The largest gap is in real estate, which can probably be explained by the significant price differences between older and newer member states. The smallest gap is found in wholesale and retail and in transport.

Excluding real estate, the highest productivity level in the CESEE countries in 2015 was in financial services and energy. The lowest was in hotels and restaurants, wholesale and retail, and construction. As in the case of FDI, there are also big differences between countries. In the analysed sectors, the differences between countries vary from 133% in ICT to 481% in construction. Construction in Slovakia is the only sector where the EU level is below the level seen in a particular CESEE country. Despite being a mostly domestic sector (FDI stock in GVA was only 8% in 2015), this sector saw an increase of 132% in productivity since accession.

Despite the notable catching up since the 1990s, with the exception of construction and transport, sectoral productivity in the EU in 2004 was above the levels seen in the CESEE countries in 2015. The most striking difference is in ICT, where productivity in 2004 in the EU was 60% higher than in 2015 in Czechia, the most productive CESEE country in this sector. Energy, and hotels and restaurants see similar gaps between EU and Slovenia, the most productive CESEE country in these sectors. Bulgaria is usually the least productive (in 7 out of the 11 analysed sectors) while Slovenia the most productive (in 7 out of 11 sectors). When excluding Romania and Bulgaria, Poland moves to the bottom of the rankings in most sectors (8 out of 11 sectors). Among the large car producers, Czechia and Hungary are the most productive.[11] At an aggregate level, Slovenia, Slovakia and Czechia seem to be the most productive countries in the region. At the other end, Bulgaria, Romania, Hungary and Poland seem to be the laggards.

It goes beyond the scope of this note to quantify the impact of FDI on aggregate productivity but it is likely that the slowdown of productivity growth in CESEE countries after the crisis is at least partially linked to subdued FDI inflows despite the recent recovery. Recent research shows that the slowdown of total factor productivity (TFP) growth since 2010 can be attributed almost entirely to 'reshoring', the tendency of some foreign firms to relocate activities back in their home country (Durán 2019).

3.5 Why Is Foreign Direct Investment so Important for the CESEE Countries?

Access to external funding is not just a matter of access to capital. Attracting foreign direct investment in these countries has been of paramount importance since it brought additional funding and new technologies, upgrading entire sectors and fostering integration into global value chains.[12] Currently, the CESEE region's integration into the regional and global value chains is significantly above the EU average.

From the beginning, it should be mentioned that FDI in the CESEE countries is highly profitable for investors. Whereas the rate of return on FDI in EU15 was as high as 6.7% in Sweden, Czechia and Lithuania had as much as 11–12%, followed by Poland, Slovakia and Latvia with around 8–10% (Eurostat data from 2015). Excluding Croatia, where the rate is negative (-0.6%) and the lowest in EU, all CESEE countries had a rate of at least 6%. These rates may slightly decrease in the near future as most of these countries saw significant increases in labour costs in recent years. Since 2012, the total amount of wages and salaries increased more strongly than the EU average (14%) in all of them. Apart from Slovenia (15%), the increase in 2012–2018 in each country was between 24% and 57%, not including the notable case of Romania where the increase was around

[11] Lithuania has higher productivity levels, but the car manufacturing sector is very small in the country.

[12] There is a vast literature on this. For FDI and long-term growth see, for example, Hansen and Rand (2006). For a general overview of theory and empirics of technology diffusion, see Keller (2004).

106%. Nonetheless, as Table A.1 shows, net earnings in CESEE are still significantly below the EU average, ranging from below 20% the EU average in Bulgaria to roughly 50% in Slovenia. Thus, even with the high growth of labour costs, the CESEE countries remain highly profitable for foreign investors.

FDI can serve local or international markets. In the case of the CESEE countries, all of them planned economies until 1990; sectors like banking or real estate were less developed than in the West. In the case of banking, for example, foreign firms contributed a reputation of solvency that would have been difficult to build for newly created firms. These two sectors attracted considerable amounts of investment in the first years of the economic liberalisation. The relatively low level of labour costs compared to the EU15 average also spurred large investments in export sectors to serve international markets. The car industry is a case in point in some countries, but manufacturing in general or wholesale trade follows similar patterns.

Whether it is to serve local or international markets, FDI is an important source of capital and jobs as well as a channel of technical change. Even during the economic transition, FDI has brought jobs and wages that would have remained abroad otherwise. Hence, FDI can be seen as a factor mitigating emigration pressures with possible important consequences in terms of the human capital stock. FDI is also a source of capital formation beyond the capacity of local savings. Even in the case of mergers and acquisitions, FDI flows entail a form of long-term commitment and usually some form of real investment. Even more direct is the impact of greenfield FDI where the investment entails the building of new production facilities from scratch. More importantly, FDI goes beyond simple capital accumulation and brings in new technologies in the form of intra-firm technological transfers, including new production techniques, new goods, production processes and management know-how.[13] Technological upgrading and increased productivity also come from the integration of the firm or plant in the new parent company's supply chain.

The benefits of FDI are not limited to the firms directly concerned. Indirect effects or potential positive spillovers may stem from a variety of mechanisms. Increased competition of purchased or newly established

[13]This is, of course, not mechanical. Borenszteina et al. (1998) explore the conditions under which FDI increases productivity more than domestic investment. Not surprisingly, the formation of human capital turns out to be a critical factor.

firms fosters efficiency and innovation among local competitors. For the same reason, spillovers can arise also upwards and downwards the value chain, exerting pressure to improve quality standards to providers higher up in the value chain and provide better goods downwards. The workforce improves its productivity not only because it operates newer and better capital but also because of learning-by-doing in a more efficient environment. FDI often improves the absorptive capacity of leading firms (close to the efficiency frontier), which in turn spill down to less performing firms.[14]

3.6 So Why Is FDI Becoming More and More Controversial in the CESEE Countries?

Despite a consensus around its benefits, foreign investment remains a sensitive issue in many countries. Criticism goes from losing control of national industries to repatriated profits, relaxing environmental standards or selling at discount national assets or natural resources in case of crisis. Recently, there has been a tendency in the region to increase the criticism of foreign investors. While some arguments may be seen as political discourse, some others may have some substance.[15]

In smaller countries, large foreign groups with 'deep pockets' may engage in anticompetitive practices to drive out of the market local competitors. This may be a theoretical possibility but it is rather difficult to verify in practice since the difference between anticompetitive practices and competitiveness is not always clear.[16] In addition, it is up to competition authorities to prevent this kind of behaviour leading to excessive market power, regardless whether it is a foreign or a domestic investment. A similar and common critique is that some investors aim taking over distribution channels and networks. While it may be true in some cases, whether the purchaser is foreign or not should probably be less relevant.

A common popular concern is the fiscal advantages granted to foreign firms for them to establish in a given country or region. If competition

[14] See Chiacchio et al. (2018) for the effect of FDI on the absorptive capacity of frontier firms and the trickle-down effect on laggards.

[15] For a more nuanced view on FDI in general, see Mencinger (2003) and references therein.

[16] In general, foreign firms often perform better in terms of capital, labour and corporate governance.

across regions or countries takes the form of better infrastructures or business environment, it could serve the general interest. In the EU, the risk of this type of behaviour on the side of governments is limited even within regions of the same country because of state aid rules. It is more difficult, however, to control competition between countries in tax rates. Hungary (9%) and Bulgaria (10%), for example, have the lowest corporate tax rate in the whole EU. In general, corporate tax rates in CESEE are slightly lower compared to EU15, with a maximum of 21% in Slovakia. The same goes for the withholding taxes on dividends. On the other hand, some of these countries imposed special levies on certain sectors such as banking, energy or telecommunications. While such taxes are also common in some Western countries, the CESEE countries focused more on assets rather than profits, to hamper the repatriation of profits.

In the case of extractive industries, a common critique is the 'looting' of natural resources in exchange of insufficient compensation. It may be fair to say that currently this phenomenon is probably more common outside the EU, in developing economies with weak institutions and pervasive corruption. However, it has also been used as an argument by certain politicians in the pre-accession phase. A related complaint is that foreign firms are granted a more relaxed interpretation of environmental standards as a form of stimulating investment. In addition, certain investors that are physically far away from the region may be less sensitive to environmental considerations. That is yet another reason to strengthen environmental standards for both domestic and foreign firms.

There may also be a reluctance to give control to foreign powers of national assets, particularly in some strategic industries, notably defence and aerospace. Beyond these particular sectors, this argument is not particularly solid and the value of the stock of intangible capital of a company—be it know-how, patent portfolios, organisational capital or alike—is a crucial element of the value of many companies, irrespective of the nationality of the purchaser. In other words, it is perfectly normal to purchase a company for its technology. In some cases, however, some monitoring may be justified.[17] If it is not the case, however, an investment

[17] In this regard, the EU has recently adopted a new EU framework for the screening of FDI in order to better scrutinise purchases by foreign companies that target Europe's strategic assets. The area remains a national competency but it will enhance cooperation among member states on these matters.

remains just an investment whether the investor resides in the country or not. Moreover, most companies involved in cross-border investment are multinational enterprises with shareholders spread over many countries. It is doubtful that this kind of enterprise has a 'nationality' so that they are going to serve any objective that is not rendering value to their shareholders.

There is also a frequent complaint about selling at discount national assets or natural resources during crises, which may be partially true but part of the normal functioning of a market.[18] Perhaps more relevant is the claim that foreign plants are the first to go in bad economic times in contrast to domestic companies. For reasons easy to understand, the withdrawal of a multinational enterprise will often lead to the closure of local plants and their separation from the multinational supply chain, with the consequent loss of opportunities and productivity.[19] While the reshoring is a real phenomenon, there are important counterexamples in which particularly the foreign branches survive the consolidation processes. In addition, past research fails to prove that a firm with a foreign owner is a less reliable employer then a comparable domestic firm.

It is also sometimes claimed that foreign plants bring with them their own network of suppliers, often foreign-owned companies themselves, which mitigate the potential channels for positive spillovers upwards and downwards the value chain. This criticism is particularly strong in the car industry, where the big producers bring with them their own Tier1 and Tier2 suppliers, which are fully integrated into the value chains of the main company. Nevertheless, casual empiricism does not support that this is a generalised phenomenon. Recent research also suggests that there have been significant positive technological spillovers towards the domestic companies in the areas close to the major foreign investments (Szabo 2019).

Finally, repatriation of profits has become an increasing criticism, particularly in the Visegrád region, partly because it leads to a sizeable gap between the GDP and Gross National Income (GNI) of these countries. Since accession, foreign-owned companies repatriated around €100

[18] Contessi et al. (2013) note that FDI inflows are countercyclical in developing countries, most likely because of the low price of local firms for potential foreign owners during recessions, particularly during large devaluations or depreciations of the local currency.

[19] Javorcik and Poelhekke (2017) show for a sample of Indonesian firms that disinvestment is associated with a drop in total factor productivity, output, mark-ups and export and import intensities.

billion in profits from both Czechia and Poland. Furthermore, in Slovakia, data suggest since 2004, almost three quarters of the income generated by foreign investors in the country was distributed as dividends. Nonetheless, the overall contribution of FDI to the economies of the CESEE countries has been significantly positive even if the outflow of dividends has been high. The total amount of wages, salaries and employers' social contributions paid by foreign firms is substantially higher than the dividends these companies distribute (Szabo 2019). Furthermore, in many countries in the region due to increased labour productivity, foreign firms offer significantly higher wages than the national average. In addition, repatriation of profits is not a region-specific phenomenon. Brada and Tomšík (2009) divide the profitability life cycle of FDI in three stages. At the entry stage foreign firms are usually losing money and do not distribute dividends. Moving into the growth stage, most earnings are reinvested in order to increase the market share. Finally, at maturity, the focus shifts to profit repatriation, either as dividends for shareholders or as seed money for other markets in other countries where investments are still in an early phase. After all, FDI is still a regular investment and, as any investment, it has to render a yield to investors.

Much of these reservations concerning FDI do not seem to have a solid base. However, it is probably fair to say that the positive effects of FDI are conditional on a series of characteristics of the recipient country, such as effective and transparent regulatory environment, absence of corruption and a functioning rule of law and trade openness. In this respect, the role of the regulatory environment is paramount (the cost of enforcing contracts and the ease to pay taxes are important factors to decide to invest in a country by foreign investors). Further, once the investment is decided, the size of the project depends on the level of protection of incumbents (the extent to which competition is limited in certain markets) and other barriers to trade and investment (e.g. discrimination against foreign firms) (Canton and Solera 2016).

3.7 Conclusions

The speed of convergence and the development of FDI in the CESEE countries are clearly interlinked. This duality has seen three main timeframes in the past three decades. The first corresponds to the early and mid-1990s, when these countries started opening their economies and, to various degrees, privatise some of their state-owned enterprises. Privatisation was seen as paramount for structural reforms to create market economies and improve productivity and economic growth. Foreign firms started entering these markets, particularly in the manufacturing-intensive countries. The second period started in the late 1990s, when most of the CESEE countries were on the path to EU accession, incorporating EU law at a fast pace. The share of FDI stock in GDP in the region more than doubled between 1997 and the first accession wave of 2004. As it became clear that certain of these countries will join, the region became an *El Dorado* of foreign investment, with annual inflows as high as 10% of GDP. The final stage started at the end of the 2010s when the share of the infusion of capital stabilised and annual FDI inflows dropped. This is the period when investments reached maturity and started providing much higher rates of return. As most FDI in the CESEE countries comes from other EU member states, countries in the region are much more dependent on the Single Market than in older member states, which have a much larger exposure to global markets. Furthermore, a lot of the non-EU foreign investment in CESEE has come particularly because of the participation of these countries in the Single Market. This may suggest that the increase of FDI is also a direct consequence of the EU membership. Access to the Single Market, the Customs Union and in some cases joining the euro and/or Schengen area are of paramount importance for foreign investors from both within and outside the EU. Nevertheless, despite a consensus that FDI can only bring benefits to the domestic economies, there has been an increasing criticism towards foreign investors in the region. However, there are very few arguments supporting a counterfactual scenario where a converging country would be better off without foreign investment.

Annex A: Some Basic Figures

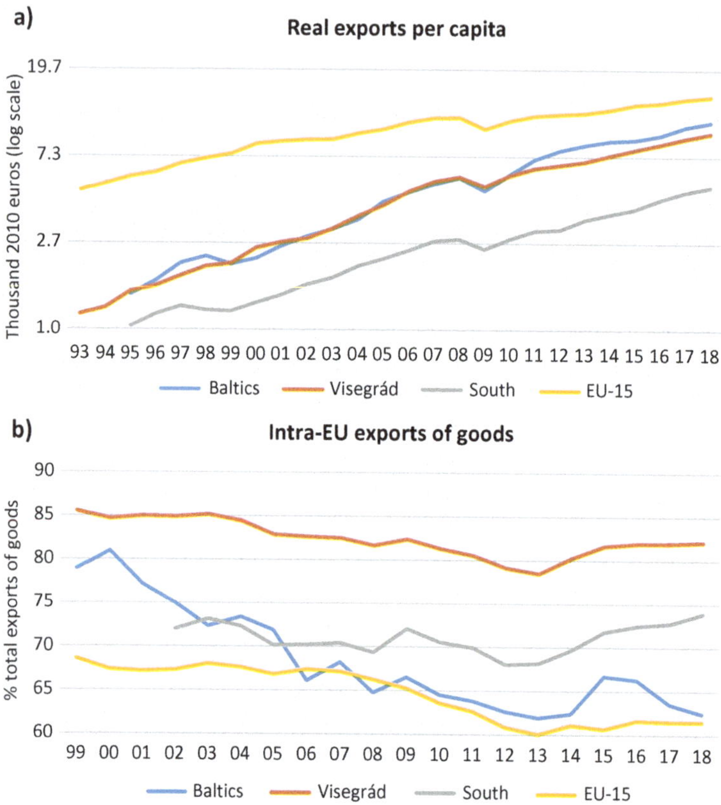

Fig. A.1 Trade and investment in CEE countries. (**a**) Real exports per capita, (**b**) share of intra-EU exports, (**c**) investment rate, excluding dwellings, (**d**) balance of FDI flows. Notes: (i) The Baltics are Estonia, Latvia and Lithuania; Visegrád countries are Czechia, Slovakia, Poland and Hungary; the South is Bulgaria, Romania, Slovenia and Croatia. (Source: Own calculations based on the AMECO database and UNCTAD)

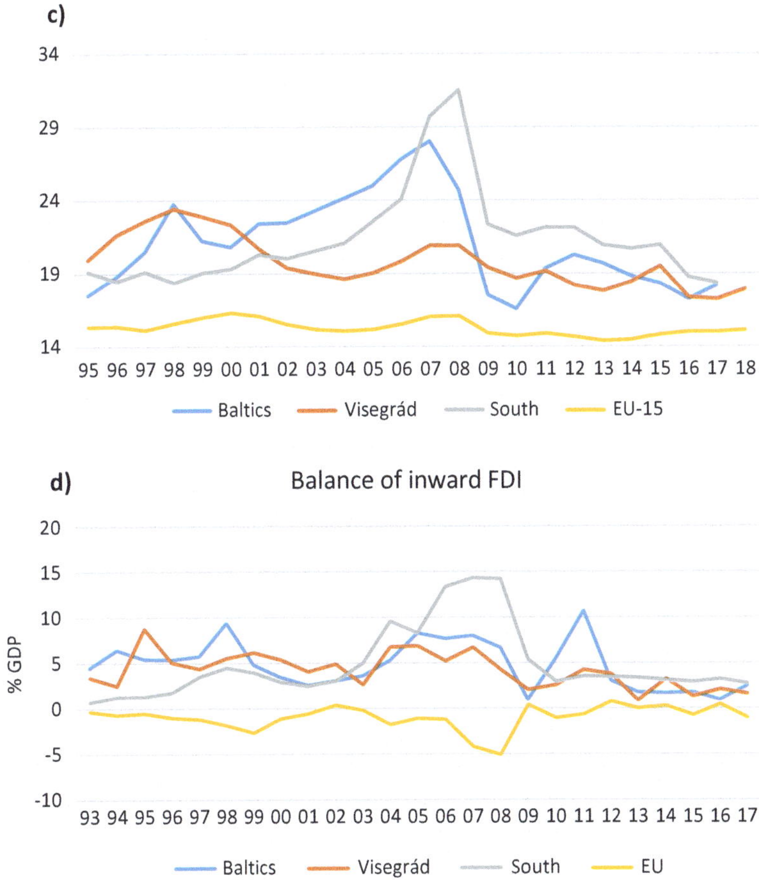

Fig. A.1 (continued)

Table A.1 Detailed data on inward and outward FDI in CESEE in 2016

MS	*GDP*		*Net annual earnings per capita (€)*	*Inward FDI*								*Outward investment*					
	Nominal (bn)	*Per capita (EU = 100)*		*Stock in billion €*	*Stock from SPEs (billion €) (%)*	*Stock/ GDP (excl. SPEs) (%)*	*FDI from other EU countries (%)*	*Share of manufac-turing in total stock (%)*	*Share of services in total stock (%)*	*Top-3 largest investors in the country*	*Return rate in 2015 (%)*	*Stock in billion €*	*Stock from SPEs (billion €)*	*Stock/ GDP (excl. SPEs) (%)*	*FDI in other EU countries (%)*	*Top-3 destination of foreign investment*	*Return rate in 2015 (%)*
BG	48.1	48	4333	40.8	0	85	78	17	63	NL CH DE	5.5	2.1	0	4	52		-1.1
CZ	176.4	88	8940	115.6	0	66	84	32	60	NL DE LU	12.2	17	0	10	92	NL SK CY	9.4
EE	21.7	77	10,638	18.7	0.5	86	83	13	79	SE FI NL	6.8	6.1	0.5	26	92	LT FI RU	5.1
HR	46.6	61	8841	26.2	0	56	87	21	70	NL AT IT	-0.6	4.8	0	10	48	NL BiH SL	-4.0
LV	25	64	6814	13.5	0	54	73	12	68	SE RU CY	7.6	1.5	0	6	68	LT EE RU	12.9
LT	38.8	75	6651	13.9	0	36	80	19	73	SE NL DE	11.2	2.5	0	7	89	NL CY LV	3.5
HU	113.9	67	6702	225.9	149.5	67	79	30	62	DE NL AT	6.0	183.1	159.4	21	71	BE IL CY	2.6
PL	426.6	68	8967	179.8	0.9	42	92	31	61	NL DE LU	9.7	26.8	0.4	6	68	LU CY CH	3.0
RO	170.4	59	5119	70.1	0	41	90	32	47	NL DE AT	5.8	0.7	0	0.4	N/A		-13.8
SI	40.4	83	12,062	13.0	0	32	85	33	61	AT LU CH	8.5	5.7	0	14	43	HR SRB BiH	0.9
SK	81.4	77	8200	45.1	0	56	93	32	58	NL AT CZ	8.2	2.5	0	3	81	CZ NL PL	7.7
EU	14,958	100	24,183	14,385	7.007	49	65	13	81 (SPEs)	US CH BMU	3.8	16,960	7845	61	57	US CH BMU	4.4

Source: Own calculations based on data from the European Commission, Eurostat, OECD, BoP data available at the national level (central bank and/or statistics institute)

Table A.2 Breakdown of the FDI stock in CESEE

	BG (%)	*CZ (%)*	*EE (%)*	*HU (%)*	*LV (%)*	*LT (%)*	*PL (%)*	*RO (%)*	*SI (%)*	*SK (%)*	*HR (%)*	*Total CESEE (million €)*
Manufacturing	4	23	2	5	1	2	35	13	3	9	4	155,921
•Car manufacturing	1	29	0	14	0	1	32	12	1	9	0	123,771
•Other manufacturing	5	21	2	3	1	2	36	13	3	9	5	32,150
Energy	12	15	1	10	2	1	25	24	2	7	1	26,028
Construction	4	7	1	4	3	2	50	21	1	3	5	17,008
Wholesale/retail	6	15	3	11	2	2	37	11	3	5	3	71,341
Transport	4	16	8	12	4	3	21	11	3	15	3	11,204
Hotels restaurants	14	12	2	11	2	1	19	11	2	1	23	4582
ICT	5	19	2	16	1	4	29	11	2	7	4	32,731
Finance	6	24	4	11	3	3	25	7	2	8	7	122,034
Real estate	7	17	7	11	4	4	30	9	1	6	3	46,610

Source: Own calculations based on data from the European Commission, Eurostat, BoP data available at the national level (central bank and/or statistics institute)

Table A.3 The share of FDI to GDP in different regional blocks around the world

FDI stock/GDP	*1992 (%)*	*1997 (%)*	*2002 (%)*	*2007 (%)*	*2012 (%)*	*2017 (%)*	*pps increase*	*Population (m)*	*FDI/ capita in 2017 ($)*
Japan	0	1	2	3	3	4	4	127	1634
Bangladesh	2	3	5	6	6	6	4	165	88
China (mainland)	7	16	15	9	10	12	5	1409	1058
Mercosur (excluding Brazil)	7	16	38	21	16	14	6	87	1548
India	1	2	5	9	12	15	14	1340	282
South Korea & Taiwan	3	4	10	11	13	15	12	75	4232
Turkey	6	6	8	23	22	21	15	80	2259
Philippines	7	10	14	14	15	25	18	105	750
Eurasian Union	0	4	22	37	23	34	34	182	3427
ASEAN (excluding. Singapore)	11	18	21	27	31	36	25	645	1360
Brazil	13	8	20	22	30	38	25	209	3724
NW Africa (Morocco, Tunisia, Algeria)	14	18	26	30	29	38	24	88	1369
Africa (whole continent)	12	13	26	28	28	40	28	1225	708
NAFTA (USA, Canada, Mexico)	11	19	20	29	28	42	31	490	19,144
Mexico	9	11	21	30	38	42	34	130	3763
Andean Community	7	16	24	27	29	47	39	101	3050
Malaysia & Thailand	17	22	32	37	43	47	30	101	3554
Australia	24	24	35	40	39	47	23	24	27,596
Central & Caribbean America	8	10	22	28	37	48	40	80	2436
EU3S (Spain, Portugal, Greece)	11	17	32	37	44	48	37	67	12,245
EU15	11	17	28	39	43	50	39	410	19,312

(*continued*)

Table A.3 (continued)

FDI stock/GDP	*1992 (%)*	*1997 (%)*	*2002 (%)*	*2007 (%)*	*2012 (%)*	*2017 (%)*	*pps increase*	*Population (m)*	*FDI/capita in 2017 ($)*
MedCasp (Azerbaijan, Israel, Jordan, Lebanon)	6	11	27	42	40	52	46	35	7313
EU	11	17	28	40	46	53	42	513	17,786
CESEE	**4**	**14**	**32**	**49**	**53**	**53**	**49**	**103**	**7541**
Egypt	26	20	24	38	28	56	31	95	1154
Vietnam	11	39	50	41	47	58	47	95	1363
EU periphery (Albania, Bosnia-Herzegovina, Georgia, Montenegro, North Macedonia, Ukraine, Serbia)	0	3	12	24	37	63	62	70	2005
EFTA	11	18	37	63	84	110	99	14	87,086
OFC8 (Bermuda, Hong-Kong, Cayman Islands, Ireland, Luxembourg, Netherlands, Singapore, Virgin Islands)	N/A	N/A	126	185	229	333	207	36	178,160

Source: Own calculations based on UNCTAD and UN statistics

Table A.4 Productivity in CESEE (gross value added per hour worked of employees in €)

	CESEE			*EU*			*Min CESEE*		*Min EU8*		*Max CESEE*	
	2004	*2015*	*Growth (%)*	*2004*	*2015*	*Growth (%)*	*2015*					
Manufacturing	€8	€13	62	€29	€41	39	BG	€7	PL	€11	SI	€26
•Car manufacturing	€9	€16	78	€29	€39	51	BG	€6	PL	€11	SI	€32
•Other manufacturing	€8	€13	56	€35	€52	37	BG	€7	PL	€11	LT	€26
Energy	€17	€25	48	€55	€76	38	RO	€17	LT	€20	SI	€43
Construction	€9	€12	39	€28	€37	33	BG	€7	HU	€9	SK	€38
Wholesale retail	€9	€12	30	€27	€33	21	RO	€6	HU	€10	SI	€24
Transport	€9	€14	52	€29	€38	31	BG	€10	PL	€12	SI	€29
Hotels restaurants	€6	€8	29	€24	€27	12	BG	€5	PL	€6	SI	€18
ICT	€23	€24	5	€60	€65	8	BG	€16	PL	€20	CZ	€38
Finance	€17	€27	56	€59	€78	32	PL	€18	PL	€18	SK	€55
Real estate	€60	€96	60	€382	€464	22	PL	€59	PL	€59	HR	€628

Source: Own calculations based on data from the European Commission, EUROSTAT, EUKlems

Note: Due to missing data, averages do not include the years 2004–2009 in Hungary, 2004–2006 in Romania and 2004–2007 in Croatia

Table A.5 FDI stock as a share of GVA

	CESEE	*CESEE*	*CESEE growth (pps)*	*EU*	*CESEE vs. EU (pps)*	*Min CESEE*		*Max CESEE*	
	2004 (%)	*2015 (%)*		*2015 (%)*		*2015 (%)*		*2015 (%)*	
Manufacturing	65	73	9	91	-18	HU	38	104	HR
•Car manufacturing	98	110	12	45	+65	HR	25	134	PL
•Other manufacturing	61	67	7	97%	-30	HU	24	107	HR
Energy	42	61	18	71	-10	HR	21	147	BG
Construction	9	25	16	11	+14	SI	5	44	BG
Wholesale retail	35	51	16	47	+5	LT	26	115	EE
Transport	12	17	5	25	-8	LT	9	66	EE
Hotels restaurants	16	26	11	13	+13	SK	7	70	BG
ICT	43	70	27	55	+15	LV	40	114	HU
Finance	189	287	99	1226	-939	RO	140	655	EE
Real estate	24	63	39	23	+40	SI	30	178	EE

Source: Own calculations based on data from the European Commission, EUROSTAT, BoP data available at the national level (central bank and/or statistics institute)

Annex B: Some Tables with Detailed Data

Annex C: Value Added, Productivity and FDI in NUTS3 Regions

Code	*NUTS 2 region*	*Significant city*	*Top employment sector*		*Change of GDP vs EU 2007–2016*	*GVA/h*	*Wages and salaries per number of employees*				*Largest foreign investor*			*FDI stock (mil. EUR)*	*GDP (mil. EUR)*	*FDI stock/ GDP (%)*
			1st sector	*2nd sector*			*Industry*	*Construction*	*Wholesale, retail, transport, hotels & rest*	*ITC*	*Controlling group*	*From*	*Rank Coface500*			
BG31	Northwestern	Pleven	Textiles	Food	2.4	15.3	2982	2714	1851	N/A	Great Wall Motors	CN	N/A	521	3486	15
BG32	Northern Central	Ruse	Textiles	Food	5.0	15.3	3818	1976	2614	2923	HSE	SI	N/A	1023	4017	25
BG33	Northeastern	Varna	Food	Textiles	4.3	16.7	4495	3269	2563	5000	Energo Pro	CZ	N/A	2568	5457	47
BG34	Southeastern	Burgas	Food	Metals	9.8	17.2	5419	3333	2582	2339	Lukoil	RU	35	2983	6685	45
BG41	Southwestern	**Sofia**	Textiles	Food	11.5	26.0	5958	4638	5902	14,901	Aurubis	DE	43	14,496	24,742	59
BG42	Southern Central	Plovdiv	Textiles	Food	4.9	14.8	4023	1789	2409	5411	Molson Coors	US	N/A	2842	7258	39
CZ01	Prague	**Prague**	Wood	Metals	2.7	67.5	16,909	10,532	18,169	27,208	Alpiq	CH	11	80,185	48,751	164
CZ02	Central Bohemia	Mlada Boeslav	Motor	Metals	2.8	47.3	11,461	3842	6525	2344	VW	DE	2	10,306	22,784	45
CZ03	Southwest	Plzeň	Metals	Motor	4.0	42.8	9261	5746	6298	7968	Robert Bosch	DE	209	7399	19,090	39
CZ04	Northwest	Ústí nad Labem	Metals	Plastics	-1.2	38.8	8724	4591	4729	5309	PKN Orlen	PL	16	4186	14,315	29
CZ05	Northeast	Liberec	Motor	Metals	4.3	41.3	8807	4643	6277	7540	IVECO	IT	234	6727	22,981	29
CZ06	Southeast	Brno	Metals	Machinery	8.2	44.2	9321	6209	7431	18,170	Automotive Lighting	DE	334	8364	27,760	30

CZ07	Central Moravia	Olomuc	Metals	Plastics	8.0	40.0	8665	5348	6061	9940	Continental	DE	58	4484	18,024	25
CZ08	Moravian-Silesia	Ostrava	Metals	Motor	6.8	43.7	9927	4963	6649	9635	Hyundai Motor Group	KR	12	8334	18,017	46
EE00	Estonia	**Tallin**	Wood	Food	5.7	43.1	11,558	8130	10,286	13,485	Ericsson	SE	245	19,924	23,615	84
HR03	Adriatic Croatia	Split	Food	Metals	-2.8	36.5	10,965	8226	7956	11,053	OTP	HU	N/A	28,108	15,750	57
HR04	Continental Croatia	**Zagreb**	Food	Wood	-0.3	36.5	10,670	7937	9373	15,156	Deutsche Telekom	DE	239		33,240	
LV00	Latvia	**Riga**	Wood	Food	7.3	35.6	8434	6446	8013	14,510	Uralchem	RU	226	14,605	27,033	54
LT00	Lithuania	**Vilnius**	Wood	Food	15.0	38.4	8278	6758	7390	14,678	PKN	PL	20	14,816	42,191	35
HU10	Central Hungary	**Budapest**	Food	Metals	2.3	38.3	10,836	5583	9535	19,548	General Electric	US	55	43,261	53,045	82
HU21	Central Transdanubia	Székes-fehérvár	Motor	Metals	8.4	34.4	9233	3309	5235	6000	Suzuki	JP	66	7795	11,646	67
HU22	Western Danubia	Gyor	Motor	Wood	15.2	37.4	10,093	3795	6035	9333	VW	DE	6	11,846	12,452	95
HU23	Southern Danubia	Pecs	Food	Electronics	3.9	30.0	6636	3774	5419	12,139	Flex	US	74	1002	6847	15
HU31	Northern Hungary	Miskolc	Electronics	Metals	6.4	31.8	7737	3691	5276	9633	Robert Bosch	DE	23	3489	8732	40
HU32	Northern Great Plain	Debrecen	Food	Electronics	5.3	29.1	6136	3366	5205	8506	Teva	IL	215	4545	10,801	42
HU33	Southern Great Plain	Szeged	Food	Plastics	8.5	30.5	6811	4047	5273	8485	Mercedes	DE	25	2776	10,374	27
PL12	Masovian	**Warsaw**	Food	Wood	26.4	42.1	7811	6050	11,524	15,734	Orange	FR	40	95,721	94,978	101
PL21	Lesser Poland	Krakow	Metals	Food	14.7	33.4	7905	4166	6207	14,380	Tesco	UK	36	8106	33,943	24
PL22	Silesian	Katowice	Metals	Motor	14.8	36.7	10,298	5570	5358	8553	ArcelorMittal	LU	21	18,718	52,498	36
PL31	Lublin	Lublin	Food	Wood	10.0	20.4	4276	3071	2895	4586	Maxima Group	LT	348	1386	16,334	8
PL32	Subcarpathian	Rzeszów	Plastics	Wood	10.7	27.8	8389	3970	3704	6971	Goodyear	US	466	3619	16,631	22
PL33	Holy Cross	Kielce	Metals	Plastics	6.8	21.8	6531	2968	3348	N/A	CELSA Group	ES	327	1665	9957	17
PL34	Podlaskie	Białystok	Food	Wood	9.1	23.3	6118	3796	4087	4889	BAT	UK	128	514	9335	6

(*continued*)

(continued)

Code	*NUTS 2 region*	*Significant city*	*Top employment sector*		*Change of GDP vs EU 2007–2016*	*GVA/h*	*Wages and salaries per number of employees*				*Largest foreign investor*			*FDI stock (mil. EUR)*	*GDP (mil. EUR)*	*FDI stock/GDP (%)*
			1st sector	*2nd sector*			*Industry*	*Construction*	*Wholesale, retail, transport, hotels & rest*	*ITC*	*Controlling group*	*From*	*Rank Coface500*			
PL41	Greater Poland	Poznan	Wood	Food	18.5	39.0	9440	4932	9102	12,797	Jerónimo Martins	PT	4	15,842	42,120	38
PL42	West Pomeranian	Szczecin	Wood	Food	10.3	36.0	7148	3815	5202	13,136	IKEA	SE	163	3530	15,899	22
PL43	Lubusz	Zielona Góra	Wood	Motor	10.0	29.6	7161	2203	3668	N/A	Krono Holding	CH	435	1795	9476	19
PL51	Lower Silesian	Wroclaw	Motor	Plastics	17.9	39.3	10,126	4628	6294	10,287	Schwarz Gruppe	DE	49	9970	35,712	28
PL52	Opole	Opole	Metals	Food	9.9	30.5	7150	3792	3734	N/A	Brenntag	DE	482	1396	8786	16
PL61	Kuyavian-Pomeranian	Bydgoszcz	Wood	Metals	10.1	27.5	7031	4098	4327	3636	Framondi	NL	264	2605	18,872	14
PL62	Warmian-Masurian	Olsztyn	Wood	Food	9.5	24.7	6712	3288	3208	N/A	VH Group	CN	130	993	11,373	9
PL63	Pomeranian	Gdansk	Wood	Metals	13.7	30.3	7172	4126	4880	12,598	Glencore	CH	200	6415	24,855	26
RO11	North-West	Cluj	Textiles	Wood	9.7	21.8	4350	2515	2965	12,343	MOL	HU	148	4108	20,065	20
RO12	Centre	Sibiu	Textiles	Motor	10.2	26.6	5406	2432	3626	5292	Daimler	DE	102	6379	19,255	33
RO21	North-East	Iasi	Textiles	Food	8.1	14.8	3579	1318	2378	6192	Delphi Technologies	UK	498	1606	17,180	9
RO22	South-East	Constanta	Textiles	Food	14.1	24.2	4386	2497	3440	6280	KazMunayGas	KZ	51	3477	17,789	20
RO31	South Muntenia	Ploiesti	Motor	Textiles	10.4	23.9	5189	1693	2514	3973	Renault	FR	14	4837	20,859	23
RO32	Bucharest-Ilfov	**Bucharest**	Food	Textiles	37.2	50.0	11,414	6121	6895	16,954	OMV	AT	31	42,021	46,262	91

RO41	South-West Oltenia	Craiova	Textiles	Food	9.5	20.2	5009	3095	3231	5880	Ford	US	181	2080	12,328	17
RO42	West	Timisoara	Motor	Textiles	12.4	27.8	4916	3680	3478	14,536	Louis Delhaize	BE	187	5605	16,539	34
SI03	Eastern Slovenia	Maribor	Metals	Wood	-2.9	54.5	17,185	13,477	11,642	9629	Renault	FR	98	2205	17,092	13
SI04	Western Slovenia	**Ljubliana**	Metals	Electronics	-7.8	64.5	19,327	16,053	17,957	19,319	Mercator	HR	144	9121	21,772	42
SK01	Bratislava Region	**Bratislava**	Motor	Other & repairs	25.9	73.5	19,652	11,677	17,843	30,268	VW	DE	7	29,041	22,283	130
SK02	Western Slovakia	Trnava	Metals	Plastics	7.0	46.0	7542	2678	4737	3883	Peugeot	FR	41	5995	24,663	24
SK03	Central Slovakia	Žilina	Metals	Wood	8.6	43.0	7658	2293	5322	4386	Hyundai Motor Group	KR	13	3836	15,696	24
SK04	Eastern Slovakia	Košice	Metals	Motor	7.9	45.7	6659	2433	3252	7217	US Steel	NL	489	3392	16,497	21

Source: Own calculations based on data from the European Commission, Eurostat, Coface Group, BoP data available at the national level (central bank and/or statistics institute)

Note: Most recent data. Data for Bulgarian regions exclude FDI in financial services. No FDI regional data for Croatia

Acknowledgements The views expressed in this chapter are those of the authors and should not be attributed in any way to the European Commission. We thank Jolita Adamonis, Judita Cuculic Zupa, Natalie Lubenets, Janis Malzubris, Ana Xavier, István P. Székely and others for many discussions, comments and suggestions.

References

Borensztein, E., De Gregorio, J., & Leee, J.-W. (1998). How Does Foreign Direct Investment Affect Economic Growth? *Journal of International Economics, 45* (1), 115–135.

Brada, J., & Tomšík, V. (2009). The Foreign Direct Investment Financial Life Cycle: Evidence of Macroeconomic Effects from Transition Economies. *Emerging Markets Finance and Trade, 45*(3), 5–20.

Canton, E., & Solera, I. (2016). *Greenfield Foreign Direct Investment and Structural Reforms in Europe: What Factors Determine Investments?* European Commission, European Economy Discussion Paper 33.

Chiacchio, F., Gamberoni, E., Gradeva, K., & Lopez-García, P. (2018). The Post-Crisis TFP Growth Slowdown in CEE Countries: Exploring the Role of Global Value Chains (European Central Bank Working Paper No. 2143).

Contessi, S., De Pace, P., & Francis, J. L. (2013). The Cyclical Properties of Disaggregated Capital Flows. *Journal of International Money and Finance, 32*, 528–555.

Durán, J. (2019). *FDI and Investment Uncertainty in the Baltics.* European Commission Economic Brief No. 043, Luxembourg: Publications Office of the European Union.

European Parliament. (2016). *Cost of Non-Schengen: The Impact of Border Controls Within Schengen on the Single Market.* European Parliament: European Parliamentary Research Service.

Hansen, H., & Rand, J. (2006). On the Causal Links Between FDI and Growth in Developing Countries. *The World Economy, 29*(1), 21–41.

Javorcik, B. S., & Poelhekke, S. (2017). Former Foreign Affiliates: Cast Out and Outperformed? *Journal of the European Economic Association, 15*(3), 501–539.

Keller, W. (2004). International Technology Diffusion. *Journal of Economic Literature, 42*(3), 752–782.

Mencinger, J. (2003). Does Foreign Direct Investment Always Enhance Economic Growth? *Kyklos, 56*(4), 491–508.

Szabo, S. (2019). *FDI in the Czech Republic: A Visegrád Comparison, European Commission Economic Brief.* Luxembourg: Publications Office of the European Union.

Weyzig, F. (2013). *International Finance and Tax Avoidance Via Dutch Special Purpose Entities.* Paper for Presentation at Research Seminar, Radboud University Nijmegen.

CHAPTER 4

The Impact of EU Cohesion Funds on Macroeconomic Developments in the Visegrád Countries After the 2008–2009 Financial Crisis

Adam Czelleng and Andras Vertes

4.1 Introduction

Following the fall of the Berlin Wall, people in the Visegrád countries (V4)[1] enthusiastically embraced freedom and regained national sovereignty, but they had to face a deep economic downturn during the

[1] The V4 group is a loose alliance of Czechia, Hungary, Poland and Slovakia. It aims to advance military, cultural, economic and energy cooperation within the group. All four countries are also NATO members. The idea of creating such an alliance originates from a summit of political leaders from Czechoslovakia, Hungary and Poland that was held in the Hungarian town of Visegrád in 1991. Visegrád was chosen to establish a historical link with a similar meeting in 1335.

A. Czelleng (✉) • A. Vertes
GKI Economic Research, Budapest, Hungary
e-mail: czelleng.adam@gki.hu; vertes.andras@gki.hu

M. Landesmann, I. P. Székely (eds.), *Does EU Membership Facilitate Convergence? The Experience of the EU's Eastern Enlargement - Volume II*, Studies in Economic Transition,
https://doi.org/10.1007/978-3-030-57702-5_4

political transition in 1989–1993. GDP declined sharply (by 15–25%), creating massive unemployment (above 10%). The pre-transition economic system of these countries was simply not competitive in the new liberalized environment, and the pace of economic and social transition was not fast enough to counterbalance this by creating new institutions and competitive firms. As a result, a decade into economic transformation, per capita GDP was still below the level people in these countries had in 1989 (Table 4.1). The only exception was Poland, albeit from a significantly lower level than the others because the introduction of Martial law in 1981 depressed the economy for the rest of the decade.

Societies in these countries looked at EU membership as a way to catch up quickly with Western living standards and to create a political and social system that matches those in the West. Hence, public support for joining the EU as early as possible was strong. The EU, however, was keen to ensure that every country that joined the EU met the institutional, legal and operational criteria set out in the 'Acquis Communautaire'. Thus, the first wave of the eastern enlargement of the EU took place only on 1st May 2004. Expectations on both sides were high, also because Europe and the world economy enjoyed a strong economic boom. This period of high hopes and enthusiasm was however brought to an abrupt end just three years later when the developed world was hit by a financial crisis, the biggest one in the history of the EU. The EU, including the V4 countries, experienced a major economic downturn. The crisis brought to the surface the unresolved structural problems of the V4 economies further amplifying the negative effects of the crisis. Policy makers in the V4 countries and in the EU had to respond quickly and decisively, and EU funds played a major role in their response.

V4 countries were among the EU member states that managed to absorb fully the financial resources allocated to them in the EU budget. Regarding the V4 countries, the highest amount of EU money both in per

Table 4.1 GDP of V4 countries (1989 = 100)

	Hungary	*Czechia*	*Slovakia*	*Poland*
1990	96.70	99.60	99.60	88.40
1993	81.80	79.20	76.70	86.90
1996	86.60	88.50	91.50	103.90

Source: Karsai (2006)

capita terms and as per cent of GDP was allocated to Hungary. Funds enabling the implementation of cohesion and agricultural policy objectives came from the European Regional Development Fund (ERDF), the European Social Fund (ESF), the Cohesion Fund (CF), the European Agricultural Fund for Rural Development (EAFRD) and the European Guidance and Guarantee Fund (EGGD). The disbursement of EU funds that amounted to financial transfers from high-income countries to low-income member states was seen as policy tool to speed up income convergence. EU money had in fact a significant economic and social impact on the region: investment, GDP, consumption and employment increased, and external and internal stability strengthened.

We analyse the role EU funds played in the economic development of the Visegrád countries. This chapter investigates how cohesion funds were spent and how these funds impacted private and public investments in the short, medium and long terms. We also aim to clarify how EU funds provided fiscal support and stimulus in the region during the recovery after the recent crisis. Our study estimates the role of EU funds in eliminating internal (budget) imbalances and reaching macroeconomic stability in Visegrád countries with a dynamic stochastic general equilibrium (DSGE) model framework.

At the time of joining the EU, V4 countries had no apparent fundamental macroeconomic economic issues, except Hungary, which faced major budgetary issues (see Vértes 2014; Vértes 2015). However, after joining the EU, some serious imbalances emerged across the region. In this chapter, we shall analyse how the spending structure of EU funds affected these economies during the crisis and in the recovery following the crisis, and what the economic policy reaction to the economic crisis and different external shocks was. The focus of our study is to analyse how the EU funds helped the recovery of the V4 countries after the crisis. As the crisis lasted for an extended period, it had a significant and lasting impact on potential growth in the region.

4.2 Literature Review

Various studies examine the role of EU funds in the recipient economies. These studies, which usually analyse the ex-post impacts of EU funds, provide important evidence to support future policy making. There are two main types of the applied methodologies: (i) micro-based counterfactual analysis and (ii) model simulations using macroeconomic or macroeconometric (estimated) models. The latter can be interpreted as an analysis of the ex-ante impact of the funds: What would be the expected effect at the macro level if the financed projects were implemented effectively and optimally? Econometric or micro-based assessment is closer to an actual, ex-post assessment of the EU funds than simulation-based macroeconomic valuations.

The micro-based counterfactual analyses have very strict assumptions and the methodological framework is described by the European Commission's Evaluation Sourcebook: 'The counterfactual situation is purely hypothetical, thus can never be directly observed. For the same reason, an effect can never be directly observed, nor can an impact (impact indicators notwithstanding). By contrast, effects and impacts can be inferred, as long as the available data allow a credible way to approximate the counterfactual. There are two basic ways to approximate the counterfactual: (i) using the outcome observed for non-beneficiaries; or (ii) using the outcome observed for beneficiaries before they are exposed to the intervention. However, caution must be used in interpreting these differences as the "effect" of the intervention. By far the most common strategy to estimate the causal effect of an intervention is to exploit the fact that some "units" have been exposed to the intervention and some other have not, according to some selection mechanism or rule' (European Commission 2013, p. 78).

Allard et al. (2008) examined how EU funds in the new member states were expected to affect economic growth. The study analysed the expected impact and not the actual one due to the small number of actual observations. In the study, the IMF's dynamic stochastic general equilibrium model, the so-called GIMF (Global Integrated Monetary and Fiscal model) was applied to analyse the impact of the transfers. GIMF is a large-scale open-economy macroeconomic model with microeconomic foundations based on optimizing forward-looking economic actors with various nominal and real rigidities. They concluded four lessons: (i) EU transfers are expected to be more effective if they were spent on public infrastructure investment rather than on income support; (ii) contribution to household welfare is highest when the funds are invested; (iii) there are just minor differences in effects under different exchange rate regimes; (iv) counter-cyclical fiscal policy is recommended from countries that receive EU funds.

Pereira and Gaspar (1999) used an individual country macroeconomic model to analyse the impact of cohesion spending. They examined the EU funds given to Portugal which was around 3.5% of GDP between 1989 and 1993. The European Union fiscal support increased GDP growth by 0.5 percentage points in the short and long run. Furthermore, the authors suggested that GDP growth was maximized when cohesion funds were spent on infrastructure. However, the impact of transfers on the current account and real exchange rate has adverse effects on long-term convergence.

Varga and in 't Veld (2011) studied the potential macroeconomic impacts of the Cohesion Policy's fiscal transfers. They applied a DSGE model (QUEST III endogenous R&D) with semi-endogenous growth and endogenous human capital accumulation. The result of the study was that structural funds caused significant output gains in the long run because of induced productivity improvements.

In 't Veld (2013) used the same QUEST model family to examine the EU fiscal consolidation assistance between 2011 and 2013 in the eurozone's core and periphery. The impact of the funds on GDP depended on two factors: how quickly the expectations were influenced and on the composition of the subsidies. Expenditure-based assistance was found to have a higher impact multiplier than revenue-based subsidies.

Banai et al. (2017) analysed the effect of EU funds on the Hungarian small and medium enterprises with micro-based counterfactual methods. In their paper, pairing was based on the propensity score and the impact was quantified through a fixed effect panel regression. The method applied in this chapter included two steps: (1) estimation of getting the subsidies for each company in the sample (2) pairing a non-subsidized company to each subsidized company. The funds of 2007–2013 had significant positive impact on employment, revenue, gross added value but no significant impact was found on productivity (proxied as revenue per employee).

For Hungary, GKI Economic Research and KPMG (2016)[2] produced a comprehensive analysis of the results of the EU programming period 2007–2013.[3] The objective of the report was to elaborate an impact analysis covering all EU financial sources and adjacent domestic investment projects according to intervention areas for the given budgetary period. Hungary was one of the EU member states that succeeded in absorbing completely the financial resources allocated to it in the common budget.

[2] The authors of this paper were members of the research team.

[3] In fact, because of the n+2 year rule of the EU, the time horizon of the report is 2007–2015.

Funds paid to beneficiaries had a significant economic and social impact in Hungary: GDP, consumption, investments and employment increased, and Hungary's external and internal stability improved. In the time frame analysed, Hungary's GDP would have decreased without EU funds and the excessive deficit procedure against Hungary could not have been terminated. Nevertheless, Hungary's competitiveness deteriorated over this time period. In spite of the rather high level of funds in per capita terms by international standards, Hungary could not keep pace with the countries of the Central and Eastern European region.

Overall, there is no consensus regarding the actual impact of the funds. The effects of EU funds are controversial as some other papers find evidence for positive impacts (e.g. Fayolle and Lecuyer 2000), some papers find positive impacts only for open economies (e.g. Everdeen et al. 2003) and some find no evidence for assisting convergence (e.g. Cappelen et al. 2013).

4.3 Scope of the Research: Countries and Data

4.3.1 *Visegrád Countries Versus Other EU Member States*

V4 countries have largely followed the same strategy to transform their economies since transition started in 1989. Hence, they have similar economic structures, they are all small, open economies, which also show strong openness of financial markets (Czelleng 2019). However, domestic economic policy decisions, especially during the time-period under investigation in this chapter, were rather different.

Since 2004, when V4 countries joined the EU, the world economy was hit by a global financial crisis and the EU was hit by the euro crisis. Hungary was among the few countries that were unable after 2004 to increase its aggregate productivity level (proxied by GDP per person employed; see Fig. 4.1). Czechia could increase its productivity level by 30%, an increase that is three times higher than the EU average. Poland and Slovakia could increase their productivity levels by more than 50%. Czechia and Poland managed to do so without increasing their public debt to GDP ratios. Hungary and Slovakia slightly increased their public debt ratios but less than the EU average. All V4 countries have public debt ratio increases between 0 and 20 percentage points but very different productivity increases. As their experience shows, with appropriate domestic policies productivity can be enhanced without significantly increasing

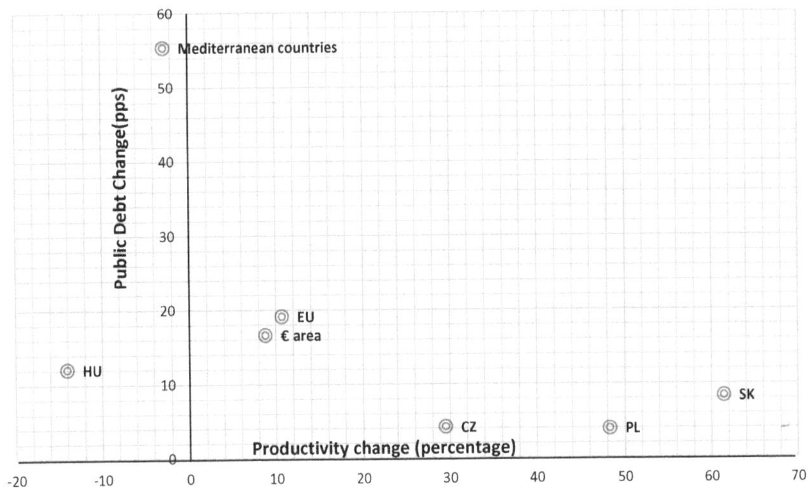

Fig. 4.1 EU members' public debt change in percentage points (vertical axis) and productivity changes in percentage points (horizontal axis); 2004–2017. The decline in Hungarian productivity is because during the analysed period no significant growth was measured while, due to the so-called Public Working Scheme, the Hungarian employment statistics were boosted (mainly with low skilled employees). (Source: Eurostat)

public indebtedness even during a crisis. Domestic policies mattered a lot in this regard.

EU funds have various effects on an economy. In the first phase, EU funds induce real economic transactions (consumption, investment). Then, it is pre-financed by the government and only months (in some cases years) later financing is covered by the European Commission. Every phase has different impact on the economy. The direct real economic effects are in the first phase when the selected investments are activated. It has a budgetary and financing impact as the government settles (pre-pays) the cost (government expenditure). There is government revenue impact in the second phase due to the balance of transfers as the EU provides the funds. Due to the administration of the funds, EU might transfer the funds two years after the end of financial framework. Due to data discrepancies, the fluctuation in the spending in different main areas (Tables 4.2, 4.3, 4.4 and 4.5) is estimated during the financial framework period

Table 4.2 Distribution of EU funds in Czechia, in million euros

	2007	*2008*	*2009*	*2010*	*2011*	*2012*	*2013*
Environment	**749.0**	**1062.4**	**1283.2**	**1486.5**	**1318.3**	**1971.2**	**2129.5**
Transport	**576.7**	**818.0**	**988.1**	**1144.6**	**1015.1**	**1517.8**	**1639.7**
R&D	**374.5**	**531.2**	**641.6**	**743.2**	**659.1**	**985.6**	**1064.7**
Employee skills	**149.8**	**212.5**	**256.6**	**297.3**	**263.7**	**394.2**	**425.9**
SMEs	**112.3**	**159.4**	**192.5**	**223.0**	**197.7**	**295.7**	**319.4**

Source: European Commission

Table 4.3 Distribution of EU funds in Slovakia, in million euros

	2007	*2008*	*2009*	*2010*	*2011*	*2012*	*2013*
Infrastructure	**328.9**	**377.3**	**362.3**	**578.8**	**542.4**	**694.8**	**615.6**
Environment	**337.0**	**478.1**	**577.4**	**668.9**	**593.2**	**887.0**	**958.3**
R&D	**194.7**	**276.2**	**333.6**	**386.5**	**342.7**	**512.5**	**553.7**
ICT	**74.9**	**106.2**	**128.3**	**148.6**	**131.8**	**197.1**	**212.9**
SMEs	**37.4**	**53.1**	**64.2**	**74.3**	**65.9**	**98.6**	**106.5**

Source: European Commission

Table 4.4 Distribution of EU funds in Poland, in million euros

	2007	*2008*	*2009*	*2010*	*2011*	*2012*	*2013*
Infrastructure	**2349.4**	**2305.0**	**2791.8**	**3567.0**	**4357.1**	**4747.9**	**4881.8**
Environment	**1348.2**	**1912.3**	**2309.8**	**2675.7**	**2372.9**	**3548.2**	**3833.1**
R&D	**1048.6**	**1487.3**	**1796.5**	**2081.1**	**1845.6**	**2759.7**	**2981.3**
E-administration	**277.1**	**393.1**	**474.8**	**550.0**	**487.8**	**729.3**	**787.9**
SMEs	**269.6**	**382.5**	**462.0**	**535.1**	**474.6**	**709.6**	**766.6**
Energy efficiency	**164.8**	**233.7**	**282.3**	**327.0**	**290.0**	**433.7**	**468.5**

Source: European Commission

(2007–2013), while the real economic effects are counted up to the end of the budgetary period (until 2015).

During the financial framework of 2007–2013, €26.7 billion was allocated to Czechia which means 2.4% of the country's GDP per annum on average; €12 billion or 2.2% of GDP per annum on average to Slovakia, €25.8 billion or 3.6% of GDP per annum on average to Hungary; and

Table 4.5 Distribution of EU funds in Hungary, in million euros

	2007	*2008*	*2009*	*2010*	*2011*	*2012*	*2013*
Infrastructure	**645.8**	**532.7**	**949.3**	**970.9**	**1418.1**	**1111.2**	**1572.1**
ICT infrastructure	**197.3**	**162.8**	**290.1**	**296.7**	**433.3**	**339.5**	**480.4**
R&D[a]	**197.3**	**162.8**	**290.1**	**296.7**	**433.3**	**339.5**	**480.4**
Employee skills	**269.1**	**222.0**	**395.5**	**404.6**	**590.9**	**463.0**	**655.0**
SMEs	**358.8**	**296.0**	**527.4**	**539.4**	**787.8**	**617.3**	**873.4**
Energy efficiency	**107.6**	**88.8**	**158.2**	**161.8**	**236.3**	**185.2**	**262.0**
Environment	**538.1**	**443.9**	**791.1**	**809.1**	**1181.7**	**926.0**	**1310.1**

Source: European Commission

[a]The spending on ICT infrastructure and R&D are similar while the distribution is estimated from the fluctuation of total EU funds

€66.5 billion or 2.6% of GDP per annum on average to Poland. The funds helped to implement different programmes. In this chapter, we aggregated them into main categories. These are E-Administration, Employee skills development, Energy efficiency, Environment, ICT, Infrastructure, R&D, SMEs, Transport.

Based on the fluctuation of total EU funds, we estimated the yearly spending on different programmes as only aggregated numbers are published. Using these estimates, we applied the following spending structure in our model.

4.4 Methodology

The applied model is a dynamic stochastic general equilibrium model augmented with various frictions. The model is calibrated on the countries in the region which allows us to analyse the impact within the same model framework. These types of models assume dynamic optimization of economic actors, that is, agents take the expected future factors into consideration when they make their decisions in the current period. The model used here is based on the Baksa-Czelleng (2019) model with minor adjustments. The applied new Keynesian dynamic stochastic general equilibrium model includes six economic actors and they can be subdivided into further subgroups. The model includes OLG (OverLapping Generations) households (also liquidity constrained households), corporates (three different types of actors in the production sector), financial sector,[4] government, monetary authority and foreign market. The detailed description can be found in the appendix.

Applied frictions and main assumptions in the model are as follows:

- Consumers' habits play an important role besides optimizing their utility.
- Production can only gradually adapt to changing circumstances. The adjustment in production and enhancement in capacities are costly.
- Investment decisions are not only based on the current cost of capital but also on expected future profitability and expected future cost of capital.
- Prices and wages are rigid. Indexation is costless for economic actors.
- We assume hybrid inflation expectations (i.e. a combination of rational and adaptive expectations).
- Economic actors are aware of the fact that the economy will receive EU funds regarding amounts and timing.

Based on the spending we can distinguish various shocks in the model. Cohesion policy interventions are simulated through shocks given to corresponding variables in the model. Table 4.6 summarizes the cohesion policy intervention and the corresponding model variable.

Table 4.6 Identification of shocks in the model

Aim of spending from EU funds	*Shock identification*
Environment	Non-productive government investment shock
Infrastructure (inc. transport)	Productive government investment shock
R&D	Technology, productivity shock
Employee skills	Technology, productivity shock
SMEs	Private investment shock
E-administration	Non-productive government investment shock
Energy efficiency	Non-productive government investment shock
ICT	Productive government investment shock

Source: Authors' own presentation

[4] Financial sector is based on Gertler-Karadi (2011).

4.5 Model Results

It is important to emphasize that, in spite of the fact that the evaluation is for a period in the past, the results should be interpreted as estimated ex-ante assessments based on the assumptions made in the model. The latter does not capture the efficiency of subsidized project selection and additionality. Corruption is not analysed by the paper either. In order to change these assumptions, one would need to conduct a micro-based analysis. This is not done here but can be the subject of future research.

The impact of cohesion funds between 2007 and 2013 for the Visegrád group is shown in Figure 4.2.

According to our estimation, the level of real GDP in Czechia was more than 2.5% higher in 2013 due to the positive impact of cohesion funds between 2007 and 2013. Czechia was massively hit by the crisis. The share of research and development and employee development spending in GDP were the highest among the V4 countries. These spending targets aim to improve productivity and thus competitiveness for a small, open economy. As a result, the long-term economic impact of the cohesion funds disbursed during the Multiannual Financial Framework (MFF) between 2007 and 2013 is estimated to be rather persistent and expected to generate 1% additional real GDP even in 2030.

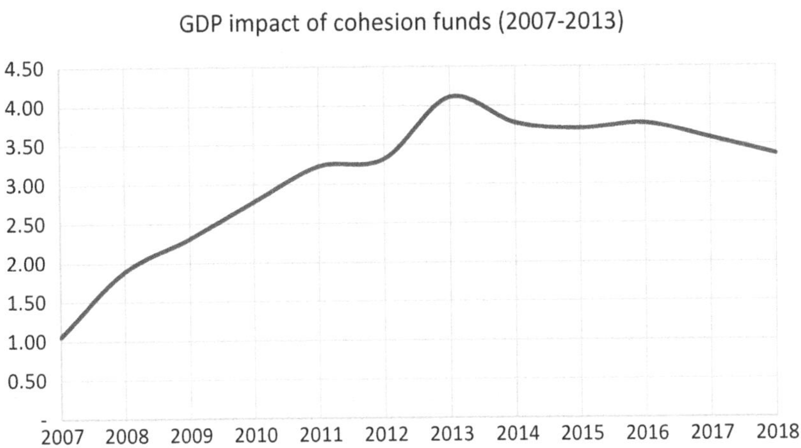

Fig. 4.2 The impact of 2007–2013 cohesion funds on the V4 group's GDP (in per cent). (Source: Eurostat and authors' own calculation)

Our estimates show that Slovakia's GDP was more than 3.8% higher in 2013 due to the cohesion fund spending between 2007 and 2013. Slovakia's real GDP returned to the pre-crisis level in 2011. The government took advantage of the cohesion funds as it tried to develop mainly real and IT infrastructure. The share of public investments was the highest among the V4 countries. The economic impact of the cohesion funds for the MFF between 2007 and 2013 in 2030 is expected to surpass 2%.

Based on the model results, Poland's GDP was more than 4.7% higher in 2013 due to the cohesion funds between 2007 and 2013. Poland spent the lowest portion on direct corporate financing among the V4 countries. This was mainly because Poland was the only country that could avert a recession in the EU after 2008. Private investments were not hit during the crisis as the credit market and profit outlook remained high. Therefore EU funds could be spent on infrastructure and competitiveness which could support private investments further in the long term. As a result, the long-term economic impact of the disbursement of cohesion funds from the MFF between 2007 and 2013 on GDP in 2030 would be greater than 3%, the highest among V4 countries.

As per our results, Hungary's GDP was more than 4.4% higher in 2013 due to the cohesion funds between 2007 and 2013. Hungary was hit hard by the crisis and the GDP returned to the pre-crisis level only in 2014. The proportion of corporate financing (especially SMEs) was the highest among V4 countries. The economic impact of the cohesion funds for the MFF between 2007 and 2013 in 2030 is expected to surpass 2%. Projects financed from the cohesion funds lead to long-term economic benefits in Hungary as well, but the positive effect is expected to be considerably less persistent than in other countries. Overall, EU funds had significant impact in the short term, but their impact seems to have evaporated quicker than in other countries. This is because Hungary spent more on corporate financing than other V4 countries to tackle insufficient market financing during the crisis. This strategy aimed to support the economy and was successful in avoiding an even larger drop in GDP, but it did not help generate additional growth in the long term.

Besides economic growth, cohesion funds also helped economies to improve their internal balances, which in turn changed investors risk assessment. The impact on the fiscal balance comes through several channels. Countries pay for being in the EU, which has a negative effect on the budget balance. Spending from EU funds impacts the budget balance in several ways. In principle, because of additionality and co-financing, EU funds should increase total public spending and thus increase the deficit. In reality, however, there was a strong substitution effect, projects funded by EU money replaced projects that had been funded previously from domestic sources. Therefore, easing the pressure on the budget balance. Cohesion funds, through financing public and private investments, research and development projects or developing employees' skills, generate higher tax revenues through several channels, not just higher economic growth and faster convergence. However, as the fiscal rules in the EU limit the fiscal deficit, these positive effects are not on the budget directly, but manifest themselves as less pressure on other items to adjust to meet the deficit target. A positive effect means more space to reduce taxes or increase expenditure in other areas.

As is the case for every recipient country, cohesion funds also have an economic impact on private sector investments. Spending from these funds aim to improve conditions for private investors which in turn is expected to increase the country's growth potential in the long run. Private investments are also supported by the substantial amount allocated to improve competitiveness through spending on research and employees' skills. The largest overall impact on GDP growth has been estimated through the impact on investments, especially on public investments during the MFF. According to our model simulations, public investment was higher by 18.4% in 2013 than it would have been without cohesion fund spending in the Visegrád countries (Fig. 4.3). Private investments are estimated to be almost 5.5% higher in 2013 than they would have been without EU funds. In the case of private investment, there is a long-term effect of EU funds while in the case of public investments the increase generated by the EU funds dissipates quickly (have significant impact only in the short term). However, it is important to emphasize that the nature of private investment seems to determine the extent and duration of the impact. Spending on competitiveness (R&D, education, etc.) might have a smaller impact in the short term but can have a significant long-term effect, just like spending on infrastructure. While on the other hand, financing private projects can generate a significant impact on the short term but the additional impact dissipates quickly. Moreover in the Visegrád countries, a significant share of public investment was spent on infrastructure, which is considered as a key incentive for private investments over a longer time horizon.

Our model calculations suggest that EU funds had the highest positive impact on private and public investments in Hungary. Public investment is

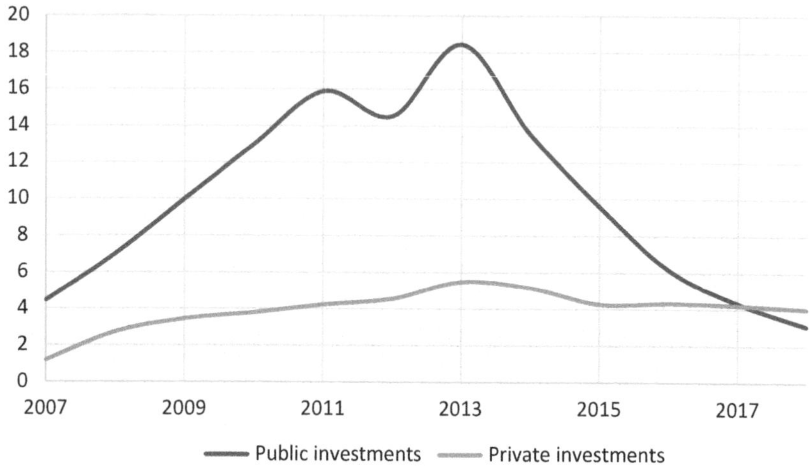

Fig. 4.3 The impact of 2007–2013 cohesion funds on private and public investments in V4 countries, percentage. (Source: Eurostat and authors' own calculation)

estimated to be higher by more than 40% while the impact on private investments was 8.5% in 2018. The reason is that due to budgetary constraints and the high debt level, the Hungarian government could manage development projects only from EU financing. Due to companies' insufficient access to financing, the impact on private investments was also significant. Private investments were also supported by the substantial amount allocated to improve competitiveness through support for research and employees' training. Poland had an above average impact on private investments in 2013 with 6.1% as a result of EU funds between 2007 and 2013 while Czechia and Slovakia have been impacted by 3.4% and 3.8% respectively. Regarding public investments, Slovakia had an impact above the average next to Hungary while public investment in Poland and Czechia would have been 14% lower in 2013 without the EU funds.

Our model simulations show significant differences regarding the long-term effects of EU funds in the V4 countries, especially on private investments. In the case of Poland and Slovakia, the impact on private investments even increased further after the end of MFF and it is expected to remain significant in 2030. In spite of a strong impact on investments during the

MFF, the long-term impact of EU funds seems less persistent in Hungary due to the above discussed reasons.

In the case of all V4 countries, our estimates suggest that significant additional tax revenue was collected between 2007 and 2018 due to cohesion fund spending related to the 2007–2013 MFF (Fig. 4.4). Furthermore, the spending is expected to have a long-term impact on tax revenues which is generated by the higher level of long-term employment and increased economic performance. The largest additional income is generated by VAT as an individual tax category (between 19% and 34% of the total) but the lion's share came from taxes related to employment (SSC and PIT together provide 42–50%).

4.6 Concluding Remarks

In this chapter, we analysed the impact of EU funds on economic developments in the Visegrád countries during and after the financial crisis. The study focused on the impact of cohesion funds on growth and the fiscal position and assumes that issues related to efficiency in project selection for EU funds, corruption and additionality of projects do not influence

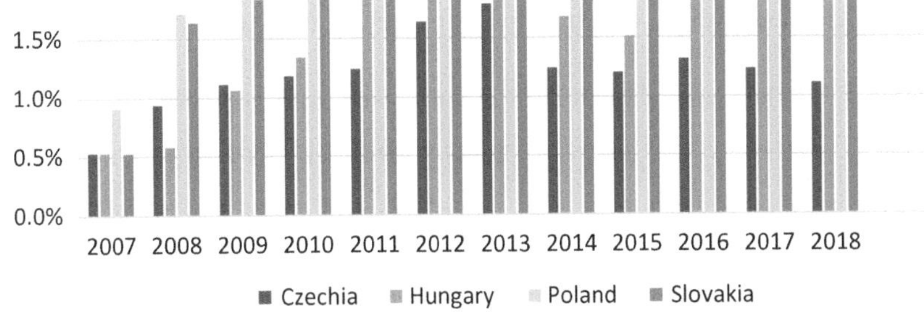

Fig. 4.4 The impact of 2007–2013 cohesion funds on tax-revenues, percentage. (Source: Eurostat and authors' own calculation)

the outcome in a major way. The analysis shows that the sizable spending from cohesion funds had a major impact on investment and growth.

Overall, EU funds had a significant positive impact on fiscal conditions. To a large extent, they substituted for expenditure that would have had to be funded from domestic sources. Moreover, they had a strong additional positive impact on tax revenues. Therefore, spending from the 2007–2013 MFF played an important role in restoring fiscal balances in the region, which in turn helped the overall economic recovery. The fact that the serious imbalances that had emerged after the countries joined the European Union were eliminated also helped improve investors' sentiment and credit rating. This gave an additional boost to the recovery.

Cohesion funds have their primary economic impact through investments. Countries which were hit massively by the crisis experienced a huge drop in private investments, because companies' profit expectations deteriorated and because companies had no adequate access to financing. Therefore, such countries spent more on direct corporate financing (through subsidies or loans) in order to complement insufficient market financing. While these actions were unavoidable to shelter countries from serious economic recessions, their long-term impact is lower than that of other forms of spending. As Table 4.7 illustrates, Hungary spent more on subsidizing firms, and thus the long-term impact of EU funds is less persistent.

Our results are in line with the literature; they confirm that the long-term impact of spending from EU funds is maximized if funds are spent on public infrastructure and on productivity-enhancing measures (innovation and employees' skills). These are the projects that are most conducive to private investment in the long term. The increased growth potential can generate additional tax revenues up to 3.5% of the total government budget in the long term, which helps improve fiscal balances. Overall, the

Table 4.7 The usage of 2007–2013 cohesion funds in the region

	Czechia (%)	*Hungary (%)*	*Poland (%)*	*Slovakia (%)*
Government spending	68	64	70	74
Productivity (innovation and employee skills)	27	20	26	21
Corporate financing	6	16	3	4

Source: European Commission

better financing position will moderate the risk premium of countries in the region, which in turn will further improve budgetary conditions.

Overall, our results suggest that EU transfers helped significantly improve the longer-term growth potential of the Visegrád countries. They also helped reduce the macroeconomic imbalances that had been accumulated prior to the crisis, and through this, they helped reduce the risk premium in the region.

Appendix A: Summary of Model

Households

$$C_t^{OLG} = MPC_t\left(Inc_t + (1+r_{t-1})B_{t-1} + (1+r_{t-1}^*)\frac{REER_t}{REER_{t-1}}B_{t-1}^*\right)$$

$$Inc_t = (1-\tau_t^L)w_t\psi S_t + Profit_t - T_t + (1-\omega)E_t\frac{Inc_{t+1}}{1+r_t}\frac{1}{1+g_{t+1}^{N.}}$$

Capital producers

$$K_t = Inv_t + (1-\delta)K_{t-1}$$

$$\frac{Q_t}{p_t^{Inv}} = 1 + S\left(\frac{Inv_t}{Inv_{t-1}}\right) + S'\left(\frac{Inv_t}{Inv_{t-1}}\right)\frac{Inv_t}{Inv_{t-1}} - \frac{1-\omega}{1+r_t}E_t\frac{p_{t+1}^{Inv}}{p_t^{Inv}}S'\left(\frac{Inv_{t+1}}{Inv_t}\right)\left(\frac{Inv_{t+1}}{Inv_t}\right)^2$$

$$ret_{t+1} = \frac{E_t\left(1-\tau_{t+1}^K\right)r_{t+1}^K + \tau_{t+1}^K\delta Q_{t+1} + Q_{t+1}(1-\delta)}{Q_t}$$

Banks

$$N_t = \theta\left[\left(ret_t - (1+r_{t-1})(1+\xi_{t-1}^{EP})\right)\frac{\eta_{t-1}}{\lambda - v_{t-1}} + (1+r_{t-1})(1+\xi_{t-1}^{EP})\right]N_{t-1} + \omega^{Bank}Q_tK_{t-1}$$

$$Q_tK_t = \frac{1}{1-\psi_t}\frac{\eta_t}{\lambda - v_t}N_t$$

Intermediate firms

$$\frac{\varphi}{\varphi-1}mc_t = 1+\frac{1}{\varphi-1}R\left(\frac{1+\hat{\pi}_t}{\left(1+\hat{\pi}_{t-1}\right)^{\gamma}}\right)+\frac{1}{\varphi-1}R'\left(\frac{1+\hat{\pi}_t}{\left(1+\hat{\pi}_{t-1}\right)^{\gamma}}\right)\frac{1+\hat{\pi}_t}{\left(1+\hat{\pi}_{t-1}\right)^{\gamma}}$$
$$+\left(1-\omega\right)E_t\frac{1}{\varphi-1}\frac{Y_{t+1}}{Y_t}\frac{R'\left(\frac{1+\hat{\pi}_{t+1}}{\left(1+\hat{\pi}_t\right)^{\gamma}}\right)\left(\frac{1+\hat{\pi}_{t+1}}{\left(1+\hat{\pi}_t\right)^{\gamma}}\right)}{1+r_t}$$

Retailer firms $j \in \{C, INv, Gov, X\}$:

$$mc_t^j = \left[\mu+\left(1-\mu\right)\left(REER_t\tilde{p}_t^{M,j}\right)^{1-\kappa}\right]^{\frac{1}{1-\kappa}}$$

$$Y_t^j = \mu\left(\frac{p_t^Y}{mc_t^j}\right)^{-\kappa}Z_t^j$$

$$\frac{\varphi_j}{\varphi_j-1}\frac{mc_t^j}{p_t^j} = 1+\frac{1}{\varphi_j-1}R\left(1+\hat{\pi}_t^j\right)+\frac{1}{\varphi_j-1}R'\left(1+\hat{\pi}_t^j\right)\frac{1+\hat{\pi}_t^j}{\left(1+\hat{\pi}_{t-1}^j\right)^{\vartheta}}$$
$$-E_t\frac{1}{\varphi_j-1}\frac{1-\omega}{1+r_t}\frac{p_{t+1}^j}{p_t^j}\frac{Z_{t+1}^j}{Z_t^j}R'\left(1+\hat{\pi}_{t+1}^j\right)\frac{1+\hat{\pi}_{t+1}^j}{\left(1+\hat{\pi}_t^j\right)^{\vartheta}}$$

$$Profit_t^j = p_t^jZ_t^j - Y_t^j - REER_tM_t^j\left(1+G(\cdot)\right)-p_t^jZ_t^jR(\cdot)$$

Government

$$Rev_t = \tau_t^C C_t + \left(\tau_t^L+\tau_t^S\right)w_tL_t\left(\tau_t^K r_t^K - \tau_t^K\delta Q_t\right)K_{t-1}+T_t+EUF_t$$
$$\mathrm{Exp}_t = TR_t + p_t^{Gov}Gov_t + p_t^{Gov}Inv_t^{Gov} + \psi_tQ_tK_t$$

Monetary policy

$$1+i_t = \left(1+i_{t-1}\right)^{\rho_i}\left[\left(1+i\right)\left(\frac{1+\pi_{t+1}^C}{1+\pi_{t+1}^{C,tar}}\right)^{\phi_\pi}\right]^{1-\rho_i}e^{\epsilon_t^i}$$

Foreign trade

$$X_t = \left(\frac{p_t^X}{REER_t}\right)^{-\theta}GDP_t^*$$

$$TB_t = p_t^X X_t - REER_t M_t$$
$$TB_t = B_t^* - \left(1 + r_{t-1}^*\right)\frac{REER_t}{REER_{t-1}} B_{t-1}^* - EUF_t$$

Equilibrium conditions

$$Y_t = Y_t^C + Y_t^{Inv} + Y_t^G + Y_t^X + Y_t R(\cdot) + p_t^{Inv} Inv_t S(\cdot) + wc_t L_t R(\cdot)$$
$$M_t = M_t^C\left(1 + G(\cdot)\right) + M_t^{Inv}\left(1 + G(\cdot)\right) + M_t^G\left(1 + G(\cdot)\right) + M_t^X\left(1 + G(\cdot)\right)$$
$$GDP_t = p_t^C C_t + p_t^{Inv} Inv_t + p_t^G G_t + p_t^X X_t - REER_t M_t$$

Parameters

- B^*—Foreign bond
- K_t—Capital
- MPC_t—Marginal propensity to consume
- $REER_t$—Real effective exchange rate
- *W*—Nominal wage
- i_t—Nominal interest rate
- r^*—Foreign interest rate
- h—Technical parameter for households' behaviour (habit parameter)
- p—Nominal prices
- *B*—Domestic bond
- *C*—Consumption
- *Debt*—Government debt
- *E*—Expectations
- EUF_t—EU funds
- *Exp*—Expenditures of the government
- *G*—Adjustment function
- *GB*—Balance for the government budget
- *Inc*—Total income for households
- *Inv*—Investments
- *L*—Labour force
- *M*—Import
- *N*—Net value
- *Profit*—Profit for final producer
- *Q*—Tobin's Q
- *R*—Rotemberg's cost function
- *Rev*—Revenues of the government

- T—Taxes
- TB—Trade Balance
- TC—Total cost
- TR—Transfers
- X—Export
- Y—Total output
- g—Growth rate
- mc_t—Marginal cost
- r—Interest rate
- ret—Return
- ν—Technical parameter for financial sector
- α—Technical parameter for production
- β—Technical parameter for households' behaviour
- δ—Amortization rate
- η—Technical parameter for financial sector
- θ—Technical parameter for financial sector
- λ—Technical parameter for financial sector
- μ—Import share in production (technical parameter)
- ξ—Yield spread between risk-free (government bond) and risky (corporate bond)
- π—Inflation
- τ—Taxation rate
- φ—Technical parameter for pricing
- ψ—Technical parameter for households
- ω—Technical parameter for household
- ϕ—Technical parameter for monetary policy

References

Allard, C., Choueiri, N., Schadler, S., & van Elkan, R. (2008). *Macroeconomic Effects of EU Transfers in New Member States* (IMF Working paper 08/223).

Baksa, D., & Czelleng, A. (2019). *Jegybanki hitelprogramok értékelése Magyarországon egy pénzügyi szektorral bővített DSGE modellben* (Working Paper).

Banai, Á., Lang, P., Nagy, G., & Stancsics, M. (2017). *Impact Evaluation of EU Subsidies for Economic Development on the Hungarian SME Sector* (MNB Working Papers 8).

Cappelen, A., Castellacci, F., Fagerberg, J., & Verspagen, B. (2013). The Impact of EU Regional Support on Growth and Convergence in the European Union. *Journal of Common Market Studies, 41*(4), 621–644.

Czelleng, A. (2019). A visegrádi országok pénzügyi integrációja: a részvény- és kötvénypiaci hozamok, valamint a volatilitás együttmozgásának vizsgálata wavelet és kopula tesztekkel. *Statisztikai Szemle, 97*(4), pp. 347–363.

European Commission. (2013). *Evaluation Sourcebook – Methods and Techniques.* Available: https://ec.europa.eu/regional_policy/sources/docgener/evaluation/guide/evaluation_sourcebook.pdf

Everdeen, S., Gorter, J., & Mooij, R. (2003). *Funds and Games.* ENEPRI Occasional Paper No. 3.

Fayolle, J., & Lecuyer, A. (2000). Regional Growth, National Membership and European Structural Funds: An Empirical Appraisal. Revue de l'OFCE (73).

Gertler, M., & Karadi, P. (2011). A Model of Unconventional Monetary Policy. *Journal of Monetary Economics, 58*(2011), 17–34.

GKI-KPMG (2016). *A magyarországi európai uniós források felhasználásának és hatásainak elemzése 2007–2013-as programozási időszak vonatkozásában* (Working Paper).

In 't Veld, J. (2013). *Fiscal Consolidations and Spillovers in the Euro Area Periphery and Core.* European Economic Papers no. 506.

Karsai, G. (2006). Ciklus és trend a magyar gazdaságban 1990–2005. In *Közgazdasági Szemle*, LIII. évf.

Pereira, A. M., & Gaspar, V. (1999). An Intertemporal Analysis of Development Policies in the EU. *Journal of Policy Modeling, 21*(7), 799–822.

Varga, J., & in 't Veld, J. (2011). Cohesion Policy Spending in the New Member States of the EU in an Endogenous Growth Model. *Eastern European Economics, 49*(5), 29–54.

Vértes, A. (2014). Tíz év az EU-ban, felzárkózás nélkül; In A. Ágh, A. Vértes, & Z. Fleck (Eds.), *Tíz év az Európai Unióban – Felzárkózázs vagy lecsúszás.* Kossuth kiadó. Budapest, Hungary

Vértes, A. (2015). The Hungarian Economy, On the Wrong Trajectory. In A. Inotai (Ed.), *Hungary's Path Toward an Illiberal System* (Vol. 63, p. no. 2). Südost-Europa.

CHAPTER 5

The Impact of the EU Cohesion Policy Spending: A Model-Based Assessment

János Varga and Jan in 't Veld

5.1 Introduction

The European Union's cohesion policy aims to reduce social and economic disparities between the various regions of the union and is one of the main policies of the EU. Cohesion policy spending has grown to become one of the largest items on the EU's budget and receives now more than one-third of total EU spending. The cohesion policy programmes of the European Union provide a framework for large fiscal transfers to the countries and regions that lag behind in terms of income

J. Varga (✉) • J. in 't Veld
DG ECFIN, European Commission, Brussels, Belgium
e-mail: Janos.VARGA@ec.europa.eu; Jan.Intveld@ec.europa.eu

M. Landesmann, I. P. Székely (eds.), *Does EU Membership Facilitate Convergence? The Experience of the EU's Eastern Enlargement - Volume II*, Studies in Economic Transition,
https://doi.org/10.1007/978-3-030-57702-5_5

per capita. These European Cohesion and Structural Funds target public and private investment in physical and human capital, and are aimed to increase economic and social cohesion among member states, enhancing a faster catch-up process of the less developed member states.

The evidence on its impact on regional differences in GDP per capita remains mixed, with large disparities across some regions persisting, and in some cases even widening. But most studies show a convergence of per capita GDP in EU member states. The 7th Cohesion Report (European Commission 2017) highlighted the significant contribution that Structural and Cohesion Funds have made to spreading growth and prosperity across the Union, while reducing economic, social and territorial disparities. The crisis has forced new reflections on how cohesion policy should be adapted to new challenges and a re-evaluation of its effectiveness in reducing disparities. To avoid fragmentation of support across too many fields and to create tangible impacts, funding priorities have been more closely linked with other key EU priorities such as the EU 2020 Strategy, with its emphasis on smart, sustainable and inclusive growth (education, knowledge and innovation, resource-efficiency, employment and economic, social and territorial cohesion).

This chapter examines the potential impact of Cohesion Funds. The assessment relies on a micro-founded Dynamic General Equilibrium (DGE) model, an extended version of the QUEST III model[1] with human capital accumulation and endogenous technological change. This version of the model has been used extensively for the analysis of structural reforms in the EU (Roeger et al. 2008, in 't Veld et al. 2018) and is particularly suitable for an evaluation of the type of structural policies that form the core of cohesion policy interventions. The model incorporates productive infrastructure investment that captures the productivity-enhancing effects of public capital. It also employs the product variety framework combined with the Jones' (1995) semi-endogenous growth framework to explicitly model the underlying development of R&D. The endogenous modelling of R&D allows us to analyse the impact of R&D promoting policies on growth. Furthermore, the human capital accumulation in the model can capture the effects of policies promoting vocational education and training. The model covers each of the EU28 member states, plus one region

[1]The QUEST III model is used by the Directorate-General Economic and Financial Affairs of the European Commission for economic policy analysis. For further references, see: http://ec.europa.eu/economy_finance/research/macroeconomic_models_en.htm

representing the rest of the world. The explicit modelling of cross-country linkages through bilateral trade relationships allows us to capture spillovers of cohesion spending and interactions between EU member states, both for the beneficiaries as well as the donor countries.[2]

Herve and Holzmann (1998) provide a detailed analysis of potential "absorption" problems of EU cohesion policy spending in receiving countries. They identify several factors that could lead to such a sub-optimal use of fiscal transfers, in particular rent-seeking activities and diversion of funds to consumption. They claim these absorption problems are of empirical relevance and that their scope may be very high. In some cases, transfers "may be unquestionably detrimental to economic growth and real convergence" (ibid, p. 14) with as most likely cause rent-seeking, protectionism and market rigidities. They also argue that absorption problems are likely to increase with the amount of transfers.

Becker, Egger, von Ehrlich (2012), using data at the NUTS3 level from the last two EU budgetary periods (1994–99 and 2000–06), find EU transfers enabled faster growth in the recipient regions, but also find evidence of optimal transfer intensity around 0.4% of a target region's GDP. Beyond treatment intensity of 1.3% of GDP, growth cannot be increased further and regions receiving in excess of this could give up EU transfers without experiencing a drop in their average per-capita growth rate. Hence, they conclude that "A reallocation of EU transfers from the 18% of regions that received more than 1.3% of their initial GDP as EU transfers to regions below that threshold would have been efficient and could have boosted regional convergence even further in the two considered programming periods" (p. 664).

Although model simulations cannot provide evidence on the positive output effects of fiscal transfers, they can shed light on the potential channels through which these policies could have an impact. Many of the mechanisms highlighted by Herve and Holzmann (1998) can be captured in a micro-founded dynamic general equilibrium model, and their relative importance can be assessed. However, the long-term growth effects of this spending will depend crucially on the precise nature of each of the projects that are funded, and only detailed project evaluations can provide evidence on that. Although a breakdown of spending into up to 123 subcategories is used in this exercise, a disaggregation to the project level of

[2] In earlier applications the model has been applied in an evaluation of Cohesion Policy over the 2000–06 and 2007–13 programme periods (see Varga and in 't Veld, 2011a, b).

cohesion expenditure is clearly not feasible with a macroeconomic model. One also should be aware that results from model simulations depend crucially on model parameterisation, and assumed productivity parameters of infrastructure and human capital investment play an essential role. Although these parameters are set in the model in a way that corresponds to what is commonly assumed in the economic literature, there is a wide range of uncertainty surrounding some of these estimates. Hence, results based on these common estimates from the literature can give an idea of the potential impact of spending on the condition that the money is directed towards productive projects and not wasted. However, incentives given by the availability of large-scale transfers could generate more rent-seeking behaviour and thus yield a lower return on investments. This indicates results should be interpreted with caution.

This chapter is organised as follows. The next section describes the core features of the model that are crucial for the analysis of this type of productive investment. Section 5.3 describes the aggregate impact of spending over the full 2000–20 period from the three programming periods, 2000–06, 2007–13 and 2014–20.

5.2 Model Description

We use a New-Keynesian dynamic general equilibrium model to evaluate the impact of EU Cohesion spending. The structure of the model is described in Roeger, Varga and in 't Veld (2008) and for applications to cohesion policy see Varga and in 't Veld (2011a, b). In this section, we give a non-technical overview of the model and Annex B of this chapter contains a more detailed model description. The model goes beyond a standard dynamic stochastic general equilibrium (DSGE) model by incorporating human capital accumulation and endogenous technological change. The model economy is populated by households, final and intermediate goods-producing firms, a research industry, a monetary and a fiscal authority. There is imperfect competition between and within domestic and foreign firms. Households provide low-, medium- and high-skilled labour services to firms. The model has an R&D sector and technological change is modelled as increasing product variety in the tradition of Dixit and Stiglitz (1977).

The model distinguishes two types of households. The first group of households have access to financial markets where they can buy and sell domestic and foreign assets (government bonds), they accumulate physical capital which they rent out to the intermediate sector and they also buy the patents of designs produced by the R&D sector and license them to the intermediate goods-producing firms. Other households are liquidity-constrained, cannot trade in financial and physical assets and consume their disposable income each period. We distinguish three skill groups of labour, low, medium and high skilled. For each skill group we assume that households supply differentiated labour services to unions which act as wage setters in monopolistically competitive labour markets. The unions pool wage income and distribute it in equal proportions among their members. Nominal rigidity in wage setting is introduced by assuming that households face adjustment costs for changing wages.

The model consists of the 28 EU member states and an additional country-block representing the rest of the world. Our primary focus is the effect of Cohesion Funds at the aggregate, country level. Since we map close to 120 intervention fields into our model variables, this approach has the advantage of being computationally tractable while we can simulate the effect of the various spending subcategories in every member state simultaneously. Although our analysis does not provide regionalised results, a more regionally disaggregated model requires significantly more assumptions for the calibration of regional interlinkages within and between countries, which would make our analysis less tractable and reliable.

In Annex B, we describe in more detail the modelling of production, human capital and the government budget constraint, which constitute the key elements for modelling the Structural Funds interventions. One particular extension to the model made here is an explicit formulation of human capital accumulation following Jones (2002) in order to account for the significant part of Structural Fund investments in various human resource programmes. For a more detailed description of the model, see Roeger et al. (2008) and Varga and in 't Veld (2011b).

5.3 Macroeconomic Impact of Cohesion Spending: 2000–20

Cohesion policy interventions are simulated in the model through shocks given to corresponding model variables. In total 86–123 different interventions are identified depending on the programming period, and each

Table 5.1 Matching fields of interventions and model variables

Field	*Method for implementing the measures*	*Variables and equations in the model (Annex B)*
Infrastructure	Increasing government investment or government consumption	I^G (Eqs. A.3, A.13) G (Eq. A.13)
Agriculture, Industry & Services	Increasing government consumptionReducing fixed costs or risk premium on tangible capital	G (Eq. A.13) FC_Y (Eq. A.2), rp_K (Eq. A.1)
RTD	Reducing the fixed costs or risk-premia faced by the users of R&D products	FC_A (Eq. A.6) rp_A (Eq. A.1)
Human resources	Raising human capital and government transfers expenditures	$h_{s,t}$(Eq. A.10) TR (Eq. A.13)
Technical assistance	Increasing government consumption	G (Eq. A.13)

Note: See the model description in Annex B for the corresponding variables and the equations shown in the parentheses above

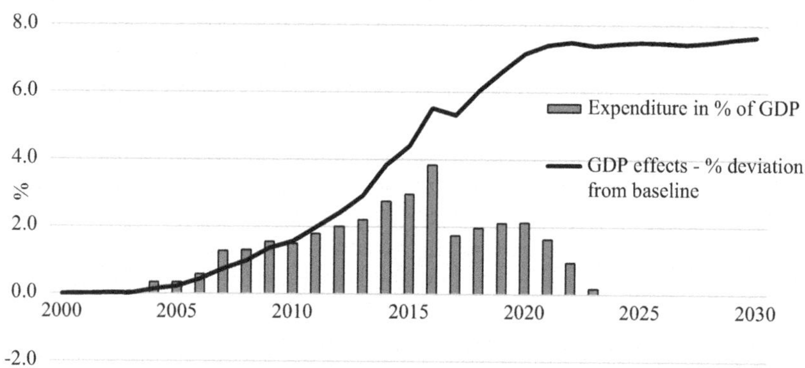

Fig. 5.1 Cohesion policy spending and GDP effects in the EU11 countries. (Source: QUEST III R&D model simulations, Varga and J. in 't Veld (2011a, b) and European Commission (2017))

of these interventions is linked to specific model variables. Table 5.1 summarises the links for the main five fields of interventions.

Figure 5.1 shows the impact of cohesion expenditure for the EU11 member states,[3] the aggregate of the countries that joined the European Union

[3]The EU11 includes Estonia, Latvia, Lithuania, Slovenia, Slovakia, Czechia, Hungary, Poland (all joined in 2004), Bulgaria, Romania (joined in 2007) and Croatia (joined in

since the 2004 enlargement excluding Cyprus and Malta and that receive the lion share of total EU cohesion policy spending. The payment profile assumed is a delayed spending profile with payments spread over 2000–23 (as in Fig. 5.1 and Table 5.2). Figure 5.2 shows the 2030 aggregate GDP effects in the EU11 countries. Detailed figures for each of the recipient countries are presented in Annex A, showing the results for all spending combined.

The comparison across countries shows that the GDP effects are roughly proportional to the funds received, when the financing of EU contributions is also taken into account. Hence, the largest recipients in terms of their baseline GDP, Latvia, Lithuania and Poland show the largest increases in GDP.

The country-specific results also show that the shares of different spending categories play an important role in the dynamic profile of the results over time. To illustrate this point, Fig. 5.3 plots the impact of cohesion spending on GDP broken down into the different categories within a single programming period. Note, that we focus on the short-, medium- and long-run effects of the different intervention fields, and these effects are qualitatively invariant with respect to the spending cycle. Without loss of generality, we can select the 2007–13 spending cycle for the analysis.[4] In Fig. 5.3, each band represents the results from a model simulation of only that particular category of spending. The lowest band shows the GDP impact of spending on agriculture, industry and services, the second band shows the GDP impact of investment in human capital, the third shows that of R&D investment, the fourth, and largest, band shows that of infrastructure spending and the last (smallest) band corresponds to technical assistance. The chart illustrates the net contribution of each field of interventions and the time profile over which the output effects for each of these categories materialise. In general, the impact of infrastructure investment (the largest category in size) comes through fastest, but this is to a large extent a reflection of statistical measurement of GDP (this government spending enters the GDP definition). R&D and human capital investment effects can even be slightly negative in the short run before generating large positive output effects in the long run. Although R&D investments also enter into

2013). Cyprus and Malta also joined in 2004 but are excluded from the EU11 aggregate of formerly communist countries.

[4] For illustrative purposes, it is also more representative to focus on a single programming period for two reasons. First, the classification of spending subcategories had changed between the programming periods; second, due to the delayed transfers of the funds, there is an overlap between the spending across the programming periods. For these two reasons, the comparison of spending categories is not straightforward across the programming periods.

Table 5.2 Simulated payment profile assumption in percentage of GDP

Years	*2000*	*2001*	*2002*	*2003*	*2004*	*2005*	*2006*	*2007*	*2008*	*2009*	*2010*	*2011*	*2012*	*2013*	*2014*	*2015*	*2016*	*2017*	*2018*	*2019*	*2020*	*2021*	*2022*	*2023*
BG	0.00	0.00	0.00	0.00	0.00	0.00	0.00	0.50	0.65	0.80	1.89	1.81	1.76	1.71	3.08	3.37	4.40	1.82	2.24	2.52	2.58	2.06	1.20	0.23
CZ	0.00	0.01	0.03	0.07	0.26	0.20	0.45	0.77	1.20	1.06	1.46	2.00	2.12	2.22	2.85	3.23	3.67	1.42	1.67	1.82	1.78	1.33	0.81	0.16
EE	0.00	0.11	0.13	0.18	0.64	0.91	1.22	1.53	1.63	3.28	2.49	2.88	2.80	2.72	3.50	3.65	4.88	1.87	2.14	2.18	1.81	1.12	0.61	0.12
HR	0.00	0.00	0.00	0.00	0.00	0.00	0.00	0.00	0.00	0.00	0.00	0.00	0.00	0.00	0.54	0.87	1.48	2.07	2.56	2.91	2.99	2.39	1.40	0.27
LV	0.00	0.11	0.18	0.23	0.79	1.28	1.09	2.30	1.80	2.35	2.06	2.09	3.30	4.42	4.58	4.04	4.83	1.86	2.02	2.04	1.95	1.52	0.90	0.17
LT	0.00	0.09	0.20	0.17	0.60	0.89	0.94	1.89	2.21	4.15	2.02	2.15	2.87	3.51	4.51	5.21	4.82	2.01	2.08	2.05	1.83	1.28	0.64	0.11
HU	0.00	0.05	0.06	0.06	0.29	0.45	0.83	1.39	1.20	2.11	2.52	3.13	3.26	3.38	3.23	2.93	5.64	2.15	2.33	2.51	2.66	2.09	1.16	0.21
PL	0.00	0.02	0.08	0.09	0.52	0.41	0.78	1.52	1.48	1.73	1.34	1.72	2.11	2.48	2.93	3.16	4.23	1.97	2.08	2.11	2.07	1.61	0.95	0.18
RO	0.00	0.00	0.00	0.00	0.00	0.00	0.00	1.30	1.17	1.42	1.32	1.24	1.20	1.16	1.83	1.96	1.97	0.84	1.43	2.07	2.37	1.87	0.99	0.18
SI	0.00	0.01	0.04	0.03	0.12	0.21	0.31	0.49	0.66	0.95	1.11	1.33	1.15	0.98	1.54	1.82	2.47	0.91	0.95	1.01	1.04	0.86	0.48	0.09
SK	0.00	0.02	0.09	0.10	0.45	0.52	0.67	1.24	1.38	0.79	1.30	1.47	1.72	1.95	2.92	3.37	3.63	2.27	2.40	2.21	1.92	1.36	0.89	0.18
EU11	0.00	0.02	0.06	0.07	0.35	0.34	0.59	1.27	1.30	1.55	1.49	1.79	2.01	2.21	2.74	2.94	3.81	1.73	1.97	2.11	2.12	1.64	0.94	0.18

Source: Varga and in 't Veld (2011a, b) and European Commission (2017)

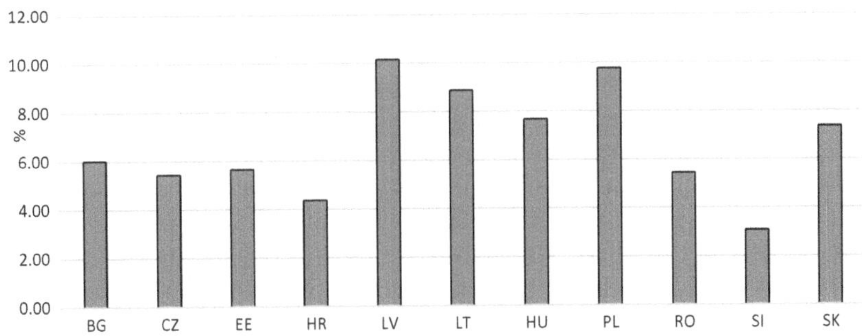

Fig. 5.2 GDP effects in the EU11 countries, 2030. Note: Percentage deviation from baseline. (Source: QUEST III R&D model simulations, Varga and in 't Veld (2011a, b) and European Commission (2017))

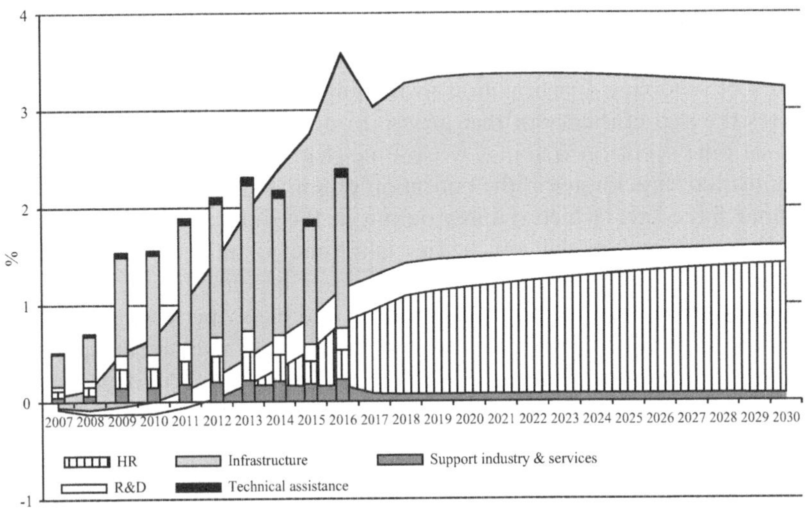

Fig. 5.3 GDP effects by intervention fields—2007–13 programmes, EU11 countries. (Source: QUEST III R&D model simulations, percentage deviations from baseline)

the measurement of GDP, these policies could drive up the wages of researchers and crowd out high-skilled employment in other sectors while their productivity-enhancing effect takes longer to materialise. Training and other human capital investments could also lower output in the short run if they lead to a temporary reduction in the active labour force.

The category *Support to agriculture, industry and services* includes interventions like support to processing and marketing of agricultural and fisheries products, agricultural waste resources management, co-financing of state aids to industries and services, supporting plant and equipment investment. These interventions are modelled as reductions in fixed costs (lowering startup costs and increasing entry of new firms) or as lower capital costs for tangible capital (increasing investment and capital accumulation). These policies have a growth-boosting effect in the short run, that is during the years of the programming period when the spending occurs, but there is some longer lasting effect on potential output even after spending has discontinued.

Expenditure on *Human resources* (*HR*) includes all spending on educational and vocational training as well as more generally defined labour market policies and spending on social inclusion. Some of these interventions are treated as unproductive government spending but most are modelled as skill enhancing. Total human capital in the model depends on the efforts individuals spend on accumulating human capital and an increase in the years of schooling (participation in training) for a respective skill group raises the skill efficiency of that group. In order to account for the additional time spent on training, we assume that the last cohort of student population stays longer in the education system and enters into the active labour force later, which reduces output in the short run. The effects of training on average skill efficiencies take time to build up, taking into account cohort effects, and the gains are only becoming apparent in the medium term, but they become significant and highly persistent. The efficiency effects depreciate according to the exit rate of working age population in the long run. This may be an underestimation of the true depreciation rate if a large part of vocational training targets unemployed or inactive people in older age groups, with a shorter remaining productive working life. A second reason why the simulated effects should be considered an upper bound of the likely outcomes is that the impact of training on skill efficiencies depends on the subsequent employment status, and human capital may depreciate faster after training if they remain unemployed/inactive or become unemployed after a short period of employment.

Support to *R&D* includes all spending on research, technological development and innovation (RTDI), including the establishment of networks and partnerships between businesses and/or research institutes. In the model, this is captured as reductions in fixed costs and reductions in intangible capital costs for the intermediate sector, the users of the output of the R&D sector. By reducing these costs, it becomes easier for new start-ups to enter the market. This is because although both existing firms and newcomers face similar problems when marketing new products, start-ups typically have less access to capital markets and have to overcome administrative hurdles (and costs) to set up a new business. By supporting innovation, high-skilled workers are reallocated in the model from the production sector to the R&D sector. Initially, this reallocation can reduce final goods production and have a negative impact on growth, but over time the positive output effects dominate as productivity increases, and this also stimulates physical investment. It is worth noting that while it takes time for these effects to become apparent, the output gains are significant and, importantly, continue to increase long after spending is discontinued (reflecting the endogenous growth nature of the modelling approach).

Infrastructure investment accounts for a large share of spending and includes investment in transport, telecommunications, energy and environmental infrastructure. All this spending is modelled as government investment with the exception of categories like social infrastructure investment and promotion of biodiversity which is treated as unproductive spending. In the short run the effects of government investment (productive) and government consumption (unproductive) are similar. Both lead to higher aggregate demand but are partly crowded out by lowering private consumption and private investment and some of the demand impulse leaks abroad through higher imports. However, in the medium term government investment raises productivity (this is in contrast to unproductive government consumption), and the output-enhancing effects of infrastructure investment become stronger in the following years. When investment is discontinued, the productivity effect slowly declines due to depreciation of public capital.

Finally, the category *Technical assistance* includes monitoring and evaluation costs and is modelled as unproductive government spending. In the model this type of spending has no positive output effects. It should be borne in mind that monitoring and evaluations serve an important purpose in avoiding that too much of the available funding goes to waste and that resources are as much as possible directed to the most "productive" projects. These benefits are however not directly quantifiable.

Varga and in 't Veld (2011a) show that the share of expenditures on infrastructure and human resources drives the GDP effects in the recipient countries. These two spending categories roughly account for up to 80% of all expenditure fields in the EU11 countries. However, there is little variation in the ratio of these intervention fields across the new Central and Eastern European member states: around 60% of all spending supported infrastructure developments while the remaining 15–20% helped human resource-related projects. Although there is more variation in R&D spending, the infrastructure and human resource-related spending rates and their combined GDP share clearly dominate the differentiated long-run effects.

5.4 Conclusions

The analysis shows there are potentially significant long-run benefits from EU cohesion policy spending in the EU11 countries. These positive benefits become stronger in the medium and long run and are able to deliver a significant improvement in incomes in the regions supported. In the short run, the additional spending could give rise to crowding out of productive private investment due to intertemporal consumption-investment decisions. Nevertheless, in the medium term the productivity-enhancing effects of infrastructure investment, R&D promoting policies and human capital investments become gradually stronger and generate large output effects in the long run. Even when the funding is terminated and spending discontinued there are permanent positive output gains.

One should stress that the results reported here are based on a macroeconomic analysis, and the long-run output gains reflect the assumed productive impact of investment in infrastructure, human capital and R&D in the model. As Tóth and Hajdu (2020) point out, countries with poor institutional quality have weak ability to control corruption risks which can lead to the inefficient use of EU funds. Therefore, our aggregate macroeconomic modelling approach gives an estimate of the *potential* effect of cohesion spending, and the results depend crucially on the underlying assumption that the subsidies are spent efficiently. The macroeconomic modelling approach should be complemented with an analysis based on micro data from individual projects. Project-based analysis could shed light on the question whether these positive impacts shown here are achievable.

Annex A: GDP Effects and Cohesion Policy Expenditures in the EU11 Member States

The cross-country comparison below shows that the GDP effects are roughly proportional to the funds received, when the financing of EU contributions is also taken into account: the largest recipients in terms of their baseline GDP, for example Latvia, Lithuania and Poland, show the largest increases in GDP. As argued in Sect. 5.3, EU11 countries spend roughly 70–80% of Cohesion Fund payments on infrastructure and human resource-related projects; therefore, the sum of these two spending categories in terms of baseline GDP dominate the differentiated country-specific long-run effects. In the following figures, the bars represent (net) cohesion spending received (as percentage of GDP) and the solid lines the simulated GDP impact (as percentage difference from baseline).

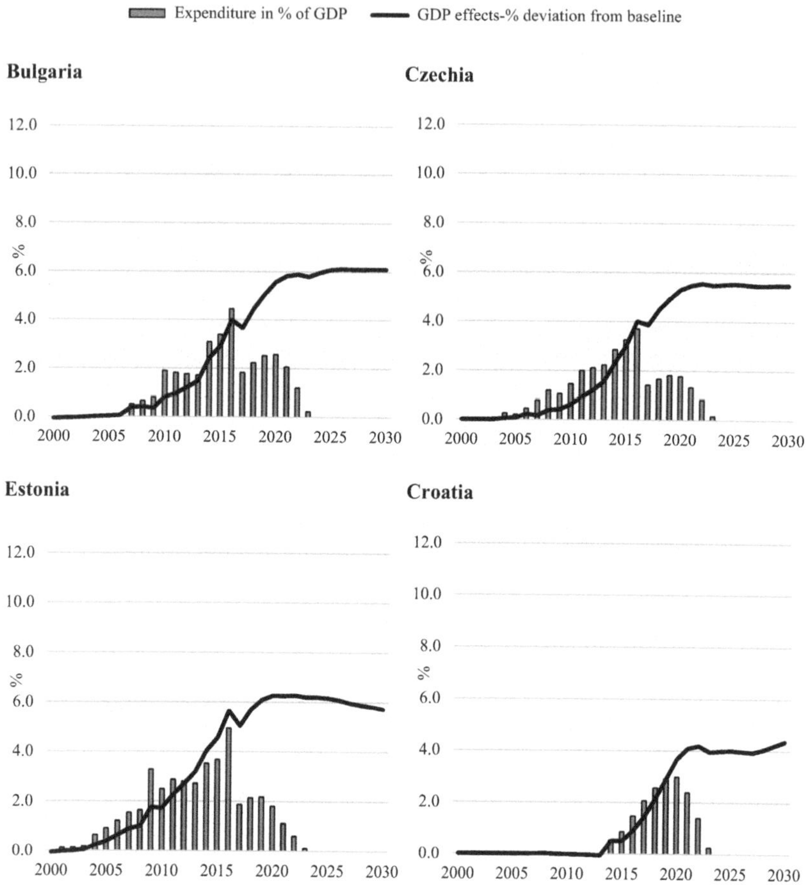

(**a**) Bulgaria, (**b**) Czechia, (**c**) Estonia, (**d**) Croatia. (Source: Varga and in 't Veld (2011a, b) and European Commission (2017))

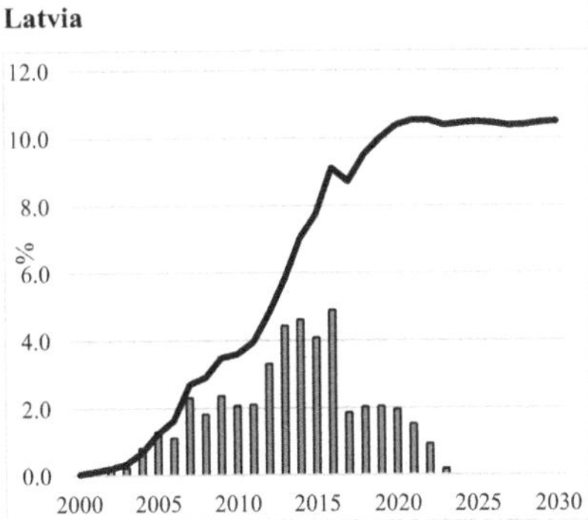
Latvia
12.0
10.0
8.0
%
6.0
4.0
2.0
0.0
2000 2005 2010 2015 2020 2025 2030

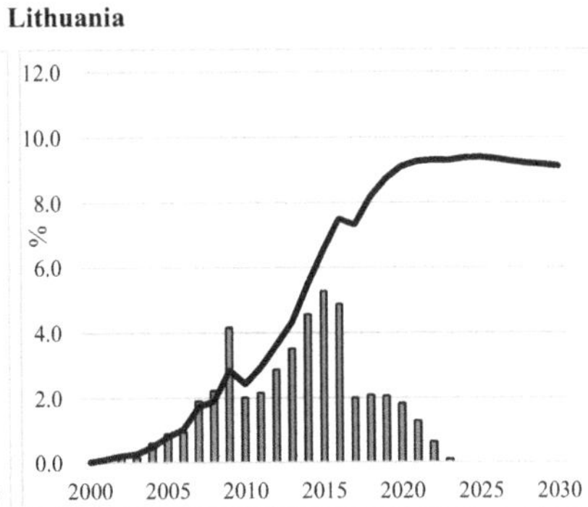
Lithuania
12.0
10.0
8.0
%
6.0
4.0
2.0
0.0
2000 2005 2010 2015 2020 2025 2030

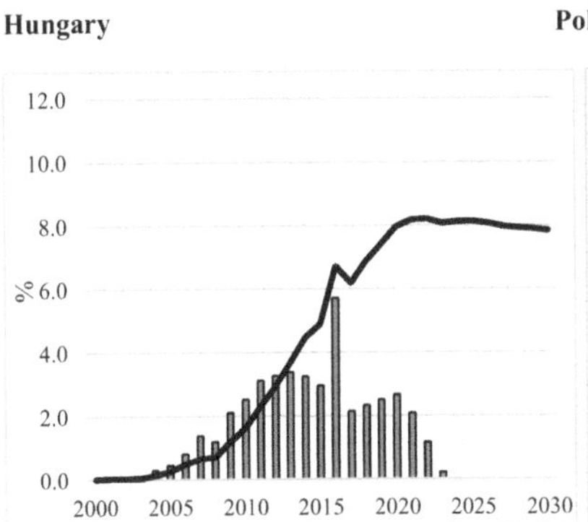
Hungary
12.0
10.0
8.0
%
6.0
4.0
2.0
0.0
2000 2005 2010 2015 2020 2025 2030

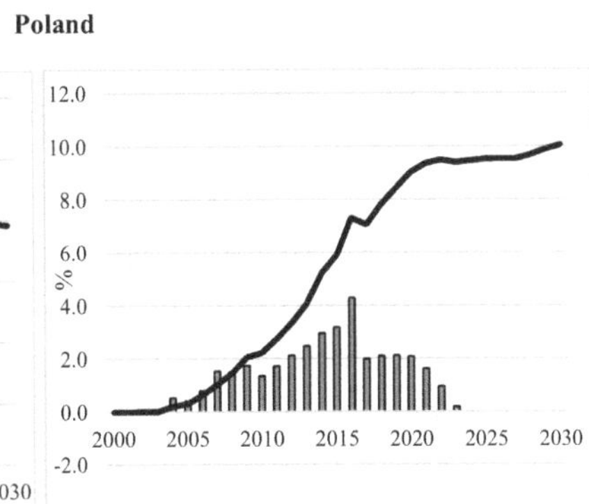
Poland
12.0
10.0
8.0
6.0
%
4.0
2.0
0.0
-2.0
2000 2005 2010 2015 2020 2025 2030

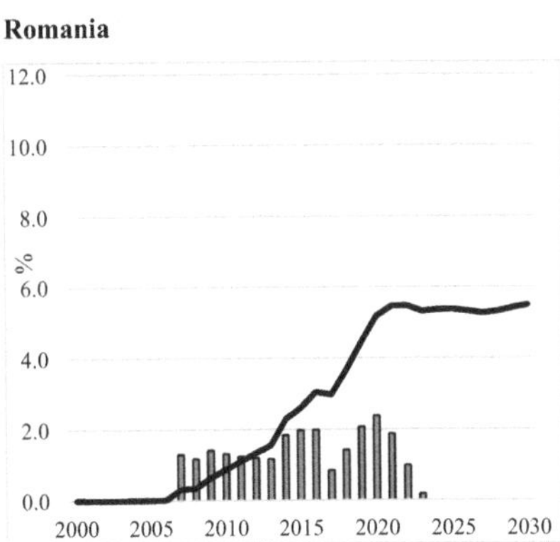
Romania
12.0
10.0
8.0
%
6.0
4.0
2.0
0.0
2000 2005 2010 2015 2020 2025 2030

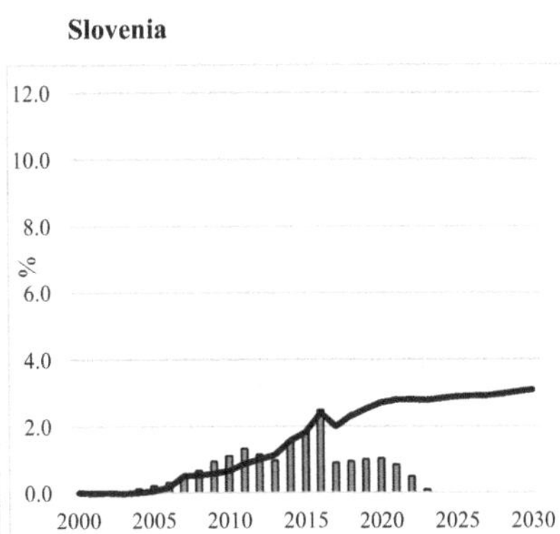
Slovenia
12.0
10.0
8.0
%
6.0
4.0
2.0
0.0
2000 2005 2010 2015 2020 2025 2030

(**a**) Latvia, (**b**) Lithuania, (**c**) Hungary, (**d**) Poland, (**e**) Romania, (**f**) Slovenia. (Source: Varga and in 't Veld (2011a, b) and European Commission (2017))

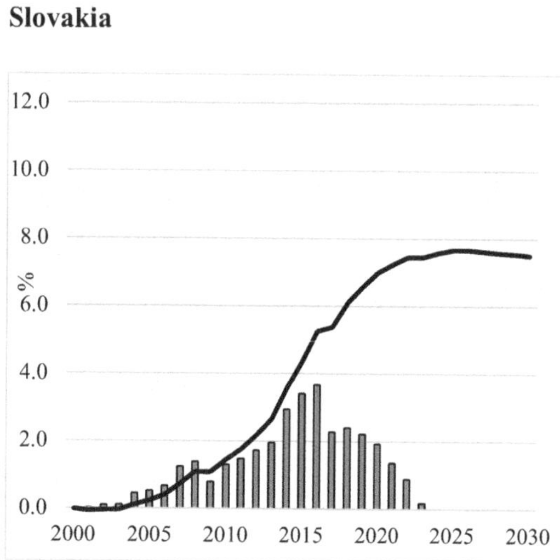

Slovakia. (Source: Varga and in 't Veld (2011a, b) and European Commission (2017))

Annex B: Model Description

In this section, we describe in more detail the modelling of production, human capital and the government budget constraint, which constitute the key elements for modelling the Structural Funds interventions. For a more detailed description of the full model, see Roeger et al. (2008) and Varga and in 't Veld (2011b). A detailed analysis of the country-level calibration can be found in D'Auria et al. (2009).[5]

[5] One difference with previous applications of this model to cohesion spending is the assumed share of liquidity-constrained households. In Varga and in 't Veld (2011b) this was set equal to the share of low-skilled workers, but due to cross-country differences in skill definitions this yielded large variations in this parameter. Currently, we set this share to 0.4, which is at the top end of the range of estimated values for the share of non-Ricardian behaviour in DSGE models which typically ranges from 0.25 to 0.4. A sensitivity analysis reported in Varga and in 't Veld (2011b) showed that the values of this parameter had no significant impact on results, because the spending is financed by transfers from abroad and hence does not affect expected future tax liabilities.

Households

A share ε of households are liquidity-constrained (so-called rule-of-thumb consumers), who cannot trade in financial and physical assets and consume their disposable income each period. The other households are non-constrained and have full access to financial markets where they can buy and sell domestic and foreign assets (government bonds), accumulate physical capital which they rent out to the intermediate sector, and they also buy the patents of designs produced by the R&D sector and license them to the intermediate goods-producing firms. Each non-constrained household maximises an intertemporal utility function in consumption ($U(C_t)$) and leisure ($V(1 - L_t)$) subject to a budget constraint. These households make decisions about consumption, labour supply (L_t), investments into domestic and foreign financial assets (B_t, $B_{F,\,t}$), the purchases of investment good (J_t) subject to adjustment costs ($\Gamma_J(J_t)$), the renting of physical capital stock (K_t), the corresponding degree of capacity utilisation (u_t), the purchases of new patents from the R&D sector ($J_{A,\,t}$), and the licensing of existing patents (A_t), and receive wage income (W_t), unemployment benefits (BEN_t), transfer income from the government (TR_t) and interest income (i_t). All firms of the economy are owned by the non-constrained households who share the total profit of the final and intermediate sector firms (PR_t^x, PR_t^Y). All households pay wage income taxes (t_w) and capital income taxes (t_K) less tax credits (τ_A) and depreciation allowances δ_K, δ_A after their earnings on physical capital and patents (i_K, i_A). There is no perfect arbitrage between different types of assets. When taking a position in the international bond market, households face a financial intermediation premium, which depends on the economy-wide net holdings of internationally traded bonds ($rp_{F,\,t}$). Also, when investing into tangible and intangible capital households require risk premia rp_K and rp_A in order to cover the increased risk on the return related to these assets. Hence, non-liquidity constrained households face the following Lagrangian

$$\max_{\left\{\begin{matrix} C_{i,t}, L_{i,s,t}, B_{i,t} \\ J_{i,t}, K_{i,t} \\ J_{A,i,t}, A_{i,t} \end{matrix}\right\}_{t=0}^{\infty}} V_{i,0} = E_0 \sum_{t=0}^{\infty} \beta^t \left(U\left(C_{i,t}\right) + \sum_{s \in \{L,M,H\}} V\left(1 - L_{i,s,t}\right) \right)$$

$$-E_0 \sum_{t=0}^{\infty} \lambda_{i,t} \frac{\beta^t}{P_t} \left(\begin{array}{c} \left(1+t_{C,t}\right) P_{C,t} C_{i,t} + B_{i,t} + B_{F,i,t} + P_{I,t}\left(J_{i,t} + \Gamma_J\left(J_{i,t}\right)\right) + P_{A,t} J_{A,i,t} \\ -\left(1+i_{t-1}\right) B_{i,t-1} - \left(1 + i_{F,t-1} + rp_{F,t}\right) B_{F,i,t-1} \\ -\sum_s \left(\left(1-t_{w,s,t}\right) W_{s,t} L_{i,s,t} - bW_{s,t}\left(1 - NPART_{i,s,t} - L_{i,s,t}\right)\right) \\ -\left(1-t_K\right)\left(i_{K,t-1} - rp_K\right) P_{I,t-1} K_{i,t-1} - t_K \delta_K P_{I,t-1} K_{i,t-1} \\ -\left(1-t_K\right)\left(i_{A,t-1} - rp_A\right) P_{A,t-1} A_{i,t-1} - t_K \delta_A P_{A,t-1} A_{i,t-1} - \tau_A P_{A,t-1} J_{A,i,t} \\ -TR_{i,t} - PR_t^x - PR_t^Y \end{array} \right) \tag{A.1}$$

$$-E_0 \sum_{t=0}^{\infty} \lambda_{i,t} \xi_{i,t} \beta^t \left(K_{i,t} - J_{i,t} - \left(1-\delta_K\right) K_{i,t-1}\right)$$

$$-E_0 \sum_{t=0}^{\infty} \psi_{A,i,t} \beta^t \left(A_{i,t} - J_{A,i,t} - \left(1-\delta_A\right) A_{i,t-1}\right)$$

The budget constraints are written in real terms with the price for consumption, investment and patents ($P_{C,t}$, $P_{I,t}$, $P_{A,t}$) and wages (W_t) divided by GDP deflator (P_t).

Final Goods Production and Public Capital

We account for the productivity-enhancing effect of infrastructure investment via the following aggregate final goods production function:

$$Y_{jt} = \left(L_{Yjt}\right)^{\alpha} \left(\int_0^{A_t} \left(x^i_{jt}\right)^{\theta} di \right)^{(1-\alpha)/\theta} \left(K_t^G\right)^{\alpha_G} - FC_Y, \text{where} \int_0^{A_t} x^i_{jt} di = K_t \tag{A.2}$$

The final good sector uses a labour aggregate (L_{Yjt}) and intermediate goods (x^i_{jt}) using a Cobb-Douglas technology, subject to a fixed cost FC_Y. Our formulation assumes that investment in public capital stock (K_t^G) increases total factor productivity with an exponent of α_G set to 0.10.

Public infrastructure investment (I_t^G) accumulates into the public capital stock K_t^G according to

$$K_t^G = \left(1 - \delta_G\right) K_{t-1}^G + I_t^G \tag{A.3}$$

where δ_G, the depreciation rate of public capital is set at 4%. Infrastructure investment is assumed to be proportional to output

$$I_t^G = \left(IGS_t + \varepsilon_t^{IG}\right) Y_t \tag{A.4}$$

where ε_t^{IG} is an exogenous shock to the share of government investment (IGS_t). It is through this shock that we simulate the increase in infrastructure investment.

Intermediate Production and the R&D Sector

The intermediate sector consists of monopolistically competitive firms that have entered the market by buying licenses for design from domestic households and by making an initial payment FC_A to overcome administrative entry barriers. Capital inputs are also rented from the household sector for a rental rate of i_K. Firms that have acquired a design can transform each unit of capital into a single unit of an intermediate input. Intermediate goods-producing firms sell their products to domestic final good producers. In symmetric equilibrium the inverse demand function of domestic final good producers is given as

$$px_{it} = \eta_t \left(1 - \alpha\right)\left(Y_{jt} + FC_Y\right)\left(\int_0^{A_t} \left(x_{jt}^i\right)^\theta di\right)^{-1} \left(x_{jt}^i\right)^{\theta - 1}, \tag{A.5}$$

where η_t is the inverse gross mark-up of the final goods sector.

Each domestic intermediate firm solves the following profit-maximisation problem:

$$PR_{i,t}^x = \max_{x_t^i} \left\{ px_{it} x_t^i - i_K P_{I,t} k_{i,t} - i_{A,t} P_{A,t} - FC_A \right\} \tag{A.6}$$

subject to a linear technology which allows to transform one unit of effective capital ($u_t k_t$) into one unit of an intermediate good.

The no-arbitrage condition requires that entry into the intermediate goods-producing sector takes place until

$$PR^{x}_{i,t} = PR^{x}_{t} = i_{A,t}P_{A,t} + \left(i_{A,t} + \pi_{A,t+1}\right)FC_{A}, \pi^{A}_{t} = \frac{P_{A,t}}{P_{A,t-1}} - 1 \tag{A.7}$$

For an intermediate producer, entry costs consist of a licensing fee $i_{A,t}P_{A,t}$ for the design or patent, which is a prerequisite of production of innovative intermediate goods, and a fixed entry cost FC_A.

Innovation corresponds to the discovery of a new variety of producer durables that provides an alternative way of producing the final good. The R&D sector hires high-skilled labour $L_{A,t}$ and generates new designs according to the following knowledge production function:

$$\Delta A_t = \nu A^{*\,\omega}_{t-1} A^{\varphi}_{t-1} L^{\lambda}_{A,t}. \tag{A.8}$$

In this framework we allow for international R&D spillovers following Bottazzi and Peri (2007). Parameters ω and φ measure the foreign and domestic spillover effects from the aggregate international and domestic stock of knowledge (A^* and A) respectively. Negative value for these parameters can be interpreted as the "fishing out" effect, that is when innovation decreases with the level of knowledge, while positive values refer to the "standing on shoulders" effect and imply positive research spillovers. Note that $\varphi = 1$ would give back the strong scale effect feature of fully endogenous growth models with respect to the domestic level of knowledge. Parameter ν can be interpreted as total factor efficiency of R&D production, while λ measures the elasticity of R&D production on the number of researchers (L_A). The international stock of knowledge is taken into account as the weighted average of all foreign stock of knowledge. We assume that the R&D sector is operated by a research institute which employs high-skilled labour at their market wage, W^H. We also assume that the research institute faces an adjustment cost of hiring new employees and maximises the following discounted profit-stream:

$$\max_{L_{A,t}} \sum_{t=0}^{\infty} d_t \left(P^{A}_{t}\Delta A_t - W^{H}_{t} L_{A,t} - \frac{\gamma_A}{2} W^{H}_{t} \Delta L^{2}_{A,t} \right) \tag{A.9}$$

Human Capital Accumulation

The labour aggregate $L_{Y,t}$ is composed of three skill types of labour force:

$$L_{Yjt} = \left(s_L^{1/\sigma_L} \left(h_{L,t} L_{Ljt} \right)^{(1-\sigma_L)/\sigma_L} + s_M^{1/\sigma_L} \left(h_{M,t} L_{Mjt} \right)^{(1-\sigma_L)/\sigma_L} + s_{HY}^{1/\sigma_L} \left(h_{HY,t} L_{HYjt} \right)^{(1-\sigma_L)/\sigma_L} \right)^{\sigma_L/(1-\sigma_L)} \tag{A.10}$$

Parameter s_s is the population share of the labour force in subgroup s (low, medium and high skilled), L_s denotes the employment rate of population s, h_s is the corresponding accumulated human capital (efficiency unit) and σ_L is the elasticity of substitution between different labour types.[6] An individual's human capital is produced by participating in education and $\Lambda_{s,t}$ represents the amount of time an individual spends accumulating human capital:

$$h_{s,t} = h_s e^{\psi \Lambda_{s,t}}, \psi > 0 \tag{A.11}$$

The exponential formulation used here adapts Jones (2002) into a disaggregated skill structure by incorporating human capital in a way that is consistent with the substantial growth accounting literature with adjustments for education.[7] The ψ parameter has been studied in a wealth of microeconomic research. Interpreting $\Lambda_{s,t}$ as years of schooling, the parameter corresponds to the return to schooling estimated by Mincer (1974). The labour-market literature suggests that a reasonable value for ψ is 0.07, which we apply here. Investments in human capital can then be modelled by increasing the years of schooling ($\Lambda_{s,t}$) for the respective skill groups.

The Government Budget Constraint

For the government sector various expenditure and revenue categories are separately modelled. On the expenditure side we assume that government consumption (G_t), government transfers (TR_t) and government investment (I_t^G) are proportional to GDP and unemployment benefits (BEN_t) are indexed to wages. The government provides subsidies (S_t) on physical

[6] Note that high-skilled labour in the final goods sector L_{HYt} is total high-skilled employment minus the high-skilled labour working in the R&D sector ($L_{A,t}$).

[7] See Barro and Sala-i-Martin (1995).

capital and R&D investments in the form of a tax-credit and depreciation allowances, which are exogenous in the model.

Government revenues (R_t^G) consist of taxes on consumption as well as capital and labour income. Fiscal transfers received from the EU are denoted by COH_t (which is negative for the net contributors). Labour taxes gradually adjust to stabilise the debt to GDP ratio in the long run according to the following rule

$$\Delta t_t^L = \tau^B \left(\frac{B_{t-1}}{Y_{t-1}} - b^T \right) + \tau^{DEF} \Delta \left(\frac{B_t}{Y_t} \right) \tag{A.12}$$

where b^T is the government debt target, τ^B and τ^{DEF} are coefficients. Therefore, government debt (B_t) evolves according to

$$B_t = (1 + r_t) B_{t-1} + G_t + IG_t + TR_t + BEN_t + S_t - R_t^G - COH_t \cdot \tag{A.13}$$

We assume that donor countries finance their contributions to the EU budget (COH<0) through increases in labour taxes.

Cohesion policy programmes are subject to the condition of additionality and co-financing. Additionality requires that Structural Funds are additional to domestically financed expenditure and are not used as a substitute for it. The co-financing principle means the EU provides only matching funds to individual projects that are part of the operational programmes and that the EU funds are matched to a certain extent by domestic expenditure. The problem with defining a proper benchmark means that in practice the principle of additionality is hard to verify and is thus not always binding. Member states are not required to create new budgetary expenditure to co-finance cohesion policy support. Existing national resources that were used to finance similar areas of interventions (and are thus concerned by the additionality requirement) can be 'earmarked' to co-finance Structural Fund transfers. Total spending increases only by the amount of Structural Fund transfers.

More formally, assume a cofinancing rate of c, that is the EU transfer COH_t has to be matched by domestically financed expenditure, $c{\cdot}COH$. The additionality and co-financing principles can be expressed as the following condition for total government spending in a beneficiary country:

$$TOTEXP_t = COH_t + \max\left(EXP_0, c \cdot COH_t\right) \tag{A.14}$$

where $TOTEXP_t$ is total expenditure, COH_t is the fiscal transfer received from the EU Cohesion Funds, EXP_0 is the domestically financed expenditure in the counterfactual situation (without Structural and Cohesion Funds) and c is the co-financing rate. Examining past additionality tables of member states, it seems that most national public expenditure concerned by additionality exceeded the co-financing needs by far. In this case $EXP_0 > c \cdot COH_t$, and total expenditure is given by

$$TOTEXP_t = COH_t + EXP_0 \tag{A.15}$$

As spending on infrastructure and education is already high in the new member states, the standard procedure in model-based evaluations has been to take domestically financed expenditure EXP_0 in the counterfactual situation (without Structural and Cohesion Funds) as the benchmark and only examine the impact of the fiscal transfer COH_t received from the EU Cohesion Funds (Varga and in 't Veld 2011b).

Acknowledgements This chapter has benefited from comments received from Michael Landesmann and István P. Székely. We also acknowledge the help and comments received from Philippe Monfort while preparing the background papers for this study. The views expressed in this chapter are those of the authors and should not be attributed to the European Commission.

References

Barro, R. J. and Sala-I-Martin, X. (1995). Economic Growth. McGraw Hill, New York.

Becker, S., Egger, P., & von Ehrlich, M. (2012). Too Much of a Good Thing? On the Growth Effects of the EU's Regional Policy. *European Economic Review, 56*(4), 648–668.

Bottazzi, L. and Peri, G. (2007). The international dynamics of R&D and innovation in the long run and in the short run. *The Economics Journal, 117*(3), 486–511.

D'Auria F., A. Pagano, M. Ratto and J. Varga (2009), "A comparison of structural reform scenarios across the EU member states: Simulation-based analysis using the QUEST model with endogenous growth". *European Economy Economic Paper* no. 392. Brussels.

Dixit, A. K. and Stiglitz, J. E. (1977). Monopolistic competition and optimum product diversity. *American Economic Review, 67*(3):297–308.

European Commission. (2017). *My Region, My Europe, Our Future.* Sixth Report on Economic, Social and Territorial Cohesion. Luxembourg: Publications Office of the European Union.

Herve, Y., & Holzmann, R. (1998). *Fiscal Transfers and Economic Convergence in the EU: An Analysis of Absorption Problems and an Evaluation of the Literature.* Baden-Baden: Nomos Verlagsgesellschaft.

in 't Veld, J, Varga, J., & Roeger, W. (2018). The Impact of Structural Reforms in the EU. In J. de Haan & J. Parlevliet (Eds.), *Structural Reforms.* Cham: Springer. 10.1007/978-3-319-74400-1_4.

Jones, C. I. (1995). R&D-Based Models of Economic Growth. *Journal of Political Economy, 103*(4), 759–784.

Jones, C. I. (2002). Source of U.S. economic growth in a world of ideas. *American Economic Review, 92*(1):220–239.

Roeger W, Varga J, & in 't Veld J. (2008). *Structural Reforms in the EU: A Simulation-Based Analysis Using the QUEST Model with Endogenous Growth.* European economy Economic Papers 351. Brussels.

Tóth, I. J., & Hajdu, M. (2020). Chapter 9: Corruption, Institutions and Convergence. In M. Landesmann & I. P. Székely (Eds.), *Does EU Membership Facilitate Convergence? The Experience of the EU's Eastern Enlargement* (Vol. II). Switzerland: Palgrave Macmillan.

Varga, J., & in 't Veld, J. (2011a). Cohesion Policy Spending in the New Member States of the EU in an Endogenous Growth Model. *Eastern European Economics, 49*(5), 29–54. 10.2753/EEE0012-8775490502. Also published as *ECFIN European Economy Economic Paper, no. 422.* http://ec.europa.eu/economy_finance/publications/economic/economic_paper/2010/pdf/ecp422_en.pdf.

Varga, J., & in 't Veld, J. (2011b). A Model-based Analysis of the Impact of Cohesion Policy Expenditure 2000–06: Simulations with the QUEST III Endogenous R&D Model. *Economic Modelling, 28*, 647–663. Also Published as *ECFIN European Economy Economic Paper, no. 387.*

PART II

Finance Channel and Financial Institutions

CHAPTER 6

Models of Financial Integration: The Experience of the Baltics and Central Eastern Europe

Lúcio Vinhas de Souza

6.1 Introduction

Financial and capital flows' liberalization can play a fundamental role in increasing growth and welfare. Typically, emerging or developing economies seek foreign savings to solve the inter-temporal savings-investment problem. On the other hand, current account surplus countries seek higher-yield opportunities to invest their savings. To the extent that

The views expressed are solely those of the author and do not necessarily represent the official views of the European Commission.

L. Vinhas de Souza (✉)
DG ECFIN, European Commission, Brussels, Belgium
e-mail: Lucio-Mauro.VINHAS-DE-SOUZA@ec.europa.eu

M. Landesmann, I. P. Székely (eds.), *Does EU Membership Facilitate Convergence? The Experience of the EU's Eastern Enlargement - Volume II*, Studies in Economic Transition,
https://doi.org/10.1007/978-3-030-57702-5_6

capital flows from surplus to deficit countries are well intermediated and, therefore, put to the most productive use, they increase welfare.[1]

Liberalization can, however, also be dangerous, as has been witnessed in many past and recent financial, currency and banking crises. It can make countries more vulnerable to exogenous shocks and sudden stops. In particular, if serious macroeconomic imbalances exist in a recipient country, and if the financial sector is weak, be it in terms of risk management, prudential regulation and supervision or in case of a large dependency of foreign inflows, capital flows can easily lead to serious financial, banking or currency crises. As the recent EU/euro area crisis has demonstrated, there are the potential risks associated with financial and capital flows liberalization. For the Baltic and Central European Countries (BCECs), beyond questions of economic allocative efficiency, this process must be understood in terms of their accession to the European Union.

The EU integration process implied sweeping liberalization and integration measures—not only capital account liberalization, but investment by EU firms in the domestic financial services, and the maintenance of a competitive domestic environment, giving this financial liberalization process strong external incentives (and constraints).

Additionally, EU membership may act as an anchor to market expectations (see Vinhas de Souza and Hölscher 2001), under certain circumstances limiting the possibilities of self-fulfilling financial crises and regional contagion.

This study's main aim is to test an underlying hypothesis that the type of financial integration chosen by the BCECs played an important role in enabling liberalization to largely deliver the welfare-enhancing outcomes that it is supposed to.

[1] The opening up and liberalization of financial services in developing countries would yield, in principle, both static and dynamic gains: static, one-shot efficiency gains from optimally allocating the available resources (i.e., developed, capital abundant nations would export capital to the developing, capital scarce ones; also domestically, deeper, more effective financial systems would facilitate the linkages between domestic savers and investors, reducing information asymmetries and scale problems), and dynamic ones because the growth rate would be shifted upwards by the increased capital stock created by the greater investment (temporarily, later adjusting again to the long-run growth trend).

6.2 EU Accession and BCECs' Banking Sectors

The process of integration of BCECs into the European Union is the single most important determinant factor in the development of their banking sectors since the 1990s. The bulk of these countries (namely, the Czech Republic, Estonia, Hungary, Latvia, Lithuania, Poland, Slovakia and Slovenia) became member states already in May 2004. Bulgaria and Romania entered the EU in 2007, and Croatia in 2013. Euro area accession is another important benchmark for EU integration.

By the early to mid-1990s, all the countries had signed Association Agreements with the European Union (frequently preceded by trade liberalization agreements with the EU, also called "Europe" trade agreements, usually with years given to the countries to prepare for their full implementation) and formally applied for EU membership. The adoption of the EU acquis pre-membership had particular implications for financial and banking liberalization, as will be described below.

Namely, financial integration, in the form of opening up of the banking sector to foreign banks, is seen as positive on a micro level as foreign banks are usually better capitalized and more efficient than their domestic counterparts. From a macroeconomic perspective, financial integration has been, on a net basis, positive for the BCECs.

In most of the BCECs, the initial stage of the creation of the two-tier banking system,[2] modelled on the Western European "universal bank" system,[3] was characterized by rather liberal licensing practices[4] and limited supervision policies (aimed at the fast creation of a de novo commercial, private banking sector). This caused a mushrooming of new banks in those

[2] In the Baltic states, already in 1987, as part of the Gorbachev reforms, the monobank Gosbak (which formed the financial system, together with an emissions bank) had spun-off five specialized banks in all URSS republics (Savings, Agriculture, Social, Industry and Construction and Foreign Trade: a somewhat similar specialization was to be found in most other centrally planned economies, with, at least, a "central bank", a savings bank and a foreign trade one).

[3] Levine (2002), after performing a panel analysis of large number of countries, concludes that either bank or market-based (i.e., via stock markets) financial systems can be growth-enhancing: what actually is relevant is the overall development of financial sector and, specially, *the quality and effectiveness of the institutional framework* (contract enforcement, investor protection, etc.).

[4] Sometimes almost comically so: as an example, in the early 1990s, Latvia allowed the creation of a bank—appropriately called Olympia Bank—just to finance the Latvian Olympic team.

countries in the early 1990s. Parallel to this, a series of banking crises, of varied proportions, affected most of those de novo domestic banking systems, due to this lax institutional framework, inherited fragilities from the command economy period (the political need to support state-owned, inefficient industries, with the consequent accumulation of bad loans and also the financing of budget deficits), macroeconomic instability, risky expansion and investment strategies and also sheer inexperience, both from the investors and from regulators. Examples of those mid-1990s crisis can be found in Latvia and Lithuania (see Fleming et al. 1996) and in Bulgaria (see Balyozov 1999). Progressively, the re-capitalization, privatization and internationalization of the banking system, coupled with the implementation of a more robust, EU-modelled institutional framework, did away with most of those problems.

The initial proliferation of mostly domestic banks was, quite naturally, followed by a process of consolidation and strengthening—parallel to the privatization of the remnant state-owned components of the financial system—of the banking sector. This consolidation process was frequently led by foreign companies, which now hold over half of the assets of the banking system in virtually all of them bar Hungary (see Table 6.1): these lower figures largely reflect deliberate policy/political decisions (as demonstrated by Hungarian Prime Minister Viktor Orbán's statement in July 2012 that "50% of Hungary's banking system should be in Hungarian hands", see Sebők 2018).

6.3 Financial Integration and Crisis

The potentially negative implications of reliance on foreign funding emerged during the region's credit boom in the mid-2000s, when foreign mostly EU banks embraced a "centralized" bank funding model and supplied their BCECs' subsidiaries with ample parent bank financing as domestic demand soared while non-existent or shallow financial and capital markets could not meet demand (see Chart 6.1). **Foreign funding to the region toppled $1 trillion by 2008 (roughly half consisting of funding for banks in the form of loans), worth a whopping 25% of the regional GDP and five times as much in terms of flows as in 2002.**[5] This fuelled a regional overheating, with ten countries in the

[5] This figure does not include FDI flows. Namely, "total funds provided to the region grew from around US$200 billion in 2002 to some US$1 trillion in 2008 or 25 percent of regional GDP. About half comprised funding for banks (in particularly their CESEE subsidiaries),

Table 6.1 Percentage of domestic banking assets from other EU MSs (different years)

Bulgaria	*Croatia*	*Czechia*	*Estonia*	*Hungary*	*Latvia*	*Lithuania*	*Poland*	*Romania*	*Slovakia*	*Slovenia*
80	77	79	95	50	59	91	54	69	89	62[a]

Source: EPRS, National Central Banks

[a]The recent post-crisis privatization of NLB (BNY Mellon now owns 62% of the capital, with a 25% residual share of capital), NKBM and A Banka (to Apollo Global Fund) has brought the Slovenian share more in line with that of the region. This happened after many years in which that country was a laggard in terms of non-state ownership of its bank system, due to the unusual ownership structure inherited from the former Federal Republic of Yugoslavia (see Moore and Zajc 2000).

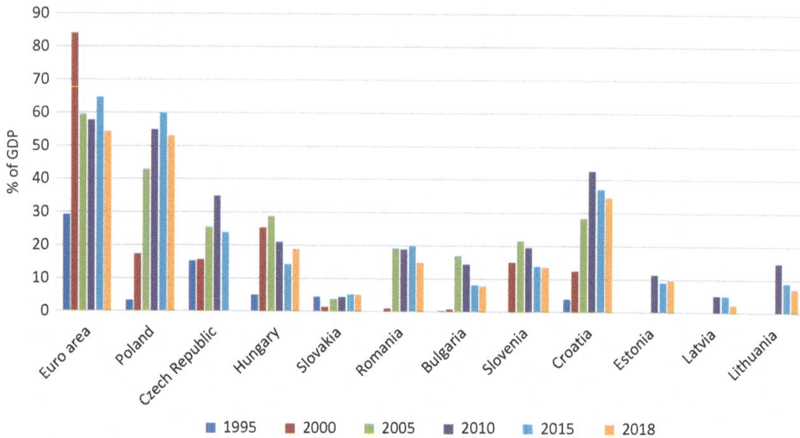

Chart 6.1 Equity market capitalization, as percentage of GDP. (Source: World Bank, CEIC, Domestic Stock Exchanges)

region exhibiting current account deficits worth 10% or more of GDP. When the global crisis hit, **around a half of the increase in inflows (or almost $400 billion) was unwound between 2008 and 2012—as growth prospects temporarily dwindled, risk reassessments took place and foreign banks needed deal with rising NPLs as well as bolstering domestic capital adequacy ratios**. This unwinding had two phases, one related to the global crisis itself and which started already in 2008, and the second one from 2011 onwards, when the global crisis morphed into the EU/euro area sovereign crisis (see IMF 2013).

Examples of the national bank crisis linked to those developments can be found in Latvia with Parex bank in 2008, in Lithuania with Snoras Bank in 2011 (and its Latvian affiliate Latvijas Krajbanka) and Ukio Bankas in 2012 (see Gallizo et al. 2018) and in Slovenia with the state recapitalizations of Nova Ljubljanska Banka and Nova Kreditna Banka Maribor in 2013, and the partial recapitalization of Abanka and its merger with Banka Celje in 2014 (see World Bank 2016).

However, it is important to stress that bank foreign ownership (by an EU MS or not) per se was not the only or main reason behind this—the

mostly in the forms of loans. The other half of the financing took the form of crossborder loans to non-banks". See IMF (2013).

Slovenian banks affected above were domestically and majority state owned; rather a heavy reliance on a certain type of foreign funding (by both domestic and foreign banks) can be a burden in the wake of the crisis, namely, short-term loans. Since the crisis, foreign banks in the region have been rebalancing their funding towards domestic sources, due to pressures arising in their own domestic markets, a reduction in credit demand in the crisis-affected countries of the region and from an EU and global regulatory reform agenda, aimed at strengthening consolidated bank balance sheets and improving the resolvability of large cross-border banking groups, as well as new guidance from Western regulators against high loan-to-deposit ratios in subsidiaries. A shift towards a funding model more balanced towards domestic deposits took place. However, even here the existence of frameworks like the Vienna Initiative (see IMF 2013) and the EU's "Capital Market and Banking Unions" (see EPSC 2015) limited outflows, compared to what happened in non-EU bank markets in the region.

Importantly, conditional on the credibility of the monetary authority, BCECs with floating exchange rates and bank systems integrated with the wider EU one through equity participations seem to have had an easier time dealing with large capital movements than countries with fixed or heavily managed exchange rates (see, for instance, Bakker and Gulde 2010; Vogel and Winkler 2012; IMF 2013; Demirgüç-Kunt et al. 2017). Conversely, BCECs with fixed exchange rates could not let the nominal exchange rate appreciate in the face of capital inflows and were therefore less able to "insulate" domestic liquidity from capital inflows (with hard currency boards having at their disposal even fewer instruments). Remarkably, in some cases the advantage of those floaters can even be observed when a comparison is made with EU member states in the so-called euro area periphery, as will be seen in the next section.

6.4 Fixer Versus Floaters Under Financial Crises

In what follows, we review the impact of the financial and economic crisis on BCECs' banks and their integration with the wider EU bank system. For that, we will use both price and quantity-based measures of financial integration across different market segments. Price-based measures could be seen as a test of the law of one price, which should hold if financial integration is complete.

We quantified price-based measures by means of sigma (σ) convergence. We quantify σ-convergence as the cross-section standard deviation (σ) of the price or yield on a given asset according to the following formula (see Babecký et al. 2010; Vinhas de Souza and Tudela 2014):

$$\sigma_t = \sqrt{\left(\frac{1}{N-1}\right)\sum_{i=1}^{N}\left[\log\left(y_{it}\right)-\log\left(\bar{y}_t\right)\right]^2}$$

where y_{it} is the yield or price on asset i at time t, and $\bar{y}_t$ is the cross-section mean yield at time t. Index I can stand for separate countries or sectors ($i = 1, 2, \ldots, N$). For the purposes of this analysis, we introduce $N = 2$, that is we examine the development of the σ-convergence over time between the euro area (EA) or Germany, on the one hand, and the individual BCECs on the other. By definition, σ takes only positive values. The lower the σ, the higher the level of convergence that has been reached. In theory, full integration is reached when the standard deviation is zero, while high values of σ reflect a very low degree of integration.

6.4.1 Price-Based Measures

By nature, interbank markets are very susceptible to increases in the perception of counterparty risk. Therefore, after the crisis, the sigma-convergence measures of interbank rates for BCECs started to increase for most countries, and more so that with the EA (see Charts 6.2–6.13). As the sovereign debt crisis became more "European" and intensified between 2010 and 2011, this indicator increased further as concerns over the impact on banks' balance sheets mounted and banks operating in the BCECs were curtailed from access to money markets. Remarkably, some of the BCECs with floating exchange rates and credible monetary authorities (Czechia, Poland) were capable of maintaining a high and rather stable level of convergence with the EA and its ultimate "core" economy, Germany, than stressed founding EA members (say, Portugal). On the other hand, BCECs' economies that were members of the EA and had "euroized" bank systems (Slovenia, Slovakia) via equity participations were also able to do that, albeit to a lesser extent, and again more than in the Iberian case, where bank systems were largely domestically held (Iberian economies are added here to provide a stressed-EA benchmark to the BCECs). As is apparent in Chart 6.14a–c, and in the next section,

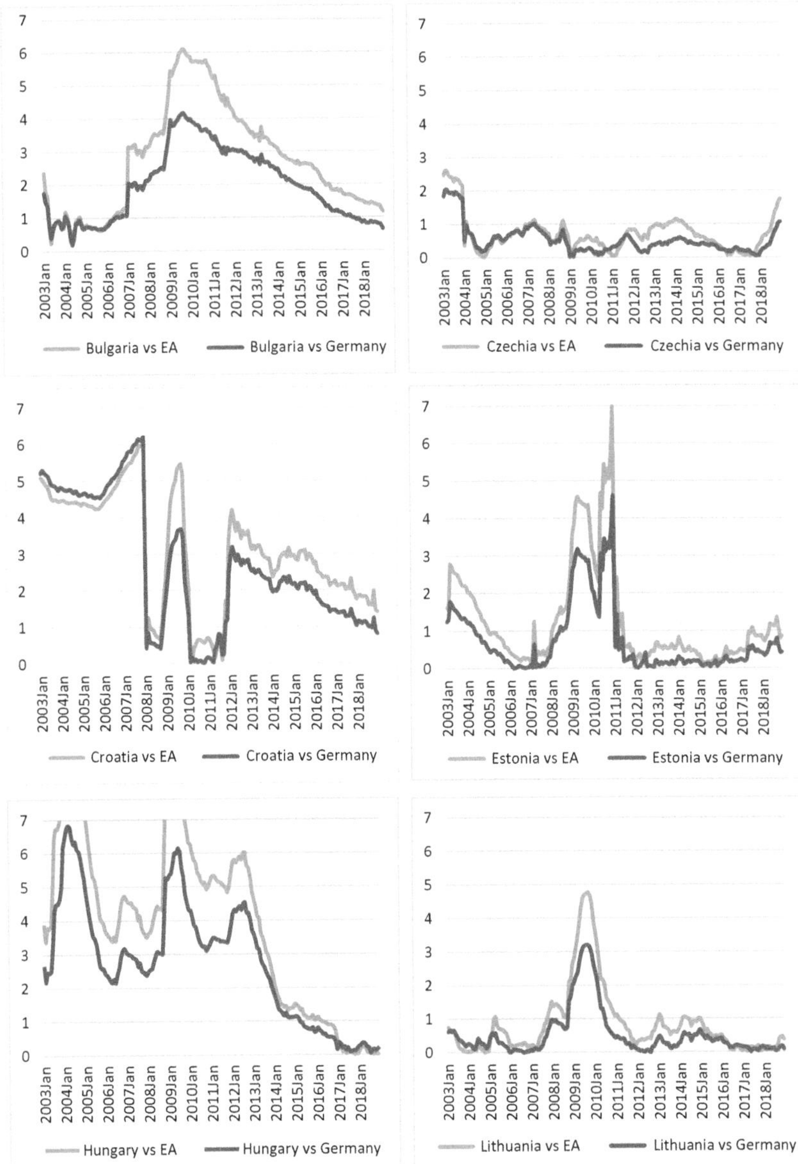

Charts 6.2–6.13 Price convergence: three-month money market rates. Note: full integration = 0; the higher the value, the lower the financial integration. (Source: ECB, authors' calculations)

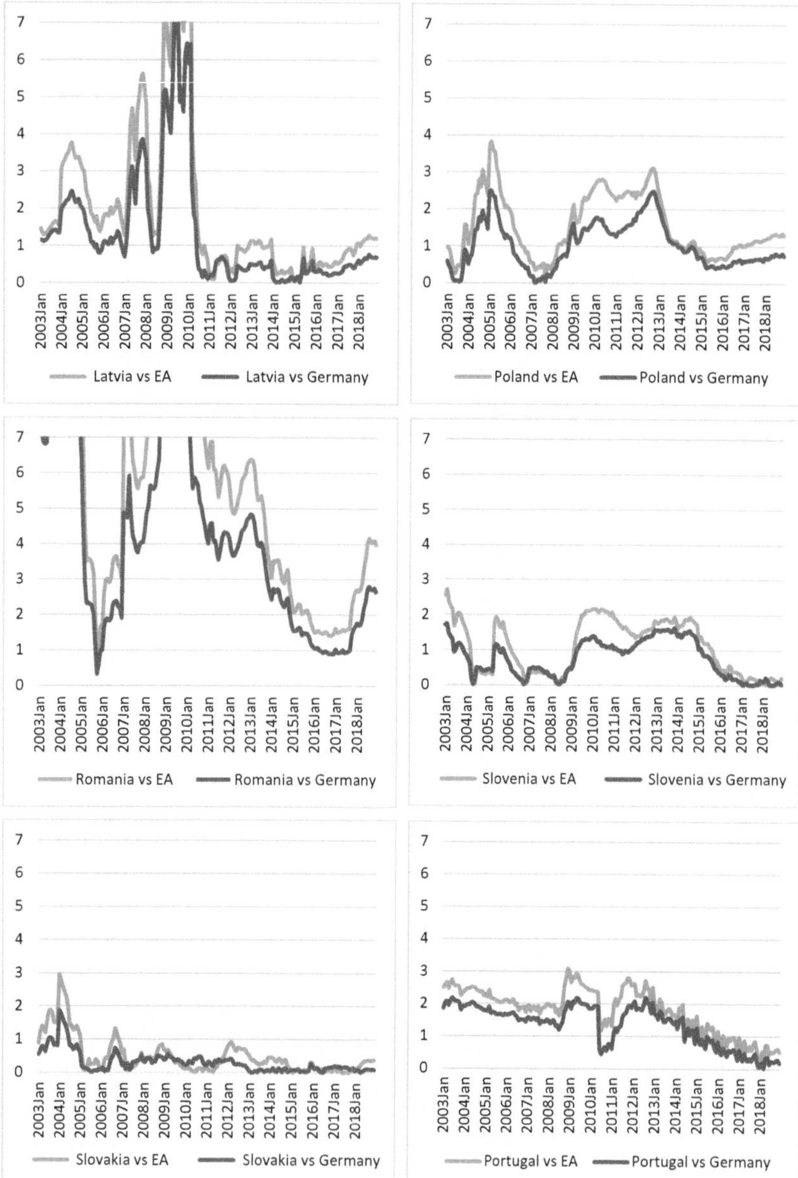

Charts 6.2–6.13 (continued)

these different outcomes were not necessarily related to the "financial depth" per se of the country in question.

6.4.2 *Quantity-Based Measures*

A complementary perspective is gained through a quantity or activity-based indicator, namely cross-border interbank activity, in total and with EA member states. A few things are apparent from Charts 6.15 to 6.26: first, for most of the BCECs, the EA dominates the interbank provision of flows, secondly, the average peak-to-trough loss in inflows for the 2005–2012 period, chosen to cover the interval from the build-up of the wave of inflows till the trough of the unwinding, was significant, at around 30% (but as low as 13–15% in Poland and Czechia), which is not that different from the 26% fall experienced by another "stressed" Iberian member of the euro area "periphery", namely Spain.

The exception to this were the Baltic countries (Charts 22–24 above): first, the relative scale of the inflows was much larger in those countries, second the inflows directed to them were dominated by non-EA banks (namely, in most cases, by Swedish banks, see Gallizo et al. 2018, which did not benefit from ECB additional liquidity provision[6]) and finally, the retrenchment of EA inflows was also much larger (over twice the average observed in other BCECs, which is partially explained by the larger economic downturn in the Baltics and the increase in NPLs, see Emter et al. 2019).

6.5 Conclusion

This chapter analysed the recent financial integration dynamics in the BCECs' economies observed since the beginning of the euro area crisis.

From their start as financially autarkic economies, the BCECs started to liberalize their highly regulated and insular financial systems already in the 1990s, before their membership in the EU. Nevertheless, EU membership (and later, euro area's) in the 2000s clearly deepened and sped-up those processes.

[6] However, even if Swedish banks were dominant, the level of concentration in the three Baltic markets was different: in both Estonia and Latvia, a single bank, Swedebank, was the clear market leader (see Scope Ratings 2019).

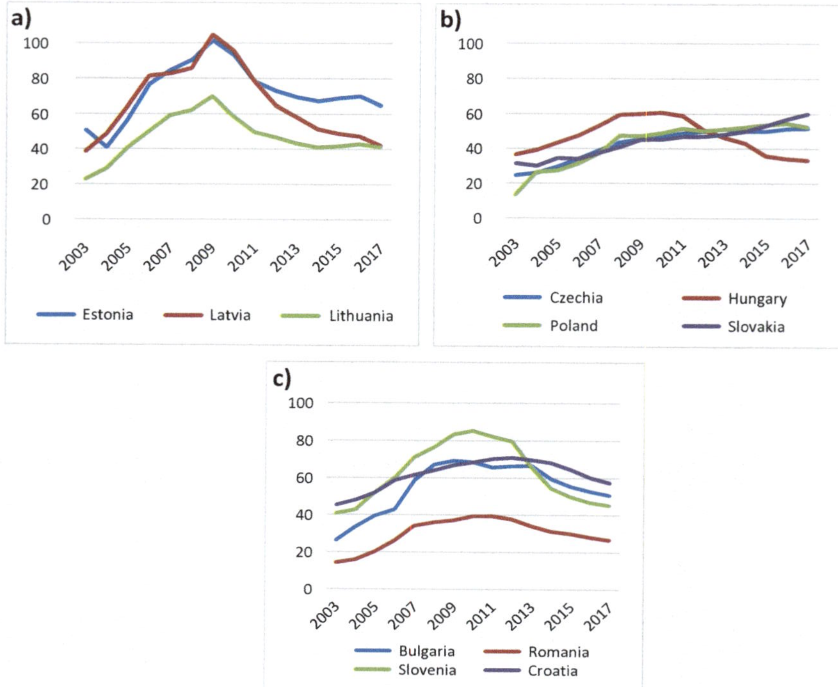

Charts 6.14 (**a–c**) A measure of "Financial Depth": domestic credit to private sector (percentage of GDP). (Source: World Bank)

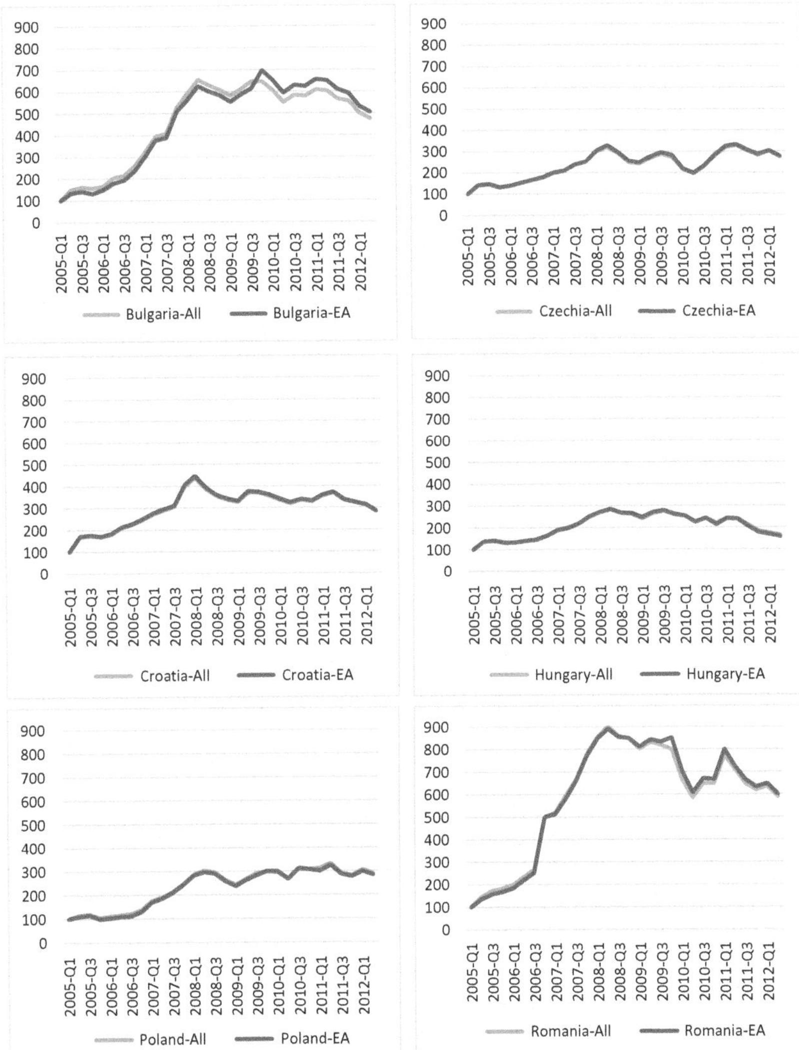

Charts 6.15–6.26 Quantity convergence-cross-border interbank integration (in percentage, with the first quarter of 2005 equal to a 100). This series shows the sigma convergence coefficient of quarterly totals of euro area originated and total foreign claims (consolidated in a ultimate risk bases) reported by the BIS for the banks in those particular jurisdictions, based at 100 at the beginning of the series (namely, the first quarter of 2005). (Source: BIS, authors' calculations)

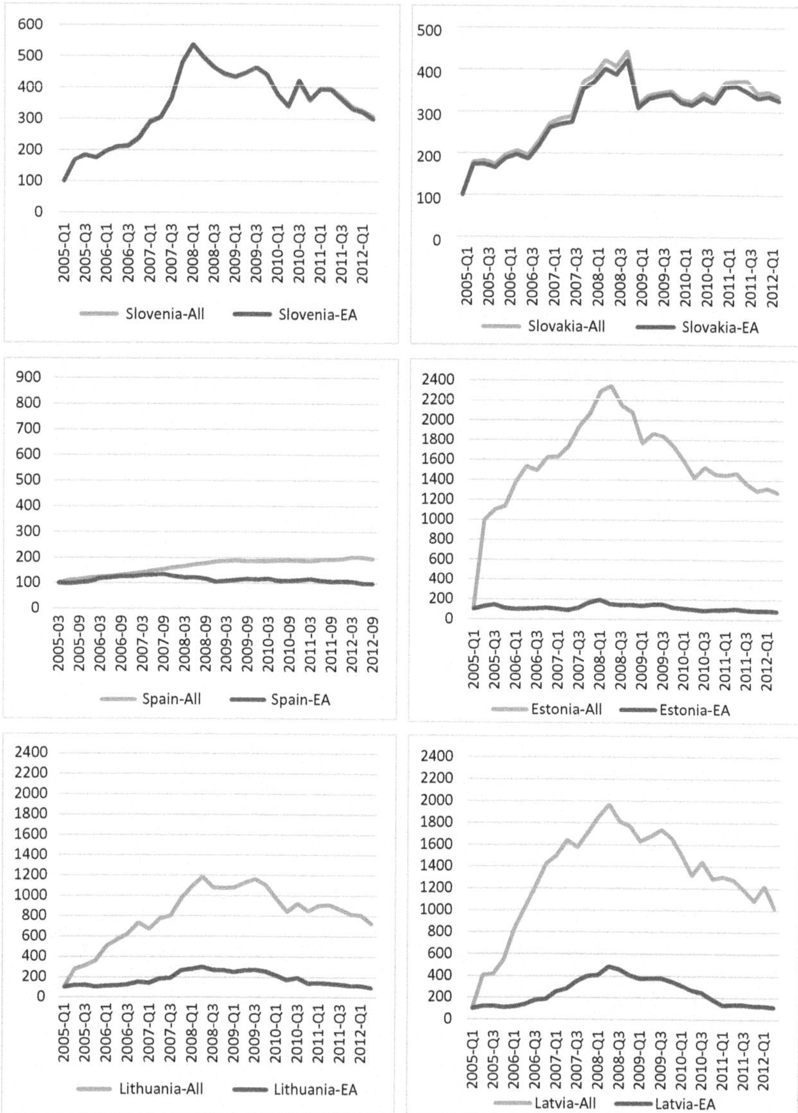

Charts 6.15–6.26 (continued)

However, this piece also demonstrated that financial integration also implies risks and a potentially enhanced sensitivity to shocks. This could be either mitigated or heightened by the specific features of national bank systems (equity participation as opposed to a debt-based integration) and by institutional frameworks such as credible national central banks. However, EU policies can also alleviate the shortcoming of financial integration and deepening via multilateral frameworks like the Vienna Initiative and via the implementation of EU priorities like the Capital Markets and Banking Unions.

References

Babecký, J., Komárek, L., & Komárková, Z. (2010). *Financial Integration at Times of Financial Instability* (Working Papers Series 9/2010). Czech National Bank, Prague.

Bakker, B., & Gulde, A. M. (2010). *The Credit Boom in the EU New Member States: Bad Luck or Bad Policies?* (IMF Working Paper 10/130).

Balyozov, Z. (1999). *The Bulgarian Financial Crisis of 1996–1997.* Discussion Paper, Bulgarian National Bank, 1999 (DP/7/1999).

Demirgüç-Kunt, A., Horváth, B., & Huizinga, H. (2017). *Foreign Banks and International Transmission of Monetary Policy: Evidence from the Syndicated Loan Market* (CEPR Discussion Paper No. 11796).

Emter, L., Schmitz, M., & Tirpák, M. (2019). Cross Border Banking in the EU Since the Crisis: What Is Driving the Great Retrenchment? *Review of World Economics, 155*(2), 287–326

European Political Strategy Center (EPSC). (2015). *Further Risk Reduction in the Banking Union-Severing the 'Doom Loop'.* Brussels.

Fleming, A., Chu, L., & Banker, M., 1996. *The Baltics – Banking Crises Observed.* Policy Research Paper n° 1647, Washington, D.C., USA: The World Bank.

Gallizo, J., Moreno, J., & Salvador, M. (2018). The Baltic Banking System in the Enlarged European Union: The Effect of the Financial Crisis on Efficiency. *Baltic Journal of Economics, 18*(1), 1–24.

IMF. (2013). *Financing Future Growth: The Evolving Role of Banking Systems in CESEE.* Washington, D.C., USA.

Levine, R. (2002). *Bank-Based or Market-Based Financial Systems: Which Is Better?* (NBER Working Paper n° 9138).

Moore, D., & Zajc, P. (2000). Implementing Bank Privatisation in Slovenia. *MOCT-MOST Economic Policy in Transitional Economics, 10*(1), 27–54.

Scope Ratings. (2019). *How Exposed Are Nordic Banks to the Baltics?*, Frankfurt, Germany.

Sebők, M. (2018). Institutional Entrepreneurship and the Mission Creep of the National Bank of Hungary. In C. Bakir & D. Jarvis (Eds.), *Institutional Entrepreneurship and Policy Change: Studies in the Political Economy of Public Policy*. Houndmills, Basingstoke: Palgrave Macmillan.

Vinhas de Souza, L. (2004). *Financial Liberalization and Business Cycles: The Experience of the New EU Member States in The Baltics and Central Eastern Europe*. Deutsche Bundesbank, Discussion Papers Series n° 23/04, Frankfurt a.M., Germany.

Vinhas de Souza, L., & Hölscher, J. (2001). Exchange Rates Links and Strategies of New EU Entrants. *The Journal of European Integration, 23*(1), 1–28. United Kingdom.

Vinhas de Souza, L., & Tudela, M. (2012). *Euro Area Periphery: Structural Reforms Have Significantly Improved External Imbalances, But Full Resolution May Still Take Years*. New York, USA: Moody's Investors Service.

Vinhas de Souza, L., & Tudela, M. (2014). Voltar a Empezar: Crisis and the Renationalization of the Iberian Financial Systems. *Comparative Economic Studies, 56*(3), 337–350. Palgrave.

Vogel, U., & Winkler, A. (2012). Do Foreign Banks Stabilize Cross-Border Bank Flows and Domestic Lending in Emerging Markets? Evidence from the Global Financial Crisis. *Comparative Economic Studies, 54*(3), 507–530.

World Bank. (2016). *Bank Resolution and Bail-in in the EU: Selected Case Studies Pre and Post BRRD*. Washington, DC: World Bank Group.

CHAPTER 7

15 Years from the Eastern Enlargement: Financial Integration and Economic Convergence in Europe

Fabrizio Coricelli and Marco Frigerio

7.1 Introduction

Fifteen years have passed since the enlargement of the EU to countries of central and eastern Europe (CEECs[1]), and thirty years have passed since the historical move of CEECs from centrally planned to market economies. It is fair to say that the anchor of EU entry, which conceivably was anticipated well before 2004, has crucially affected the dynamics of

[1] We denote with CEECs the following countries: Bulgaria, Croatia, Czech Republic, Estonia, Hungary, Latvia, Lithuania, Poland, Romania, Slovak Republic and Slovenia.

F. Coricelli (✉)
University of Siena, Siena, Italy

Paris School of Economics, Paris, France

M. Frigerio
University of Milan, Milan, Italy

M. Landesmann, I. P. Székely (eds.), *Does EU Membership Facilitate Convergence? The Experience of the EU's Eastern Enlargement - Volume II*, Studies in Economic Transition,
https://doi.org/10.1007/978-3-030-57702-5_7

development of CEECs after 1990. Indeed, the development paths of CEECs, which eventually entered the EU, diverged from those of other transition countries that remained tightly connected with the Russian economy (Campos and Coricelli 2002). One of the most remarkable features of the development of CEECs has been the process of convergence with the incomes per capita of old EU members. Furthermore, such a process was supported by large inflows of capital from advanced EU members and by a unique experience of foreign ownership of domestic banking sectors. Indeed, in contrast with the experience of emerging economies in the rest of the world, international financial integration by CEECs took place mainly through flows of cross-border bank credit and through direct investments by foreign banks leading to acquisition of large shares of domestic banking sectors. These features were likely relevant for the apparent positive effects that financial integration had on economic growth by CEECs.

In spite of these positive developments, CEECs were badly hit by the Global Financial Crisis (GFC) of 2008. CEECs were not immune by the typical boom-bust cycle that typically characterized emerging economies in the rest of the world. Several CEECs suffered the phenomenon of sudden stop in capital flows, which was previously observed especially in Latin America. Putting together the pre- and post-GFC periods, an interesting question is whether the growth model of most CEECs, based on a rapid process of financial integration through cross-border bank loans and sale of the local banking sector, can be positively judged. Is it possible that CEECs have been victims of the phenomenon of "too much credit"? Recent economic literature has indeed pointed out several channels through which excessive credit growth can hurt the real economy. All these channels are related to the presence of a threshold or an upper bound to credit beyond which credit has a negative effect on the real economy. First, studies have identified thresholds for government debt (e.g. Arcand et al. 2015). Second, Mian and Sufi (2018) argued that when there is excessive household credit, real growth may suffer. Finally, Coricelli et al. (2012) found that when leverage at the firm level passes a given threshold firm productivity goes down. For CEECs the public debt channel has not played an important role, whereas the other two channels have been highly relevant.

In this chapter, after briefly reviewing the real convergence process characterizing CEECs and the attendant process of financial integration, we analyze firm-level data in order to assess the efficiency of the financial development-cum-financial integration process followed by many CEECs. Rather than simply focusing on the behavior of real output, we emphasize the relationship between credit developments and the efficiency of the allocation of resources. Indeed, in the long run, such efficiency or inefficiency of resource allocation crucially affects sustained growth of output and productivity.

Our analysis complements previous work based on macro data and the possibility of a nonlinear relationship between debt and growth (Arcand et al. 2015).

7.2 Is Europe Different? Convergence of New Member States from the 2004 Enlargement

One of the many puzzles in the international economics literature goes under the name of "Lucas puzzle." The Lucas puzzle arises from the observation that international capital flows do not go from rich to poorer countries, as traditional neoclassical growth theory would predict. The experience of the EU seems to contradict the Lucas puzzle. In particular, emerging European countries involved in the so-called eastern enlargement of the EU in 2004 display a clear pattern of convergence in their incomes per capita relative to the richer incumbent EU members. More important, such convergence process took place in parallel with large net capital inflows, originating mainly from the rich part of the EU. Absolute (beta) convergence is illustrated by the negative correlation between growth rates and initial incomes per capita (Fig. 7.1).[2]

7.2.1 *Financial Development and Financial Integration*

After enlargement, CEECs displayed a remarkable increase in their financial development, measured as the ratio of domestic credit to the private sector in terms of GDP. From 2003 to 2008 the credit-to-GDP ratio doubled on average. Even though the ratio declined in the post-crisis period, especially after the 2011–12 sovereign debt crisis in the euro area, it remained well above the pre-boom period (2003 in Fig. 7.2a).

The dynamics of credit was determined by the behavior of credit from foreign banks, both through credit from their subsidiaries or through

[2] Campos et al. (2019) show that among all enlargements of the EU, the Eastern enlargement had the largest effect on productivity and incomes per capita of new entrants.

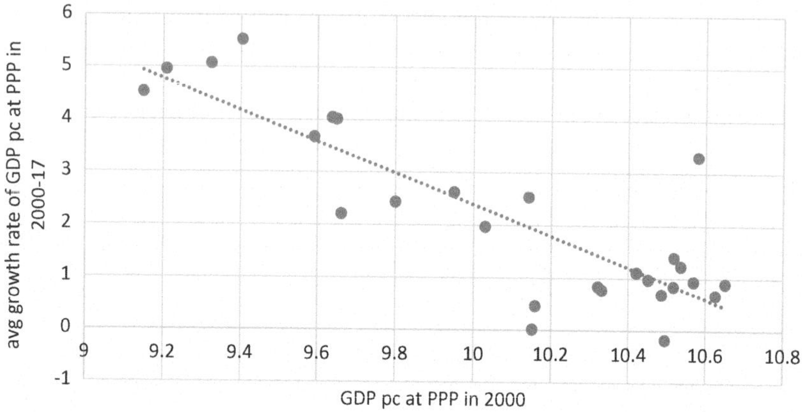

Fig. 7.1 Real convergence in the EU, 2000–17. Note: GDP pc PPP = GDP per capita at purchasing power parity; avg. growth rate 2000–17 = average rate of growth of GDP per capita at PPP. (Source: IMF, WEO database, 2019)

cross-border flows (Fig. 7.2b). Again, even though the decline post-crisis was sizable (more than 20 percentage points in terms of GDP), by 2016 the claims of foreign banks on the domestic non-financial private sector was more than 20 percentage points in terms of GDP above their 2003 levels. This suggests that part of the credit boom prior to the global financial crisis reflected an equilibrium phenomenon of increased financial deepening.

However, while the behavior of total credit might be consistent with an equilibrium phenomenon, the distribution of credit between household and enterprise credit displayed some anomalies. Indeed, during the credit boom that preceded the global financial crisis, a large part of the increase in total credit to the private sector in CEECs derived from a very large increase in household credit, especially during the pre-crisis period (Fig. 7.3).[3]

As a result, in CEECs the share of household credit over total credit significantly increased during the period 2004–08. As noted above, in light of recent literature on the relationship between credit and growth, it

[3] The data for CEECs here refer to new member states from the 2004 enlargement and thus exclude Bulgaria, Croatia and Romania.

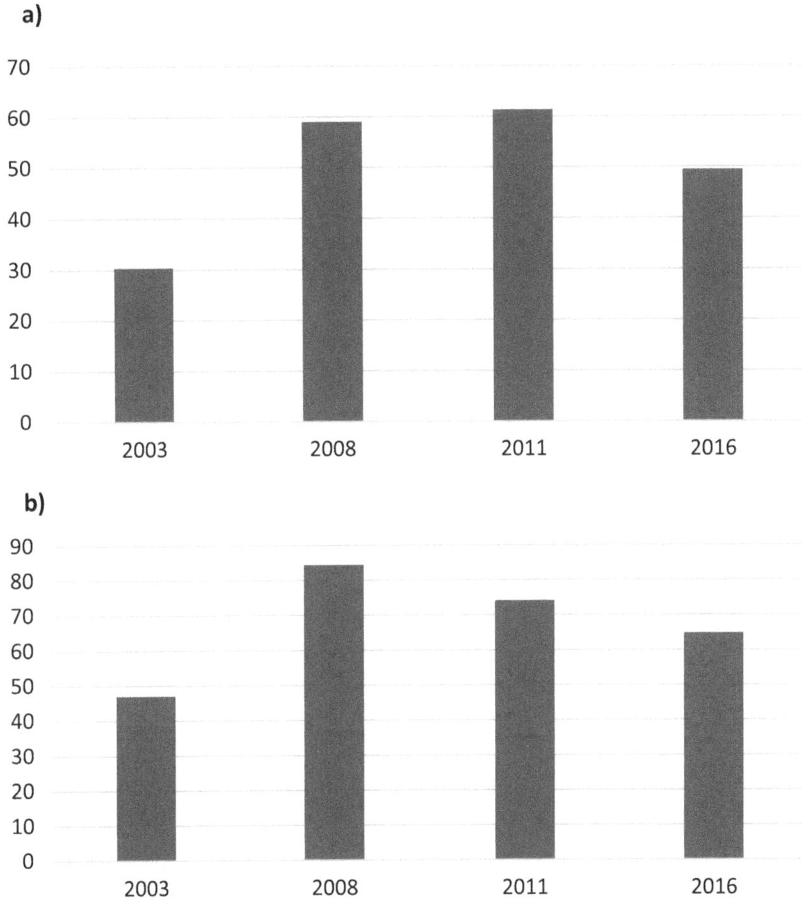

Fig. 7.2 Financial development and financial integration in CEECs after enlargement. (**a**) Domestic credit to the private sector (% of GDP), (**b**) claims of foreign banks (% of GDP) (cross-border plus local loans of foreign banks). (Source: Financial development indicators, World Bank, 2019)

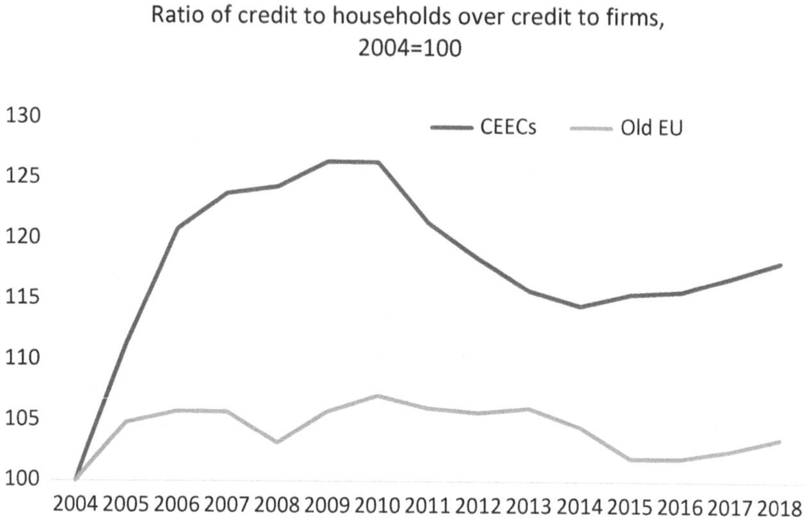

Fig. 7.3 Credit to household and firms. (Source: BIS and World Bank)

appears that the distribution of credit in CEECs was inefficient from the point of view of its impact on economic growth.

7.2.2 Capital Flows and Current Account Imbalances

A second relevant stylized fact is that convergence of emerging Europe with respect to old EU member states took place in the context of large net flows of capital from rich to poorer European countries. In other words, the "Lucas puzzle" did not apply to Europe.

Figure 7.4 associates incomes per capita (the yearly log of GDP per capita in purchasing power parity) to the yearly observations of the current account of the balance of payments in terms of GDP during the period 2000–17, as an indicator of net capital flows. It is apparent that poorer countries received large flows of capital, as evidenced by large deficits of the current account, while richer countries displayed sizable surpluses in their current account.

The relationship is particularly strong if one focuses on the pre-crisis period, as shown in Fig. 7.5., in which incomes per capita are taken in the

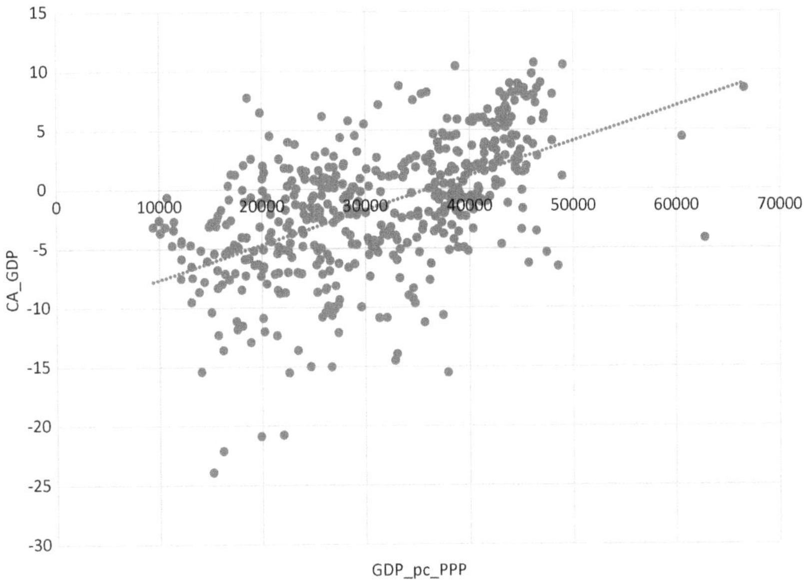

Fig. 7.4 Current account and GDP per capita: yearly observations 2000–17. Note: GDP_pc_PPP = GDP per capita at purchasing power parity; CA/GDP = current account balance in % of GDP. (Source: IMF, WEO database, 2019)

initial year, to avoid the two-way causality between incomes per capita and capital inflows.

This provides additional evidence of the "Europe is different" view, which was widespread before the Great Recession. With the Great Recession the picture drastically changed, with large reversals of capital flows.

7.3 The Global Financial Crisis and the Great Recession

Interestingly, the Great Recession did not interrupt the process of convergence. In spite of the sharp fall in output in 2008–09 in Emerging Europe, convergence continued during the period 2009–17, though with a larger dispersion relative to the pre-crisis period (Fig. 7.6.).

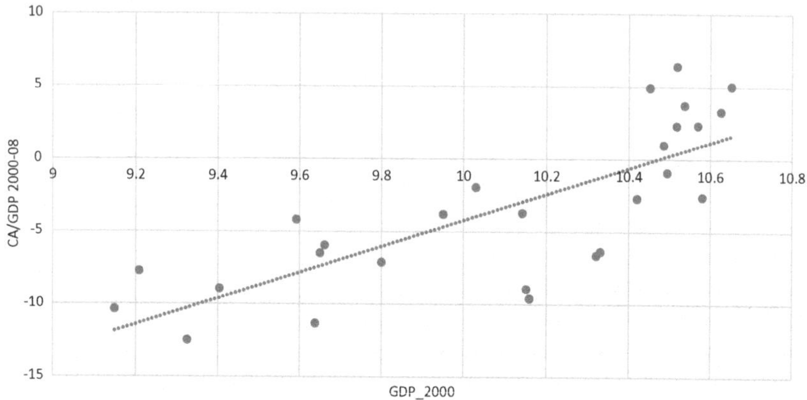

Fig. 7.5 Initial GDP per capita and subsequent capital flows, EU countries. Note: ln GDP _2000 = log of GDP per capita at PPP in the year 2000; CA/GDP 2000–08 = average value of the current account balance in % of GDP during the period 2000–08. (Source: IMF, WEO database, 2019)

In contrast with the pre-crisis period, however, such convergence was not accompanied by capital flows from rich to poorer countries (Fig. 7.7). Indeed, there were several instances of sudden stop in capital flows and attendant large reversals in the current account of the balance of payments.

The reversal for new member states from central-eastern Europe has been spectacular, on average of the order of ten percentage points of GDP. The current account has improved as well for old member states, but by a small amount and fully driven by Southern Europe, which was severely affected by the sovereign debt crisis of 2011–12 ignited by the Greek crisis (Fig. 7.8).

In summary, countries involved in the so-called eastern enlargement of the EU in 2004 experienced a process of economic convergence toward the richer old member states. This convergence was accompanied by a rapid process of financial deepening determined by large credit flows from foreign banks. Economic convergence, financial deepening and financial integration were all elements of the experience of EU membership of central-eastern European countries.[4] Nevertheless, CEECs went through the phenomenon of sudden stop in capital inflows through a spectacular

[4] Brezigar-Masten et al. (2008) show that financial integration affects the real economy depending on the existing depth of the domestic banking sector.

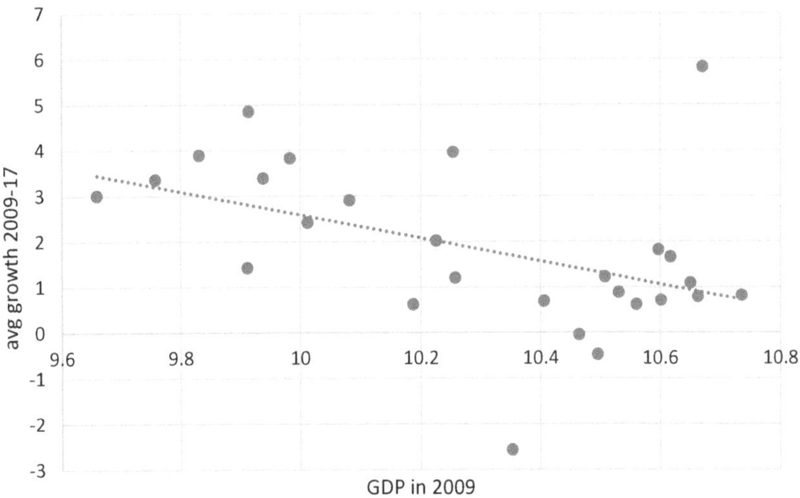

Fig. 7.6 Convergence in post-crisis EU. (Source: IMF, WEO database, 2019)

adjustment in their current accounts of the balance of payments. There were large losses in terms of reductions in GDP, but the recovery process was more favorable than that observed in old EU members. This allowed CEECs to continue their process of convergence toward richer EU members. However, going beyond the macroeconomic data, it is interesting to ask whether the rapid growth of credit, often a truly credit boom, led to improvements in productivity and efficiency in the allocation of resources across firms in CEECs.

In spite of a common experience of financial deepening and closer financial integration with old EU member states, not all new member states went through a process of boom and bust of credit. Indeed, as shown in the next section, there were notable exceptions, involving several new member states. Therefore, we can exploit such variation to identify the effects of credit booms on efficiency. We will also include in the analysis the experience of the old EU members and emerging economies not belonging to the EU (Turkey, Russia, Ukraine, Bosnia and Serbia).

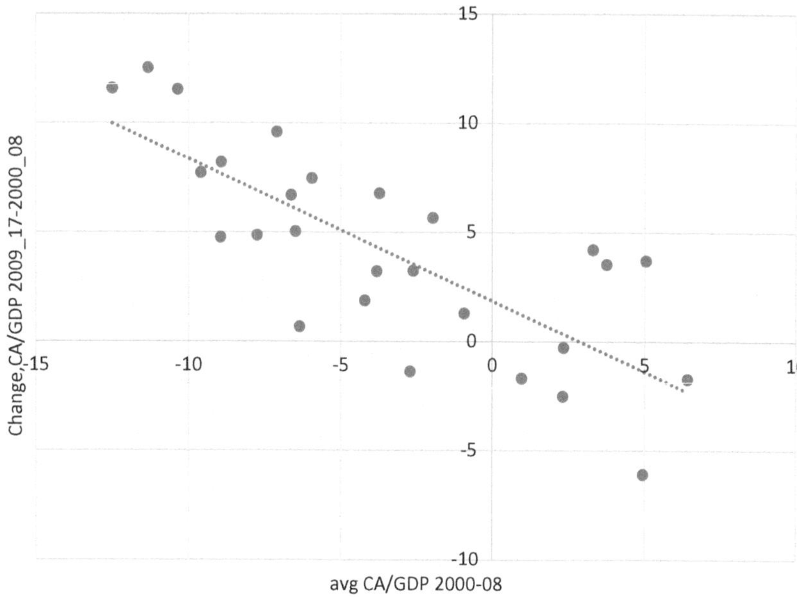

Fig. 7.7 Capital flows reversals. Note: Avg CA/GDP = average of the ratio of the current account of the balance of payments divided by GDP; change in CA/GDP 2009_17-2000_08 = change in the current account balance in % of GDP, comparing the average for the years 2000–08 and the period 2009–17. (Source: IMF, WEO database, 2019)

7.4 Evidence from Micro Data: Credit Boom-Bust and Misallocation of Resources

As we argued above, financial integration for CEECs has taken place through large capital inflows in the form of bank loans. Furthermore, foreign banks, mainly from the euro area, have dominated local financial sectors. In many, but not all, countries such a process coincided with credit booms and subsequent busts following the global financial crisis. During the credit boom episodes, construction and real estate absorbed significant shares of credit, potentially inducing adverse effects on overall productivity of the economy.

This process, common as well to several southern European countries, has been singled out as a main cause of resource misallocation, with an

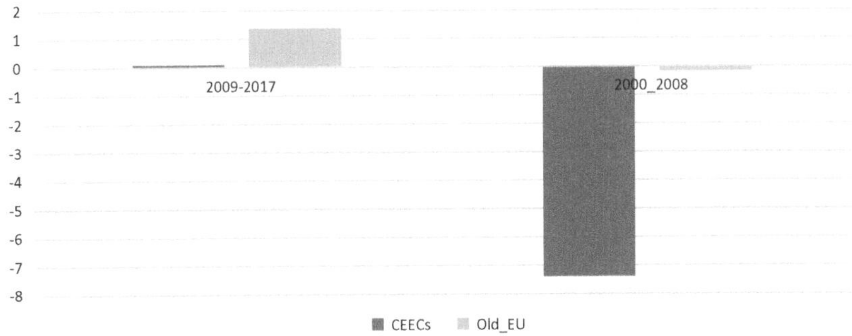

Fig. 7.8 Current account reversal: CEECs versus old member states. Note: Average value of the current account balance for the periods 2009–17 and 2000–08 for the two groups of countries. (Source*:* IMF, WEO database, 2019)

excessive absorption of resources by these service sectors at the expense of more productive manufacturing industries (Borio et al. 2015). However, establishing the optimal relative size of services relative to manufacturing is a daunting task, especially for countries that begun their development as market economies with compressed service sectors and over-sized industrial sectors.

Nevertheless, the issue of misallocation of resources and its connection with credit booms, fueled by large capital inflows, goes beyond the intersectoral allocation of resources. Indeed, a perhaps more fundamental issue for productivity growth relates to misallocation within industries. For instance, this is the focus of the recent work by Gopinath et al. (2017) on southern European countries (Spain).

We follow the work by Hsieh and Klenow (2009) (HK from now on) and Restuccia and Rogerson (2008) to analyze how aggregate productivity is affected not only by the dynamics of productivity in each firm but also by the allocation of inputs to firms with different productivity levels. The main idea of HK is that in an undistorted, though not perfectly competitive market, Revenue Total Factor Productivity (TFPR), given by the product of prices and physical TFP (TFPQ) should be equalized across firms, as more competitive firms set lower prices to gain market shares (on the distinction between revenue productivity and physical productivity, see Foster et al. 2008).

With distortions, TFPR may vary across firms and resources (productive inputs) end up being disproportionally absorbed by less productive firms. Indeed, the variation of TFPR is a measure of resource misallocation. There are many sources for such misallocation, ranging from product market, labor market, taxation to financial markets. In this chapter we focus on the relationship between credit markets and misallocation.

Several studies have analyzed such relationship, among them Banerjee and Munshi (2004) and Banerjee and Duflo (2005) and Greenwood et al. (2010). Interestingly and related to our work, Buera and Shin (2007) study the potential effects of financial crises on misallocation.

We focus on firm-level data from the commercial database ORBIS over the period 2004–14. We use firm-level data to compute misallocation at the industry and country levels. We divide the sample in Eastern and Western Europe. CEECs are now a subset of Eastern European countries. For most of our analyses we use the four-digit level of sectoral aggregation

Credit Boom 2003-2007	No Credit Boom
Western Europe	*Western Europe*
ICELAND	AUSTRIA
IRELAND	BELGIUM
LUXEMBOURG	DENMARK
SPAIN	FINLAND
UNITED KINGDOM	FRANCE
Eastern Europe	GERMANY
BOSNIA	GREECE
BULGARIA	ITALY
CYPRUS	MALTA
ESTONIA	NETHERLANDS
LATVIA	NORWAY
LITHUANIA	PORTUGAL
ROMANIA	SWEDEN
RUSSIA	SWITZERLAND
SERBIA	*Eastern Europe*
SLOVAKIA	CROATIA
SLOVENIA	CZECH REPUBLIC
TURKEY	HUNGARY
UKRAINE	POLAND

Fig. 7.9 Country classification by credit dynamics

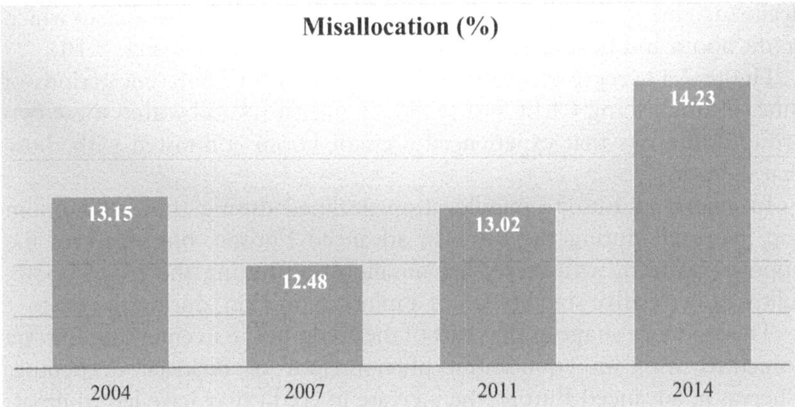

Fig. 7.10 Misallocation, whole sample. (Source: Our calculations on Orbis database)

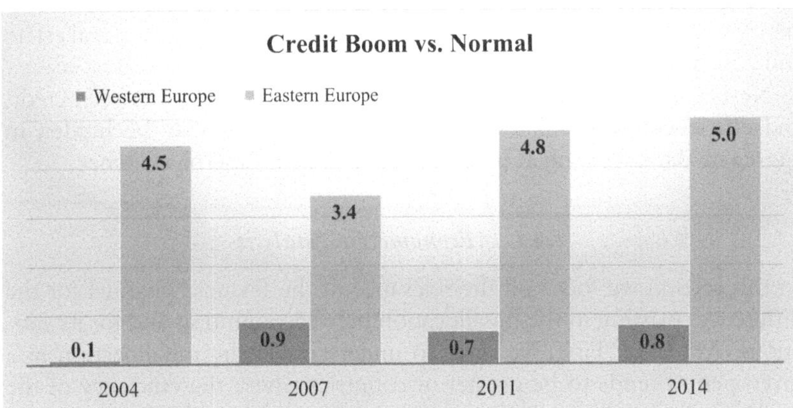

Fig. 7.11 Misallocation. Difference between credit boom versus normal countries. (Source: Our calculations on Orbis database)

and concentrate on European countries, even though for comparison with emerging economies in some cases we include Asian countries (see Fig. 7.9 for the list of countries considered).

First, the dynamics over time of misallocation indicates misallocation increased after the crisis, whereas during the boom period misallocation declined. This result is entirely due to emerging Europe, the area in which credit boom and bust characterized most of the countries (Fig. 7.10).

Figure 7.11. reports the levels of misallocation in different periods of time, distinguishing CEECs from old EU members and within these two groups countries that experienced a credit boom contrasted with those that did not.

In emerging Europe misallocation declined during the credit boom and increased during the bust. In advanced Europe, one observes the opposite pattern, with increasing misallocation during the credit boom, followed by relative stability, if not a minor reduction, during the bust.

This evidence suggests that part of the credit boom in emerging Europe coincided with an equilibrium phenomenon of financial deepening, whereas in advanced Europe the increase in credit may have led to misallocation of resources by letting less productive survive and expand through easy credit low-productivity firms. It should be kept in mind that the notion of misallocation is a within-industry effect and not an across industry effect. This means that the credit boom may have induced loss of efficiency by artificially supporting low-productivity sectors, such as real estate and construction.

Nevertheless, to gain better insight on the relationship between credit and efficiency of the allocation of resources, which may be hidden in aggregate data, we look at micro data and at econometric evidence.

7.4.1 *Econometric Analysis*

In this section we focus on the relevance of the financial channel for the differences existing in the misallocation between countries and for its variations over time. First, we want to understand if the misallocation in a given period tends to be greater in countries where the efficiency of the banking system is lower. Second, we want to understand whether increased misallocation may have been affected by changes in the efficiency of the credit system or, more simply, by the trend in bank credit.

To do this, we analyze the potential interaction between characteristics of individual industries and characteristics at the country level. We will compare the different allocative efficiency in industries that are more (less) dependent on external finance within countries where credit markets are more (less) advanced, or where credit has grown faster (slower) over the years considered.

The dependent variable in the econometric analysis is the index of misallocation derived from firm-level data. Misallocation refers to four-digit industries and varies both across industries and across countries. We present two sets of estimates, one using industry fixed effects and the other specifying industry-level variables that can capture the effect of financial factors on misallocation. In the appendix we describe the whole set of variables used in the econometric analysis.

As discussed above, we also try to get insights on the role of financial factors by looking at country-level characteristics of financial development, including the possible event of credit boom prior to the financial crisis. To avoid problems of reverse causality between financial development and misallocation, in line with the approach introduced by Rajan and Zingales (1998), we capture the effect of financial development interacting it with the dependence on credit of the various sectors. In addition to the variable "external dependence" proposed by Rajan and Zingales, we use alternative measure of dependence on external finance, such as the debt-to-capital ratio[5] and the debt-to-value-added ratio. For the country-level variable we use private credit over GDP as indicator of financial depth.

Tables 7.1, 7.2 and 7.3 present the results of the econometric analysis. We first analyze the year 2007 as indicative of the pre-crisis situation. The dependent variable is a measure of efficiency: higher values imply lower misallocation. In the econometric analysis we distinguish advanced European countries from both CEECs and non-EU emerging countries, which we denote as Eastern Europe.

Table 7.1 reports both the specification without fixed effects and the specification with industry and country fixed effects. The main result is that higher financial depth tends to reduce efficiency, as shown from the interaction term. Industries with higher financial dependence are less efficient when the credit-to-GDP ratio is higher.

The interaction effect is robust to the inclusion of industry and country effects. In the specification without fixed effects one can note that the negative effect of higher credit is observed in Western Europe but not in CEECs. However, including industry and country fixed effects, the adverse effect of credit depth is found for CEECs.

[5] The ratio is computed with Interest Bearing Debt in the numerator, and total assets net of current liabilities in the denominator. The higher the debt-to-total-capital ratio, the more the company is financing its operations with debt compared to internal funds. See also Fernandez de Guevara and Maudos (2009) and Inklaar and Koetter (2008)

Table 7.1 Estimation results

No fixed effects

	(1)	(2)	(3)	(4)	(5)	(6)
	Whole	West. Eur.	CEEC	Other east.	Manuf.	Services
Interaction	-0.0753**	-0.0842*	-0.0468	0.2245	-0.0636***	-0.0703
	[0.032]	[0.043]	[0.087]	[0.111]	[0.014]	[0.044]
ExtDep1	-0.0530	-0.0449	-0.0410	-0.2465**	-0.0183	-0.0218
	[0.034]	[0.056]	[0.052]	[0.047]	[0.020]	[0.050]
Credit GDP	0.0444***	0.0477***	0.0598	0.0488*	0.0466***	0.0396**
	[0.011]	[0.012]	[0.069]	[0.013]	[0.011]	[0.017]
N	4578	2327	1676	575	2038	2540
r2	0.03	0.04	0.02	0.05	0.04	0.02

Fixed effects for both country and industry

	(1)	(2)	(3)	(4)	(5)	(6)
	Whole	West. Eur.	CEEC	Other east.	Manuf.	Services
Interaction	-0.0855**	-0.0340	-0.1294**	0.7450	-0.0841***	-0.0772*
	[0.035]	[0.066]	[0.050]	[0.315]	[0.020]	[0.041]
N	4578	2327	1676	575	2038	2540
r2	0.46	0.55	0.51	0.75	0.42	0.44

Period: 2007

Dependent variable: $EFF_{s,c,y}$

Industry characteristics: *ExtDep1*

Country characteristics: *Credit_GDP*

Standard errors in brackets

* $p < 0.1$, ** $p < 0.05$, *** $p < 0.01$

Nevertheless, it should be kept in mind that our analysis refers to intra-industry effects and it thus neglects misallocation due to inter-sectoral inefficient allocation, for instance through an excessive absorption of resources by low-productivity sectors such as real estate and construction.

Furthermore, Table 7.1 provides a static picture focusing on observations for one year. A more relevant perspective is to analyze dynamic effects, related to the growth rates of credit rather than its levels. In particular, we are interested in analyzing the efficiency implications of credit booms and bust, associated to deviations of credit growth from normal trends.

Table 7.2 Dynamic analysis

No fixed effects

	(1)	*(2)*	*(3)*	*(4)*	*(5)*	*(6)*
	Whole	West. Eur.	CEEC	Other east.	Manuf.	Services
Interaction	-0.1029***	-0.2661***	-0.0198	-0.3524*	-0.0245	-0.1308***
	[0.031]	[0.088]	[0.030]	[0.114]	[0.098]	[0.044]
ExtDep1	0.0128	0.0271**	-0.0182	0.1236	0.0006	0.0165
	[0.009]	[0.011]	[0.011]	[0.056]	[0.019]	[0.011]
Delta_Credit_Cycle	0.0953***	0.0965**	0.0759	0.2967**	0.0703	0.1039**
	[0.029]	[0.037]	[0.045]	[0.050]	[0.048]	[0.042]
N	4578	2327	1676	575	2038	2540
r2	0.02	0.00	0.03	0.06	0.03	0.01

Fixed effects for both country and industry

	(1)	*(2)*	*(3)*	*(4)*	*(5)*	*(6)*
	Whole	West. Eur.	CEEC	Other east.	Manuf.	Services
Interaction	-0.0906**	-0.2597**	-0.0137	-0.1762	-0.0218	-0.1282***
	[0.036]	[0.097]	[0.038]	[0.151]	[0.116]	[0.045]
N	4578	2327	1676	575	2038	2540
r2	0.14	0.18	0.28	0.60	0.18	0.13

Period: 2004–07

Dependent variable: $Delta\_EFF_{s,c,y}$

Industry characteristic: *ExtDep1*

Country characteristic: *Delta_Credit_Cycle*

Standard errors in brackets

* $p < 0.1$, ** $p < 0.05$, *** $p < 0.01$

We focus on the dynamics of credit by computing the deviation of the credit-to-GDP ratio from its trend (see also Gourinchas et al. 2001).

As dependent variable we consider now the change in efficiency. Before the global financial crisis, the increase in credit was accompanied by misallocation of resources, as indicated by the negative coefficient of the interaction term (Table 7.2). In contrast with results from levels, now the negative effects of credit growth on efficiency are entirely due to Western Europe.

Table 7.3 Estimation results

No fixed effects

	(1)	(2)	(3)	(4)	(5)	(6)
	Whole	West. Eur.	CEEC	Other east.	Manuf.	Services
Interaction	0.0417*	0.0426***	0.0928**	-0.0534*	-0.0344	0.0760***
	[0.023]	[0.014]	[0.037]	[0.016]	[0.042]	[0.023]
ExtDep1	-0.0153	-0.0077	-0.0310	-0.0032	-0.0003	-0.0151
	[0.012]	[0.012]	[0.026]	[0.016]	[0.010]	[0.014]
creditless1	-0.0178	-0.0168***	-0.0520***	0.0416***	0.0143	-0.0343***
	4578	2327	1676	575	[0.020]	[0.012]
N	0.00	0.00	0.01	0.02	2038	2540

Fixed effects for both country and industry

	(1)	(2)	(3)	(4)	(5)	(6)
	Whole	West. Eur.	CEEC	Other east.	Manuf.	Services
Interaction	0.0461*	0.0404*	0.1064**	-0.1473*	-0.0262	0.0757***
	[0.026]	[0.019]	[0.042]	[0.037]	[0.048]	[0.027]
N	4578	2327	1676	575	2038	2540
r2	0.10	0.16	0.22	0.65	0.11	0.10

Period: 2007–11

Dependent variable: $Delta\_EFF_{s,c,y}$

Industry characteristic: *ExtDep1*

Country characteristic: *Creditless_Country*

Standard errors in brackets

* $p < 0.1$, ** $p < 0.05$, *** $p < 0.01$

Finally, we investigate whether the deleveraging process that followed the global financial crisis brought an improvement in efficiency (Table 7.3). To measure the magnitude of the unwinding of the previous credit boom we identify the nature of the adjustment post-crisis by separating countries that did not recover the level of financial depth achieved in the pre-crisis period from the others. Another way to represent such classification is to identify countries that experienced a "creditless" recovery and those that did not.

We denote a *Creditless_Country* with a dummy variable taking the value 1 for countries that had a ratio of private credit to GDP in 2011 lower than the value in 2007. According to this measure, creditless countries are

Estonia, Lithuania, Latvia, Ukraine, United Kingdom, Luxembourg, Iceland, Norway.

Results summarized in Table 7.3 indicate that the deleveraging process brought about efficiency gains in all countries, except for other Eastern Europe. Moreover, the effect was particularly strong in CEECs.

Note that in all three specifications of the econometric analysis, the effect of credit or credit dynamics is interacted with the relevance of credit for each industry. While this allows a proper identification of the credit effect, it makes the interpretation of the results more complex. In all specifications, the direct effect of credit has a positive effect on efficiency. If firms have all very low exposure to external finance, higher financial depth and more rapid credit growth would improve the allocation of resources. However, when dependence is high, the effects of higher credit or more rapid credit growth induce lower efficiency. Therefore, this suggests the presence of some form of nonlinearity of the effect of credit on efficiency.

This result complements the findings obtained at the macro level, indicating the presence of a threshold of indebtedness after which growth and productivity are adversely affected by larger credit. Firm-level data permit to highlight a channel through which less financially dependent firms may achieve higher productivity, while larger credit keeps alive less efficient firms. However, the fact that at the country level misallocation increases after the bust of a credit boom suggests that lack of credit may hurt firms with low level of indebtedness, by making their financial constraints effectively binding. By contrast, in industry with high dependence on external finance, the contraction of credit may induce some cleansing effect, leading to better allocation of resources. In the aggregate, the negative effect of a financial crisis on misallocation of resources seems to dominate.

7.5 Concluding Remarks

Entry in the EU ratified the complete shift of former transition countries to the state of market economies. At the time of entry, however, CEECs had incomes per capita sharply lower than old EU members. Accession to the EU helped CEECs narrowing the initial incomes gap. At the same time, entry in the EU fostered rapid financial integration. While most emerging countries in other parts of the world typically received large flows of capital in the form of portfolio investments, foreign bank loans dominated capital inflows in CEECs. Financial integration with old EU members was very rapid and for several CEECs it was associated with large imbalances in the current account of the balance of payments.

The global financial crisis induced a sudden stop to capital inflows and determined a large, and in some cases spectacular, reversal of the current account deficit. This chapter investigated whether and how the pattern of credit boom and bust that accompanied the first decade of participation in the EU of CEECs affected the productivity of the economy and the efficiency of resource allocation. The novelty of our analysis is the focus on microeconomic data and the emphasis on the concept of misallocation of resources popularized by the contribution by Hsieh and Klenow (2009). Using the comparison between CEECs and old EU members, we concluded that the rapid expansion of credit that preceded the global financial crisis likely produced negative effects on productivity through a worsening of the allocation of resources even within industries. The process of deleveraging partly reversed the increased misallocation during the boom period in industries more dependent on credit, but in the aggregate, it increased the levels of misallocation. Interestingly, the evidence suggests that the relationship between credit and efficiency is nonlinear, with adverse effects emerging only when the exposure to credit is sufficiently high. However, looking at the dynamics of credit, we found that rapid credit growth exerted negative effects on efficiency in old EU members, but not in CEECs, suggesting that part of the rapid credit growth in CEECs prior to the global financial crisis was an equilibrium phenomenon. Of course, our analysis does not rule out that inefficiencies of rapid credit growth were present also in CEECs in the allocation of resources *across* sectors and not *within* sectors.

Appendix: Variables Used in the Econometric Analysis

The dependent variable in the regressions relates to firm-level output. The ORBIS database contains a high number of observations relating to the Operating Revenues (Turnovers) of each company, while the availability of observations relating to Value Added (VA) is much lower (about one third). In order to avoid losing many observations, we assume that the VA is a fixed percentage of the Operating Revenues within each industry. In other words, we assume that firms, to generate a certain amount of revenue, use a given quantity of intermediate goods, which vary according to the industry to which the firm belongs. Therefore, the physical productivity of each firm depends on its ability to generate value added for a given use of capital and labor, while the use of intermediate goods only depends on the technological characteristics of the industry.

Regarding the other variables, capital is measured by fixed assets, taking an average book value of the beginning and the end of the year values. For labor we use cost of employees item. As noted in Hsieh and Klenow (2009), it is likely that the wage per labor unit will vary from firm to firm mainly due to the difference in hours worked or in human capital rather than to differences in workers' incomes. Therefore, it can be assumed that the Cost of Employees is equal to the product of a common wage per unit of actual work and the actual labor units, which also capture the difference in hours worked and human capital. In some countries this item is not available so in such a case we use the item Number of Employees (average values between the beginning and the end of the year). Finally, we derive an estimate of input shares. Again, we assume that these shares are variable with respect to the different industries but constant with respect to countries. Assuming a Cobb-Douglas production function we obtain the labor share as the ratio of the Cost of Employees to the Operating Revenues (Turnover), and the capital share as the complement to 1.

References

Arcand, J. L., Berkes, E., & Panizza, U. (2015). Too Much Finance? *Journal of Economic Growth, 20*(2), 105.

Banerjee, A., & Duflo, E. (2005). Chapter 7: Growth theory through the lens of development economics. In P. Aghion & S. Durlauf (Eds.), *Handbook of Economic Growth* (Vol. 1A, pp. 473–552). Elsevier.

Banerjee, A., & Munshi, K. (2004). How Efficiently Is Capital Allocated? Evidence from the Knitted Garment Industry in Tipur. *Review of Economic Studies, 71*, 19–42.

Borio, C, Kharroubi, E, Upper, C., & Zampolli, F. (2015). *Labour Reallocation and Productivity Dynamics: Financial Causes, Real Consequences* (BIS Working Papers, No 534).

Brezigar-Masten, A, Coricelli, F., & Masten, I. (2008). Non-Linear Growth Effects of Financial Development: Does Financial Integration Matter? *Journal of International Money and Finance*, Elsevier, *27*(2), 295–313.

Buera, F., & Shin, Y. (2007). *Financial Frictions and the Persistence of History: A Quantitative Exploration*. Manuscript: Northwestern University.

Campos, N. F., & Coricelli, F. (2002). Growth in Transition: What We Know, What We Don't, and What We Should. *Journal of Economic Literature*, American Economic Association, *40*(3), 793–836.

Campos, N. F., Coricelli, F., & Moretti, L. (2019). Institutional Integration and Economic Growth in Europe. *Journal of Monetary Economics*, Elsevier,, *103*(C), 88–104.

Coricelli, F., Driffield, N., Pal, S., & Roland, I. (2012). When Does Leverage Hurt Productivity Growth? A Firm-Level Analysis. *Journal of International Money and Finance*, Elsevier, *31*(6), 1674–1694.

Fernandez de Guevara, J., & Maudos, J. (2009). Regional Financial Development and Bank Competition: Effects on Firms' Growth. *Regional Studies, Taylor & Francis Journals*, *43*(2), 211–228.

Foster, L., Haltiwanger, J., & Syverson, C. (2008). Reallocation, Firm Turnover, and Efficiency: Selection on Productivity or Profitability? *American Economic Review*, *98*, 394–425.

Gopinath, G., Kalemli-Özcan, Ş., Karabarbounis, L., & Villegas-Sanchez, C. (2017). Capital Allocation and Productivity in South Europe. *The Quarterly Journal of Economics*, *132*(4), 1915–1967.

Gourinchas, P. O., Valdes, R., & Landerretche. (2001). Lending Booms: Latin America and the World. *Economía*, Latin American and Caribbean Economic Association, 1(2), 47–99.

Greenwood, J., Sanchez, J., & Wang, C. (2010). Financing Development: The Role of Information Costs. *American Economic Review*, *100*(4), 1875–91.

Hsieh, C., & Klenow, P. (2009). Misallocation and Manufacturing TFP in China and India. *The Quarterly Journal of Economics*, *124*(4), 1403–1448.

Inklaar, R., & Koetter, M. (2008). Financial Dependence and Industry Growth in Europe: Better Banks and Higher Productivity. In *GGDC Research Memorandum GD-100, Groningen Growth and Development Centre*. Groningen, The Netherlands: University of Groningen.

Mian, A. R., & Sufi, A. (2018). *Finance and Business Cycles: The Credit-Driven Household Demand Channel* (NBER Working Paper, n. 24322).

Rajan, R., & Zingales, L. (1998). Financial Dependence and Growth. *American Economic Review*, *88*(3), 559–586.

Restuccia, R., & Rogerson, R. (2008). Policy Distortions and Aggregate Productivity with Heterogeneous Plants. *Review of Economic Dynamics.*, Elsevier for the Society for Economic Dynamics, *11*(4), 707–720.

PART III

Migration Channel and Labour Market Institutions

CHAPTER 8

Labour Markets, Demography, Migration and Skills

Michael Landesmann and Hermine Vidovic

8.1 Introduction

Labour market developments in the 'new member states' since the beginning of the 'transition' in 1989/1990 reflect a number of far-reaching structural adjustment processes, due both to the 'transition' itself (from a planned to a market economy) as well as the deep impact of the East-West European integration process, culminating in EU accession. What were the main features of these—historically rather unique—processes of structural change and adjustment? We single out the following:

We gratefully acknowledge the contributions by Isilda Mara, wiiw, to sections 8.4 and 8.5 of this chapter and to Sandra Leitner and Robert Stehrer, both also wiiw, to section 8.8. The support of Beate Muck and other members of the wiiw statistical staff are also gratefully acknowledged.

M. Landesmann (✉) • H. Vidovic
Vienna Institute for International Economic Studies (WIIW), Vienna, Austria
e-mail: landesmann@wiiw.ac.at; vidovic@wiiw.ac.at

M. Landesmann, I. P. Székely (eds.), *Does EU Membership Facilitate Convergence? The Experience of the EU's Eastern Enlargement - Volume II*, Studies in Economic Transition,
https://doi.org/10.1007/978-3-030-57702-5_8

- Sectoral structural change
- Productivity catching-up and changing skills demand
- Spatial reorganisation and cross-border production linkages
- Demographic dynamic strongly influenced by migration flows
- Convergence in labour market institutions and labour market policies

The legacy of the socialist/communist period was that sectoral structures differed quite substantially from those found in advanced Western European economies. The main difference was the strong emphasis in the Communist period on industrial development and the relative neglect of the services sector. It was thus expected that a turn towards a market economy would lead to a retrenchment of the relative share of manufacturing (and particularly of 'heavy industry') and a strong increase of employment in a variety of (especially market) services activities. Apart from this change, we also have to take note that some of the CEESE (Central-Eastern and South-Eastern European) economies still had—due to their generally lower stage of economic development—a high share of the population living in the countryside and engaged in agriculture and related activities. This was expected to also induce a change regarding a shrinkage of people working in the primary sector.

A second component of 'transition' (and of 'integration' with the more advanced Western European region) was an expectation of catching-up in productivity levels, which is a necessary condition for catching-up processes in income levels. Such productivity catching-up has implications for employment, both regarding how output growth translates into employment growth and also how the differential scope for productivity catching up across sectors translates into changing sectoral employment patterns. We shall explore this in more detail in Sects. 8.2 and 8.3 of this chapter. Linked to this is the issue of the changing demand for skills and qualifications which accompanies productivity catching-up, technology transfer and changing sectoral employment patterns (Sect. 8.7).

A third feature of labour market developments refers to the spatial dynamic of economic activity in CEESE (Sect. 8.6 of this chapter). This has much to do with the reorientation of production linkages from an earlier structure of international specialisation and integration amongst the Council for Mutual Economic Assistance (CMEA) countries (i.e. the 'Soviet bloc') towards the development of close economic relationships with Western Europe and the EU in particular. This integration process led to important relocations of economic activity and hence to uneven labour market developments across regions within each of the CEESE economies. Thus, on the one hand, there was a relocation of economic activity through cross-border production linkages to the regions in closer proximity to the Western borders (there was also the increased intensity of purchases by final consumers across the borders) and, on the other hand, capital cities became major attractors of higher-end activities. The latter was in parts a function of the speed by which the gap in tertiary (in particular business services) activities was closed, and this was easier in agglomerations in which high purchasing power combined with higher skill levels and centres of administration, research and education, all of which attracted headquarter activities by the larger foreign and domestic companies operating in CEESE economies.

The fourth element which is due to both, differences in developmental (and thus income) levels and the rather rapid progress in East-West economic and political integration (culminating in EU membership leading to free mobility of labour), was the strong push and pull factors behind the sizeable migration flows between Eastern and Western Europe. Income gaps were very high and hence the expected returns on migration were high inducing especially the young (more mobile) members of the labour force to migrate. This significantly affected the age profile of the population and thus the development of the labour force and the overall activity rate. The gradual evolution of more liberalised access to Western Europe (in steps through visa liberalisation, student mobility and, in the last instance, full access to the labour market after transitory periods through EU membership) furthermore facilitated these strong migration flows. Apart from migration, transition also created an initial shock to birth rates which also had an impact on the age profile of the population. From a labour market point of view we were able to observe a transition over a twenty to thirty years period from a 'surplus labour' to a 'labour shortage' regime in many of the CEESE economies that joined the European Union (the EU11). This will be discussed in Sects. 8.4, 8.5 and 8.8 of this chapter.

Finally we come to labour market institutions and labour market policies: The transition from the Communist regime towards a liberalised market-based regime had—as expected—a strong impact on how labour markets function both institutionally and in terms of policy. In the Communist period, employment was guaranteed, there was a strong concentration of work forces in large plants and the participation rate of women was high. Trade unions were 'official unions' (i.e. part of the regime) and lost their legitimacy after 1989. Further, wages were set and not negotiated. It was thus expected that quite different arrangements would emerge in the labour market once transition took place. Union membership declined rapidly, and wages became a function of direct interactions between employers and workers depending on the supply-demand constellations on the labour market. In fact, what could be observed was a move towards a more liberalised regime in labour markets compared to what characterised labour markets in Western (and Northern) continental European labour markets. As regards labour market policies there was *grosso modo* a convergence process to those which characterise Western Europe, although some differentiation (also amongst EU11 countries) persisted. We shall analyse these in Sect. 8.9 of this chapter.

The approach taken in this chapter hence is that developments in CEESE countries that joined the European Union in three waves over the period 2004–2013 have to be understood as the result of the unfolding of three types of forces that interacted with each other: (i) the 'transition' from being centrally planned economies to becoming market-based economies; (ii) the dramatically changing international environment which led to a strong reorientation of their economic linkages (trade, production, finance, labour mobility) from a formerly relatively closed economic bloc (the CMEA) towards a close integration with the international (but particularly wider European) economy; and (iii) the expectation and then realisation of EU membership. There were clear interdependencies between these three forces, and these forces had different degrees of importance in the different phases of economic, social and political developments which the CEESE economies transgressed since 1989. Thus (iii) clearly conditioned the way how transition proceeded, especially once it became clear that EU membership would be a realistic outcome of negotiations. On the other hand, progress in and the particular direction of transition was part of the conditions imposed to lead to a successful outcome of EU accession processes. The redirection of international economic linkages (i.e. ii) was an immediate result of the programmes of 'transition' adopted, and any progress in negotiations with the EU and prospects of accession deepened the extent of economic integration with Western European economies across all the various tracks (trade, finance, labour mobility, etc.). Hence the position in this chapter is that the impact of EU Enlargement on economic developments in CEESE economies has to be analysed and comprehended in the context of these three interacting forces.

8.2 Labour Market Dynamics and Economic Growth: Longer-Term Patterns Before and After Enlargement

As mentioned in the introduction, employment patterns from 1989 onwards were characterised by dramatic macroeconomic and structural changes in CEESE economies: immediately after 1989, with the implementation of swift reform packages to move the economy towards a market-based economy (through abrupt trade and price liberalisation, as well as the introduction of a variety of privatisation schemes). As regards employment, there was the impact of a slump in economic activity widely recognised as the 'transformational recession' (Kornai, 1995). This went along with a particularly strong fall of industrial employment as the strong dependence of industrial production on traditional CMEA production linkages collapsed, as well as a fall in participation rates of women in the labour markets (which were traditionally high in Communist countries).

After the initial recessions, economic development stabilised and GDP growth moved on a positive trajectory (although interrupted at times by 'secondary transition recessions'[1]) and we can observe rather distinct patterns in the relationship between GDP growth and employment growth—both in different phases and in comparison with EU incumbent countries (Fig. 8.1).

Figure 8.1 shows employment and GDP growth (average per annum growth rates) over various periods: 1996–1999, 1999–2004, 2004–2008, 2008–2013 and 2013–2017. Three groups of Central and Eastern European countries are distinguished: the Central European economies (Czech Republic, Hungary, Poland, Slovenia and Slovakia; henceforth called CEE-5), the three Baltic States (Estonia, Latvia, Lithuania) and the two economies that joined in 2007 (Bulgaria and Romania; BG, RO). We also depict in this and in most future graphs also two groups of the 'old member states' (OMS): an 'EU-South' group (Greece, Portugal, Spain) and an 'EU-North' group (AT, BE, DE, DK, FI, FR, IE, NL, SE, UK) for comparative purposes.

What we see in these graphs is that (almost without exception) the gap between GDP growth and employment growth is much more accentuated

[1] Such 'secondary transition recessions' were often a function of unsustainable exchange rate regimes and misguided monetary policies which often led to exchange rate collapses with ensuing banking crises.

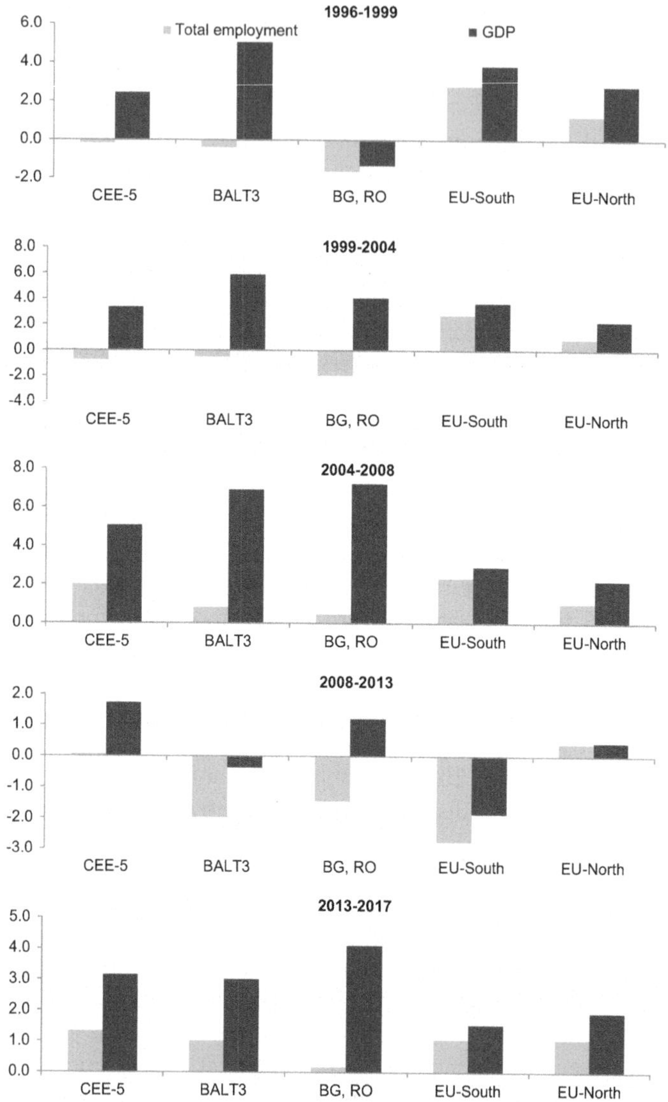

Fig. 8.1 Growth of GDP and employment (from national accounts), p.a. averages. Note: CEE-5 until 1999 excl PL. 1999–2004 for CEE-5 refers to 2000–2004. Definition of county groups: CEE-5: CZ, HU, PL, SI, SK. BALT3: EE, LT, LV. EU-South: EL, ES, PT. EU-North: AT, BE, DE, DK, FI, FR, IE, NL, SE, UK. (Source: wiiw Annual Database incorporating national statistics and Eurostat)

in the EU11 economies than in either the EU-South or the EU-North countries. Another way of saying this is that the 'employment elasticity' (i.e. the way employment reacts to changing production levels) is smaller in the EU11 countries than in the EU15. This is true in all periods and particularly in the boom period after the first round of accession and before the outbreak of the economic crisis. In this period we also see a marked acceleration of GDP growth. Prior to this period, that is in the periods 1996–1999 and 1999–2004, there was also positive GDP growth[2] but negative employment growth. One spoke of this phase as one of 'jobless growth'. The CEE countries also weathered the economic crisis period better than the OMS (with the exception of the Baltics) and then resumed relatively fast GDP growth (2013–2017) but again with a significantly lower employment elasticity than the EU-Southern and EU-Northern economies.

If we want to explain the low 'employment elasticity' of the new member states, one can simply state that it reflects the other side of the coin of real income catching-up driven by productivity catching-up. Thus, if the difference in the growth rates of GDP and aggregate employment were the same in the EU15 and in the CESEE countries, there would be no catching-up of productivity levels between the two groups of economies. This is, of course, arithmetically correct but does not provide much insight into the underlying processes.

A more sophisticated argument was developed in Landesmann et al. (2004) and will be discussed in the following section.

8.3 Sectoral Employment Structures: Convergence and Divergence

In this section we examine sectoral employment structures and see whether and to which extent employment structures converged to those of the more advanced economies (EU-North) and how they compare to those in the EU-South. Let us point to some of the striking distinguishing features and the patterns of development over time.

As regards the share of total employment in agriculture (sector A) there was generally a process of convergence to 'EU-North' of all the CEE

[2] Some economies experienced severe balance of payments and exchange rate crises in the late 1990s, foremost Bulgaria which moved to a currency board regime in order to contain hyperinflation. The result was a sharp contraction of GDP over a number of years.

country groups although at different speeds: thus CEE5 and Baltics start (on average) with an 'excess' of people employed in agriculture (compared to EU-North) of 6–7 ppts and 10 ppts respectively in the mid-1990s, and they then both differ in the shares of employment in agriculture only by 3 ppts and 4 ppts from EU-North in the most recent period 2014–2017. By now the EU-South has, on average, a higher share of employment in agriculture than the CEE5 and the Baltics. Bulgaria and Romania on the other hand remain with a share of the workforce in agriculture at about (on average) 18% but this has come down from about 30% in the mid-1990s.

The picture is quite different as regards employment in manufacturing (the main segment of sector C): here we see a relative strength of the CEECs relative to both EU-North and EU-South. The most dramatic deviation we observe for the CEE5 who show a share of employment in industry 10 ppts above that in the EU-North, but also Bulgaria and Romania and the Baltics show a positive employment share differential of about 6 ppts and 4 ppts respectively compared to the EU-North. No such positive differential is recorded for the EU-South. Furthermore, the differential grew over time, from the mid-1990s to 2014–2017, in all the CEE economies. This confirms the picture of Central and Eastern Europe having become 'industrial hubs' in the context of the development of European manufacturing, a topic to which we shall return later. A last point on the issue of manufacturing: we can see that the positive deviation from EU-North grew particularly over the period 2005–2008, that is after the Enlargement. EU accession did stimulate—in the context of overall economic growth—the development of cross-border production networks in the manufacturing sector. The economic crisis period 2009–2013 shows some contraction, but the positive growth in the share differential resumes again in the recovery period 2014–2017.

As regards employment in the services sectors, we distinguish between three groups of services sectors: tradable services (TS), non-tradable services (NTS) and non-market services (NMS). In all these services areas the CEEs have a smaller share of employment than the EU-North; however there is convergence over time in tradable and non-tradable services, but not in non-market (i.e. publicly provided) services where the deficit is even growing. This seems to indicate that, as regards market services, CEECs are converging with the more advanced North-EU countries, but not so in publicly provided services where there is a significant and widening gap. This indicates that CEECs follow a different model as regards provision of health, education and so on, that is services that are characteristic of the 'welfare model' of advanced Western and Northern EU economies (Fig. 8.2).

We are now in a position to present a 'structural' explanation of the U-shaped employment pattern which could be observed in CEE economies over the entire period, starting from the 'transition phase' to the most recent period. As we saw in Fig. 8.1, aggregate employment growth was negative over the transition period until the early 2000s, after which it became positive. Furthermore, CEE economies showed a very low employment elasticity (employment response to output growth) for most of the transition period, followed by an improvement more recently.

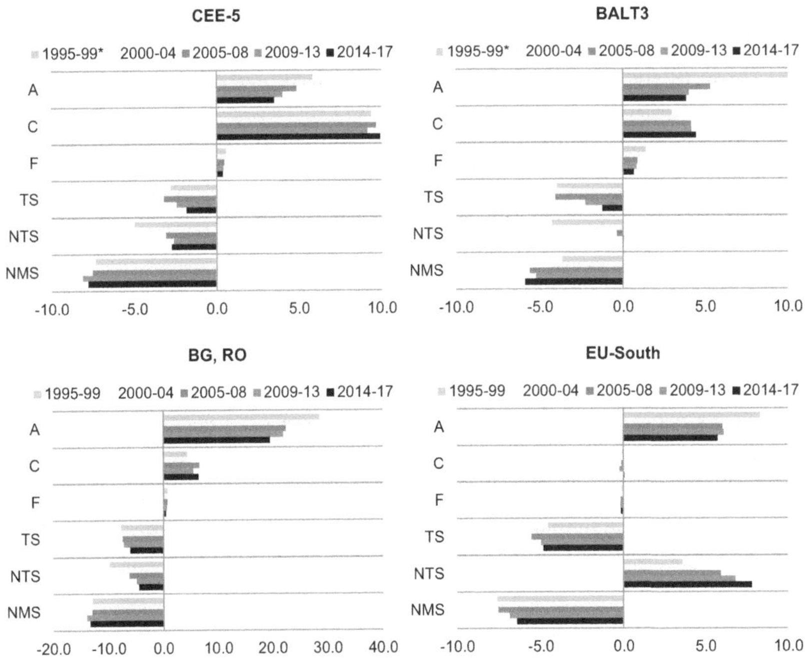

Fig. 8.2 Employment shares difference to the EU-North. (in percentage points). Note: CEE-5 until 1999 excl. PL. BALT3 until 1999 excl. LV. Sectors: A (Agriculture, Forestry, Fishing), C (Manufacturing), F (Construction), TS (Tradable Services), NTS (Non-tradable Services), NMS (Non-market Services). (Source: wiiw Annual Database incorporating national statistics and Eurostat)

Rather complex structural convergence processes lay behind the relative output and employment performances in CEECs: at the outset of transition, the CEE countries had a wide range of industries in which labour productivity gaps to Western European industries were particularly high and in which, consequently, there was a strong potential for productivity catching-up (particularly in manufacturing industries and—in many CEE countries—in agriculture). On the other hand, the services industries were strongly underrepresented in comparison with Western European countries. The CEE countries however underwent not only a convergence process of productivity levels at the aggregate level but also a structural convergence process in the output composition of their economies, that is the representation of different sectors in the aggregate economy became more similar to those in the advanced Western European countries. Thus, the shares of heavy manufacturing industry and of agriculture declined and those of the services industries (particularly market services, such as retail trade, business and financial services) increased. Services industries are more labour-intensive, and hence, a shift in the output structure towards services increases the employment elasticity of aggregate economic growth. The initial overrepresentation of industries in which productivity catching-up was fast (manufacturing and agriculture), followed by a phase of convergence in output structures (with labour-intensive services industries gradually gaining in importance) thus showed up in a very low employment-output elasticity in the initial phase after transition, followed by a recovery of that elasticity afterward. This led to the U-shaped pattern of aggregate employment growth observed in the CEE countries over the longer period from 1990 to 2008. More recently, many CEE economies have moved into a 'labour shortage' regime, which has to an important extent been due to the large outflow of population from the CEE countries, particularly of young and skilled workers. This phenomenon will be covered further in the following section.

8.4 Demographic Trends and Migration Flows

This section discusses the rather dramatic trends in demography which characterised the CEECs since the beginning of transition and which became a major factor also in labour market developments. Demography has been shaped by the shock of the transition process itself, but also significantly by intra-EU migration flows (see also Brücker et al. 2009).

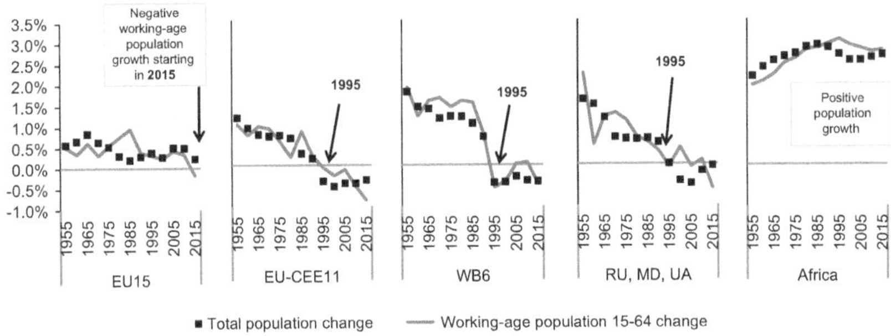

Fig. 8.3 Total and working-age population growth, 1955–2015, percentage. Note: RU (Russia), MD (Moldova), UA (Ukraine); EU-CEE11 refers to the EU-CEE member countries. (Source: UN Statistics, 2017; own calculations; five-yearly average annual growth rates)

Figure 8.3 shows the (average per annum) population growth rates and the growth rates of the working-age (15–64 years) population in five-yearly intervals from 1955 onwards. The dramatic collapse of population growth from the early 1990s onwards (following the beginning of the 'transition') is clearly visible in the EU-CEE11 (the new member countries including Croatia), as well as in other Eastern European economies (the Western Balkan economies—WB6—and the group comprising Russia, Ukraine and Moldova).[3] In the EU15 population growth remained—on average—positive. As regards working-age population, the situation is more dismal (both in the EU-CEE11 and in the EU15) reflecting the changing age profile of the population that we shall discuss further below.

The more recent period 2011–2017 is depicted in Fig. 8.4. The change in population over this period is decomposed in 'natural change' (the net of birth and death rates over the period) and 'net migration flows'. We can observe a lot of country differentiation with some countries experiencing a net population loss of 5–12% over this period (two of the Baltic countries, plus Bulgaria, Croatia, Romania and Hungary) while others show stagnant (Poland) or positive population growth (Slovenia, Slovakia and Czech Republic). Amongst the OMS, Greece and Portugal were the countries with population losses and all three EU-Southern countries (i.e.

[3] For comparative purposes Fig. 8.3 also includes the information regarding African demographic developments, the main non-European neighbouring region of the EU.

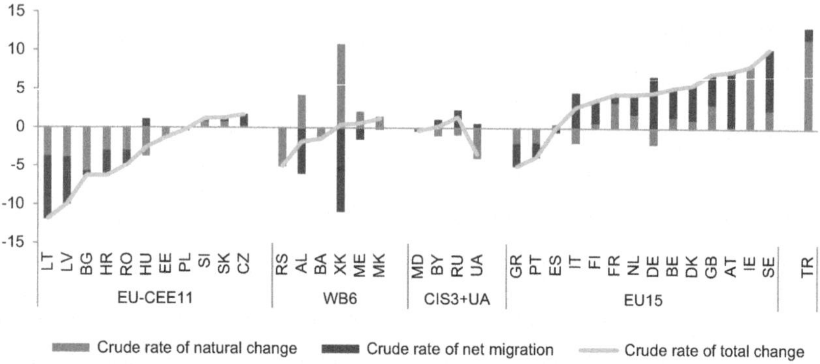

Fig. 8.4 Average population change by individual countries, cumulative in percentage, 2011–2017. (Source: Eurostat)

including Spain) lost population through net migration. The other EU15 countries were net beneficiaries of migration flows, while the Baltics as well as Southeast European countries experienced heavy losses both due to negative natural population growth and significant net emigration flows. Overall, 4.2 million people emigrated from the EU-CEE11 since 2014 of which 2.2 million after the financial crisis.

Figure 8.5 gives the breakdown of net migration from the EU-CEE11 countries to other EU countries over the period 2008–2017 by country of origin. We can see that the biggest contributors to net migration flows were Poland and Romania, but also Latvia and Lithuania had sizeable emigration flows in absolute numbers (and, of course, high rates in relation to the population) and more recently Croatia. In general, one observes a 'hump' of emigration slightly before and after accession. The migration flows from EU-CEE11 to other EU countries continue to fluctuate in total around 150–200,000 per annum.

8.5 The Impact of Migration Flows on Age Profiles and on Labour Markets

As a result of these demographic developments reported in Sect. 8.4 age profiles of the populations of the EU15 and the EU-CEE11 (and also those of the Western Balkan countries) have converged since 1990 (see Fig. 8.6).

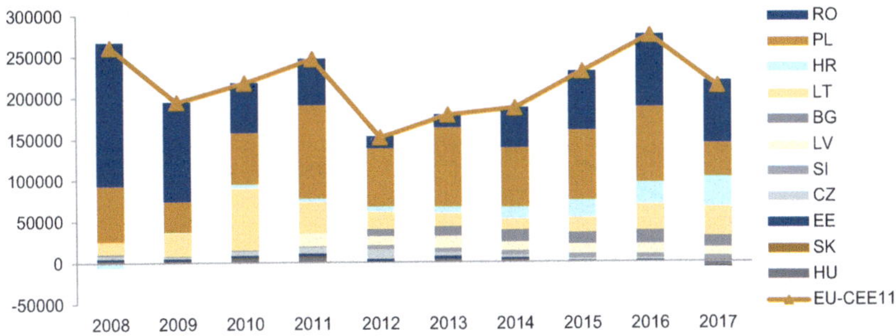

Fig. 8.5 Net migration from EU-CEE11, 2008–2017. (Source: Eurostat)

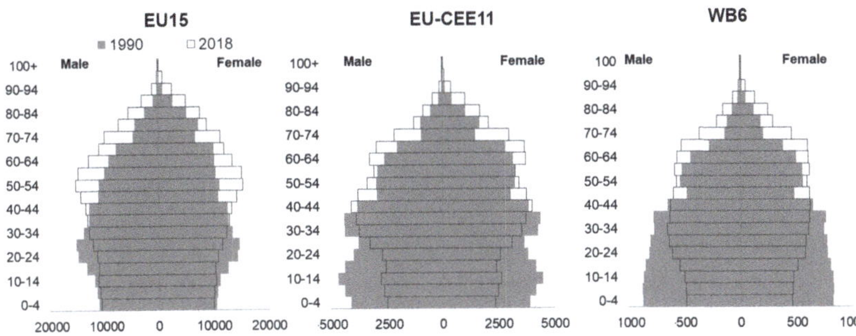

Fig. 8.6 Age structure in EU15, EU-CEE11 and WB6. (Source: UN Statistics, 2017)

The changes in the age profile (showing a dramatic ageing process in both the EU11 and the WB6) not only are the result of falling birth rates and rising life expectancy, but also reflect the age profile of the migrants leaving the country who are predominantly young. This is reflected in Fig. 8.7, which shows the age profiles of the three segments of the population in the EU15 economies: natives, migrants from inside the EU, and migrants from outside the EU. What we can see is that the bulk of the immigrant population in the EU15 population, both from outside and inside the EU, is in the age group 20–54 (peaking in the age groups 25–39); hence they significantly contribute to the working-age population in the receiving countries and reduce the dependency ratio.

We shall now return to the labour market developments in the EU11 countries and focus on the more recent phenomenon of labour market

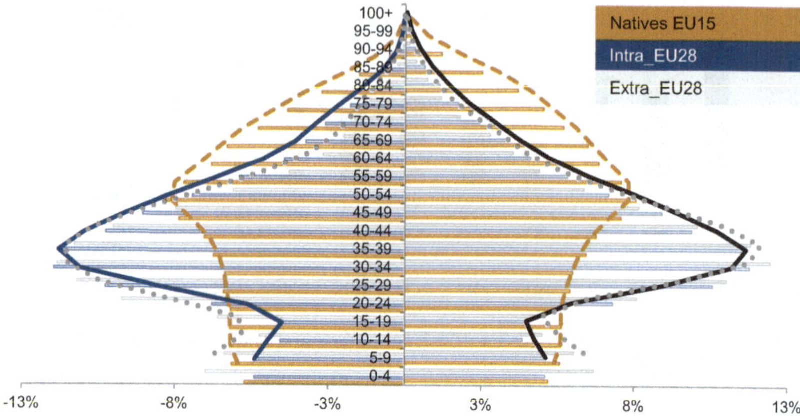

Fig. 8.7 Age structure in EU15: natives; migrants intra-EU and from outside the EU. (Source: Eurostat; own calculations males on the left, females on the right)

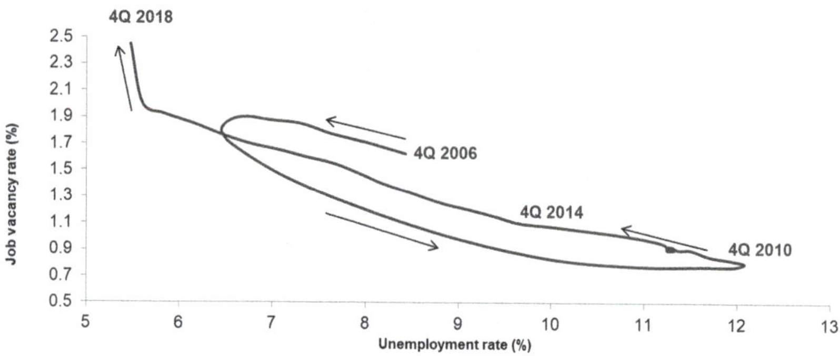

Fig. 8.8 Beveridge curve, 4Q 2006—4Q 2018 (four-quarter average rates). (Source: Eurostat)

tightening. Figure 8.8 draws the so-called Beveridge curve over the period 2006–2018. What we see is that EU11 labour markets recovered in the pre-crisis period due to high GDP growth (see earlier Fig. 8.1), unemployment rates fell below 7% for the region as a whole and the job vacancy rate rose. Then followed the financial and economic crisis and by 2010:Q4 the unemployment rate reached 12% for the region as a whole. From then on the labour market situation recovered with the unemployment rate falling by end 2018 to 5.5% which is significantly lower than in the EU15 (where it hovers around 8%). The vacancy rate shot up. Hence one can speak of moving towards a 'labour force constrained growth' scenario in many of the EU11 countries. This is—as was demonstrated above—due to unfavourable developments in natural population growth, but also—varied by country—significantly due to emigration flows from the region and especially linked to the age profile of the emigrants. On top of this, the evidence shows that the skill distribution of EU11 migrants in the EU-15 is double peaked, in the sense that both lower skilled and high skilled migrants tend to migrate; the latter accentuates skill shortages back home (see Jestl et al. 2015).

Figure 8.9, extracting data from a survey of employers in the different EU member countries, shows the reasons given by employers for filling their vacancies. Amongst the EU-CEE countries particularly the category 'lack of applicants' features prominently.

In response to the labour market tightening, also labour force participation rates increased substantially in many of the EU11 economies (see Table 8.1):

We shall in Sect. 8.8 report on an exercise that projected the likely binding constraint which the population (and migration) dynamic exerts on the labour supply and thus on the likely long-term growth performance of CEESE economies. Before that we still want to reflect on the differences between the two regions in Central and Eastern Europe, the EU11 and the Western Balkan countries. For this comparison, we refer to two variables that are commonly used in economic migration analysis as

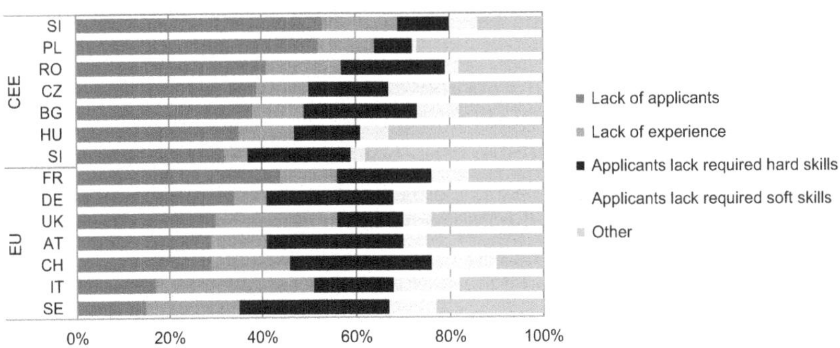

Fig. 8.9 Main difficulties faced by employers to find workers, 2018. (Source: Manpowergroup, '2018 Talent Shortage Survey')

Table 8.1 Activity rates (in age group 15–64)

	2000	2005	2008	2012	2013	2014	2015	2016	2017	2018
EU28	:	69.6	70.7	71.7	72.0	72.3	72.5	72.9	73.3	73.7
EU15	69.0	71.0	72.2	72.9	73.2	73.3	73.4	73.8	74.0	74.3
Euro area	67.6	69.8	71.2	72.0	72.2	72.3	72.5	72.8	73.1	73.4
Belgium	65.2	66.7	67.1	66.9	67.5	67.7	67.6	67.6	68.0	68.6
Bulgaria	61.6	62.1	67.8	67.1	68.4	69.0	69.3	68.7	71.3	71.5
Czechia	71.2	70.4	69.7	71.6	72.9	73.5	74.0	75.0	75.9	76.6
Denmark	80.0	79.8	79.3	77.2	76.6	76.6	76.9	77.5	77.9	78.2
Germany (until	71.0	73.8	75.9	77.2	77.6	77.7	77.6	77.9	78.2	78.6
Estonia	70.5	70.7	74.2	74.8	75.1	75.2	76.7	77.5	78.8	79.1
Ireland	67.5	70.8	74.8	71.1	71.8	71.8	72.1	72.7	72.7	72.9
Greece	63.9	66.4	66.7	67.5	67.5	67.4	67.8	68.2	68.3	68.2
Spain	65.1	70.0	72.7	74.3	74.3	74.2	74.3	74.2	73.9	73.7
France	68.8	69.7	69.9	70.7	71.1	71.0	71.3	71.4	71.5	71.9
Croatia		63.3	65.8	63.9	63.7	66.1	66.9	65.6	66.4	66.3
Italy	59.9	62.5	62.9	63.5	63.4	63.9	64.0	64.9	65.4	65.6
Latvia	67.1	69.1	74.2	74.4	74.0	74.6	75.7	76.3	77.0	77.7
Lithuania	71.2	68.7	68.4	71.8	72.4	73.7	74.1	75.5	75.9	77.3
Hungary	59.9	61.3	61.2	63.7	64.7	67.0	68.6	70.1	71.2	71.9
Netherlands	74.9	75.1	77.8	79.0	79.4	79.0	79.6	79.7	79.7	80.3
Austria	71.3	71.4	73.9	75.1	75.5	75.4	75.5	76.2	76.4	76.8
Poland	66.1	64.4	63.8	66.5	67.0	67.9	68.1	68.8	69.6	70.1
Portugal	71.1	73.2	73.9	73.4	73.0	73.2	73.4	73.7	74.7	75.1
Romania	69.6	62.3	62.9	64.8	64.9	65.7	66.1	65.6	67.3	67.8
Slovenia	67.4	70.7	71.8	70.4	70.5	70.9	71.8	71.6	74.2	75.0
Slovakia	69.5	68.9	68.8	69.4	69.9	70.3	70.9	71.9	72.1	72.4
Finland	76.8	74.7	76.0	75.2	75.2	75.4	75.8	75.9	76.7	77.9
Sweden	75.3	78.7	79.3	80.3	81.1	81.5	81.7	82.1	82.5	82.7
United Kingdor	75.2	75.4	75.8	76.1	76.4	76.7	76.9	77.3	77.6	77.9
Albania				64.9	59.6	61.5	64.2	66.2	66.8	68.3
Bosnia and Herzegovina				53.9	53.5	54.2	54.6	54.2	54.5	54.2
Montenegro	:	:	:	58.8	58.6	61.6	62.6	63.4	63.5	64.7
North Macedor	:	:	63.5	63.9	64.9	65.3	64.9	64.5	65.3	65.4
Kosovo				38.2	41.5	42.5	38.4	39.6	43.8	41.6
Serbia	:	:	:	60.2	61.7	63.4	63.7	65.6	66.7	67.8

Source: Eurostat and SEE Jobs Gateway.

Source: Eurostat and SEE Jobs Gateway

the important economic ‘push’ and ‘pull factors’: differences in unemployment rates and differences in wage rates between country of origin and (potential) country of destination.

Figure 8.10a and b shows the very different situation of the two source regions in Eastern Europe, the EU11 and the WB6 in relation to the EU15. In both regions the unemployment rate has fallen since 2010; however, while the unemployment rate now lies just above 5% in the EU11 and is thus substantially below that of the EU15, the unemployment rate in the WB6 still hovers above 15%. Similarly, we see a closure of the wage gap between the EU11 and the EU15 (from about 43% to close to 60% over the period 2005 to 2017), while the wage gap between the EU15 and the WB6 countries remains at about 40%, and with respect to the EU11 a wage gap with the Western Balkan countries opens up. Hence, while the ‘push’ and ‘pull’ factors declined dramatically in the relationship between the EU15 and the EU11 and thus indicate a fall in future EU11–EU15 migration flows, this is not (yet) the case in the Western Balkans.

The comparison between the EU11 and the Western Balkan countries and their different labour market developments with respect to

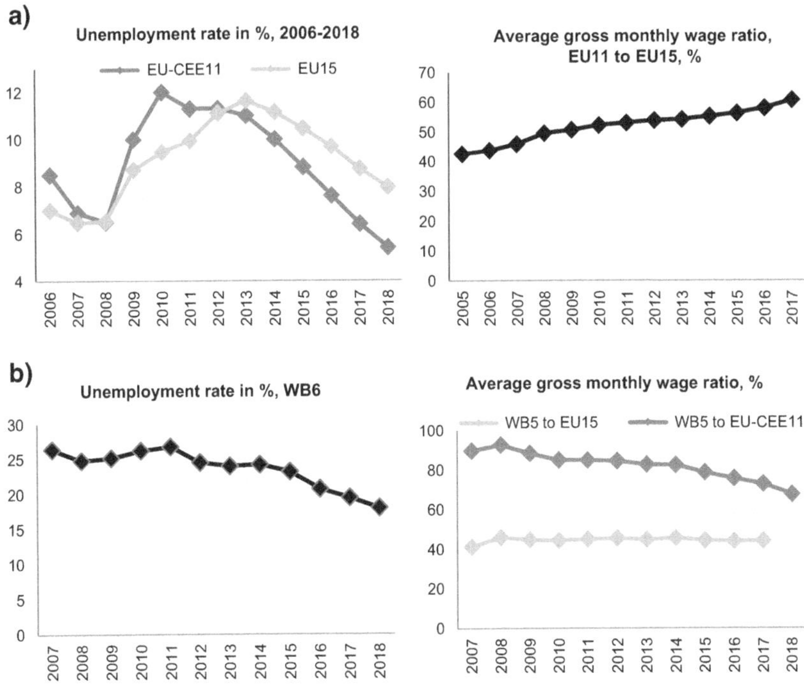

Fig. 8.10 (**a**) Unemployment rates and average gross monthly wage ratio in EU11 and EU15. (Source: wiiw database, Jobs Gateway (2018)). (**b**) Unemployment rates and average gross monthly wage ratios in Western Balkans compared to EU15 and EU11. (Source: wiiw database, Jobs Gateway, wiiw Handbook of Statistics; WB5 refers to WB6 without Kosovo for which wage rate data were not available)

unemployment and wage levels can be interpreted as evidence for the impact which full EU membership (including full labour market access) can have on wage convergence, on the one hand, and on interacting labour supply and labour demand developments across (old and new) member countries. As the Western Balkan countries are still removed from a proper EU accession process the interaction effects are limited to outward labour mobility but there is much less evidence for wage and income convergence (in fact Fig. 8.10b shows wage divergence between the Western Balkan countries and the EU11).

8.6 Spatial Patterns in CEESE Labour Markets

Uneven regional development in CEESE economies have been analysed in many studies and publications (Iammarino et al. 2019; Petrakos et al. 2005) and are covered also in Chaps. 4 vol. I and 3 vol. II of this book. We shall first summarise what has been found in this respect across the CEE region and then come to a specific topic which explains strong regional agglomeration effects of industrial employment in some of the CEE economies.

At the regional level, a change in regional development patterns could be expected from the outset of the 'transition' as the opening of the CEESE economies towards Western Europe would change the regional orientation of economic activity in the transition economies. However, a number of additional factors were at work, leading to important agglomeration tendencies of economic activity at the regional level. This led to a very significant strengthening of the economic importance of capital cities and a sharp increase in regional inequality. In most of the CEESE countries, the levels of intra-country regional income inequality surpassed those observed in Western Europe.

What were the explanatory factors in these developments? Without any claim to completeness, the following factors have played important roles, leading to a sharp increase in regional inequality and tendencies towards agglomeration of economic activity (particularly in capital cities).

One factor is the aforementioned catching-up process in tertiary activities, which were traditionally underrepresented in the CEESE economies and which, in the early phases of transition, could develop most easily in capital cities or strong urban agglomerations. Such urban agglomerations provide the sophisticated markets and the necessary concentration of people with higher-level skills and, furthermore, the scope for complementarities between tertiary activities necessary to support the development of a vibrant services sector. Thus, CEE capital city (or metro) regions are outliers in the shares of tertiary educated in the population compared to the countries as a whole, or in patenting and R&D expenditure, in firm start-ups, in public transport infrastructure and of course in GDP per capita (for statistical evidence on this, see, e.g. European Commission 2017, Ch. 1; Lavalle et al. 2017).[4]

[4]Taking the last indicator, GDP per capita, the gaps (measured as ratios) between urban regions and the country as a whole and to rural regions in particular would be for the EU-15

The other factor that has supported the tendency towards regional inequality is the strong concentration of FDI activity in regions bordering Western European economies. Such locations have facilitated the easy integration into cross-border production networks and have been able to make use of the more developed logistics and transport infrastructure in their neighbouring Western European regions. Cross-border production linkages were thus responsible that CE-5 economies contributed significantly to the Central and Eastern European region becoming increasingly the 'Central European Manufacturing Core' (a term coined by Stehrer and Stöllinger 2015). The complementarity between Western European (particularly German) high value-added, high-quality manufacturing capabilities and the low-waged, but relatively well-skilled labour force found in the ex-Communist countries (which had provided the background to the training and employment of a sizeable industrial work force) led to this strong agglomeration of industrial activity in Central (and Eastern) Europe (see Fig. 8.11).

As infrastructure might improve more widely, further labour supply pools may be tapped, and uneven land prices may also attract FDI to a wider range of regions; this—supported by appropriate regional and labour market policies—could somewhat reduce the degree of regional inequality in the future. However, regions with entrenched structural problems are a more persistent cause for regional inequality. These include regions that suffer from their geographical position away from the border to Western Europe but also from the legacy of past heavy industrialisation in the socialist period. Lagging regions also include poor agricultural regions that have not been able to sufficiently attract new activities. Such regions have suffered from (at times massive) emigration and a deterioration of the demographic profile as young people leave, and also from an

respectively 1.12 and 1.38, while for the EU11 this gap would amount to 1.68 and 2.35. Of course, there are various problems with comparisons of GDP per capita between urban (and particularly metropolitan) regions and other regions, due to the non-availability of region-specific price levels to construct proper PPP measures of real income levels; further the distortions that arise between GDP and GNP due to the profit reporting of companies that have headquarters in capital cities, but also due to the impact of often a significant share of commuters in the working population. There are also other factors that can lead to biases in such real income comparisons at the regional level.

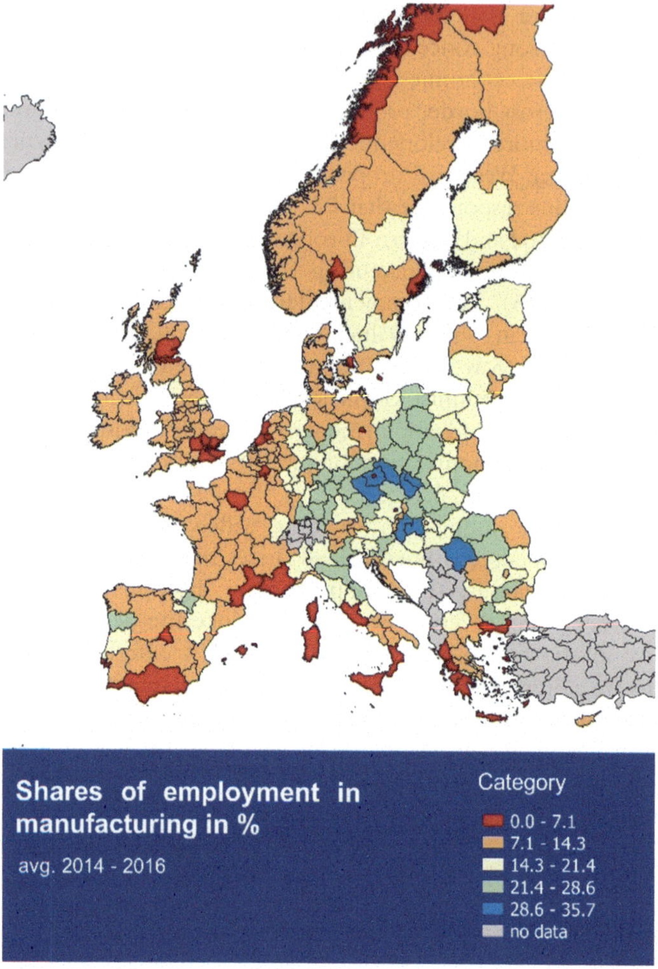

Fig. 8.11 Regional employment in manufacturing. (Source: Eurostat, own calculations)

erosion of the skill base as the better trained are more mobile. They remain 'poverty-trapped' regions faced with social misery and a number of authors have also pointed to political implications of such traps (Martin 2008; Rodriguez-Pose 2018).

8.7 Educational Attainment in the Labour Markets: A Comparison Between EU11 and EU-North and EU-South

Structural developments and human capital formation (decisions by private individuals and changing educational and training structures) have impacted on the position of groups with different educational attainment levels in EU11 labour markets. Figure 8.12 compares these with the developments in the EU-North and the EU-South. Figure 8.12a–d shows the composition of population and employment by educational attainment groups (Fig. 8.12a and b), the employment and activity rates (Fig. 8.12c and d) and unemployment rates (Fig. 8.12e). In the following we point to some distinguishing and differentiating features in the labour market situation of these educational groupings between the EU11 and the EU-North and the EU-South. There are also some differences in this respect between the CEE5 and the Baltics and Bulgaria and Romania but these are minor.

The educational categories distinguished in Fig. 8.12a–d are the following: 'low' refers to people/employees who have not completed secondary education, 'medium' those with completed secondary education and 'high' those with a college or university degree. This is a standard tripartite distinction derived from the international International Standard Classification of Education (ISCED) classification and used in many studies for cross-country comparisons.[5] A more disaggregated classification is almost impossible to use for cross-country analysis as institutional educational structures are quite diverse in different countries.

So what are the 'stylised facts' that emerge from Fig. 8.12a–e?

First of all, we see a preponderance of 'medium educated' in the working-age population and in the employment structure of the EU11 economies compared with both the EU-South and the EU-North. On the other hand, a very low representation of the 'low educated' (which are much more strongly represented in EU-South). Both these features are in parts still the legacy of education under the Communist regimes where a strong effort was made to educate the entire population up to (at least) completion of secondary schooling. The high representation of medium-educated has been a comparative strength of many of the EU11 countries which still also have a significant tradition of vocational training

[5] 'Low' refers - according to ISCED classification 2011 - to ISCED 0-2, 'Medium' to ISCED 3-5, and 'High' to ISCED 6-8.

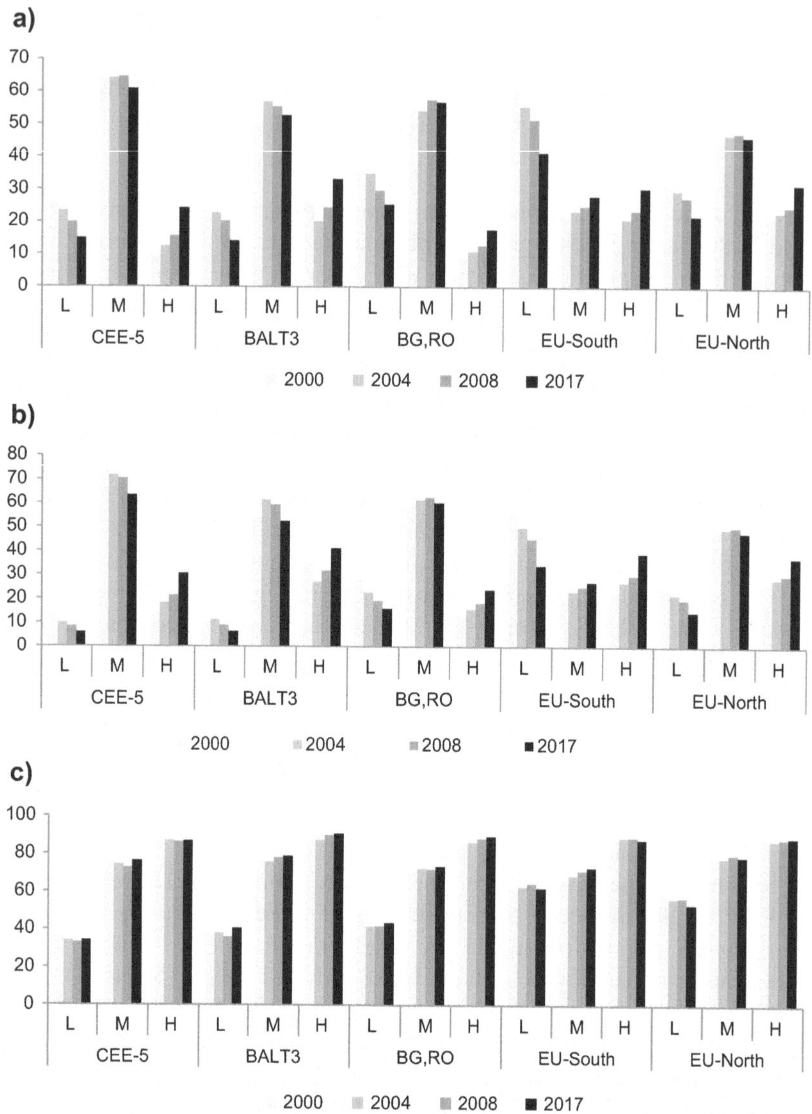

Fig. 8.12 (**a**) Educational structure of working-age population (working-age population 15–64, LFS; working-age population = 100). (**b**) Employment structure by educational attainment (employed 15–64, LFS; total employment = 100). (**c**) Activity rates by educational attainment (labour force in percentage of working-age population 15–64, LFS). (**d**) Employment rates by educational attainment (employed in percentage of working-age population 15–64, LFS). (**e**) Unemployment rates by educational attainment (unemployed in percentage of labour force 15-64, LFS). Note: L-low educated, M-medium educated, H-high educated. (Source: Eurostat)

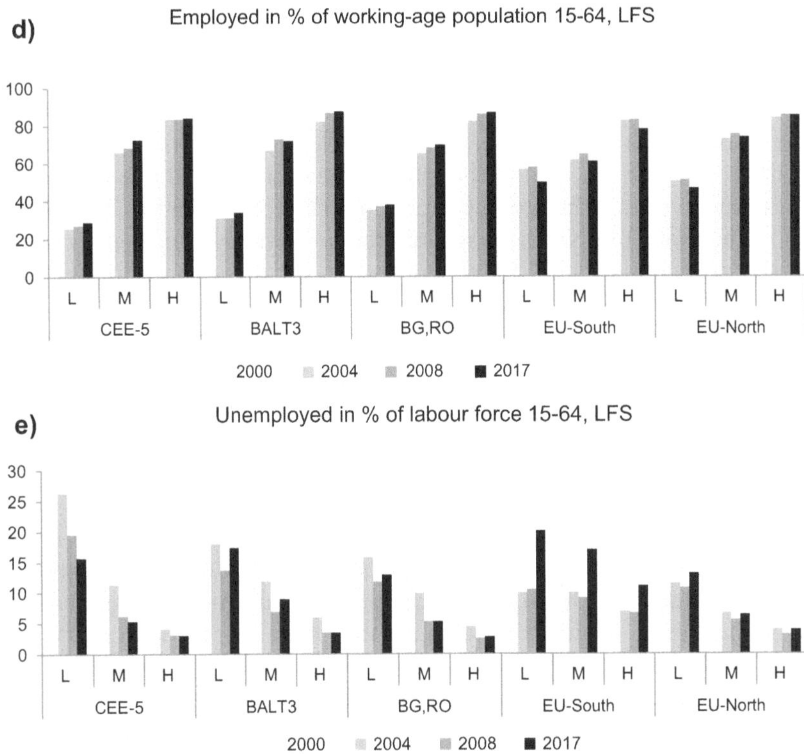

Fig. 8.12 (continued)

institutions; it is one of the factors that explains the attraction of CEE-5 economies for industrial production. We can also observe in Fig. 8.12b that employment developments are 'skill biased' that is there is a decline in the shares of the low skilled and a relatively sharp increase of the employment shares of the high skilled. This is true for all the economies. A more detailed sectoral analysis would reveal that at the upper end this is particularly due to the demand for people with tertiary degrees in advanced service activities. It also reflects, however, changes on the supply side that more young people obtain tertiary degrees compared to the older age cohorts in the population.

The information contained in Fig. 8.12c–e can be summarised thus: all the three indicators indicate that the low skilled are in a particularly unfavourable position in EU11 labour markets compared to the position of this group in EU-South or EU-North: they show significantly lower employment and activity rates in the EU11 and significantly higher unemployment rates. Hence, although their shares in the population are lower in the EU11 than in the EU15 (particularly compared to the EU-South), the ones that exist occupy a very unfavourable position in the CEE labour markets.[6] On the other side, especially for the CEE-5 and the Baltic countries, we can see a rather good performance (better than in the EU-South and in line with EU-North) as regards employment rates and activity rates of the medium-educated. Employment rates for the highly educated are fully in line with those in EU-North.

8.8 Projecting Working-Age Population and Labour Demand to 2050: Reaching 'tipping points'

In this section we refer to a recently completed study (Leitner and Stehrer 2019) that uses Eurostat's population projections together with projections of labour demand (a function of GDP and labour productivity growth) to arrive at a time profile when sharp quantitative 'labour constraints' will be felt in all the CEESE countries and also in most of the EU15 countries. When the projected labour demand crosses the (projected) availability of the labour force then this point will be called the 'tipping point'.

The exercise reported in Leitner and Stehrer (2019) uses existing Eurostat population projections that are basically projections derived from past trends regarding fertility rates (based on trends for the period 1977–2014), mortality rates (age and gender specific assessments) and net migration flows (trend extrapolations based on migration patterns observed for the period 1996–2015). This allows the authors to arrive at a base scenario that projects population growth over the period 2015–2050.

[6] Specific attention has to be paid to the special situation of the Roma population in those countries in which their share is relatively high (Hungary, Slovakia, Bulgaria, Romania). The evidence is that they have significantly and persistently lower educational attainment levels than the rest of the population and that they tend to be concentrated in left-behind regions. Some of the much worse position of the low skilled in the labour markets of the EU11 (as compared to the situation in the EU-15) is due to the unresolved issue of educational and labour market integration of this highly disadvantaged ethnic group.

See European Union, FRA (2012); Kahanec (2014); Kertesi and Kezdi (2011a, b); Milcher and Fischer (2011); Ringold (2000).

Around this base scenario, other scenarios are explored—such as high- and low-migration scenarios, and changes in fertility and mortality rates.

In order to arrive at projections of the labour supply, assumptions are made about activity rates (assumed to converge over the period to a long-term level of 75%) which, together with projections regarding the working-age population, yield a projection of labour supply. For the EU28 as a whole, the projections for working-age population under the different scenarios can be seen from Fig. 8.13, and for individual countries in the base scenario in Fig. 8.14a.

We can see that sizeable reductions of working-age populations are expected, particularly for the Central and Eastern European countries and also the Southern EU economies. In order to get an impression of the role that net migration flows play in these projections, the authors added a 'zero migration' scenario (net migration declines to zero over the projection period) for a comparison with the baseline scenario (see Fig. 8.14b). As one would expect this reduces the population decline in net emigration countries (Latvia, Lithuania, Bulgaria, Romania), but leads to sharply declining populations in net immigration countries such as Germany, Austria, Belgium, Italy. However, over the projection period also some of the EU11 countries that have become net immigration countries (Hungary, Czech Republic, Slovakia, Estonia) would lose out.

In order to project aggregate 'labour demand' the study projected country-specific GDP growth rates (for the EU28 as a whole these amounted to 1.4% per annum over the period 2002–2017) and trend growth rates of labour productivity (for the EU28 this amounted to 0.8% per annum over the same period). Putting the two together one obtains

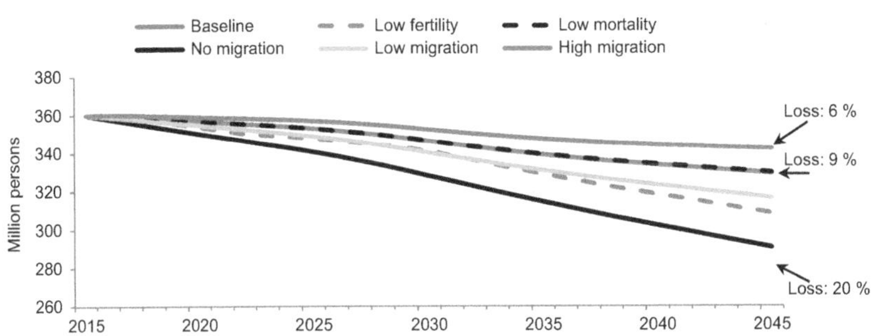

Fig. 8.13 EU28 working-age population (15–64)—projections under different scenarios. (Source: Eurostat's population projections)

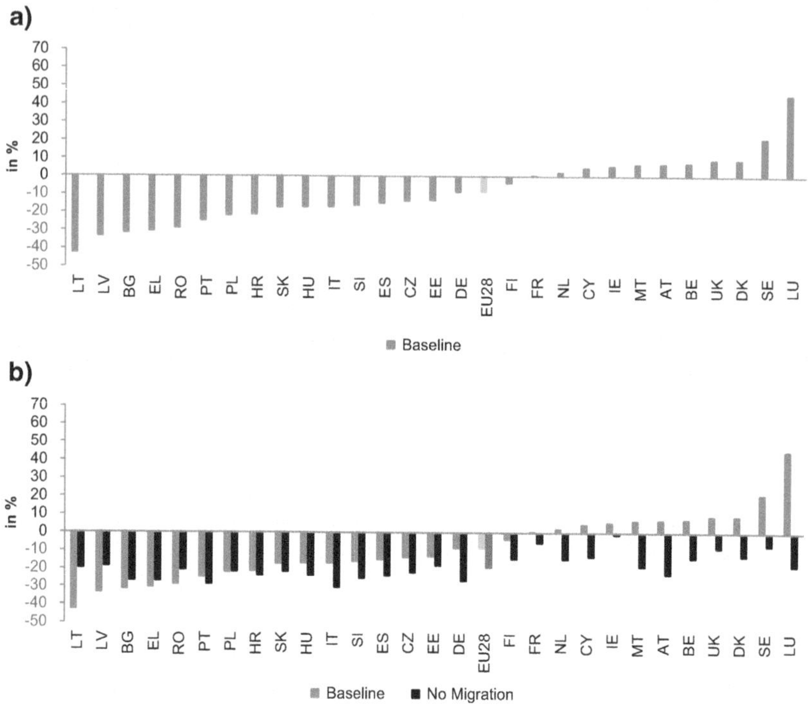

Fig. 8.14 (**a**) Projections of working-age populations (15–64) under the baseline scenario (cumulative change: 2015–2045). (**b**) No migration scenario compared to baseline scenario (working-age population (15–64) projected to shrink in all EU countries. Cumulative change: 2015–2045). (Source: Eurostat's population projections)

estimates of labour demand growth (for the EU28 as a whole: 0.6% per annum). Putting the 'labour supply' and 'labour demand' trajectories together one obtains the 'tipping point', that is when employment is actually constrained by labour supply. For the EU28 as a whole such a tipping point can be seen in Fig. 8.15, which would be reached in the baseline scenario in 2029. For the individual EU member countries these points are shown in Fig. 8.16. We can see that 'tipping points' will be reached for about half the EU member countries over the next ten years, and most of the EU11 countries would reach these over the next five to six years. This is in line with the labour shortage situation apparent already now in a number of EU11 countries which we already discussed in the previous

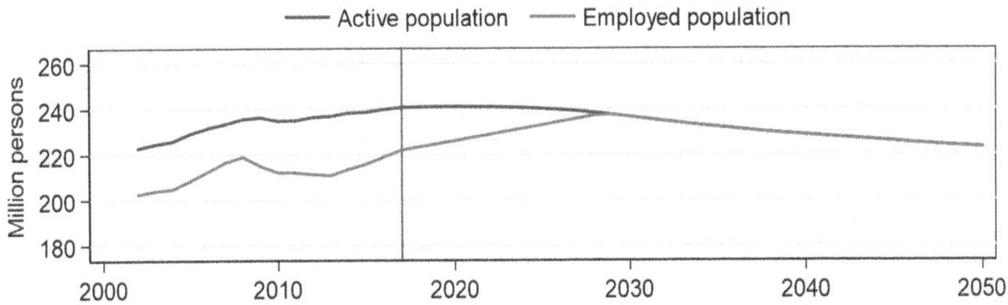

Fig. 8.15 Baseline scenario for EU28—labour supply constraint—tipping point reached in 2029. Note: Vertical red line refers to 2017

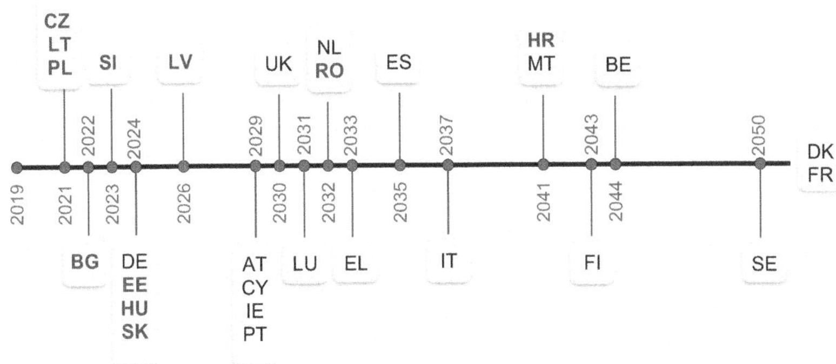

Fig. 8.16 Half of all EU countries will reach the tipping point within the next ten years

section and which is borne out by current labour market statistics (vacancy rates, wage developments).

Of, course, the above is a rather mechanical exercise based mostly on extrapolations and should be subjected to sensitivity analysis, which has been conducted in the Leitner and Stehrer (2019) study. We mention some results of these sensitivity exercises:

- Reducing net migration flows leads (as one would expect) to earlier tipping points for the net immigration countries in Western Europe and to more favourable outcomes in some of the CEE countries (BG, RO, LT, LV) but makes things worse in the CEE5 which have already become net immigration countries. Increasing net migration flows above the baseline has the opposite effect.

- Higher activity rates (increasing participation rates and also delaying retirement age) push tipping points backwards and so do higher labour productivity growth rates—the latter can be linked to the active debate regarding the impact of 'robotisation' and 'digitisation'.

Despite these *caveats* the exercise illustrates the likely move into a severe 'labour constraint' environment in many of the CEE economies over the coming decade if current trajectories are followed.

There are additional points that should be considered regarding the set-up of the exercise though most of these would move the 'tipping points' forward. Firstly, the analysis is conducted at an aggregate level and shortages of particular types of workers would be staggered, that is some occur earlier and some later. Secondly, the transmission of shortages happens through increased labour costs that would infringe on profitability and competitiveness and could delay necessary labour-saving investment. These are issues that could be further investigated. Nonetheless, we believe that the 'labour shortage' scenario is a real one for many countries in Central-Eastern Europe and has to be seen as one of—if not 'the'—most important factor constraining the future growth dynamic of the new member states.

8.9 Labour Market Institutions and Policies

Rigid and inflexible labour markets have been considered an important source of high and persistent unemployment in Europe during the 1990s, particularly when compared with the United States. Measuring flexibility or rigidity of labour markets was subject to numerous studies at that time—for example Nickell (1997), Blanchard and Wolfers (1999) and the OECD in its Job Study (1994). Since then there has been a controversial debate among economists on whether or not flexible labour markets lead to higher employment and better overall economic performance.

In view of the EU aspirations and the subsequent adoption of the euro, labour market flexibility became also an important research issue in the then candidate countries (see Boeri and Keese 1992; Boeri and Garibaldi 2006; Cazes and Nesporova 2003). Following the OECD methodology, Riboud et al. (2002) examined the role of labour market institutions—job security provisions, support programmes for the unemployed and other related policies—in a group of EU accession countries (Czech Republic, Estonia, Hungary, Poland, Slovak Republic and Slovenia) in the 1990s and compared the results with those obtained for the OECD including the then EU countries. In the following we shall present a quick overview of the main features of EU-CEE countries regarding labour market institutions and policies and point to differences resp. similarities with other EU member countries.

- Employment protection legislation (EPL) has been adjusted to 'European standards' in all EU-CEE countries in view of their EU entry and was further tightened in response to the crisis. According to the latest available information EU-CEE countries are less restrictive than other EU countries with regard to individual dismissals but (slightly) more restrictive with respect to collective dismissals and temporary contracts (see OECD 2013).
- As regards expenditures on labour market policies in general is concerned (see Fig. 8.17) there remained still a significant gap compared with the EU-CEE countries: in 2016, the latest year for which data are available, expenditures varied between 0.13% of the GDP in Bulgaria and 1.17% in Hungary, while the respective value in the EU15 was exceeding the 2% mark.
- Unemployment benefit systems of the EU-CEE countries, which were very generous at the beginning of the transition, were subject to numerous changes with respect to tougher eligibility conditions, shorter entitlement periods and lower benefit payments. Reforms

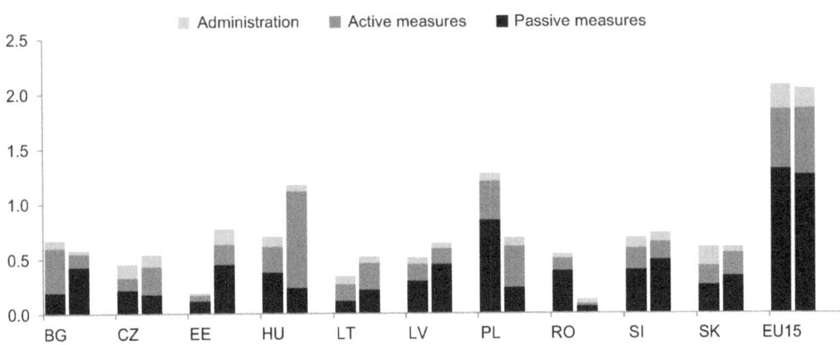

Fig. 8.17 Expenditures on labour market policies, in percentage of GDP, 2005 and 2016. (Source: DG EMPL)

were carried out prior to and immediately after EU accession, but particularly in response to the crisis unemployment insurance is now altogether less generous than in the EU15. The coverage of unemployment benefit recipients increased and converged to EU-South, but remains far below countries such as Austria or some Scandinavian countries.

- In parallel with the passive labour market policy measures the transition countries introduced active labour market policy (ALMP) measures starting from the early phase of transition. With the exception of Hungary, where expenditures on ALMPs reached 0.87% of the GDP in 2016 owing to a comprehensive public works programme, spending in all EU-CEE countries was still far below the EU15 level (0.6%). The priorities of ALMPs differ from country to country: while the Czech Republic and Poland support employment and rehabilitation and employment incentives, Slovenia and especially Hungary focus on direct job creation, Lithuania and Slovakia on employment incentives and Latvia on training. For comparison, the main focus of the EU15 active labour market policy measures lies on training and employment incentives.
- During the transition period and beyond, union density and consequently the bargaining power of trade unions on wage setting and employment have been declining in the EU-CEE countries dramatically, particularly in the private sector. On the other hand, the coverage of workers by collective agreements exceeded and still exceeds union density in almost all countries, but is much lower than in the Scandinavian countries or Austria and in the Southern EU countries (Portugal and Spain). The average coverage rate in the EU-CEE countries (28%) is only half that of the EU14 excluding Greece. In contrast to the Western European countries where wage bargaining is conducted at sectoral level, in most EU-CEE countries wages are increasingly set at company level.
- Minimum wages in the EU-CEE are around one-third the levels of the other EU countries in absolute terms (see Fig. 8.18) and none of the countries—not even the best performers Czech Republic or Slovenia—is classified in the group with the highest levels of minimum wages. But in terms of minimum wages relative to the mean value of average wages most of the EU-CEE countries have already caught up with the other

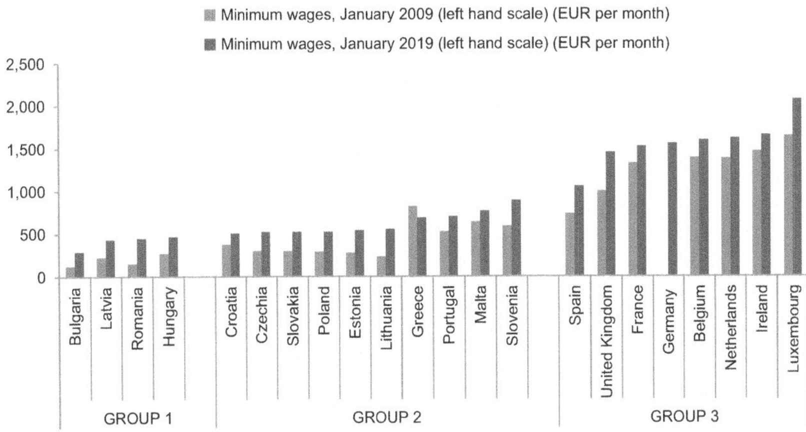

Fig. 8.18 Minimum wages, January 2009 and January 2019 (EUR per month). Note: Group 1, where national minimum wages were lower than EUR 500 per month in January 2019, Group 2, where national minimum wages were at least EUR 500 but lower than EUR 1000 per month and Group 3, where national minimum wages were at least EUR 1000 per month in January 2019. (Source: Eurostat)

EU countries. In the absence of strong social partners and collective agreements minimum wages became an important wage policy tool in the EU-CEE countries (see also Bodnár et al. 2018).

8.10 Conclusions

This chapter attempted to give an overview of the many changes that affected labour market developments in the CEE economies since the transition towards becoming market economies in 1989. Of course, a very important factor was the move towards integration with the incumbent EU economies, culminating in EU Enlargement in 2004, 2007 and 2013 respectively of different (groups of) CEE economies.

Integration with the EU was a process that happened in spurts and characterised economic, social and institutional developments in the CEE region. Hence, already in 1989/90 the dismantling of the 'Soviet bloc' led to a dramatic reorientation of trade and production linkages away from the CMEA economic relationships and towards those with the Western European economies which became and remained the most important trading partners.

This reorientation as well as the shift from a planned economy towards a market economy meant a dramatic shake-up in industrial structures, the regional distribution of economic activity and, most relevant for this chapter, employment patterns and the demand for different skills and qualifications. Furthermore, on the labour supply side, the high wage and income gaps with the advanced Western European economies as well as the 'transition shock' that affected the labour market situation and demographic developments initiated migration flows which—with phases of ebbs and flows (largely depending on migration policy arrangements with EU countries)—held on up to the present day. These demographic and migration developments had a strong impact on the development of the available labour force in CEE economies, leading to a dramatically changing age profile and a situation where these economies shifted from being 'labour surplus' economies (which characterised the early periods of transition with relatively high rates of unemployment) to becoming—by now—'labour shortage' economies. A number of EU11 experience at times acute shortages of workers in specific qualification segments and show some of the lowest unemployment rates in the EU as a whole.

Together with these structural shifts in labour demand and labour supply, young people in education and training adjusted their choices regarding qualifications. CEE economies had—a legacy from the Communist period—a rather low share of workers with an educational attainment level lower than completed secondary schooling. Nonetheless, the part of the labour force with low qualifications occupies a very precarious position in the labour markets. Just like in other European economies but in an even more pronounced manner, this group of persons shows extremely low activity and employment rates and conversely high unemployment rates compared to the other groups in the labour force. Because of the general improvement in the labour market and due to migration flows, unemployment rates of this group have come down more recently. Underlying this uneven incidence of unemployment lie also regional and ethnic issues (such as the position of Roma in a number of CEE economies). The relatively high levels of employment (and relatively low unemployment rates) of the 'medium-educated' reflect in part the holding up in the demand for industrial workers in CEE economies. Demand side developments favoured the 'highly educated' (those with some completed tertiary education) and reflect a strong 'skill bias' which characterises economic developments in CEE economies as it does in other advanced economies. The additional factor here—leading to at times acute supply shortages—is the high international (and particularly intra-EU) mobility of young, highly talented and qualified persons in CEE, leading to high outward migration (either as students or later on when they already completed their training and education).

Let us add some further remarks concerning patterns of intra-country and international mobility of the labour force: standard economic analysis used to welcome high spatial mobility of the labour force as this would allow a better allocation of persons to jobs and thus support market clearing. The experiences of CEE economies (but also developments in other advanced economies analysed by economic geographers; see Martin 2008; Rodriguez-Pose 2018) also point to the negative sides of high intra-country and international labour mobility. Migration of the young and better qualified can have long-running hysteretic impacts on the development of regions, leading to the degradation of a significant share of regions to the status of 'peripheral' or 'lagging' regions highly dependent on long-run transfers. This works via the impact of outward migration on the age and skill structure of the remaining population, the loss of capabilities also in administrative and policy-making structures in such regions and also the reverse dynamic implied by the loss of agglomeration economies (loss of purchasing power, of production capacities, of complementarities across activities, etc.) To avoid such strong polarisation in regional development, economic geographers increasingly advocate the importance of strengthening second- and third-tier growth poles (see, e.g. Camagni and Capello 2017) and this seems to have had an impact also on recent formulations of EU regional policy (see e.g. Radosevic 2017; Foray et al. 2009).

An important characteristic of the important role of East-West economic integration was the dynamic of spatial patterns of economic activity within the countries. A number of factors was responsible for these: the disintegration of the CMEA linkages and the reorientation of trade and production linkages towards Western Europe had a very important effect on the location patterns of economic activity by regions: the border regions to Western European EU economies showed dynamism and an attraction for foreign investors. Also cross-border purchases by and sales to final consumers between the richer consumers in the West and the cheaper suppliers in the East intensified (also in service areas). On the other hand, the regions further away from the Western border regions which had often been centres of industrial activity (especially of heavy industry supplying other CMEA economies) had to bear the brunt of regional decline. This led to a very pronounced pattern of unbalanced regional development and to a regional 'periphery' in CEE economies (regional inequality indicators show higher levels of inequality in CEE economies than in most Western European economies) and this, in turn, affected regional disparities in labour markets. Unemployment rates in Eastern regions far exceeded unemployment rates in regions bordering the West and also the age and skill profile of 'peripheral regions' deteriorated due to international and intra-country migration flows. This in turn initiated vicious cycles of further deepening regional inequalities.

The other interesting feature of regional inequality is the very strong position of capital cities in CEE economies. The reasons stated in the chapter for the very big gaps between capital cities and the rest of the economies were the following: capital cities provided—given agglomeration advantages—a focal point to make up the deficit of ex-Communist countries in tertiary activities. This also made capital cities a major point of attraction for the highly educated, for headquarter locations of the large domestic and foreign companies and for the development of administrative (and also educational and research) centres. The result was virtuous circles so that CEE capital cities (and—in the bigger economies—also other larger cities) developed a gap in income per capita compared to the rest of the country which exceeded that observed in most of the Western European economies (with the exceptions of London and Paris).

Let us also return to another dynamic unleashed by European integration and EU membership (or in expectation of such membership) and that is the development of cross-border production linkages and the integration of the Central European members of the CEE into Global Value Chains (GVCs). We can deduce the importance of EU membership (or the expectation of such membership) from the fact that countries which remained outside the EU or countries which had a low chance to join within a clearly defined time horizon were at a great disadvantage to be integrated into such GVCs. An important example is the countries of the Western Balkans that underwent a dramatic process of deindustrialisation and have remained real laggards in the process of integration into GVCs (see recent reports by IMF 2019, and OECD 2019). There is no doubt that the integration of CEE economies into cross-border value chains were an extremely important factor in facilitating a process of 'reindustrialisation' after the initial collapse of industry at the beginning of transition. CEE economies now are an important part of the 'Central European Manufacturing Core' (Stehrer and Stöllinger 2015). Companies from the more advanced EU partner countries (Germany, Austria, Sweden) have been principal drivers in setting up these cross-border value chains and this has led to a strong agglomeration process of industrial activity into this part of the European Union. One worry that exists is that CEE economies do not show sufficient dynamism in moving 'up-stream' into the higher value-added components of the 'functional specialisation' which characterises GVCs (see Stöllinger 2019).

We also reviewed the development of labour market institutions and policies in the CEE countries. Here one can speak of a relatively strong convergence process (speeded up also by the impact of the international financial crisis post-2008) with Western European labour market institutions and policies, although some important differences persist and there is also differentiation amongst the NMS in this respect. Thus, the role of trade unions remains very weak—given the dismantling of labour market institutions that characterised the Communist period—and they are unlikely to play the role which they attained in the more advanced Western and Northern European economies. This has implications for wage settings which in some countries is characterised by a strong impact of electoral cycles. Similarly there is still a significant deficit in the building up of efficient labour exchanges and publicly provided training and retraining institutions which would facilitate forward-looking policies with respect to skill acquisition and jobs-qualifications matching given the challenges of structural change.

Finally, and in the light of the principal question asked in this volume, we can conclude by saying that the various phases of integration of the CEE economies with the European economy at large and with the EU in particular had a tremendous impact on labour markets, on sectoral and regional employment patterns, skill demands, inter-country and intra-country mobility and demography, as well as on institutions and behavioural responses. The features of these integration processes show both convergence, but also strong asymmetries developing in the course of such convergence processes, at times seriously contributing to imbalances in a number of dimensions (regional, skills and incomes). Looking forward in time, as the overall convergence process proceeds further, one can expect such imbalances to weaken and follow the patterns we observe in the rest of Europe. However, heterogeneity will persist regarding how countries' labour markets and policy structures are organised and hence—from an analytical point of view—Europe remains an arena in which the effectiveness of policy and institutional differences can be compared and analysed in a 'real world experimental setting'.

References

Blanchard, O., & Wolfers, J. (1999). *The Role of Shocks and Institutions in the Rise of European Unemployment: The Aggregate Evidence* (NBER Working Paper 7282).

Bodnár, K., Fadejeva, L., Lordache, S., Malk, L., Paskaleva, D., Pesliakaitė, J., Todorović Jemec, N., Toth, P., & R. Wyszyński (2018). *How do Firms Adjust to Rises in the Minimum Wage? Survey Evidence from Central and Eastern Europe* (ECB Working Paper Series, No 2122).

Boeri, T., & Garibaldi, P. (2006). Are Labour Markets In The New Member States Sufficiently Flexible for EMU? *Journal of Banking and Finance, 30*, 1393–1407.

Boeri, T., & Keese, M. (1992). *Labour Markets and the Transition in Central and Eastern Europe*. OECD Economic Studies No. 18, Spring.

Brücker, H., et al. (2009). *Labour Mobility Within the EU in the Context of Enlargement and the Functioning of the Transitional Arrangements. Study for the European Commission: Final Report*. Nuremberg: European Integration Consortium.

Camagni, R., & Capello, R. (2017). *Second Rank Cities in Europe: Structural Dynamics and Growth Potential*. London: Routledge Publ.

Cazes, S., & Nesporova, A. (2003). *Labour Markets in Transition. Balancing Flexibility and Security in Central and Eastern Europe*. Geneva: ILO.

European Union, Agency for Fundamental Rights (FRA). (2012). *The situation of Roma in 11 EU Member States; Survey Results at a Glance*. Luxembourg: Publications Office.

European Commission. (2017). *My Region, My Europe, Our Future; Seventh Report on Economic, Social and Territorial Cohesion*. Luxembourg.

Foray, D., David, P. A., & Hall, B. (2009). Smart Specialisation – The Concept. *Knowledge Economists Policy Brief n°9*. http://ec.europa.eu/invest-in-research/pdf/download_en/kfg_policy_brief_no9.pdf

Iammarino, S., Rodriguez-Pose, A., & Storper, M. (2019). Regional Inequality in Europe: Evidence, Theory and Policy Implications. *Journal of Economic Geography, 19*, 273–298.

IMF. (2019). *Lifting Growth in the Western Balkans: The Role of Global Value Chains and Services Exports*. Washington, DC: IMF European Department.

Jestl, S., Landesmann, M., & Leitner, S. (2015). *Migrants and Natives in EU Labour Markets: Mobility and Job-Skill Mismatch Patterns*. Research Report No. 403, The Vienna Institute for International Economic Studies (wiiw), Vienna.

Kahanec, M. (2014). Roma Integration in European Labor Markets. In *IZA World of Labor* (39 pp).

Kertesi, G., & Kezdi, G. (2011a). The Roma/Non-Roma Test Score Gap in Hungary. *American Economic Review: Papers and Proceedings, 101*, 519–525.

Kertesi, G., & Kezdi, G. (2011b). Roma Employment in Hungary After the Post-Communist Transition. *The Economics of Transition, 19*(3), 563–610.

Milcher, S., & Fischer, M. (2011). On Labour Market Discrimination Against Roma in Southeast Europe. *Papers in Regional Science, 90*(4), 773–788.

Kornai, J. (1995). Chap. 2 Transformational Recession: The Example of Hungary. In C. T. Saunders (Ed.), *Eastern Europe in Crisis and the Way Out*. London: Palgrave Macmillan.

Landesmann, M., Vidovic, H., & Ward, T. (2004). Economic Restructuring and Labour Market Developments in the New EU Member States. *wiiw Research Report 312*. Vienna: wiiw.

Lavalle, C., et al. (2017). *European Territorial Trends – Facts and Prospects for Cities and Regions*. Luxembourg: Publications Office of the European Union.

Leitner, S. M., & Stehrer, R. (2019). Demographic Challenges for Labour Supply and Growth. *wiiw Research Report No. 439*. Vienna: wiiw.

Martin, R. L. (2008). National Growth Versus Spatial Equality? A Cautionary Note on the New 'Trade-Off' Thinking in Regional Policy Discourse. *Regional Science Policy and Practice, 1*, 3–13.

Nickell, S. (1997). Unemployment and Labor Market Rigidities: Europe versus North America. *Journal of Economic Perspectives, 11*(3), 55–74.

OECD. (2013). *Calculating Summary Indicators of EPL Strictness: Methodology*. Paris: July.

OECD. (1994). *The OECD Jobs Study, Facts, Analysis*. Paris: Strategies.

OECD. (2019). *Unleashing the Transformation Potential for Growth in the Western Balkans*. Paris.

Petrakos, G., Rodriguez-Pose, A., & Rovolis, A. (2005). Growth, Integration and Regional Disparities in the European Union. *Environment and Planning A, 37*, 1837–1855.

Radosevic, S. (2017). Assessing EU Smart Specialisation Policy in a Comparative Perspective. In S. Radosevic, A. Curaj, R. Gheorghiu, L. Andrescu, & I. Wade (Eds.), *Advances in the Theory and Practice of Smart Specialisation*. London: Academic Press.

Riboud, M., Sánchez-Páramo, C., & Silva-Jáuregui, C. (2002). Does Eurosclerosis Matter? Institutional Reform and Labor Market Performance in Central and Eastern European Countries in the 1990s. In *World Bank Social Protection Discussion Paper No. 0202*. Washington, DC: The World Bank.

Ringold, D. (2000). *Roma and the Tranisition in Central and Eastern Europe: Trends and Challenges*. Washington, DC: The World Bank.

Rodriguez-Pose, A. (2018). The Revenge of the Places That Don't Matter (and What to Do About It). *Cambridge Journal of Regions, Economy and Society, 11*, 189–209.

Stehrer, R., & Stöllinger, R. (2015). The Central European Manufacturing Core: What Is Driving Regional Production Sharing?, *FIW-Research Report* 2014/15 (2).

Stöllinger, R. (2019). *Testing the Smile Curve: Functional Specialisation in GVCs and Value Creation* (wiiw Working Paper, 163).

PART IV

Institutional Channel

CHAPTER 9

Corruption, Institutions and Convergence

Empirical Analysis of Public Tenders of the Old and New EU Member States

István János Tóth and Miklós Hajdu

9.1 Introduction

Promoting economic convergence between the old and the new European Union member countries was one of the main aims of EU enlargement. Many papers only concentrate on the economic and social aspects of convergence (e.g., reducing differences among countries in GDP per capita,

I. J. Tóth (✉)
Corruption Research Center Budapest (CRCB), Budapest, Hungary

Institute of Economics, CERS, HAS, Budapest, Hungary
e-mail: istvanjanos.toth@crcb.eu

M. Hajdu
Corruption Research Center Budapest (CRCB), Budapest, Hungary

Corvinus University of Budapest, Budapest, Hungary
e-mail: miklos.hajdu@crcb.eu

M. Landesmann, I. P. Székely (eds.), *Does EU Membership Facilitate Convergence? The Experience of the EU's Eastern Enlargement - Volume II*, Studies in Economic Transition,
https://doi.org/10.1007/978-3-030-57702-5_9

in regional inequality and in life expectancy) and do not attach sufficient importance to institutional aspects. Recently, more research has focused on the institutional conditions of the economic convergence (Huemer et al. 2014; Heckelman 2015; Masuch et al. 2016; Savoia and Sen 2016; Alesina et al. 2017; EBRD 2017; The World Bank 2017; Masuch et al. 2018; Schönfelder and Wagner 2019). We also believe that the latter aspects play a substantial role in economic development and that institutional convergence influences economic convergence in the long run. Only modern institutions with high level of integrity can create a favourable environment for stable and sustainable economic growth and convergence. Moreover, only stable institutions with a high level of integrity allow social policies to be effective and to reduce social inequalities. Only stable, modern institutions, which effectively fight or control corruption risks, can establish economic convergence. However, measuring institutional convergence and analysing its effects on economic performance are very difficult. There are no simple ways to create indicators of or proxies for institutional quality, integrity or the effectiveness of fighting corruption.

In this chapter, using a new method based on hard data at micro level, we deal with the measurement of institutional convergence among the teen EU member states in Central Eastern and Southeastern Europe and the Baltics that joined the EU since 2004 (EU10) as well as four Southern European EU countries. We only focused on one aspect of institutional quality: the ability of institutions in a country to control corruption risks in public procurement. We analysed this ability in certain European countries using a contract-level dataset. The data range from 2006 to 2018 with more than 3.6 million observations downloaded from the European Union TED database. As regards transparency, we compared European results with procurement data from Paraguay and Uganda, and as regards corruption risks we made a comparison with data from Colombia. We considered control of corruption risk as a proxy for or aspect of institutional quality. We then used countries with high institutional quality (with a high ability to control corruption) as a benchmark to measure the performance of the test countries. We ran logit estimations by year and by country and used the odds ratio of these estimations as an indicator of the level of convergence. We also analysed the impact of EU subsidies on the level of corruption risks at both the European level and the country level.

Our findings partially support earlier research on the weak performance of the Southern European EU countries (Alesina et al. 2017; Schönfelder and Wagner 2019) and demonstrate the considerable difference in institutional convergence among the EU10 countries. Slovakia, Estonia and

Lithuania have achieved strong institutional convergence and by now have reached institutional quality in control of corruption risks which is as high as in benchmark countries. Poland has attained some convergence, and its institutional quality still remains relatively weak. Latvia has had relatively weak convergence but has managed to reach a high level of institutional quality due to its favourable starting position. Other countries like Hungary, the Czech Republic and Romania have seen a low level of convergence starting with weak institutional quality. Thus, they now have institutions with a weak ability to control corruption risks. Slovenia and Bulgaria have displayed the weakest performance, with divergence from the benchmark countries and a rather low level of institutional quality. These results show that institutional reforms at the national level matter and that EU policies promoting these reforms are necessary but not sufficient conditions for successful institutional convergence.

The impact of EU funding is controversial. At the European level, our findings indicate a significant negative effect: the level of corruption risk is higher for EU-funded contracts than for non-EU-funded ones. At the country level, the results show major differences in this regard: in some countries (Slovakia, Bulgaria and Romania), the impact of EU funding is rather positive. Here, the convergence is stronger for EU-funded contracts than for non-EU-funded ones, but in other new accession countries, these impacts are insignificant or negative.

The rest of this chapter is structured as follows. In Sect. 9.2, we provide a brief overview of the literature. In Sects. 9.3 and 9.4, we describe the conceptual framework and the data we have used in our empirical analysis. In Sect. 9.5, we first describe trends in perception indicators for institutional quality. This is followed by an econometric analysis of control of corruption risks based on micro-level (contract-level) data on public tenders. In Sect. 9.7, we present our conclusions.

9.2 Literature

Researchers tend to associate convergence or integration with a reduction of differences in economic development between developed and developing countries or with a reduction of inequalities in terms of socio-economic indicators. The vast majority of empirical research on convergence is also focused on analysing social and economic trends, such as differences in income or productivity between countries. Furthermore, many of the international initiatives to reduce inequalities around the world are concentrated on these aspects of integration. However, without structural changes in the institutional framework towards good governance, these projects may remain unsuccessful.

The literature investigating the effects and successes of aid for developing countries also discusses this problem. Bauer (1981) concluded that such supports actually hinder convergence instead of bringing about development. Funds received from national governments or international organizations may have positive effects on the level of corruption.

Findings are not straightforward in this respect. Several studies showed that foreign aid has positive correlation with the level of corruption or there is no significant negative correlation between them (Alesina and Dollar 2000; Svensson 2000; Knack 2001; Knack 2004; Alesina and Weder 2002; de la Croix and Delavallade 2014). Other research brings empirical evidence on sub-national level: the exogenous revenues (as subsidies or direct financial aid) may induce more corruption in municipalities as the incumbents can seek rents without leaving their voters disappointed (Brollo et al. 2013). Moreover, this rent-seeking activity proves to be attractive for individuals leading to deteriorating performance on the part of official bodies. These two effects may strengthen each other during an election, when the office-holder can grab more rents and use the acquired resources to increase his/her re-election chances in the meantime. The effects of financial aids can be very similar to what is referred to as Dutch disease: increase in the economic development of a specific sector (i.e., a boom in extraction of natural resources) causes a decline in other sectors. The international aid and subsidies may effect a decrease in political stability and a rise in corruption, among other consequences, mostly in countries where the traditions of the rule of law and democratic institutions are not very well established (Holden 2013). In contrast, other studies concluded that foreign aid had positive impact on the quality of governance, and it decreased the level of corruption (Goldsmith 2001; Tavares 2003; Charron 2011; Okada and Samreth 2012; Ali et al. 2019).

Rose-Ackerman claims that corruption is present in cases when private wealth and public power are both existent and decision-makers are open to influence by forbidden (financial) means (Rose-Ackerman 1978). The literature, dealing with the problem of corruption in theoretic point of view, attaches great importance to the decisions of the actors, especially to the decisions of the officials (Burguet et al. 2016). As corrupt transactions are illegal, the actors involved in them need to trust each other not to reveal their activities (Rose-Ackerman 2001a). Corrupt officials also betray the public trust; however, corruption can be indirectly controlled by offering people the option to complain about the corrupt activities of the government and state institutions. These actions can be facilitated by supplying appropriate information on the work of the state administration, and on that basis, the media, private organizations and individuals can push for public accountability (Lambsdorff 2007). An open government is more vulnerable to popular dissatisfaction but is also more trustworthy, as it can be encouraged by demands for accountability among sceptical citizens who are aware of its activities.

Post-socialist European countries find themselves in a special situation from this point of view, as democratization may enhance corruption if it is followed by diminished state controls and confusion among the citizens about proper behaviour in a context of increased freedom (Rose-Ackerman 2001b). In addition, people tend to assume that official state actors prior to the transition were self-serving players within an irrational regulatory environment, and these public attitudes are inherited by the new democratic governments: citizens who have no faith in public institutions rather place their trust in interpersonal relations instead of relying on public establishments and laws.

Empirical research on institutional convergence is quite scarce, perhaps because of the lack of quantitative data that are suitable for a cross-national comparison. Most studies rely on perception measures on the quality of institutions like the Worldwide Governance Indicators (WGI) and Doing Business studies produced by the World Bank, reports by the World Economic Forum and indices reported by organizations like Transparency International. Also, their findings are generally in line with each other.

Several studies address the critique of perception-based measurement and perception-based indicators. Wallace and Haerpfer (1999), Sik (2002), Thompson and Shah (2005), among many others, provide such analyses. A detailed analysis conducted by Heywood and Rose (2013) and United Nations (2016) summarized these critical approaches. Measuring corruption risks is difficult because corruption is a soft social phenomenon. Understandings of it may vary, so perceptions cannot be aggregated. Moreover, perceptions may be strongly influenced by media coverage of scandalous cases. Controversially, the existence of a well-functioning free press may raise the perception of corruption (Wallace and Haerpfer 1999). In addition, the wording of the questions and the interview situation itself can strongly influence people's responses as regards their perceptions.

Finally, the direction of the distortion of the corruption-perception method is ambivalent.

Heywood and Rose (2013) argue that perception-based measurements of corruption, which became the most widely used method in the 1990s, may be reliable but not necessarily valid, as outcomes may reflect factors that are not related to corruption itself. The final outcomes of such researches—like the Corruption Perceptions Index (CPI) produced by Transparency International—provide evidence of qualitatively different domains of corruption, but they do not handle these biases well. For example, if there is a country with a low level of petty corruption but severe political corruption, it is questionable whether their impacts on the final indices are in line with their actual importance. Heywood and Rose (2013) also claim that non-perceptual approaches have a narrower scope and suffer from problems of definition. Such measures may not specifically differentiate between corruption and other deficiencies. In addition, in those rare situations when hard (objective) data are available and deviations from an expected distribution are analysed, researchers must assume that such abnormalities are evidence of corruption, rather than indications of specific circumstances. This assumption can only be validated if such analyses are backed up with official investigations of corruption.

Schönfelder and Wagner (2019) investigated whether institutional convergence occurred during the European integration process based on perception indicators of the World Bank and the OECD. They found that there was some convergence because of improvements among new member states and candidate countries, but they found divergence among old member states due to deterioration in the quality of institutions in the Southern European EU countries (Greece, Italy and Portugal). According to their results, the quality of institutions in euro-area countries converged only in the areas of product market and business regulation but not in the area of governance.

Alesina, Tabellini and Trebbi (2017) showed that the quality of public administration and that of the legal system did not converge in Europe. In areas where EU member states retained unconstrained sovereignty, Europe often provided benchmarks and incentives for harmonization and for the dissemination of best practices, particularly with the so-called Lisbon Strategy. Nevertheless, Southern Europe's institutions were falling further behind those of Northern Europe. They concluded that the obstacle to convergence might not be heterogeneity in fundamental cultural traits, but other cleavages, such as national identities.

Guiso, Herrera and Morelli (2016) concluded that cultural differences cause difficulties when nations must integrate their economic activities, as in the case of creating the euro area. They argued that the slow-moving nature of cultural norms should be changed through a process of convergence of institutions when the cultural clash leads to particularly costly outcomes, such as political stalemates, which prolong and exacerbate a crisis. An excellent example of the latter analysed in their study is the German-Greek clash during the recent Greek crisis.

Jurlin and Čučković (2010) found that differences in institutional quality between the new and old EU members remained rather high between 2006 and 2009 and that the new EU members did not make improvements following their accession. For Bulgaria, Romania, Croatia, Macedonia and Serbia, the analyses indicated rather substantial progress in the quality of institutions, suggesting compliance with the formal convergence criteria.

Iancu (2009) analysed the essence and role of institutions in modern economic systems, the main issues concerning institutional convergence in relation to EU integration, institutional capital and the impact of the quality and effectiveness of institutions on closing the economic gap between countries in the context of the implementation of the European integration strategy. His analysis found that a boost in the quality of institutional capital significantly influences economic development.

Our study implements a methodology based on hard (objective) data related to corruption risks in public procurement in EU member states. This type of research investigates the occurrence of conditions which may make it easier to carry out corrupt transactions (Fazekas et al. 2014, 2016; Fazekas and Tóth 2016). It supposes that entities that would like to take part in corruption arrange these circumstances to facilitate their fraudulent activities (Tóth and Hajdu 2016). However, the presence of conditions conducive to corruption does not necessarily mean that corrupt transactions have actually happened.

Apart from the objectivity of such data, another advantage is that it is available at the micro level, since it is a feature of every public procurement contract. Corruption risk indicators can thereby be aggregated not only to the level of countries, but also to that of the institutions which issued the public tenders, the winning companies, different intra-national regions or even towns or villages. In addition, changes in time can be observed on a finer basis than yearly comparisons depending on the number of public procurement contracts. Charron et al. (2016) and Fazekas

(2017) found that public procurement data can be useful in assessing the quality of government at the regional level.

Broms et al. (2017) used public procurement data for a subnational analysis on the level of municipalities in Sweden. They found that if one party dominates local politics, then procurement quality decreases and corruption risk increases. The indicator they used to measure public procurement quality is the same as what we intended to use in our study: the single bidding ratio.

Several studies have found that one of the most important corruption risk indicators in public procurement is the share of tenders with a single bid, or in other terms, the share of procurement contracts awarded with no competition. Even the lack of competition may also result from a shortage of firms with proper competencies and capacities in certain sectors (Heggstad et al. 2010; Charron et al. 2016; Tóth and Hajdu 2016). Coviello and Gagliarducci (2010) investigated the relationship between local public procurement corruption measured by number of bidders and number of terms in which mayors held office in Italy. Fazekas and Tóth (2016) and Fazekas, Tóth and King (2014, 2016) created a composite corruption risk index based on several elementary indicators that characterize public procurement (e.g., transparency of type of procurement and length of submission and decision periods), and the single bid received turned out to be the most important element.

In addition, there are many further indicators related to public procurement data that can be interpreted in terms of corruption risks and quality of the institutional environment. The values of procurement contracts can be analysed from several perspectives. Firstly, the distortion of prices can be investigated using fraud analytics and forensic accounting tools, for example, by testing whether the first digits of the contract values follow Benford's distribution or if the prices are rounded or not (Miller 2015; Nigrini 2012; Spann 2013). A non-competitive environment in public procurement may result in prices that are determined by issuers and winning companies instead of by market conditions; an analysis of prices from this perspective can thereby be a fruitful area of public procurement corruption research (Tóth and Hajdu 2017b).

Secondly, it can be supposed that if there is no real competition for a tender, then the final contract values will be close to the estimated prices. The core assumption behind this consideration is that intense competition between bidders should produce stronger price competition, thus leading to lower prices in the end. Consequently, the degree of the price drop in the final contract price compared to the estimated value can be regarded as a proxy measure for the intensity of competition (Tóth and Hajdu 2017a).

Empirical results confirm that an analysis of contract prices is an important aspect of investigating public procurement. For example, in the Czech Republic, there is statistical evidence for the manipulation of contract values to avoid bidding, and there is also a higher fraction of anonymously owned firms among the winners of such manipulated contracts (Pertold and Palguta 2017). These findings are in line with those of investigations into the effects of the introduction of discretionary thresholds in Hungary. An amendment to the Hungarian Public Procurement Act in 2011 established a new type of procedure with low transparency, which can only be launched below a certain threshold (Ft25 million, or approx. €75,000), and this caused more distorted prices within contracts which did not exceed this price limit in the service sector. It has also been empirically demonstrated that after removing the obligation to use open bidding for contracts under a certain anticipated value in Hungary in 2011, contract values were strategically set below the threshold to avoid open tenders (Tóth and Hajdu 2017b; Szűcs 2017).

9.3 The Framework of Analysis and Indicators

Out of the options listed above in the literature, we focus on the risks of corruption in public procurement. The risk of corruption is measured by monitoring the lack of competition during the public procurement procedure.

We consider that institutional convergence in country *i* in year *t* is $IC_{i,t}$, which is given as follows:

$$IC_{i,t} = CCR_{i,t} / CCR_{bc,t} \tag{9.1}$$

where $CCR_{i,t}$ is the level of control of corruption risks in test country *i* in year *t* and $CCR_{bc,t}$ is the level of control of corruption risks in the best-performing countries in a given year *t* (the benchmark countries), where $0 < CCR_{i,t} < 1$, $0 < CCR_{bc,t} < 1$ and $0 < IC_{i,t}$. A value of *CCR* close to zero indicates a low level of control of corruption risks, i.e., poor institutional quality, and a value of *CCR* close to 1 indicates a high level of control. Whereas it is evident that control of corruption is stronger in the benchmark countries than in the test countries ($CCR_{bc,t} > CCR_{i,t}$), a value of IC close to 1 represents perfect convergence and an IC value of much lower than 1 means imperfect convergence, where control of corruption risks is higher in the best-performing countries than in the test countries. $IC > 1$ means that the institutional quality of a test country is better than that of the benchmark countries.

Theoretically, we can observe a value of IC_i for every year t ($t = 0,1,2,\ldots.n$). However, this is a difficult and complicated way to measure the goodness or quality of institutions to obtain indicators that are proxies for good performance. To avoid these difficulties, we focused on measuring corruption risks instead of attempting to measure quality of control. We observed the level of corruption risks ($CR_{i,t}$) in country i in year t, and we set control of corruption risks (CCR) as the inverse of corruption risks (CR): $CCR_{i,t} = 1/CR_{i,t}$. Another novelty of our approach is that we use hard data instead of perception data to measure corruption risks. Thus, our solution was not based on observing the perceived control of corruption empirically (as the World Bank does) or perceived control of corruption risks. Instead, we focused on measuring the level of corruption risks itself for each country i and each year t ($CR_{i,t}$) based on micro-data. Then, we calculated institutional convergence ($IC_{i,t}$) as the rate of observed levels of corruption risks in the benchmark and test countries:

$$IC_{i,t} = CR_{bc,t} / CR_{i,t} \tag{9.2}$$

where $0 < CR_{bc,t} < 1$ and $0 < CR_{i,t} < 1$

We measured the level of corruption risk in a simple way: we calculated the share of contract award notices where there was no competition (i.e., there was only one bidder) out of the total number of contract notices. We used a dummy variable for every contract, $SB\,[0,1]$, which has a value of 1 if there was no competition during the tendering procedure and 0, where a contract was signed after a competition (i.e., there was more than one bidder). Clearly, the likelihood of a competitive or non-competitive tender is linked to several factors, not just how the institutions that manage the tendering procedures (i.e., the issuers) can control corruption risks. The type of contracting authority (issuer), the size of contract (the net contract value), the sector of the purchased goods or services by public tender and asynchronicity in business cycles also matter. Due to these possible factors, we used estimations, in which we controlled for the industrial sector for goods or services purchased through public tenders, size of the contract, date of the contract (year) and type of issuer. For every test country i and year t we ran the following logit estimation separately:

$$\ln\left[SB_{i,j,t}^{*} / \left(1 - SB_{i,j,t}^{*}\right)\right] = \beta_{0,i,t} + \beta_1 S_{i,t} + \beta_2 SECTOR_{i,j,t} + \beta_3 SIZE_{i,j,t} + \beta_4 TYPE_{i,j,t} + \varepsilon \quad (9.3)$$

We run the estimate for each i test country on a combined sample of i test country and benchmark countries. The $SB_{i,j,t}^{*}$ is the estimation of occurrence of a single bidder for contract j in the sample analysed that contains country i in year t. $S_{i,t}$ is a dummy variable [0,1], which has value 0 for every test country i and 1 for benchmark countries in year t, $SECTOR_{i,j,t}$, $SIZE_{i,j,t}$ and $TYPE_{i,j,t}$ are the sector of purchased goods or services (based on the common procurement vocabulary, CPV codes[1]) and the logarithm function of net contract value and type of contracting authority in every country i, in contract j and in year t, respectively. We ran estimation (9.3) separately for every given country i and for every year t, and we used *the odds ratio* in the estimations instead of the beta coefficients as a result. The *odds ratio* concerning $S_{i,t}$ provides us with clear information on the difference in the level of corruption risks between benchmark countries and those of the test countries: how much lower is the rate of the estimated share of contracts signed after a non-competitive procedure (with single bidder) and that of the estimated share of contracts signed after a competitive procedure in the benchmark countries than in the test county i:

$$OR_{S_{i,t}} = \frac{SB^{*}_{benchmark,t}}{1 - SB^{*}_{benchmark,t}} \Big/ \frac{SB^{*}_{test,i,t}}{1 - SB^{*}_{test,i,t}} \quad (9.4)$$

Where $SB^{*}_{test,i,t}$ is the estimated share of contracts signed after a non-competitive procedure in test country i in year t.

In other words, we can interpret the odds ratio concerning $S_{i,t}$ as the rate of odds of corruption risks in the benchmark countries and those in the test countries. The value of this *odds ratio* thus provides us with an excellent indicator of institutional convergence (IC), where a value of 1 or close to 1 means perfect or advanced convergence (relatively low level of

[1] The description of CPV codes see: https://ec.europa.eu/growth/single-market/public-procurement/digital/common-vocabulary_en

corruption risks *or* relatively high level of control of corruption risks in test country *i*) and a much lower value means weak convergence or lack of convergence (relatively high level of corruption risks *or* low level of control of corruption risks in test country *i*). Then we can plot the *IC* values by year and by country to present the trends for convergence by country.

In addition to the aforementioned, we consider another aspect of the analysis. It is not only interesting how effective an institution is in controlling corruption risks, but also what impact the choice between types of procedure (with or without a call for bids) has on corruption risks. To deal with this issue, we created a dummy variable (*LTR*, lack of transparency) that divides tenders into two groups:

$LTR\,[0,1] =$ 0 if the tender was issued with an announcement

1 if the tender was issued with no announcement.

Then, for every test country *i* and period *p* we ran the following logit estimation separately:

$$\ln\left[SB_{i,j,p}{}^{*} / \left(1 - SB_{i,j,p}{}^{*}\right)\right] = \beta_{0,i,p} + \beta_1 LTR_{i,j,p} + \beta_2 SECTOR_{i,j,p} + \beta_3 SIZE_{i,j,p} + \beta_4 TYPE_{i,j,p} + \varepsilon \qquad (9.5)$$

As before, we used the odds ratio (*OR*) in the estimations instead of the beta coefficients as a result:

$$OR_{LTR} = \frac{SB^{*}_{LTR=1}}{1 - SB^{*}_{LTR=1}} \Big/ \frac{SB^{*}_{LTR=0}}{1 - SB^{*}_{LTR=0}} \qquad (9.6)$$

Therefore, the period analysed (2006–2018) was divided into two parts (P[1,2]): the first from 2006 to 2011 ($P = 1$) and the second from 2012 to 2018 ($P = 2$). With this method, we were able to observe the changes that took place in the relationship between *LTR* and *SB* in each country. If the value OR_{LTR} is significant and greater than 1 and a contracting authority chooses one of the unrestricted public procurement procedures ($LTR = 1$), the likelihood of non-competitive tenders ($SB = 1$) also increases, thus suggesting a higher risk of corruption. If $OR_{LTR} \approx 1$, it shows that when the tendering procedure was carried out with no announcement this did not raise the odds of non-competitive tenders. In this case, even with *LTR* = 1, more than one bidder submitted their bids, so the competition criterion was not violated, at least not formally. If $OR_{LTR} < 1$, we are dealing with a special situation. In an open procedure, tenders tend to be characterized more by a lack of competition than in a non-transparent procedure. In this case, the open procedure (*LTR* = 0) is more likely to have no competition (*SB* = 1) than the non-transparent procedure. In this case, either the general rule (conducting a non-transparent procedure requiring more than one bidder to submit a bid) or the effect of the contracting authority's pro-competitive measures (properly alerting potential companies to the tender and inviting them to submit a bid) decrease the likelihood of non-competitive tenders. This mechanism will result in a higher rate of competitive tendering than if the contracting authority only published a call for bids and waited for the companies to respond spontaneously.

We used the following specification to compare the effect of *LTR* on the incidence of *SB* between the two periods (from 2006 to 2011, where *P* = 1 and from 2012 to 2018 where *P* = 2):

$$\begin{aligned}\ln\left[SB_{i,j}^{*}/\left(1-SB_{i,j}^{*}\right)\right] &= \beta_0+\beta_1 LTRP1_i+\beta_2 LTRP2_i+\beta_3 SECTORP1_{i,j}\\ &+\beta_4 SECTORP2_{i,j}+\beta_5 SIZEP1_{i,j}+\beta_6 SIZEP2_{i,j}\\ &+\beta_7 TYPEP1_{i,j}+\beta_8 TYPEP2_{i,j}+P+\varepsilon \qquad (9.7)\end{aligned}$$

Where *LTRP1* is equal to *LTR* if *P* = 1 otherwise it has zero value, and *LTRP2* is equal to *LTR* if *P* = 2 otherwise it has zero value. The other variables are defined in the same way.

For the next step, we used the Wald test to analyse the identity of the two coefficients β_1 and β_2 to estimate SB (H_0: $\beta_1 - \beta_2 = 0$). If the difference between the two parameters is significant and $\beta_1 > \beta_2$, then this indicates an improvement from the first period to the second. In this case, conducting tender procedures with no announcement (*LTR* = 1) has a smaller impact on restricting competition in the second period than before. Conversely, if $\beta_1 < \beta_2$, that means if a tender took place without a call for bids, it would be more likely that this would entail a restriction of competition in the second period than before. Therefore, the central government should adjust the regulations on non-open procedures (to require or encourage more bidders in these cases) and observe and evaluate the contracting authorities' decisions when they choose non-open procedures. In this case, the contracting authorities' decisions on the type of procedure result in a restriction of competition and indicate poor control of corruption risks at an institutional level. Of course, the higher values of β_1 and β_2 indicate the greater weight of this problem and the lower values of β_1 and β_2 show a lower weight.

9.4 Data

The novelty of our chapter is that we use hard data at the micro level (public procurement contract data) instead of soft perception data at the country level to analyse institutional convergence in a comparative study. This solution has three advantages. First, the microdata can be aggregated according to different aspects, and this approach thus provides a rich analytical opportunity. Second, the hard data, which came from the administrative process of public procurement, are more reliable than soft, usually expert survey-based data. Third, the creation of indicators based on microdata is based on a completely clear procedure. The raw data, the final composite indicators and the data transformation steps could be made transparent by using a simple method, for instance by publishing the Stata do files.[2]

First, in this section, we deal with perception data from the World Bank and the World Economic Forum, and then we proceed to microdata on public procurement from the European Union TED database.

9.4.1 Perception Data

Among the indicators published by the World Bank, we used the "Control of Corruption" and "Rule of Law" indicators, in addition to the "Public Institutions" indicator issued by the World Economic Forum. We downloaded these data from the World Bank webpage (https://info.worldbank.org/governance/wgi/#home) and the World Economic Forum webpage (www3.weforum.org/docs/GCR2017-2018/GCI_Dataset_2007-2017.xlsx). As regards the World Bank, we had data from 1996 to 2017, while we had data from 2004 to 2017 from the World Economic Forum. We included Austria, Belgium, Denmark, Finland, Germany, Ireland, the Netherlands, Norway and Sweden as the benchmark countries in the analysis and Bulgaria,

[2] Our detailed results see: http://www.crcb.eu/?p=2245

Table 9.1 Main statistics for the perception indicators under analysis

Indicators	*Mean*	*Median*	*Standard deviation*	*N*
Control of corruption, benchmark countries	1.9643	2.0226	0.1044	171
Control of corruption, test countries	0.3497	0.3317	0.4134	209
Rule of law, benchmark countries	1.7941	1.8475	1.1991	171
Rule of law, test countries	0.5699	0.6362	0.4285	209
Public institutions, benchmark countries	5.6030	5.6289	0.4111	126
Public institution, test countries	3.9124	3.8450	0.5589	154

Source: The World Bank and The World Economic Forum authors' own calculations

the Czech Republic, Croatia, Estonia, Hungary, Lithuania, Latvia, Poland, Romania, Slovakia and Slovenia as the test countries.

Clearly, the results of aggregate data for the indicators under analysis show huge differences between the benchmark and test countries (see Table 9.1): the benchmark countries perform better. Additionally, the findings also indicate that the benchmark countries were not totally homogeneous during the period under analysis. The indicators for the test countries suggest a more heterogeneous group than those of the benchmark countries. The standard deviation for the indicators is higher for the latter—in certain cases, four times higher.

9.4.2 *Microdata of Public Procurement Contracts*

We relied on the European Union TED database (https://bit.ly/2ya51hd), from which we downloaded the datasets for 2006, 2007, 2008, 2009–2017 and 2018 separately. Additionally, for comparative purposes, we drew on data from the Colombian public procurement database as well as from Paraguay and Uganda. We combined the EU TED data and used the combined dataset of 6,355,766 observations (records) of contract award notices from 2006 to 2018. After a multi-stage data cleaning and sampling process, we employed a dataset with 3,643,735 records in the analysis (see Annex Tables 9.6, 9.7 and 9.8).

The number of contract award notices under analysis by year increased significantly during the period under examination. This trend can be observed in most of the countries analysed. The TED dataset contains contract award notices above a certain threshold, and these thresholds changed over the period under analysis (see Annex Tables 9.9 and 9.10).

Thus, these threshold changes were partially caused by the rise in the number of contracts.

We used a detailed sector specification with 31 categories based on the CPV codes of purchased goods and services. We measured the size of the contract with the logarithm function of the net contract value. To avoid transactions in which unit prices are recorded instead of contract value or there could be suspicious data for contract prices, we used only a net contract price above €100 and below €50 million. Thus, we excluded 147,039 cases from the estimations. The TED lists issuers in the field of type of contracting authority in ten categories. We used only nine categories since we combined "5. European Union institution/agency" and "5A. other international organization" because there were few cases in these categories.

9.5 Trends

9.5.1 Perception Data

Regarding the indicator of Control of Corruption proposed by The World Bank, the trends of benchmark countries show strong stability, amongst these countries only Austria has a decreasing tendency. In Austria, the control of corruption was weakening from 2007 to 2012. On the contrary, amongst the test countries, there are very different tendencies: the leading countries as Estonia, Czech Republic, Lithuania and Latvia have strongly improving trends, while the control of corruption strongly weakened in Hungary during the analysed period. The average trend of benchmark countries shows stability while that of test countries shows a slight strengthening trend (see Fig. 9.1a). The standard deviation of Control of Corruption in the test countries points out a possible inhomogeneity of data in the analysed period: this was much higher in 1996 and in 1998 than in the next years concerning these countries. From 2000 to 2017 there is a stability in standard deviation and the only slight difference between the trends of test and benchmark countries (see Fig. 9.1b).

The World Bank's Rule of Law indicator shows a stable trend for the benchmark countries, and, in contrast, among the test countries, there are increasing trends, except in Hungary, where the rule of law strongly deteriorated from 1996 to 2017. In contrast to Hungary, the leaders among the test countries, Estonia, Lithuania and Latvia, show a strong improvement in the rule of law, and Croatia shows strong progress as well. In

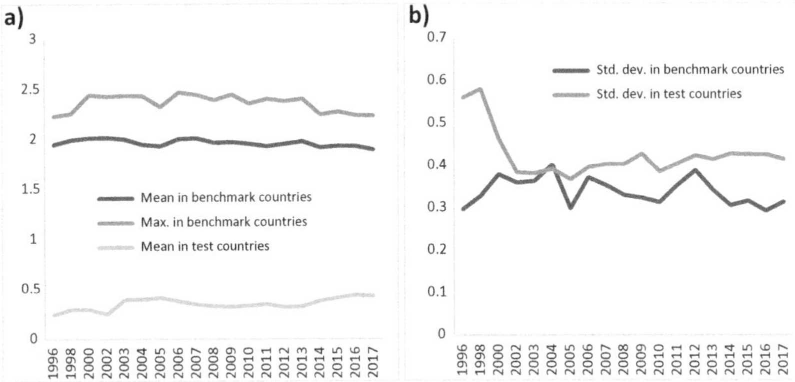

Fig. 9.1 (a, b) The World Bank's Control of Corruption indicator in the test and the benchmark countries, 1996–2017. (a) Mean and maximal values. (b) Standard deviations. (Source: The World Bank, authors' own calculations)

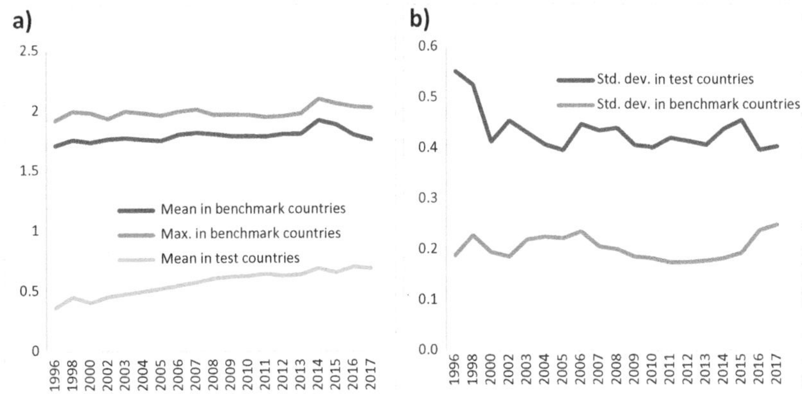

Fig. 9.2 (a, b) The World Bank's Rule of Law indicator in the test and the benchmark countries, 1996–2017. (a) Mean and maximal values. (b) Standard deviations. (Source: The World Bank, authors' own calculations)

other countries (Bulgaria and Poland), there is stability, with high variance in the case of Poland and with very small variance in the case of Bulgaria. The growing trend among the test countries in the rule of law is much stronger than in control of corruption, while the standard deviation for the rule of law indicator is almost twice as high in the test countries as it is in the benchmark countries over the period (see Fig. 9.2a, b).

The World Economic Forum (WEF) indicator, which measures the quality of public institutions, shows a clear lack of homogeneity in the period under analysis: the values of this indicator by country in 2004 and 2005 are much higher, especially among the test countries (see Fig. 9.3a, b). In addition, the standard deviation trends are very strange: there are huge differences between the test and benchmark countries in 2004–2005, which suddenly disappear in 2006. We think that it is better to see and interpret the data for this indicator only from 2006 to 2017 and not analyse the data for 2004 and 2005.

The WEF data show strong stability and little variance among the benchmark countries from 2006 to 2017. As regards the test countries, we see the same stability with the highest variance. There are only two countries with a strong decreasing trend: Hungary and Slovakia. In contrast, Estonia, a leader in this respect, shows a slight improvement. As regards average trends, there is no convergence between the test and benchmark countries (see Fig. 9.3a), and the differences in standard deviations remain almost the same over the period (see Fig. 9.3b).

We calculated the level of convergence in the following way: we considered the maximum value of each indicator from each year and subtracted the value for test countries by country and by year from these maximum

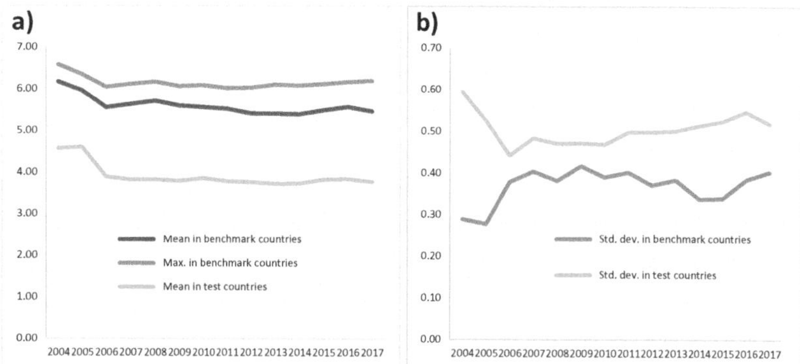

Fig. 9.3 (a, b) The World Economic Forum: Public Institutions in test countries and in benchmark countries, 2004–2017. (a) Mean and maximal values. (b) Standard deviations. (Source: WEF, authors' own calculations)

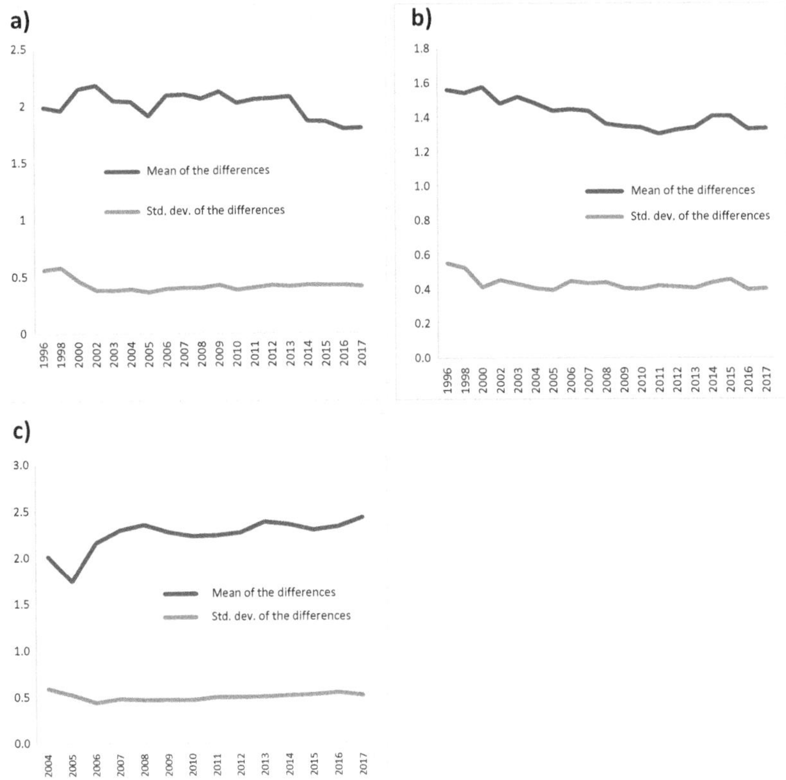

Fig. 9.4 (a–c) Trends of convergence to the benchmark countries by Control of Corruption, Rule of Law and Public Institutions indices, 1996–2017. (a) Control of Corruption. (b) Rule of Law. (c) Public Institutions. (Source: The World Bank, authors' own calculations, WEF)

values. Consequently, we obtained an indicator that shows the distance of the value for the test country under analysis in the given year from the best value for the benchmark country in the same year. We then calculated the standard deviation of these distances. The results are shown in Fig. 9.4a–c. As regards control of corruption and the rule of law, there are trends with slight convergence in the period under analysis, while there is a divergence for public institutions: the test countries are moving away from the benchmark countries in this respect.

9.5.2 *Public Procurement Data*

9.5.2.1 The Share of Contracts Without Competition

In this part of the analysis, we look at the trend for corruption risks (i.e., the share of contracts signed with no competition) over the period under analysis. Figure 9.5a shows a considerable increase in corruption risks in the entire sample: the share of non-competitive contracts grew from 15% to 30%. We must add an important feature to this: at the same time, the share of records (contract award notices) with missing data or suspicious data in the number of bidders variable decreased considerably: from 17.9% to 2.6% (see Fig. 9.5b). Therefore, the data quality of the TED database significantly improved from 2006 to 2018 from this perspective. We must deal with this phenomenon because the lack of information in the number of bidders variable can be interpreted as a sign of data concealment, which may be a consequence of a hidden and irregular behaviour on the part of the actors involved in public tenders, such as different forms of corrupt activity. We thus computed an alternative indicator (SB_MAX), where we considered a record with missing data in the number of bidders variable, such as a contract award notice with no competition [SB_MAX=1 if *SB* = 1 or SB = missing value]. This indicator shows a more stable trend over the

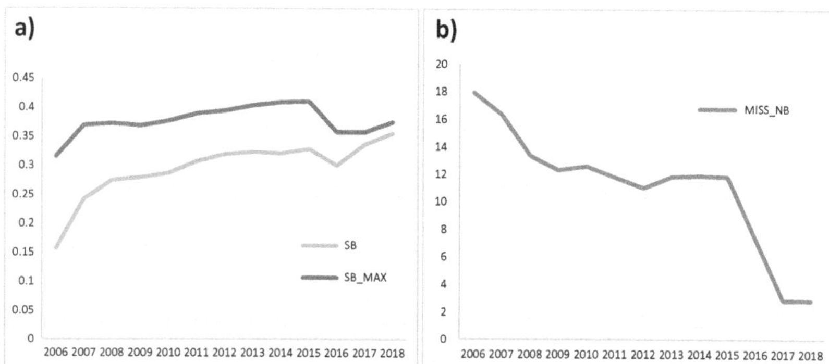

Fig. 9.5 (a, b) The trend of corruption risks and share of contracts with missing value in the variable of number of bidder, 2006–2018, percentage. (Source: WEF, authors' own calculations. Notes: SB: average share of contracts with single bidder (SB) by year, SB_MAX: average share of contracts with single bidder by year where a contract with missing data in the number of bidders variable considered as a contract award notice with no competition, MISS_NB: average share of contracts with missing value in the variable of number of bidders by year, N: 3,643,039)

Table 9.2 The list of countries chosen as benchmark countries with an average share of contracts without competition, 2006–2018, percentage

	Benchmark countries	*Single bidder (SB) Mean 2006–2018, %*	*N*	*Max value of single bidder (SB_MAX) Mean 2006–2018, %*	*N*
1	Austria (AT)	11.1	20,876	15.2	21,900
2	Belgium (BE)	15.1	37,266	19.2	39,155
3	Germany (DE)	13.3	223,923	16.4	232,253
4	Denmark (DK)	10.9	17,009	17.2	18,306
5	Ireland (IE)	10.1	7188	14.2	7529
6	Netherlands (NL)	12.0	25,598	15.6	26,696
7	Norway (NO)	10.5	9230	13.4	9539
8	Sweden (SE)	10.4	27,476	12.4	28,111
	Total	12.8	368,566	15.9	382,246

Source: TED, authors' own calculation

period, only changing from 30% to 41%. After this step, we chose eight benchmark countries, where the average values of SB_MAX by year were the lowest during the period under analysis. We finally used these countries as benchmark countries (see Table 9.2) during the analysis.

As regards the test countries, our results clearly indicate that there is a high level of corruption risks in the period under analysis (see Table 9.3), and, surprisingly, the data quality is far better in the new EU member states than in the Southern European countries (Greece, Italy, Spain and Portugal). These preliminary findings also reflect the poor institutional quality of the latter countries from the perspective of the quality of the data disclosure protocol used in each country under analysis (see Fig. 9.6b).

Of the benchmark countries, the share of contracts signed with no competition rose from 2006 to 2018 (see Fig. 9.6a), as measured by both corruption risk indicators (SB and SB_MAX). In addition, in 2017, due to the decreasing rate of contracts with missing data (see Fig. 9.6b), they reached the same level. The results show significant improvement of data quality in the benchmark country and test country subsamples as well. The share of records with missing data indicates that the data quality was better in the benchmark countries than in the test countries (see Fig. 9.7) over time.

We have no information on the validity of our assumption concerning the categorization of contracts with missing data, that is, whether the

Table 9.3 List of countries chosen as test countries with an average share of contracts with no competition, 2006–2018, percentage

	Test countries	*Single bidder (SB) mean, % 2006–2018*	*N*	*Max. value of single bidder (SB_MAX) mean, % 2006–2018*	*N*
	New EU member countries				
1	Bulgaria (BG)	25.8	88,874	27.1	90,375
2	Czech Republic (CZ)	37.7	92,657	39.7	95,741
3	Estonia (EE)	28.5	13,580	35.5	15,053
4	Hungary (HU)	33.3	66,065	34.7	67,450
5	Latvia (LV)	21.7	106,934	21.7	107,009
6	Lithuania (LT)	29.2	59,180	29.3	59,242
7	Poland (PL)	45.5	1,230,367	46.7	1,257,310
8	Romania (RO)	31.4	94,669	31.4	94,682
9	Slovenia (SL)	51.1	91,805	51.8	93,155
	Slovakia (SK)	40.5	19,386	41.1	19,604
	Southern European countries				
10	Spain (ES)	17.7	154,255	38.4	206,060
11	Greece (GR)	26.4	31,848	48.4	45,449
12	Italy (IT)	26.3	160,672	36.8	187.493
13	Portugal (PT)	19.2	15,830	54.5	28,095
	Total	38.2	2,226,122	41.9	2,366,718

Source: TED, authors' own calculations

missing data in the number of bidders variable can be considered as a contract signed with no competition ($SB = 1$) or a wrong categorization. We have thus decided to use the original data (SB) instead of the expanded version of our corruption risk indicator (SB_MAX). We excluded any contracts from further analysis where the number of bidders values were missing. We are aware that this decision, in certain cases, where the quality of data was relatively poor (especially in the Southern European countries), led to results that overestimated convergence towards the benchmark countries. This effect does not matter in the new EU countries, where the quality of data was much better compared to the Southern European countries (See Fig. 9.7).

After we used the share of contracts with a single bidder as a proxy for corruption risks, our results indicated that corruption risk trends show

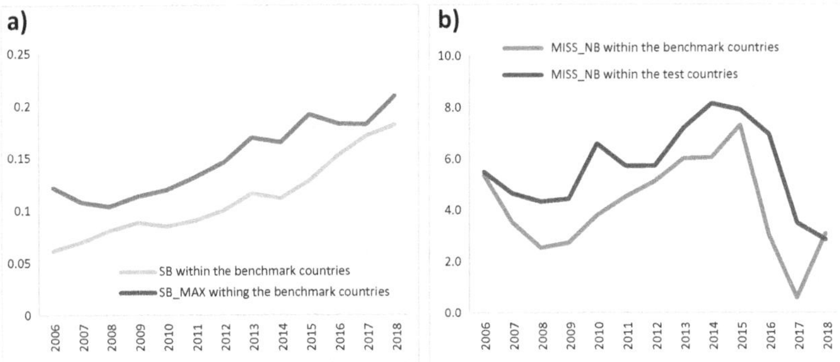

Fig. 9.6 (a, b) Corruption risk trends in the benchmark country sample and share of contracts with missing values in the number of bidders variable in both the test country sample and the benchmark country sample, 2006–2018, percentage. (Source: TED, authors' own calculations. Notes: SB: average share of contracts with single bidder (SB) by year, SB_MAX: average share of contracts with single bidder by year where a contract with missing data in the number of bidders variable considered as a contract award notice with no competition, MISS_NB: average share of contracts with missing value in the variable of number of bidders by year, N: 2,750,210)

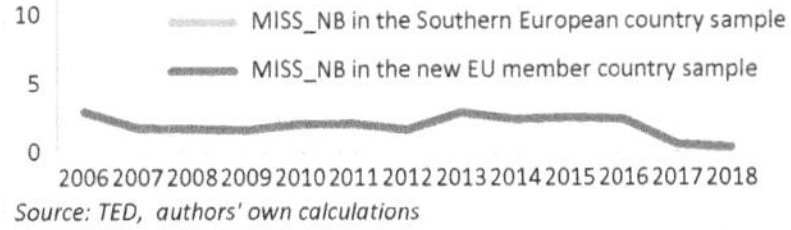

Fig. 9.7 Share of contracts with missing values in the number of bidders variable in both the new EU member country sample and the Southern European country sample, 2006–2018, percentage. (Source: TED, authors' own calculations. Notes: MISS_NB: average share of contracts with missing value in the variable of number of bidder by year, N: 2,366,718)

great variability across the new accession countries under analysis (see Fig. 9.8b–f). While the level of corruption risks decreased significantly in Estonia and Lithuania and especially in Slovakia (from 0.27 to 0.25, from 0.33 to 0.21 and from 0.51 to 0.19, respectively) in the period under analysis, there was a reverse trend in most of the new EU countries: corruption risks increased in Hungary (from 0.28 to 0.35), Poland (from 0.25 to 0.49), the Czech Republic (from 0.29 to 0.47), Bulgaria (from 0.15 to 0.33) and especially in Slovenia (from 0.22 to 0.62) and Romania (from 0.21 to 0.43). It is important to add that the significant fall in corruption risks in Slovakia is not a unique case. If we calculate the same indicator using Colombian public procurement data, we see the same significant drop from a level of 0.6 to 0.2 (see Fig. 9.8g). This could also mean that rapid success in reducing corruption risk is possible and may stem from a feasible anti-corruption policy.

9.5.2.2 The Share of Contracts with Few Competitors

After an analysis of the share of contracts without competitors, we also wished to calculate the share of contracts with weak competition. To achieve this goal, we defined an indicator which measures the share of contracts with only two or three competitors (FC). This has the value 1 if there were only 2–3 bidders and 0 if the number of bidders was higher.

The results show a clear rise in the share of contracts with few competitors in the case of the test and benchmark countries and the Southern European countries as well (see Fig. 9.9a, b, c, d, e and f) In contrast, we can see a certain stability in Romania and a slight increase in Bulgaria with a relatively low share (26–37%) of these contracts (see Fig. 9.9b).

The number of contracts with few competitors was relatively stable with high variance in Slovakia and the Czech Republic (Fig. 9.9c) and with low variance in Lithuania, Latvia and Estonia (Fig. 9.9e, f). There is a strong increase in Poland, Hungary and Slovenia: from 30% to 71%, from 45% to 71% and from 33% to 76%, respectively (Fig. 9.9d, f). A comparison of the European data with public procurement data from Colombia (Fig. 9.9g) shows that contracts with few competitors were issued less frequently (25%) in the latter than in the benchmark European countries (33%).

Fig. 9.8 (a–g) Corruption risk trends in different European countries (2006–2018) and Colombia (2016–2018) based on TED data and the Colombian public procurement database. (Source: TED, authors' own calculation, Colombian public procurement database with authors' own calculations)

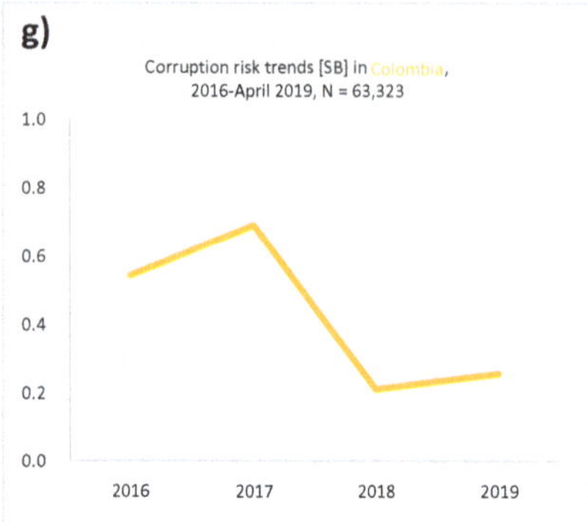

Fig. 9.8 (continued)

These results demonstrate a weakening trend in the intensity of competition, which characterizes not only the majority of European test countries, but benchmark countries as well.

9.5.2.3 *The Share of Contracts with Announcement, and Without Announcement*

In the first step of the analysis of the microdata on public procurement contracts, we looked at the trends for transparent procedures. The corruption literature emphasizes that the occurrence of corrupt transactions strongly depends on the cost of corrupt activities, that is, the probability of detection and, in the case of detection, the penalty (Rose-Ackerman 1978; Becker and Stigler 1974; Lambsdorff 2007). Whereas transparency enhances the effectiveness of control, and thus raises the probability of detection, transparency of public tenders may decrease the probability of corrupt activities. As regards public procurement, tenders with an announcement (i.e., open procedures) are more transparent, as any company on the market can apply for such tenders, unlike those tenders where there is no call for bids, that is, tenders without transparency. Naturally, this is only an additional factor for reducing corruption risks in public procurement because the substantial element of an anti-corruption policy—that is, to reduce the probability of corrupt practices—is to ensure competition. There is a strong probability that there is no competition besides the call for bids. In this section, we provide an overview of the trends for public tenders with open and non-open procedures.

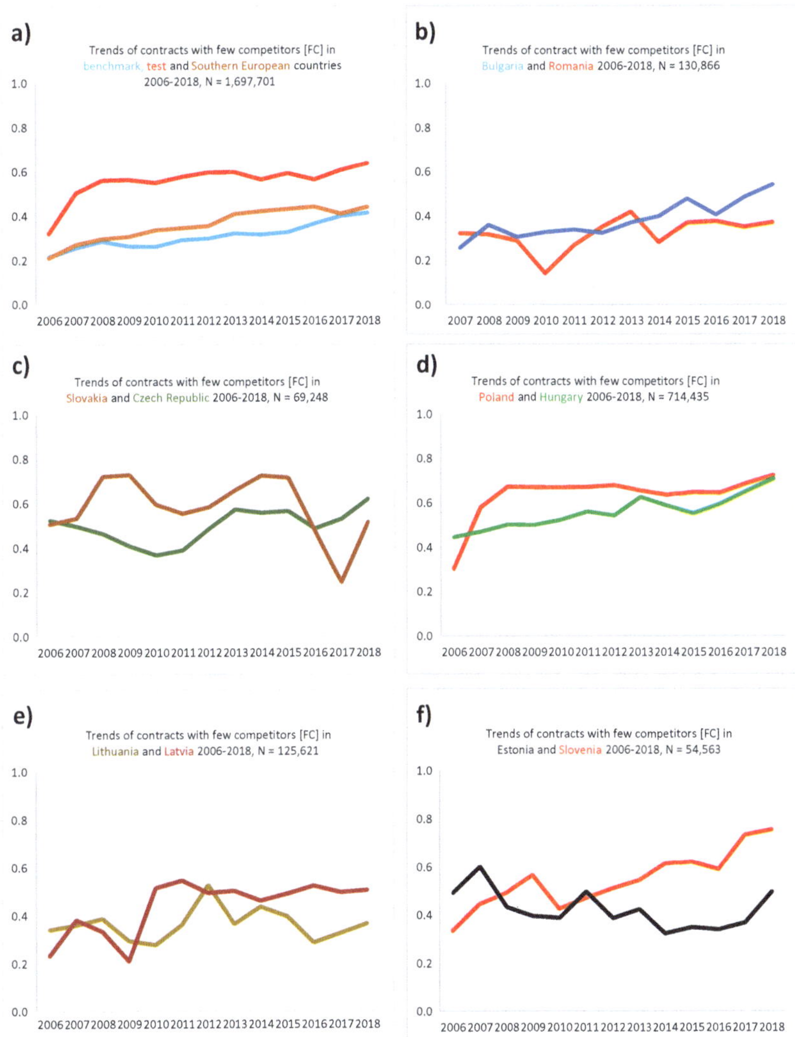

Fig. 9.9 (a–g) Trends for contracts with few competitors in different European countries (2006–2018) and Colombia (2016–2018) based on TED data and the Colombian public procurement database, annual averages. (Source: TED, authors' own calculation, TED and the Colombian public procurement database with authors' own calculations)

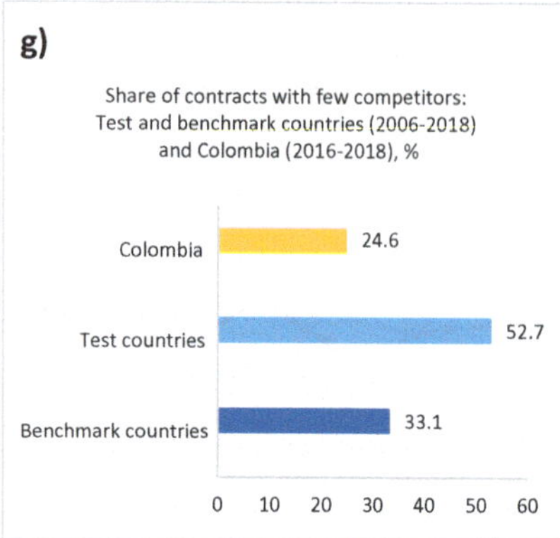

Fig. 9.9 (continued)

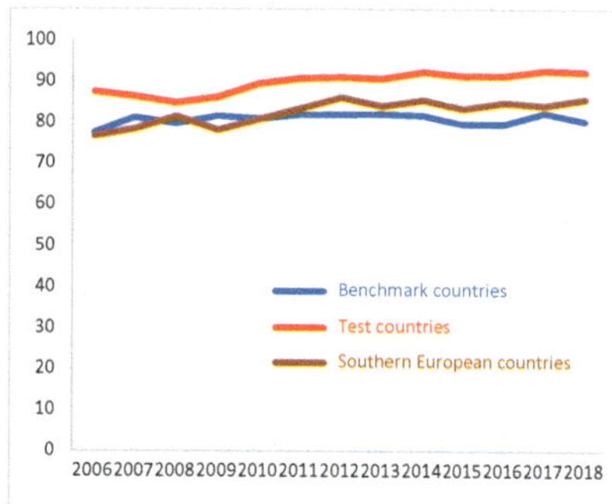

Fig. 9.10 The share of contracts with an announcement in the test and benchmark countries, 2006–2018, percentage. (Source: TED, authors' own calculation. Note: N = 3,643,039)

The trend for the share of contracts with an announcement shows a certain increase from 2006 to 2018 at the European level: in 2006, 83% of the contracts were signed after a procedure with an announcement, and in 2018 this figure was already 88%. There is no substantial difference from this perspective between the benchmark and test countries (see Fig. 9.10). Moreover, the share of contracts with an announcement was higher by 5–6 percentage points over the period in the test countries than in the benchmark countries as well as in the Southern European countries. The new accession countries have the highest values in the period analysed. There are considerable differences between the test countries in this regard: Poland and Lithuania have high values with stable trends. In contrast, Estonia, Slovakia, Hungary and Slovenia have a relatively low share

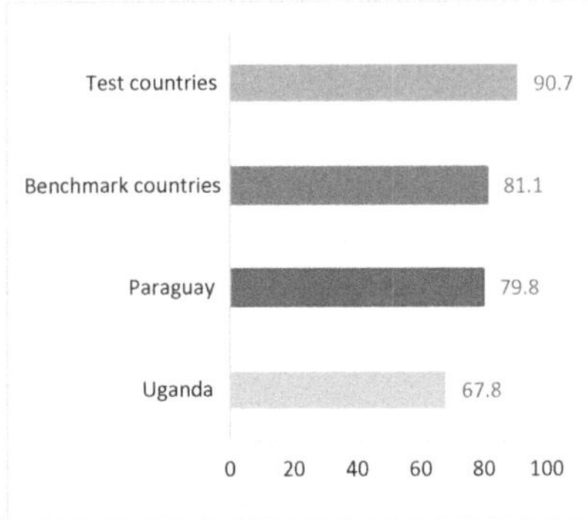

Fig. 9.11 The share of contracts with an announcement in the test countries, the benchmark countries (2006–2018), Paraguay (2010–2018) and Uganda (2015–2018), percentage. (Source: TED and national procurement databases with authors' own calculations)

of contracts with an announcement at the beginning of the period, and their data show high variability. In terms of the aggregate data for the whole period, 89% of the contracts were signed after a procedure with an announcement in the test countries, and that figure was 81% in the benchmark countries. It is important to add that the two developing countries (Paraguay and Uganda) performed well in this respect, their figures being 80% and 68%, respectively (see Fig. 9.11).

As described above, the weight of tenders with no announcement is low and shows a decreasing trend from the first period (2006–2011) to the second period (2012–2018) in most countries analysed (see Table 9.4).

Table 9.4 shows that in most countries the likelihood of tenders with a lack of transparency ($LTR = 1$) decreased from the first period to the second. Only Austria, Bulgaria and Portugal are exceptions to this trend. In Portugal, the proportion of these tenders has increased remarkably (from 10.4% to 42.1%) because the share of open procedures dropped and the share of negotiated procedures with a call for bids rose from 1.2% to 34.9%. At the same time, the share of tenders with no competition ($SB = 1$) grew significantly in almost all countries: from 8% to 15% in the case of the benchmark countries, from 38% to 43% in the test countries and from 17% to 27% in the Southern European countries. In the non-transparent procedure subsample ($LTR = 1$), the share of tenders with no competition increased in almost all the countries. The share of these tenders only decreased in the Czech Republic, Estonia, Lithuania, Latvia, Poland and Romania.

Table 9.4 Share of contracts with no announcement and no competition in the two periods, percentage

	First period (2006–2011)			*Second period (2012–2018)*		
Country name	*Contracts with no announcement (LTR = 1)*	*Single bidder (SB = 1)*	*SB = 1 if LTR = 1*	*Contracts with no announcement (LTR = 1)*	*Single bidder (SB=1)*	*SB=1 if LTR=1*
Benchmark countries						
Austria (AT)	13.0	7.3	24.6	18.3	14.1	30.9
Belgium (BE)	17.9	11.1	19.5	15.3	17.5	27.1
Germany (DE)	16.7	7.6	18.9	17.5	16.3	27.9
Denmark (DK)	45.5	6.9	4.8	39.6	12.8	13.1
Ireland (IE)	26.6	5.0	3.4	21.7	12.7	10.1
Netherlands (NL)	32.7	8.8	12.6	35.1	13.3	18.8
Norway (NO)	22.3	7.6	7.0	17.4	11.5	13.9
Sweden (SE)	18.6	8.5	9.1	5.9	10.8	12.6
All benchmark countries	19.3	8.0	22.9	18.7	15.2	24.0
New EU member countries (test countries)						
Bulgaria (BG)	7.6	16.4	46.6	12.7	28.3	59.1
Czech Republic (CZ)	24.6	30.7	59.6	24.9	40.1	51.0
Estonia (EE)	41.6	36.5	58.6	23.7	23.3	39.1
Hungary (HU)	34.8	29.9	39.7	18.2	35.7	50.1
Latvia (LV)	11.4	25.1	77.2	4.6	20.2	54.7
Lithuania (LT)	25.0	28.4	38.3	18.7	29.8	32.0
Poland (PL)	7.7	42.9	75.1	4.2	47.0	64.5
Romania (RO)	18.5	28.2	46.7	22.6	34.1	44.2
Slovenia (SL)	23.8	24.2	35.8	7.8	56.2	60.9
Slovakia (SK)	32.9	57.6	66.3	14.8	31.2	76.2
All test countries	12.0	38.4	60.0	8.0	42.8	54.8
Southern European countries						
Spain (ES)	14.3	11.8	34.6	13.3	22.3	55.0
Greece (GR)	11.3	18.0	26.4	3.0	33.0	33.9
Italy (IT)	28.6	21.7	25.6	14.6	30.1	47.0
Portugal (PT)	10.4	10.3	30.1	42.1	24.5	67.3
Mean	19.8	16.8	27.8	15.0	26.7	50.9
All Southern European countries	19.8	16.8	27.8	15.0	26.7	50.9

Source: TED, authors' own calculation

9.6 Results of Estimations

The results shown in the previous section underline that new EU members had different ways of controlling corruption risks in public tenders. These trends not only depend on the effect of institutional quality, but also on several other factors, such as the internal structure of public tenders by size, sector and characteristics of contracting authority (the type of issuer), and, clearly, these latter factors may change year by year. If we wish to measure, at least approximately, the effect of institutional quality in terms of control of corruption risks in test countries and, based on this, convergence towards institutional quality in developed (benchmark) countries, we must control our findings with these latter factors independent of institutional quality. In this section, we report on this task using the concept described in Sect. 9.3.

First, we focused on the role that the lack of transparency ($LTR = 1$) plays in ensuring that a tender is conducted with no competition ($SB = 1$), that is, with a high risk of corruption. We estimated the impact of LTR on the occurrence of the single bid, and we used the sector, logarithm function of the net contract value and type of issuer as control variables as per eq. 5. We compared the impact of LTR on SB between the two periods (2006–2011 and 2012–2018) as per Eq. (9.6).

An administrative decision on an open procedure ($LTR = 0$ or $LTR = 1$) may be (i) the result of a centralized regulation or (ii) may be an autonomous decision made by the issuer. In the first case, control of corruption is linked to a central government policy, and, in the second case, it is an outcome of institutional integrity. If control of corruption is realized for non-open procedures ($LTR = 1$), then there may be two causes: (ii) it is caused by regulations on public tenders or (ii) it may be an impact of issuer behaviour that promotes market competition. That is, the issuer itself takes action and attempts to persuade market players to participate in tenders. The high coefficient value of LTR indicates that government needs to think about changing regulations on non-open procedures, for instance, specifying the number of competitors that must be involved in such a tender.

Table 9.5 shows that the impact of LTR on SB rose slightly from the first period to the second in only three benchmark countries: Denmark, Ireland and Norway. In other countries, there was no change in this regard (in Belgium and the Netherlands) or this impact decreased (in Austria, Germany and Sweden). Nonetheless, the results demonstrate that the decision to launch an open or non-open procedure has a considerable impact on the likelihood of non-competitive tenders, mostly in Germany,

Table 9.5 The estimated impact of lack of transparency on lack of competition in the two periods (2006–2011 and 2012–2018) and the Wald test to determine the strength of the effect in the two periods, 2006–2018

	First period	*Second period*	*Wald test*		
	2006–2011	*2012–2018*	*Value*	*Sign.*	*N*
	Odds ratio	*Odds ratio*			
Bulgaria	5.04	8.56	29.34	0.000	85,601
Czech Republic	5.71	5.18	3.76	0.053	89,535
Estonia	7.27	4.34	14.32	0.000	13,118
Hungary	2.94	2.53	8.62	0.033	62,496
Lithuania	15.83	3.56	501.03	0.000	78,829
Latvia	4.29	2.85	40.26	0.000	54,829
Poland	4.57	2.98	372.63	0.000	1,156,802
Romania	2.40	2.40	0.00	0.995	89,154
Slovakia	2.92	12.99	153.66	0.000	18,501
Slovenia	2.84	1.50	79.21	0.000	87,411
Test countries	2.88	2.10	592.79	0.000	1,736,557
Greece	0.92	1.65	15.48	0.000	28,345
Italy	1.48	2.87	390.38	0.000	149,533
Portugal	11.05	11.57	0.07	0.787	14,875
Spain	7.04	7.38	0.93	0.335	137,356
Southern European countries	2.54	4.14	386.92	0.000	330,361
Austria	7.13	2.17	63.37	0.000	19,421
Belgium	2.52	2.76	0.89	0.345	35,127
Denmark	0.57	1.11	18.00	0.000	15,500
Germany	3.95	3.22	18.89	0.000	200,876
Ireland	0.57	1.57	7.94	0.005	6023
Netherland	3.10	3.17	0.04	0.841	20,456
Norway	0.88	1.61	4.31	0.038	8529
Sweden	2.02	0.81	17.12	0.000	25,110
Benchmark countries	2.96	2.50	24.57	0.000	331,748
All countries under analysis	2.36	2.09	144.34	0.000	2,398,666

Note: The estimations by countries are controlled by size of contract (ln of net contract value), sector and type of issuer

Source: TED, authors' own calculation
N = 2,985,782

the Netherlands, Belgium and Austria. In these countries in the second period, the fact that a tender was announced in a non-open procedure ($LTR = 1$) significantly increases (by 2.2–3.2 times) the likelihood of this tender being conducted with no competition. These findings suggest that governments in these countries should deal with regulating the legal framework of non-open tenders and should analyse issuer decisions on non-open tenders.

As for the test countries, there is a positive trend in this regard in five countries: Hungary, Lithuania, Latvia, Poland and Slovenia. There is no significant change in Romania and the Czech Republic, and there is a significant deterioration in Slovakia and Bulgaria. In almost all the countries, except Slovenia in the second period, LTR has a strong effect on the likelihood of the presence of a single bid. The case of Bulgaria and Slovakia is extreme: the issuer's decision to use a non-open procedure in the second period raises the odds of a single bid 8.6–13 times, respectively. This result demonstrates that in almost all the test countries (especially in Slovakia, Bulgaria and also in Spain and Portugal), the government should change the regulations on non-open procedures to achieve highest level of competition and lower level of corruption risks in public procurement.

Second, we ran logit estimations based on equitation (9.3), where we controlled for the effect of the institutional ability to control corruption risks by market characteristics (sector of purchased goods or services), size of contract (logarithm function of net contract value) and type of issuer (contracting authority), and we ran the estimations separately by year and by test country.

The results of the estimations show that there is a slow convergence of the test country sample to the benchmark country sample and using SB instead of SB_MAX we are slightly underestimating the strength of convergence (see Fig. 9.12a). There are different paths for new EU member states as regards institutional convergence (see Fig. 9.12b–f). The worst example is Slovenia with poor institutional quality (see Fig. 9.12e) and a tendency of divergence from the benchmark countries, while Slovakia had the best results with almost perfect institutional convergence and a high level of institutional quality at the end of the period under analysis (see Fig. 9.12b).

In other V4 countries, such as Hungary and the Czech Republic, we saw weak convergence with a low ability to control corruption risks with values in 2018 of 0.44 and 0.28, respectively. Hungary managed to control corruption risks at 44% of the level of the benchmark countries and the Czech Republic was able to do the same at 28% of the benchmark level at the end of the period (see Fig. 9.12b, c). The other example is Poland with a convergence trend, but the results of this trend are rather weak: at the end of the period, Poland had a value of 0.22. This means that Poland

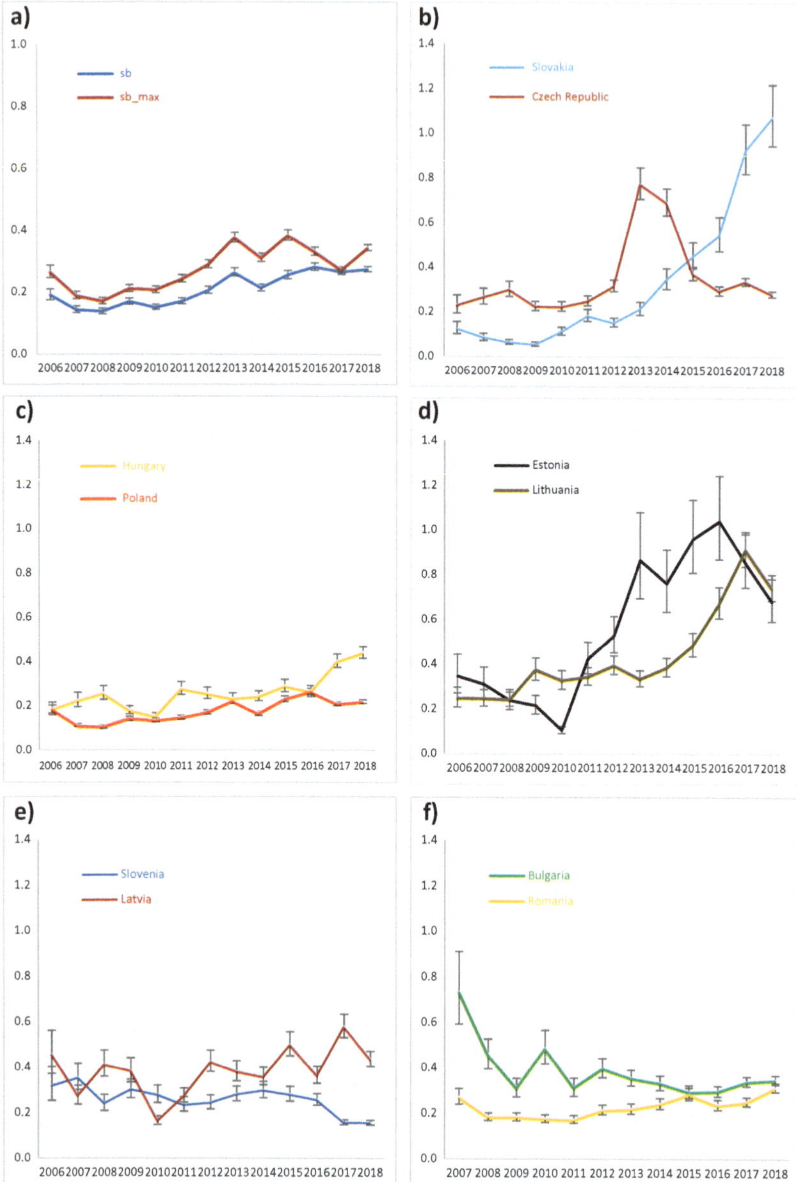

Fig. 9.12 (a–h) Institutional convergence: convergence of the test countries towards countries with high institutional quality measured by level of corruption risks in public tenders, 2006–2018. (a) New EU member states. (b) Czech Republic and Slovakia. (c) Hungary and Poland. (d) Estonia and Lithuania. (e) Latvia and Slovenia. (f) Bulgaria and Romania. (g) Portugal and Spain. (h) Greece and Italy. (Source: Authors' own calculations based on TED data. Note: N = 2,985,782)

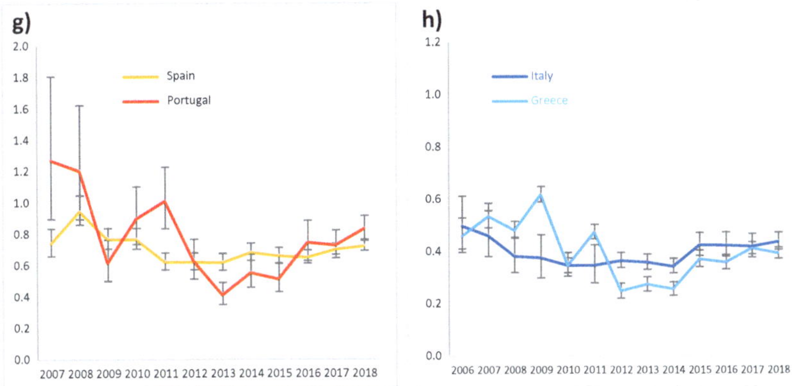

Fig. 9.12 (continued)

succeeded in controlling corruption risks at only 22% of the level of the benchmark countries (see Fig. 9.12c).

The other typical sub-group of the new EU member states is two Baltic states (Estonia and Lithuania) with strong and almost perfect convergence: in 2016–2018, they reached the level of the benchmark countries as regards the ability to control corruption risks (see Fig. 9.12d). The institutional convergence in these countries was considerable with values in 2018 of 0.68 and 0.74, respectively. The fourth group consists of Bulgaria and Romania with very poor convergence and a low or moderate level of institutional quality (see Fig. 9.12f). The benchmark countries controlled corruption risks three times more effectively than these two countries.

As regards the Southern European countries, our findings partially support those of Alesina, Tabellini and Trebbi (2017) and Schönfelder and Wagner (2019). These countries rather show a decreasing trend at the beginning of the period and then an increasing one towards the end with relatively high institutional quality (with values of 0.72 and 0.83 in Spain and Portugal, respectively) and relatively low institutional quality (with values of 0.39 and 0.44 in Greece and Italy, respectively). This means that control of corruption is 2.3–2.6 times higher in the benchmark countries than in Italy or Greece (see Fig. 9.12g, h).

Finally, we measured the impact of EU funding on level of corruption risks in contracts in two ways. First, we ran a logit estimation of corruption risk exclusively for the subsample of new accession countries. In the estimations, we controlled for the impact of EU funds by year, sector, type of issuer, net contract value and country. Then, we calculated our indicator of institutional convergence (IC) among test countries taking into consideration only EU-funded contracts in these countries. The logit estimation shows a significant positive impact of EU funds on the level of corruption risks. In the new accession countries, the odds of a contract with no competition is 36% higher among EU-financed contracts than among contracts financed by national sources (see Table 9.11). Taking into consideration EU-funded contracts in the test countries only, we re-calculated institutional convergence. The findings show that in certain countries (Slovakia, Bulgaria and Romania), control of corruption is more effective in the case of EU funds than in contracts financed by national sources (see Table 9.11). In other countries, there is an inverse situation: control of corruption is stronger among contracts financed by national sources (Estonia, the Czech Republic, Lithuania, Latvia, Poland and Slovenia). The results demonstrate that the impact of EU funds varies country by country and year by year (see Tables 9.12, 9.13 and 9.14). In addition, the results show slightly stronger convergence in the sub-sample of new member states in the case of EU-funded tenders than for non-EU-funded ones, even though new member states are still very far from the benchmark countries at the end of the period in this respect (see Fig. 9.13). Obviously, the occurrence of stronger control of corruption in the case

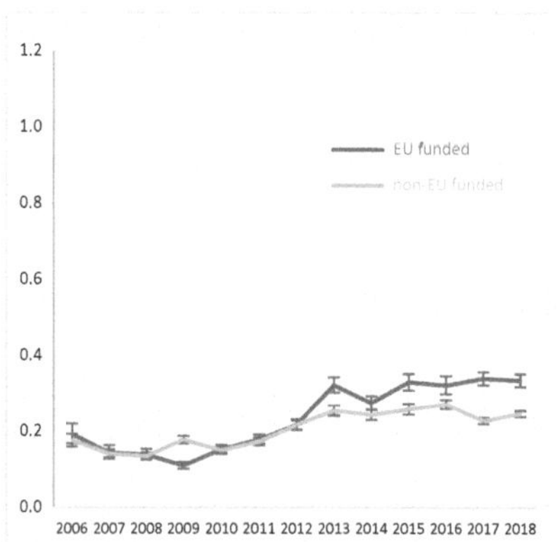

Fig. 9.13 Institutional convergence: convergence of test countries towards countries with high institutional quality measured by level of corruption risks in public tenders by EU funding, 2006–2018. (Source: Authors' own calculations based on TED data. Note: N = 2,564,225)

of EU subsidies relates to the intensifying pressure of the European Commission on national anti-corruption policies as regards the national public procurement system, which can be seen, for instance, in the content analysis of the EU Country Reports (see Figs. 9.14, 9.15, 9.16 and 9.17).

9.7 Conclusions

Our findings demonstrate that institutional convergence is a real possibility. The good examples of Slovakia, Estonia and Lithuania provide us with evidence that in 13 years almost perfect institutional convergence can be implemented from a low level of control of corruption risks almost to the levels in benchmark countries. The other group of countries—the worst examples—are Italy, Greece, Bulgaria and Slovenia, with very poor convergence or rather divergence. In the third group of countries (the Czech Republic, Hungary, Latvia, Poland and Romania), there was a slight and slow institutional convergence and low institutional quality at the end of the period under analysis.

The results for the impact of the non-open procedure on lack of competition show that in a number of benchmark and test countries, the government should deal with the undesired impact of non-open procedures, which severely restricts market competition. The findings show that in almost all countries, the government should consider changing the regulations on non-open procedures. In this regard, except for Slovenia, there is a weak convergence among new EU member states towards developed EU countries.

A content analysis of the EU Country Reports shows (see Annex Figs. 9.14, 9.15, 9.16 and 9.17) that in the case of the new EU member countries during the period under analysis the EU increasingly dealt with the topic of corruption and public procurement and nudged governments to use more effective measures and tools to control corruption risks in public procurement. These recommendations generated some institutional reforms at the national level and raised institutional quality. Only in Slovakia, Bulgaria and Romania, the control of corruption is more effective for EU-funded contracts than for those financed by national sources (see Table 9.11). Other countries—except Hungary, where there is no significant difference—are experiencing the opposite: control of corruption is stronger for contracts financed by national sources. These results basically confirm the results of previous analyses: with the exception of some countries (such as Bulgaria and Romania), in the new member countries the EU-funded tenders have higher level of corruption risks than the nationally funded ones (Fazekas and Tóth 2017). In addition, our results indicate that EU measures promoting institutional reforms to reduce corruption risks were limited during the period under analysis and policies were rather necessary but did not set sufficient conditions for real and effective reforms at the national level. While in Slovakia, Estonia and Lithuania the effects of the EU intertwined with the aims and measures of national governments (for instance, introduction of a good e-procurement system, introduction of a transparent control system for public tenders and improvement of data disclosure practices of the public procurement authority), in the other new EU member countries there were no such effective measures. In these countries (Hungary, Romania, the Czech Republic, Bulgaria and Slovenia), the impacts of EU policy on strengthening control of corruption risks in the entire public procurement system were insufficient. Poor political support from the national governments led to an imitation of institutional reforms rather than actual institutional reforms. The consequence of that situation—as can be seen in our findings—was poor institutional convergence and a relatively low level of institutional quality.

Annex

The TED Database and the Sampling

The TED database contains 6,355,766 records from 2006 to 2018 (see Table 9.6). However, out of these, 178,603 records are duplicates. These are part of the same contracts since they include the purchase of multiple services. Therefore, we excluded these from the sample under examination. The remaining 6,177,163 contracts show a yearly growth (see Table 9.7): from 240,161 in 2006 to 711,155 in 2018.

Then, of the remaining 6,177,163 records, we removed those where the net contract value was missing or the contract value was 0 euros. The TED database is rather deficient in this regard, as a total of 1,994,015 records were classified as meeting the categories outlined above, thus amounting to 31.4% of records lacking basic data.

In order to homogenize the data sample, we pulled out contracts that were framework agreements, since their basic characteristics, especially the contract value, implementation and so on, differed from those of simple contracts. In total, we found 671,847 framework agreements. Furthermore,

Table 9.6 Number of records in the TED database by year, 2006–2018

Year	*Freq.*	%	*Cum.*
2006	240,410	3.78	3.78
2007	312,987	4.92	8.71
2008	361,168	5.68	14.39
2009	398,527	6.27	20.66
2010	444,009	6.99	27.65
2011	476,733	7.50	35.15
2012	499,032	7.85	43.00
2013	500,221	7.87	50.87
2014	522,344	8.22	59.09
2015	542,597	8.54	67.62
2016	538,181	8.47	76.09
2017	708,840	11.15	87.24
2018	810,717	12.76	100.00
Total	6,355,766	100.00	

Table 9.7 Number of contracts in the TED database by year, 2006–2018

Year	*Freq.*	%	*Cum.*
2006	240,161	3.89	3.89
2007	312,548	5.06	8.95
2008	360,720	5.84	14.79
2009	397,986	6.44	21.23
2010	442,045	7.16	28.39
2011	474,805	7.69	36.07
2012	497,047	8.05	44.12
2013	498,948	8.08	52.20
2014	521,331	8.44	60.64
2015	541,708	8.77	69.41
2016	525,606	8.51	77.91
2017	653,103	10.57	88.49
2018	711,155	11.51	100.00
Total	6,177,163	100.00	

notices published in TED failed to include multiple important data. We examined four of these in detail: (i) number of bidders; (ii) names of issuers; (iii) names of winners; and (iv) estimated value of the contract. If out of these four, at least three were missing, we did not include them in our analysis. In total, 1566 cases matching the above criteria were found. All in all, 3,644,735 records were used in our analysis (see Table 9.8).

Table 9.8 Number and share of contract award notices (records) included in the analysis, 2006–2018, number and percentage

Year	*Notices (records) included in the analysis*	*Notices (records) excluded from the analysis*	*Total*
2007	205,807	107,180	312,987
2008	226,281	134,887	361,168
2009	229,694	168,833	398,527
2010	253,738	190,271	444,009
2011	266,901	209,832	476,733
2012	276,187	222,845	499,032
2013	273,950	226,271	500,221
2014	291,577	230,767	522,344
2015	282,131	260,466	542,597
2016	298,763	239,418	538,181
2017	409,946	298,894	708,840
2018	452,321	358,396	810,717
Total	3,644,735	2,711,031	6,355,766

Threshold Changes in the EU TED Database

From 2015, the number of contracts in the TED database has significantly increased. This stems from Public Procurement Directive 2014/24/EU[3] in 2014, which replaced Directive 2004/18/EC.[4] The new law lowered the threshold above which tenders must be added to the TED database.

For public procurement, EU law sets harmonized rules for tenders whose monetary value exceeds a certain amount and which are presumed to be of cross-border interest. For tenders lower than that given value, national rules apply which must respect general principles of EU law (https://bit.ly/2VViHK4). The changes are the following (see Table 9.9).

[3] Directive 2014/24/EU of the European Parliament and of the Council. Section 2, Article 4. https://eur-lex.europa.eu/legal-content/EN/TXT/HTML/?uri=CELEX:32014L0024&from=EN

[4] Directive 2004/18/EC of the European Parliament and of the Council. Section 1 Article 7. https://eur-lex.europa.eu/legal-content/EN/TXT/HTML/?uri=CELEX:32004L0018&from=EN#d1e2159-114-1

Table 9.9 Threshold changes in the EU TED database, 2004–2014, €

	2004/18/EC	*2014/24/EU*
For public works contracts	6,242,000	5,186,000
For public supply and service contracts awarded by central government authorities (except defence and security)	162,000	134,000
For public supply and service contracts awarded by sub-central contracting authorities	249,000	207,000
Social and specific services	–	750,000

Source: https://eur-lex.europa.eu/legal-content/EN/TXT/HTML/?uri=CELEX:32014L0024&from=EN

https://eur-lex.europa.eu/legal-content/EN/TXT/HTML/?uri=CELEX:32004L0018&from=EN #d1e2159-114-1

For procurements under Directive 2009/81/EC on defence and sensitive security procurement, the applicable thresholds are €5,548,000 for works contracts and €443,000 for supplies and services contracts. https://ec.europa.eu/growth/single-market/public-procurement/rules-implementation/thresholds_en

Table 9.10 EU thresholds for public contracts from 1 January 2018 to 31 December 2019, €

	Works	*Supplies*	*Services*		
			Social and specific services	*Subsidized services*	*All other services*
Central government authorities	5,548,000	144,000	750,000	221,000	144,000
Sub-central contracting authorities	5,548,000	221,000	750,000	221,000	

Source: Commission Delegated Regulation (EU) 2017/2365 of 18 December 2017 amending Directive 2014/24/EU in respect of the application threshold for the procedures for the award of contracts

The European Commission revises the threshold every two years.[5] For example, Table 9.10 shows the new threshold value for 2018–2019 (according to Commission Delegated Regulation (EU) 2017/2365 of 18 December 2017).

[5] Tenderio (2014). Guide to country specific elements on public procurement: Estonia. p. 16. Available at: https://blog.tenderio.com/guide-to-country-specific-elements-on-public-procurement-estonia/

Consequently, the significantly lowered thresholds according to the 2014 law have resulted in far more tenders in the TED database from 2015.

Results of Estimations

Table 9.11 The impact of EU subsidies on level of corruption risks, new accession countries, 2006–2018, odds ratios

Country	*Impact of EU funds odds ratio*	*Sign.*	*Standard error*	*Pseudo R^2*	*N*	*Share of contracts financed by EU, %*
Bulgaria	0.577	0.000	0.018	0.1008	80,448	9.5
Czech Republic	1.724	0.000	0.035	0.1094	76,466	30.2
Estonia	1.129	0.046	0.068	0.1302	12,597	29.0
Hungary	1.042	0.113	0.027	0.0742	59,839	18.7
Latvia	1.970	0.000	0.066	0.1036	53,042	13.0
Lithuania	1.476	0.000	0.039	0.0428	73,494	11.2
Poland	1.623	0.000	0.013	0.0381	1,100,557	9.1
Romania	0.721	0.000	0.022	0.1139	87,380	8.6
Slovenia	1.190	0.000	0.062	0.0940	82,046	2.9
Slovakia	0.728	0.000	0.041	0.1446	15,786	23.9
All new accession countries+	1.358	0.000	0.008	0.0450	1,641,835	10.6

Note: The estimations by countries are controlled by size of contract (ln of net contract value), year, sector and type of issuer

+: the estimation is controlled by size of contract, year, sector, country and type of issuer

Source: Authors' own calculations based on TED data

Table 9.12 Institutional convergence, 2006–2018 (odds ratios are in each column)

	Hungary	*Hungary*	*Slovenia*	*Slovenia*	*Slovakia*	*Slovakia*	*Czech Rep.*	*Czech Rep.*	*Poland*	*Poland*
		EU financed		*EU financed*		*EU financed*		*EU financed*		*EU financed*
2006	0.186***	0.234***	0.320***	0.402***	0.126***	0.131***	0.231***	0.449**	0.183***	0.148***
	(0.014)	(0.033)	(0.038)	(0.116)	(0.014)	(0.028)	(0.020)	(0.149)	(0.009)	(0.012)
2007	0.225***	0.198***	0.354***	0.241***	0.087***	0.117***	0.267***	0.290***	0.110***	0.113***
	(0.016)	(0.031)	(0.029)	(0.065)	(0.008)	(0.037)	(0.018)	(0.073)	(0.005)	(0.010)
2008	0.257***	0.220***	0.242***	0.421***	0.065***	0.113***	0.301***	0.488***	0.105***	0.076***
	(0.015)	(0.028)	(0.018)	(0.116)	(0.005)	(0.028)	(0.018)	(0.096)	(0.004)	(0.006)
2009	0.180***	0.145***	0.302***	0.406***	0.055***	0.059***	0.225***	0.100***	0.142***	0.064***
	(0.009)	(0.012)	(0.021)	(0.076)	(0.005)	(0.011)	(0.011)	(0.008)	(0.005)	(0.003)
2010	0.153***	0.141***	0.280***	0.460***	0.113***	0.098***	0.224***	0.140***	0.135***	0.141***
	(0.008)	(0.010)	(0.020)	(0.090)	(0.009)	(0.013)	(0.011)	(0.009)	(0.004)	(0.006)
2011	0.278***	0.239***	0.236***	0.200***	0.183***	0.150***	0.249***	0.177***	0.148***	0.158***
	(0.014)	(0.019)	(0.016)	(0.042)	(0.014)	(0.018)	(0.012)	(0.011)	(0.004)	(0.007)
2012	0.256***	0.256***	0.245***	0.155***	0.152***	0.156***	0.316***	0.260***	0.171***	0.184***
	(0.013)	(0.022)	(0.015)	(0.025)	(0.010)	(0.021)	(0.013)	(0.014)	(0.005)	(0.007)
2013	0.234***	0.246***	0.282***	0.177***	0.213***	0.237***	0.773***	1.007	0.222***	0.251***
	(0.011)	(0.018)	(0.017)	(0.019)	(0.015)	(0.027)	(0.036)	(0.065)	(0.006)	(0.010)
2014	0.244***	0.259***	0.300***	0.226***	0.345***	0.716***	0.690***	0.776***	0.165***	0.202***
	(0.011)	(0.020)	(0.018)	(0.034)	(0.024)	(0.083)	(0.031)	(0.045)	(0.005)	(0.008)
2015	0.290***	0.247***	0.281***	0.327***	0.449***	1.608***	0.371***	0.317***	0.231***	0.294***
	(0.014)	(0.019)	(0.017)	(0.038)	(0.030)	(0.182)	(0.015)	(0.017)	(0.007)	(0.012)
2016	0.266***	0.467***	0.258***	0.131***	0.543***	1.300	0.294***	0.124***	0.264***	0.428***
	(0.012)	(0.068)	(0.012)	(0.031)	(0.039)	(0.348)	(0.010)	(0.009)	(0.007)	(0.023)

(*continued*)

Table 9.12 (continued)

	Hungary	*Hungary*	*Slovenia*	*Slovenia*	*Slovakia*	*Slovakia*	*Czech Rep.*	*Czech Rep.*	*Poland*	*Poland*
		EU financed		*EU financed*		*EU financed*		*EU financed*		*EU financed*
2017	0.402***	0.674***	0.158***	0.220***	0.923	1.937***	0.336***	0.190***	0.209***	0.310***
	(0.015)	(0.064)	(0.005)	(0.042)	(0.056)	(0.418)	(0.009)	(0.009)	(0.004)	(0.010)
2018	0.441***	1.009	0.157***	0.214***	1.071	5.891***	0.280***	0.175***	0.219***	0.258***
	(0.014)	(0.091)	(0.005)	(0.041)	(0.070)	(1.316)	(0.006)	(0.008)	(0.004)	(0.009)

Note: Results from logit estimations and odds ratios, controlled by ln of net contract value, sector and type of issuer. Standard errors are in parentheses

*$p<0.1$; **$p<0.05$; ***$p<0.01$

Source: Authors' own calculations based on TED data

Table 9.13 Institutional convergence, 2006–2018 (odds ratios are in each column)

	Lithuania	*Lithuania*	*Latvia*	*Latvia*	*Estonia*	*Estonia*	*Bulgaria*	*Bulgaria*	*Romania*	*Romania*
		EU financed		*EU financed*		*EU financed*		*EU financed*		*EU financed*
2006	0.249***	0.293***	0.458***	0.413***	0.347***	0.381***	–	–	–	–
	(0.023)	(0.046)	(0.048)	(0.076)	(0.044)	(0.125)	–	–	–	–
2007	0.247***	0.118***	0.275***	0.191***	0.310***	0.321**	0.735***	0.528*	0.273***	0.344***
	(0.018)	(0.014)	(0.021)	(0.031)	(0.035)	(0.153)	(0.081)	(0.178)	(0.018)	(0.071)
2008	0.242***	0.135***	0.413***	0.241***	0.239***	0.503**	0.457***	0.454***	0.185***	0.308***
	(0.016)	(0.017)	(0.029)	(0.038)	(0.022)	(0.153)	(0.034)	(0.083)	(0.008)	(0.037)
2009	0.376***	0.298***	0.384***	0.145***	0.216***	0.401***	0.311***	0.293***	0.185***	0.462***
	(0.025)	(0.036)	(0.027)	(0.018)	(0.021)	(0.091)	(0.021)	(0.045)	(0.009)	(0.054)
2010	0.328***	0.354***	0.166***	0.056***	0.106***	0.282***	0.486***	1.096	0.177***	0.372***
	(0.021)	(0.033)	(0.010)	(0.005)	(0.008)	(0.039)	(0.038)	(0.223)	(0.009)	(0.035)
2011	0.344***	0.292***	0.275***	0.214***	0.424***	0.356***	0.313***	1.062	0.173***	0.240***
	(0.020)	(0.023)	(0.016)	(0.020)	(0.036)	(0.038)	(0.020)	(0.211)	(0.008)	(0.019)
2012	0.395***	0.352***	0.425***	0.355***	0.529***	0.551***	0.398***	0.628***	0.216***	0.346***
	(0.021)	(0.027)	0.024	(0.032)	(0.041)	(0.056)	(0.022)	(0.065)	(0.011)	(0.033)
2013	0.334***	0.294***	0.382***	0.413***	0.866	0.747*	0.354***	0.641***	0.220***	0.643***
	(0.018)	(0.021)	0.022	(0.044)	(0.097)	(0.122)	(0.018)	(0.056)	(0.011)	(0.069)
2014	0.385***	0.404***	0.359***	0.671***	0.762***	0.524***	0.333***	0.566***	0.242***	0.442***
	(0.021)	(0.033)	(0.020)	(0.069)	(0.070)	(0.079)	(0.016)	(0.049)	(0.012)	(0.040)
2015	0.485***	0.503***	0.501***	0.610***	0.960	0.662***	0.294***	0.651***	0.285***	0.398***
	(0.027)	(0.045)	(0.027)	(0.060)	(0.083)	(0.084)	(0.014)	(0.064)	(0.014)	(0.028)
2016	0.673***	0.675***	0.365***	0.289***	1.040	1.628**	0.297***	0.269***	0.237***	0.322***
	(0.035)	(0.095)	(0.019)	(0.046)	(0.095)	(0.351)	(0.011)	(0.027)	(0.011)	(0.041)
2017	0.913**	0.471***	0.580***	0.0376***	0.855**	1.354**	0.339***	0.398***	0.251***	0.675***
	(0.040)	(0.047)	(0.026)	(0.047)	(0.061)	(0.189)	(0.011)	(0.253)	(0.010)	(0.080)
2018	0.741***	1.244	0.436***	0.315***	0.681***	0.498***	0.347***	0.752***	0.314***	0.678***
	(0.029)	(0.200)	(0.017)	(0.037)	(0.048)	(0.087)	(0.010)	(0.698)	(0.009)	(0.078)

Note: Results from logit estimations and odds ratios, controlled by ln of net contract value, sector and type of issuer. Standard errors are in parentheses
$^{*}p<0.1$; $^{**}p<0.05$; $^{***}p<0.01$
Source: Authors' own calculations based on TED data

Table 9.14 Institutional convergence, 2006–2018 (odds ratios are in each column)

	Greece	*Italy*	*Portugal*	*Spain*
2006	0.459***	0.499***	+	0.961
	(0.051)	(0.034)	+	(0.077)
2007	0.535***	0.461***	1.272	0.743***
	(0.045)	(0.024)	(0.228)	(0.045)
2008	0.481***	0.382***	1.204	0.948
	(0.034)	(0.017)	(0.183)	(0.048)
2009	0.618***	0.376***	0.618***	0.770***
	(0.042)	(0.015)	0.067	(0.033)
2010	0.346***	0.347***	0.900	0.769***
	(0.023)	(0.014)	(0.093)	(0.033)
2011	0.474***	0.348***	1.012	0.625***
	(0.037)	(0.014)	(0.099)	(0.027)
2012	0.249***	0.365***	0.628***	0.624***
	(0.015)	(0.015)	(0.064)	(0.027)
2013	0.275***	0.359***	0.414***	0.621***
	(0.015)	(0.014)	(0.036)	(0.027)
2014	0.257***	0.343***	0.556***	0.685***
	(0.014)	(0.013)	(0.053)	(0.028)
2015	0.371***	0.425***	0.514***	0.663***
	(0.022)	(0.016)	(0.046)	(0.025)
2016	0.359***	0.424***	0.748***	0.654***
	(0.024)	(0.014)	(0.065)	(0.021)
2017	0.413***	0.420***	0.730***	0.704***
	(0.023)	(0.012)	(0.045)	(0.018)
2018	0.393***	0.438***	0.835***	0.724***
	(0.017)	(0.011)	(0.038)	(0.016)

Note: Results from logit estimations and odds ratios, controlled by ln of net contract value, sector and type of issuer. Standard errors are in parentheses

p*< 0.1;*p*< 0.05; ****p*< 0.01

+: Due to the small number of cases, we omitted the year 2006. In this year, TED had a total of 645 contracts from Portugal, of which 29 had only one bidder

Source: Authors' own calculations based on TED data

Two Issues in EU Country Reports: Corruption and Public Procurement

The Appearance of the Word "Corruption" in the European Commission Country Reports, 2006–2018

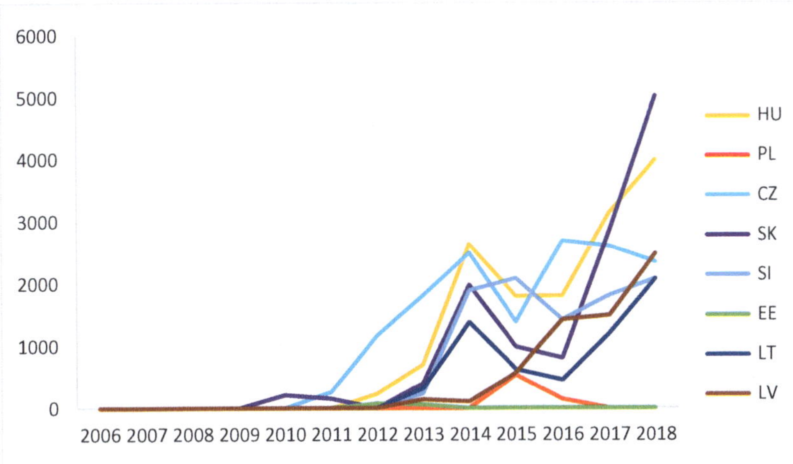

Fig. 9.14 Number of characters in sentences that contain the word "corruption" in the Country Reports (from 2006 to 2010 the ERAWATCH Country Reports and from 2011 to 2018 the European Semester Country Reports) of the European Commission for the eight new accession countries, 2006–2018. (Source: Authors' own calculations. Note: N = 104)

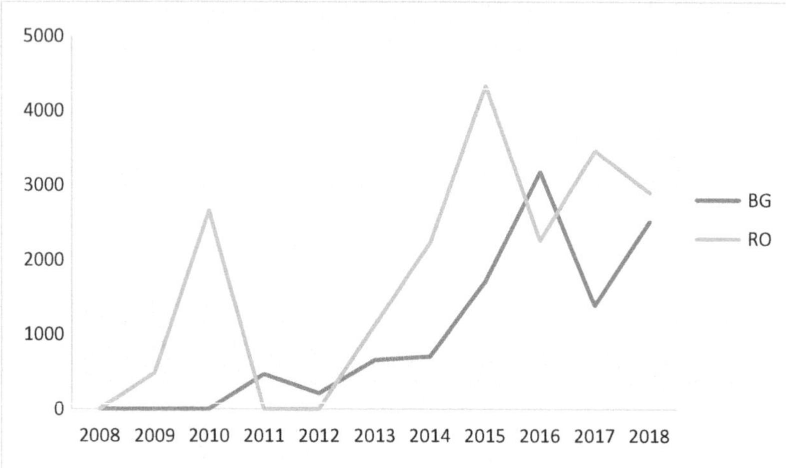

Fig. 9.15 Number of characters in sentences that contain the word "corruption" in the Romania and Bulgaria Country Reports (from 2006 to 2010 the ERAWATCH Country Reports and from 2011 to 2018 the European Semester Country Reports) of the European Commission, 2008–2018. (Source: Authors' own calculations. Note: N = 22)

The Appearance of the Phrase "Public Procurement" in the EU Country Reports, 2006–2018

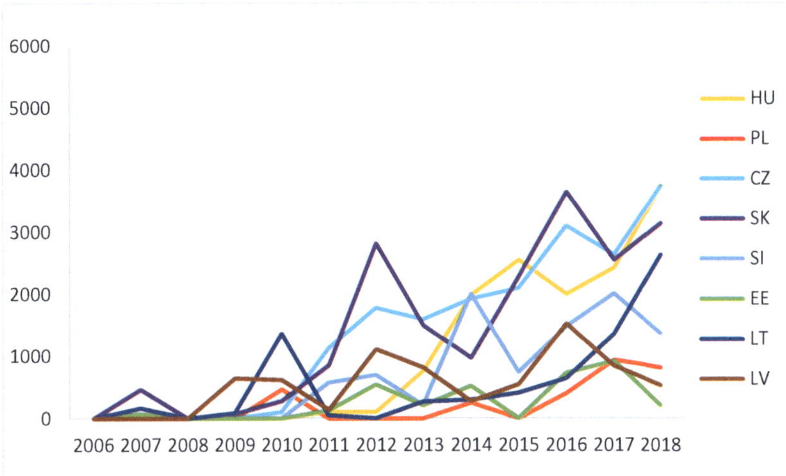

Fig. 9.16 Number of characters in sentences that contain the phrase "public procurement" in the Country Reports (from 2006 to 2010 the ERAWATCH Country Reports and from 2011 to 2018 the European Semester Country Reports) of the European Commission for the eight new accession countries, 2006–2018. (Source: Authors' own calculations. Note: N = 104)

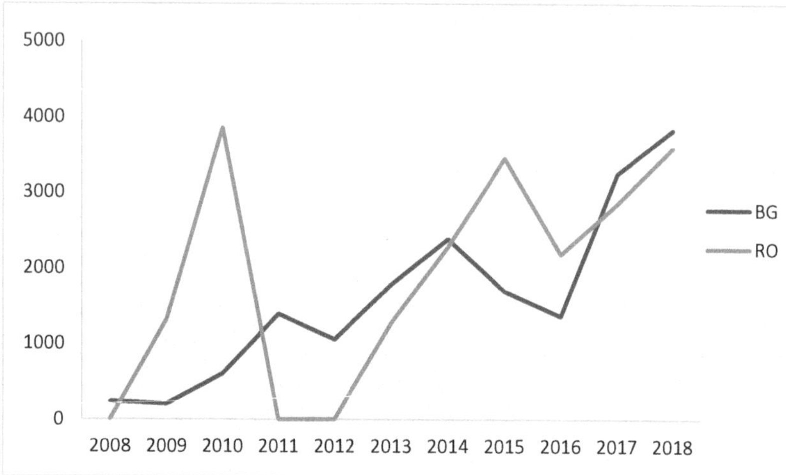

Fig. 9.17 Number of characters in sentences that contain the phrase "public procurement" in the Romania and Bulgaria Country Reports (from 2008 to 2010 the ERAWATCH Country Reports and from 2011 to 2018 the European Semester Country Reports) of the European Commission, 2008–2018. (Source: Authors' own calculations. Note: N = 22)

References

Alesina, A., & Dollar, D. (2000). Who Gives Foreign Aid to Whom and Why? *Journal of Economic Growth, 5*(1), 1381–4338. https://www.jstor.org/stable/40216022

Alesina, A., & Weder, B. (2002). Do Corrupt Governments Receive Less Foreign Aid? *American Economic Review, 92*(4, September), 1126–1137.

Alesina, A., Tabellini, G., & Trebbi, F. (2017). Is Europe an Optimal Political Area? *Brookings Papers on Economic Activity*, (Spring), 169–213.

Ali, M., Khan, L., Sohail, A., & Puah, C. (2019). The Relationship Between Foreign Aid and Corruption: A Case of Selected Asian Countries. *Journal of Financial Crime, 26*(3), 692–704. https://doi.org/10.1108/JFC-08-2018-0089.

Bauer, P. T. (1981). *Equality, the Third World, and Economic Delusion*. Cambridge, MA: Harvard University Press.

Becker, G. S., & Stigler, G. J. (1974). Law Enforcement, Malfeasance, and Compensation of Enforcers. *The Journal of Legal Studies, 3*(1), 1–18.

Brollo, F., Nannicini, T., Perotti, R., & Tabellini, G. (2013). The Political Resource Curse. *American Economic Review, 103*(5), 1759–1796.

Broms, R., Dahlström, C., & Fazekas, M. (2017). *Procurement and Competition in Swedish Municipalities. Gothenburg.* Retrieved March 5, 2019, from https://bit.ly/2DSCkbK

Burguet, R., Ganuza, J.-J., & Montalvo, J. G. (2016). *The Microeconomics of Corruption: A Review of Thirty Years of Research* (Barcelona GSE Working Paper Series, Working Paper No. 908). Barcelona: Graduate School of Economics. Retrieved March 5, 2019, from https://bit.ly/2JCF3bj

Charron, N. (2011). Exploring the Impact of Foreign Aid on Corruption: Has the 'Anti-Corruption Movement' Been Effective? *The Developing Economies, 49*, 66–88. https://doi.org/10.1111/j.1746-1049.2010.00122.x.

Charron, N., Dahlström, C., Fazekas, M., & Lapuente, V. (2016). Careers, Connections, and Corruption Risks: Investigating the Impact of Bureaucratic Meritocracy on Public Procurement Processes. *The Journal of Politics, 79*(1), 89–104.

Coviello, D., & Gagliarducci, S. (2010). *Building Political Collusion: Evidence from Procurement Auctions* (IZA Discussion Papers No. 4939). Bonn: IZA. Retrieved March 6, 2019, from http://ftp.iza.org/dp4939.pdf

de la Croix, D., & Delavallade, C. (2014). Why Corrupt Governments May Receive More Foreign Aid. *Oxford Economic Papers, 66*(1), 51–66. https://doi.org/10.1093/oep/gpt004.

EBRD. (2017). *Transition Report 2017–18.* London: European Bank for Reconstruction and Development. Retrieved March 6, 2019, from https://bit.ly/2vawssJ

Fazekas, M. (2017). *Assessing the Quality of Government at the Regional Level Using Public Procurement Data.* Brussels. Retrieved March 5, 2019, from https://bit.ly/2VPCJpx

Fazekas, M., & Tóth, I. J. (2016). From Corruption to State Capture: A New Analytical Framework with Empirical Applications from Hungary. *Political Research Quarterly, 9*(2), 320–334. https://doi.org/10.1177/1065912916639137.

Fazekas, M., & Tóth, I. J. (2017). Corruption in EU Funds? Europe-wide evidence of the corruption effect of EU-funded public contracting. In J. Bachler, P. Berkowitz, S. Hardy, & T. Muravska (Eds.), *EU Cohesion Policy. Reassessing Performance and Direction* (pp. 186–205). London/New York: Routledge. https://www.taylorfrancis.com/books/e/9781315401867

Fazekas, M., Tóth, I. J., & King, L. P. (2014). *Anatomy of Grand Corruption: A Composite Corruption Risk Index Based on Objective Data.* Budapest. Retrieved March 5, 2019, from http://econ.core.hu/file/download/mtdp/MTDP1403.pdf

Fazekas, M., Tóth, I. J., & King, L. P. (2016). An Objective Corruption Risk Index Using Public Procurement Data. *European Journal on Criminal Policy and Research, 22*(3), 369–397. Retrieved March 5, 2019, from https://doi.org/10.1007/s10610-016-9308-z.

Goldsmith, A. A. (2001). Foreign Aid and Statehood in Africa. *International Organisation, 55*(1), 123–148. https://www.jstor.org/stable/3078599

Guiso, L., Herrera, H., & Morelli, M. (2016). Cultural Differences and Institutional Integration. *Journal of International Economics*, (99), 97–113. https://doi.org/10.1016/j.jinteco.2015.11.005.

Heckelman, J. C. (2015). Economic Freedom Convergence Clubs. In R. J. Cebula, J. Hall, F. G. Mixon Jr., & J. E. Payne (Eds.), *Economic Behavior, Economic Freedom, and Entrepreneurship* (pp. 102–114). Cheltenham: Edward Elgar Publishing. https://bit.ly/2GeX6D0

Heggstad, K., Frøystad, M., & Isaksen, J. 2010. *The Basics of Integrity in Procurement: A Guidebook*. Bergen: Chr. Michelsen Institute. Retrieved March 5, 2019, from http://bit.ly/2n1shZp

Heywood, P. M., & Rose, J. (2013). Close But No Cigar: The Measurement of Corruption. *Journal of Public Policy, 34*(3), 507–529.

Holden, S. (2013). *Avoiding the Resource Curse: The Case of Norway*. Oslo: University of Oslo, Department of Economics. Retrieved March 5, 2019, from https://bit.ly/2rs7MtU

Huemer, S., Scheubel, B., & Walch, F. (2014). *Measuring Institutional Competitiveness in Europe* (Working Paper Series, No. 1556). Frankfurt am Main: European Central Bank. Retrieved March 6, 2019, from https://www.ecb.europa.eu/pub/pdf/scpwps/ecbwp1556.pdf

Iancu, Aurel. (2009). *Institutional Convergence*. Bucharest: INCE – CIDE. Retrieved March 5, 2019, from http://www.workingpapers.ro/2009/wpince090101.pdf

Jurlin, K., & Cuckovic, N. (2010). Comparative Analysis of the Quality of European Institutions 2003–2009: Convergence or Divergence? *Financial Theory and Practice, 34*(1), 71–98.

Knack, S. (2001). Aid Dependence and the Quality of Governance: Cross-Country Empirical Tests. *Southern Economic Journal, 68*(2), 310–329. https://doi.org/10.2307/1061596. https://www.jstor.org/stable/1061596.

Knack, S. (2004). Does Foreign Aid Promote Democracy? *International Studies Quarterly, 48*(2), 251–266. https://www.jstor.org/stable/3693571

Lambsdorff, J. G. (2007). *The Institutional Economics of Corruption and Reform: Theory, Evidence and Policy*. Cambridge: Cambridge University Press.

Masuch, K., Moshammer, E., & Pierluigi, B. (2016). *Institutions, Public Debt and Growth in Europe* (ECB Working Paper Series, No. 1963). Frankfurt am Main: European Central Bank. Retrieved March 6, 2019, from https://bit.ly/2NMBNNe

Masuch, K., Anderton, B., Setzer, R., & Benalal, N. (2018). *Structural Policies in the Euro Area* (Occasional Paper Series, No. 210). Frankfurt am Main:

European Central Bank. Retrieved March 6, 2019, from http://www.ecb.europa.eu/pub/pdf/scpops/ecb.op210.en.pdf

Miller, S. J. (Ed.). (2015). *Benford's Law: Theory and Applications.* Princeton: Princeton University Press. https://www.jstor.org/stable/j.ctt1dr358t

Nigrini M. J. (2012). *Benford's Law Applications for Forensic Accounting. Auditing and Fraud Detection.* Hoboken: Wiley. https://bit.ly/38sZCBL

Okada, K., & Samreth, S. (2012). The Effect of Foreign Aid on Corruption: A Quantile Regression Approach. *Economics Letters, 115*(2), 240–243. https://doi.org/10.1016/j.econlet.2011.12.051.

Pertold, F., & Palguta, J. (2017). Manipulation of Procurement Contracts: Evidence from the Introduction of Discretionary Thresholds. *American Economic Journal: Economic Policy, 9*(2), 1–44. https://doi.org/10.1257/pol.20150511.

Rose-Ackerman, S. (1978). *Corruption: A Study in Political Economy.* New York: Academic Press.

Rose-Ackerman, S. (2001a). Trust, Honesty, and Corruption: Reflection on the State-Building Process. *European Journal of Sociology*, (42), 27–71. Retrieved March 5, 2019, from http://www.ssrn.com/abstract=283429

Rose-Ackerman, S. (2001b). Trust and Honesty in Post-Socialist Societies. *Kyklos, 54*(2/3), 415–444. https://doi.org/10.1111/1467-6435.00161.

Savoia, A., & Sen, K. (2016). Do We See Convergence in Institutions? A Cross-Country Analysis. *Journal of Development Studies, 52*(2), 166–185. https://doi.org/10.1080/00220388.2015.1060315.

Schönfelder, N., & Wagner, H. (2019). Institutional Convergence in Europe. *Economics: The Open-Access, Open-Assessment E-Journal, 13*(3), 1–23. https://doi.org/10.5018/economics-ejournal.ja.2019-3.

Sik, E. (2002). The Bad, The Worst and the Worst. In S. Kotkin & A. Sajo (Eds.), *Political Corruption in Transition* (pp. 91–114). New York: Central European University Press.

Spann, D. D. (2013). *Fraud Analytics: Strategies and Methods for Detection and Prevention.* Hoboken: Wiley.

Svensson, J. (2000). Foreign Aid and Rent-Seeking. *Journal of International Economics, 51*(2), 437–461. https://doi.org/10.1016/S0022-1996(99)00014-8.

Szűcs, F. (2017). *Discretion and Corruption in Public Procurement.* Job Market Paper. University of California at Berkeley. Retrieved March 5, 2019, from https://bit.ly/2KTvmFB

Tavares, J. (2003). Does Foreign Aid Corrupt? *Economics Letters, 79,* 99–106. https://doi.org/10.1016/S0165-1765(02)00293-8.

The World Bank. (2017). *World Development Report – 2017.* Governance and Law. Washington, DC: The World Bank. https://www.worldbank.org/en/publication/wdr2017

Thompson, T., & Shah, A. (2005). *Transparency International's Corruption Perceptions Index: Whose Perceptions Are They Anyway?* Mimeo. The World Bank. Retrieved October 22, 2019 from https://bit.ly/34kNCk4

Tóth, I. J., & Hajdu, M. (2016). *Korrupciós Kockázatok, Átláthatóság, Közbeszerzések – Magyar Közbeszerzések 2009–2015 közötti adatainak elemzése* [Corruption Risks, Transparency, Public Procurement – Analysis of Hungarian Public Procurement Data 2009–2015]. In T. Kolosi, & I. G. Tóth (Eds.), *Társadalmi Riport 2016* (pp. 33–53). Budapest: TÁRKI. Retrieved March 5, 2019, from https://bit.ly/2dA9XlI

Tóth, I. J., & Hajdu, M. (2017a). *Intensity of Competition, Corruption Risks and Price Distortion in Hungarian Public Procurement – 2009–2016* (Working Paper Series: CRCB-WP/2017:2). Budapest: CRCB. Retrieved March 5, 2019, from https://bit.ly/2prJVsW

Tóth, I. J., & Hajdu, M. (2017b). *Versenyerősség, társadalmi veszteségek és a 25 millió forintos értékhatár rejtélye 2009–2016 közötti magyar közbeszerzések statisztikai vizsgálata* [Intensity of Competition, Social Loss and the Enigma of the €25 Million Threshold: Statistical Analysis of Hungarian Public Procurement from 2009 to 2016]. Budapest. Retrieved March 5, 2019, from https://bit.ly/2wWe6Me

United Nations. (2016). *African Governance Report IV.* Addis Ababa: United Nations Economic Commission for Africa. Retrieved March 5, 2019, from https://bit.ly/33hFgs5

Wallace, C. D., & Haerpfer, C. W. (1999). *Corruption and Economic Development in Post-Communist Central and Eastern Europe* (IHS Working Paper).

CHAPTER 10

Climate Change and EU Membership: The Journey of Central and Eastern Europe Towards a Carbon-Free World

István P. Székely

10.1 Introduction

Soviet-type central planning and economic isolation of the Soviet-bloc from the rest of the world is part of the shared history of Central Eastern and South Eastern Europe. Besides a strong negative impact on growth potential and human capital (Székely and Kuenzel 2020), central planning

Currently, EU Fellow at the University of Colorado, Boulder, CEUCE. Principal Advisor, European Commission, DG ECFIN and Honorary Professor, Corvinus University of Budapest. Views expressed here are those of the authors and do not necessarily represent the views of any of the institutions the author is associated with.

I. P. Székely (✉)
DG ECFIN, European Commission, Brussels, Belgium

Corvinus University of Budapest, Budapest, Hungary
e-mail: istvan-pal.szekely@ec.europa.eu

M. Landesmann, I. P. Székely (eds.), *Does EU Membership Facilitate Convergence? The Experience of the EU's Eastern Enlargement - Volume II*, Studies in Economic Transition,
https://doi.org/10.1007/978-3-030-57702-5_10

also had a devastating impact on environment and made these economies among the most energy intensive and polluting ones on earth (Carter and Turnock 2001, Chandler 2018, Ürge-Vorsatz et al. 2006). This was due to the inordinate share of heavy (and military) industry and the use of highly energy intensive and environmentally unfriendly technologies. In fact, the impact of economic activities on the environment and on human health was among the most neglected aspects of economic and social development under Soviet-type central planning.

Thus, a rather unexpected and unintended positive side effect of the collapse of this system and economic transition was a sudden downward shock to CO_2 emission at the global level.[1] In fact, the collapse of the Soviet-bloc had an as long and almost as strong dampening effect on the global trend of CO_2 emission than the second oil shock in the late 1970s (Fig. 10.1). It is ironic though that this "positive" effect lasted only shortly as another centrally controlled (albeit much more reliant on global trade and market mechanisms) economy, China, sparked a so far most forceful new spur in CO_2 emission, taking away all the gains from economic transition in Central-Eastern and South-Eastern Europe (CESE).

With the EU now putting the fight against climate change in the forefront, and with the 15th anniversary of the start of the eastern enlargement of the EU, it is perhaps fitting to look into how this region did on reducing the CO_2 intensity of its economy. With part of the region joining the EU, another part aspiring to do so and the rest of the region staying outside the EU for long (if not for ever), it is also interesting to see whether (the aspiration for) EU membership had any traceable impact on developments in this regard.

10.2 The Journey

Soviet-type central planning in the past put the CESE countries on a high carbon emission path similar to that of high-income countries. As the Soviet-type central planning system made these economies rather isolated from the world economy, the adjustment that started in the world economy after the first oil shock in 1973–74 was delayed and only started after the second oil shock in the late 1970s (Fig. 10.2). Thus, CESE countries, including those that later joined the EU (EU11), entered economic

[1] For an analysis of the impact of transition in the countries that formerly were Soviet Republics from a de-modernization perspective, see York (2008). He also analyses the impact of the size of the army on CO_2 emission, albeit not that of military industry.

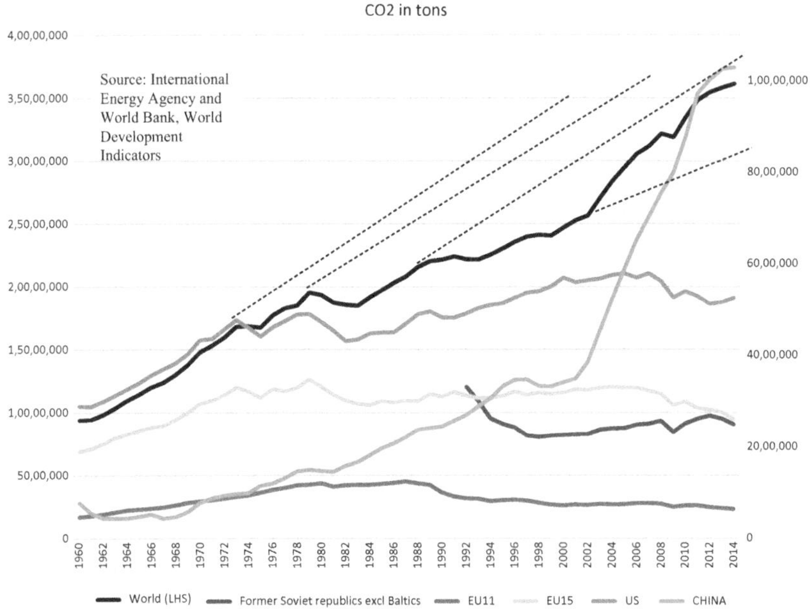

Fig. 10.1 CO_2 emission in the world, 1960–2014. (Sources: International Energy Agency and World Bank. Note: Former Soviet Republics are the countries that were formed after the collapse of the USSR, excluding the three Baltic countries that are in the EU11 group)

transformation with very high levels of CO_2 emissions, much higher than their overall development at that point in time would have suggested.

High carbon emission was driven by the high energy intensity of the economy (Fig. 10.3, Chandler 2018). In this regard, EU11 countries followed the same trend as the EU until the beginning of economic transition in the late 1980s.[2]

The energy mix was more carbon intensive in EU11 than in the EU, but the two groups followed very similar declining trends regarding the CO_2 intensity of energy use (Fig. 10.4). This set apart EU11 countries

[2] When we talk about EU and EU11 countries regarding a period in the past, we mean the countries that today are members of the EU, or the countries that joined the EU since 2004 from the region. Comparable GDP data (PPP) are only available since 1990, so we use per capita numbers to describe trends prior to economic transition, as they are available for a longer period starting in 1960.

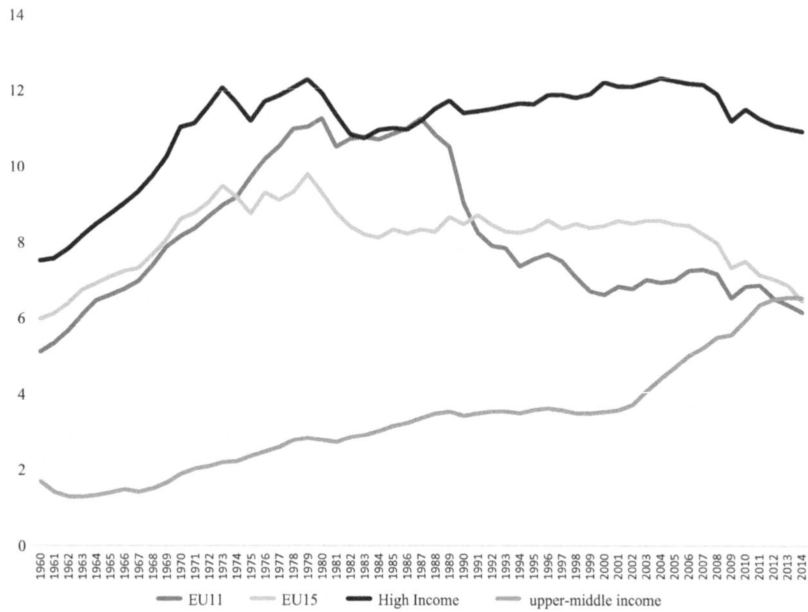

Fig. 10.2 Per capita carbon emission 1960–2014. (Sources: International Energy Agency and World Bank)

from upper-middle-income countries in other parts of the world, as those countries continuously increased their reliance on high carbon energy sources (mostly coal).

Transition leads to a rapid shrinking of the highly energy-intensive heavy industry in the CESE region, which resulted in a large and immediate decline in CO_2 emission (Fig. 10.1, Chandler 2018). This trend was driven by declining energy intensity of the economy (Fig. 10.5), as the energy mix changed only gradually. Connectivity of the energy systems of EU11 countries to Western Europe was very poor at the beginning of economic transition, and generation capacities did not allow any fast reorientation towards less carbon-intensive energy sources either.

The journey of EU11 countries towards a modern market economy, after accession as EU members, was characterized by a rapid decline in the energy and CO_2 intensity of their economies. By 2014, they have become as energy efficient as high-income countries on average, and rapidly approached the EU average, which is one of the lowest among

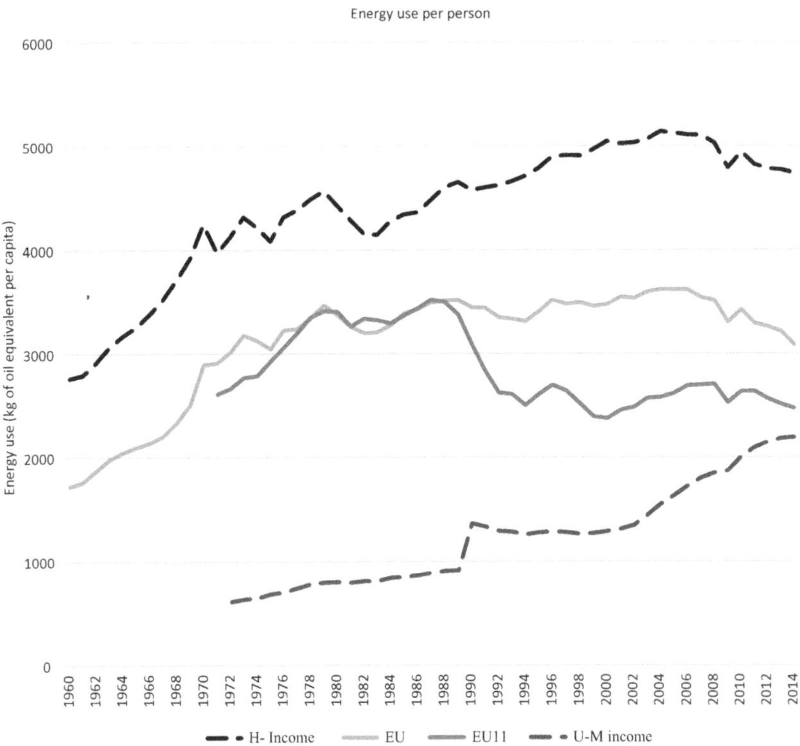

Fig. 10.3 Per capita energy use 1960–2014. (Sources: International Energy Agency and World Bank)

high-income countries. As their energy mix also adjusted at a pace similar to that of the EU, they rapidly approached the carbon-intensity levels of high-income countries. This has been a unique trend in the world, not followed by other upper-middle-income converging economies (Fig. 10.6). In fact, the trend in the carbon intensity of the latter group flattened out since the turn of the century, because they increased their reliance on high-carbon energy sources (mostly coal, Fig. 10.4).

The uniqueness of this journey in the global context becomes even more apparent if we show it along the carbon Kuznets curves (Fig. 10.7). The first part of the journey, until 1995 (from the first red dot to the second one in the figure), was clearly driven by the collapse of the previous

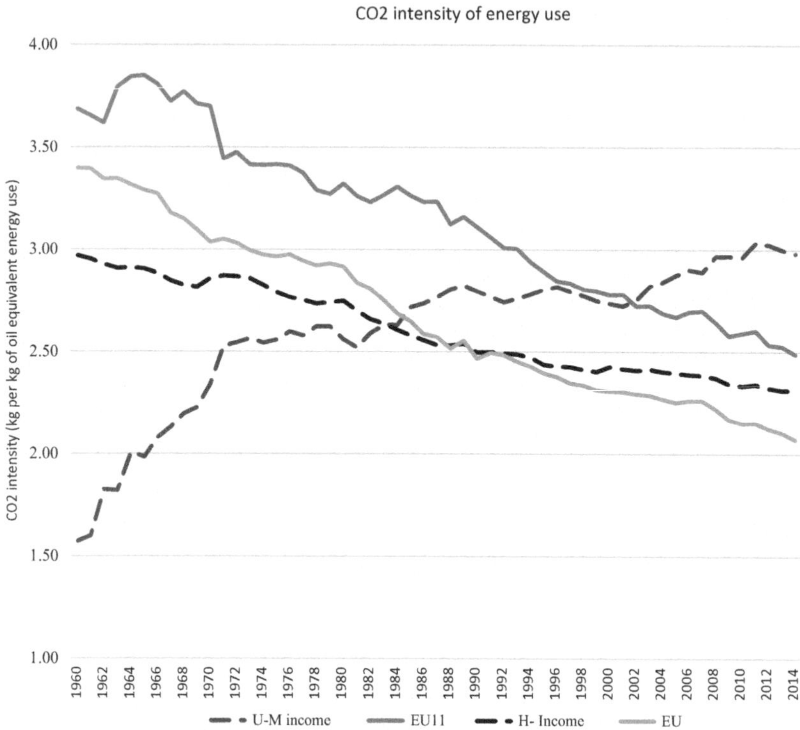

Fig. 10.4 CO_2 intensity of energy use 1960–2014. (Sources: International Energy Agency and World Bank)

economic system (as the curve also moves to the left). However, from there on, it was driven by a rapid restructuring and the re-industrialization of the economy. From the turn of the century, the decline in carbon intensity is less dramatic but still very rapid, faster than in any other group.

The prospect of EU membership and later the membership itself was a major force behind this development. It promoted a rapid increase in FDI, which not only boosted trade but also brought in modern technology. Thus, FDI allowed EU11 countries to reindustrialize their economies rapidly while keeping it on a fast declining trend of carbon intensity. EU environmental legislation and standards also had major impact, but this kicked in later, after joining the EU. In the first phase, the investment

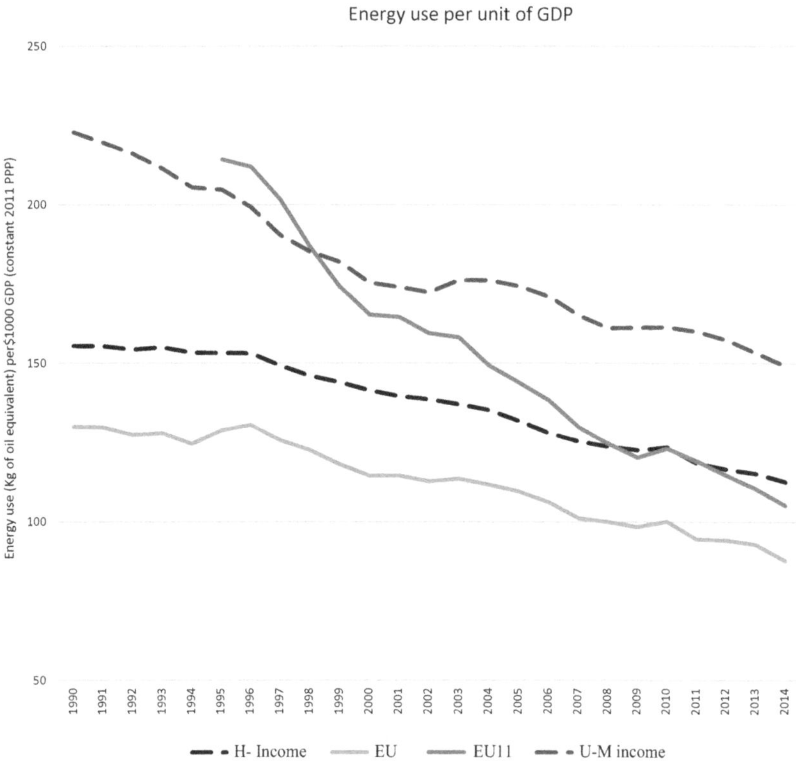

Fig. 10.5 Energy intensity of the economy: energy use per unit of GDP, 1990–2014. (Sources: International Energy Agency and World Bank)

channel (Székely and Kuenzel 2020) and the private sector (FDI) probably played a much more important role.

While the prospect and later the reality of EU membership were undoubtedly a major force behind the gradual decarbonization of EU11 economies through several channels, the globally unique trend observed in EU11 was unique more to Europe than exclusively to EU11. Similar trends were observable in Southern-Eastern Europe (Balkans) and in the former Soviet Republics (Fig. 10.8).

Part of the similarity stems from a shared initial position, the extreme high energy intensity and high carbon intensity of energy production in a centrally planned economy, which also characterized most parts of the

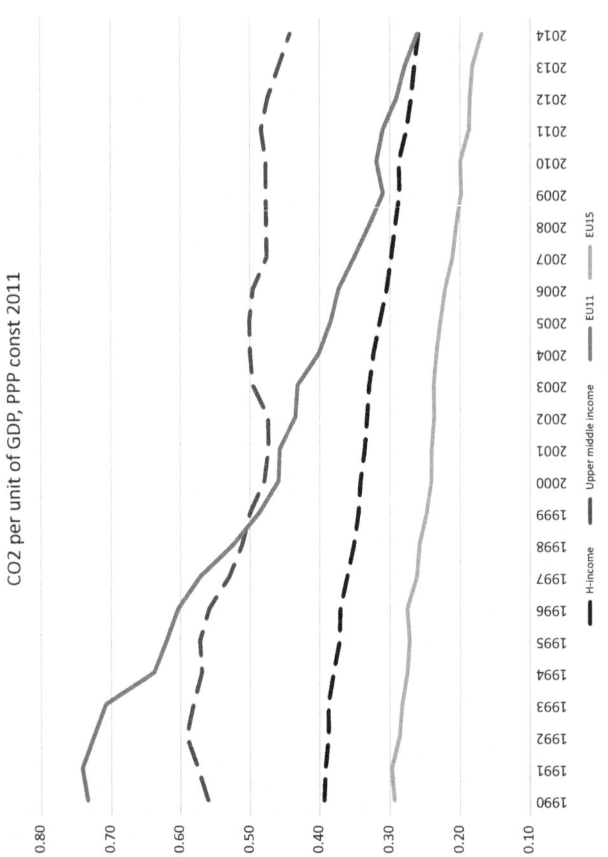

Fig. 10.6 Carbon intensity of the economy: CO_2 emission per unit of GDP, 1990–2014. (Sources: International Energy Agency and World Bank)

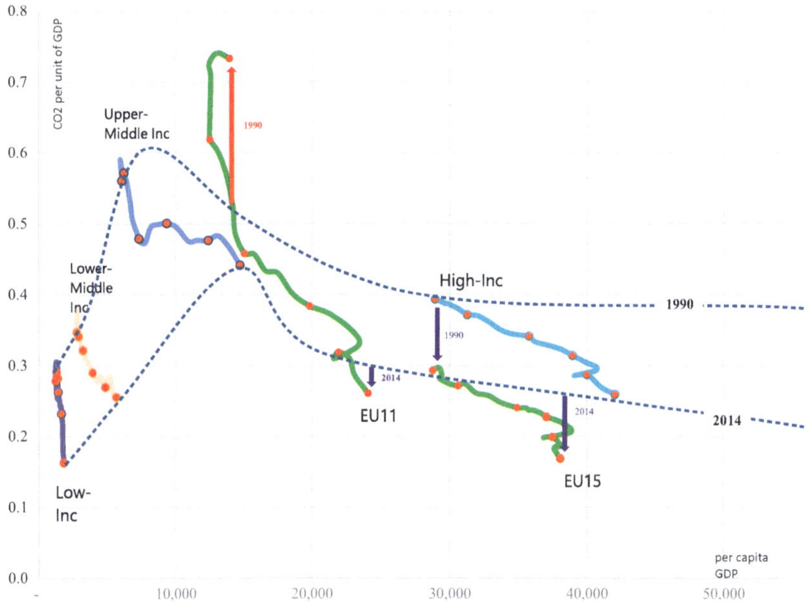

Fig. 10.7 Carbon emission Kuznets curves 1990–2014. (Sources: International Energy Agency and World Bank. Note: This a scatter plot of CO_2 emission per unit of GDP (in constant 2011 PPP, vertical) and per capita GDP (in constant 2011 PPP, horizontal))

former Yugoslavia. Another important common driving force was FDI, or the investment channel, which apparently also worked for EU candidate countries, bringing in modern technology (Székely and Kuenzel 2020).

Despite apparent similarities of the carbon-intensity path of the countries that were former Soviet Republics to that of EU11, Jorgenson et al. (2012) conclude that this path during the period 1992–2005 was unsustainable. The conclusion is based on an econometric analysis which suggests that the (negative) coefficient of per capita GDP in an equation for CO_2 intensity of GDP is time variant; it is increasing over time (becoming less negative). The reform and development paths of these countries were very different from those of EU11, with important implications for factors that directly influence energy and carbon intensity (Ürge-Vorsatz et al. 2006). Moreover, these countries did not have the perspective of EU membership in that period and were not engaged in adopting EU

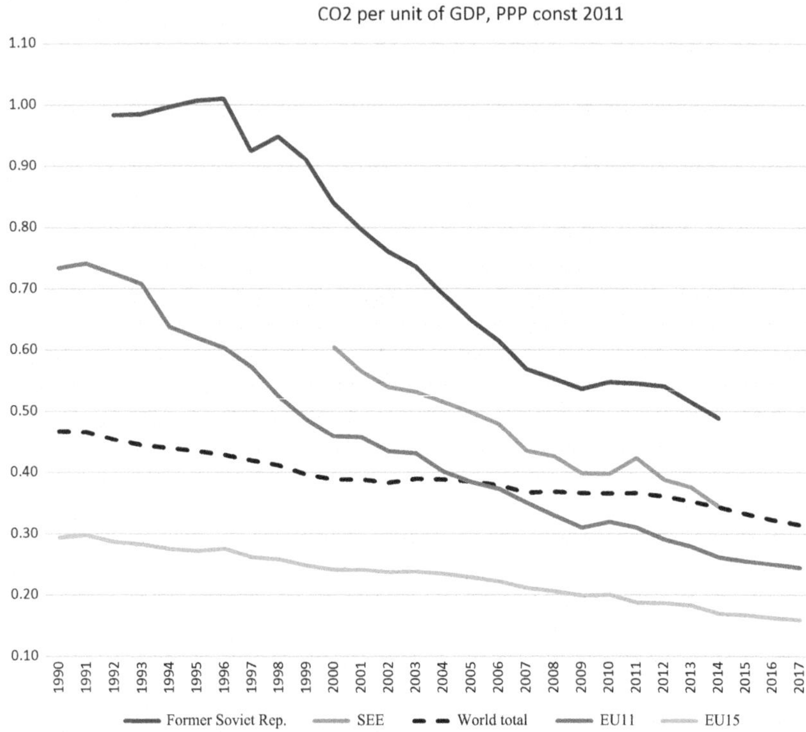

Fig. 10.8 Carbon intensity of European economies, 1990–2017. (Sources: International Energy Agency and World Bank. Note: Former Soviet Republics are the countries that were formed after the collapse of the USSR, excluding the three Baltic countries that are in EU11. The series for world total is extended to 2015–17 by using data published by Global Carbon Project. The series for EU11 and EU15 are extended by using Eurostat data. In both cases, these are approximations as methodologies applied and historical data from these sources are somewhat different)

standards and norms, as were EU11 countries. On the other hand, their trade openness did not increase rapidly and they did not get a major inflow of FDI, as did EU11 countries. This may perhaps be the reason why Jorgenson et al. (2012) did not find these factors significant in explaining changes in CO_2 intensity. Nevertheless, the apparent differences among the first phase, which was dominated by the collapse of the old system, and the second one, which was characterized by a more gradual decline in CO_2 intensity, call for a different model specification. Perhaps, some sort of regime-switch model might have produced more reliable estimates for the post-collapse period.

What is perhaps most special about EU11 is that the rapid re-industrialization and increase in export openness of these economies did not break the former trend. Improving connectivity of their energy systems, modernization of power generation, transportation and insulation of buildings, all heavily financed by EU funds, EU financial support to the phasing out of coal and gradual compliance with EU environmental standards all contributed in this regard.

Regarding energy generation, Jorgenson et al. (2017) shed some light on the role of the EU in bringing about this rather unique path of convergence. They analysed CO_2 emission levels for 1360 fossil-fuel power plants in the 25 post-Soviet transition nations in CESE and Eurasia in 2009. Using multilevel regression modelling and controlling for plant size, age, heat rate, capacity utilization rate and coal as the primary fuel source, factors that were positively associated with plant-level emissions, they found that plant-level emissions were lower, on average, in the transition nations that joined the European Union (EU). Moreover, the associations between plant-level emissions and EU accession were stronger for the countries that joined the EU in 2004 relative to those that joined in 2007.

Their findings also suggest that export-oriented development was positively associated with plant-level CO_2 emissions in CESE. Vlčková et al. (2015) offer a detailed analysis of how trade reorientation, changes in product stricture (and thus production structures) and expansion of trade impacted CO_2 emission on the production side. Besides the factor endowments of EU11 countries, particularly skills, FDI played an important role in bringing about a relatively low carbon intensity structure, and thus limiting the negative impact from increased exports and manufacturing production. Their analysis is confined to the Visegrad 4 countries (Czech Republic, Hungary, Poland and Slovakia), but offers a broader insight into the overall development in EU11 in this regard.

Regarding the overall impact of rapid economic convergence, the CO_2 emission-moderating impact of EU membership was strong enough to counterbalance this negative impact stemming from increased trade openness EU membership brought about (Székely and Kuenzel 2020) and to keep EU11 countries on a declining trend of CO_2 intensity. Put differently, EU membership allowed EU11 countries to benefit from trade and

FDI globalization while remaining on a declining trend of CO_2 intensity that was rather similar to the trends observed in the rest of the EU and in other high-income countries.

However, as Fig. 10.8 shows, the extra dynamism EU membership injected into the process seems to have faded by the middle of the previous decade. Since 2014, EU11 seems to follow the same trend as the rest of the EU and in fact, the rest of the world as a whole. This slow-down in EU11; the longer-term trend in EU15, which was commendable but not that different from the trend in other high-income countries (Fig. 10.6); and the pressing need to act more decisively at the global level explain why a new impetus from Europe was so much needed.

By 2014, most EU11 countries positioned themselves below the global carbon Kuznets curve, close to EU15 countries, which are among the least carbon-intensive economies in the world, and are more developed than EU11 countries (Fig. 10.9).

Figure 10.9 also shows the differences among EU11 countries, some being located above the global carbon Kuznets curve, one even being close to the highly carbon-intensive upper-middle-income countries in South-East Asia. As Fig. 10.10 shows, the difference between the least and most carbon-intensive economies in EU11 in 2014, Latvia and Estonia, was almost threefold. Interestingly, both were parts of the former USSR that promoted a highly energy- and carbon-intensive economy. They are also neighbours with rather similar climate conditions.[3] As the analysis in Ürge-Vorsatz et al. (2006) shows, the differences among EU11 countries (and between EU11 and the countries that were former Soviet republics) in this regard are stemming from their Soviet-type central planning legacy.[4]

[3]As Fig. 10.11 shows, high carbon intensity of the economy in Estonia is explained by both, high energy intensity and high carbon intensity of energy use. The latter is due to heavy reliance on domestic oil shale, while the former is attributable to the relatively high energy use in transportation and by households.

[4]Ürge-Vorsatz et al. (2006) also mention some of the positive legacies of Soviet-type central planning, such as the high share of public transport in total transport, the wide prevalence of district heating and cogeneration (the utilization of the waste heat of power or industrial plants as district heating) and the relatively large share of multi-family houses in urban areas. However, some of these positive legacies were combined with negative ones, such as highly polluting buses or very low standards of energy efficiency for buildings, thus many of these positive legacies were more potential than real. After EU accession, some of the schemes funded by structural funds were targeted precisely on these weak elements of the system, allowing EU11 countries to turn this part of their legacy into a truly positive one. On the other hand, a rapid increase in car ownership eroded some of the initial advantages in the area of transportation.

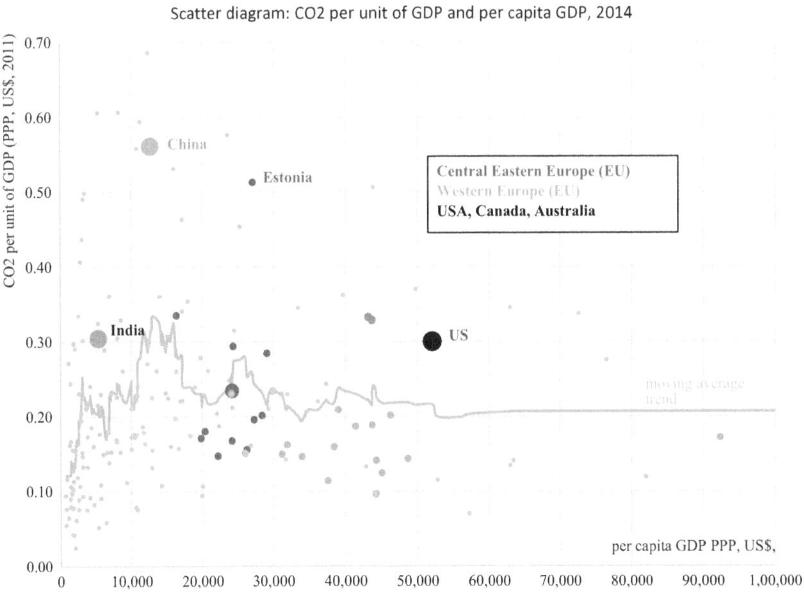

Fig. 10.9 Carbon emission Kuznets curve, 2014. (Sources: International Energy Agency and World Bank. Note: This a scatter plot of CO_2 emission per unit of GDP (in constant 2011 PPP, vertical) and per capita GDP (in constant 2011 PPP, horizontal))

Figure 10.10 also shows that Poland and the Czech Republics are also significantly more carbon intensive than the rest of the group. In light of this, it is not surprising that some EU11 countries pointed to the challenges involved in moving towards a carbon-neutral economy when EU leaders discussed the new Green Deal of the EU recently.

If we decompose carbon intensity into energy intensity of GDP and carbon intensity of energy, it is only Poland where the problem is purely related to the energy mix (reliance on coal), while in the other cases, both energy intensity and carbon intensity of energy play a role, with Estonia standing out on both fronts (Fig. 10.11).

While this shows a rather large difference in levels in 2014, the trend decline in Poland and the Czech Republic since the beginning of transition was very similar if not faster than in Hungary, which is among

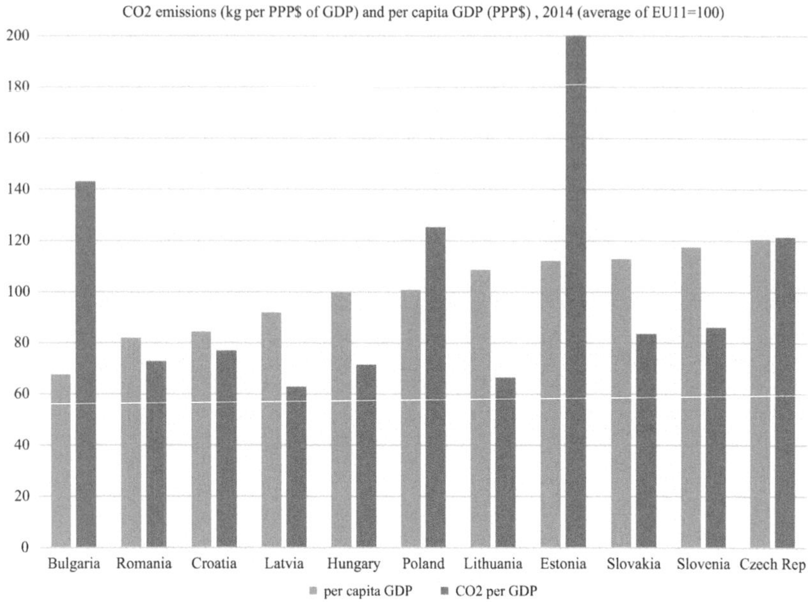

Fig. 10.10 Carbon intensity of EU 11 countries, 2014. (Sources: International Energy Agency and World Bank)

the least carbon-intensive economies in the region (Figs. 10.12, 10.13 and 10.14).

Coal-based energy production results in high CO_2 emission, and it also contributes to air pollution, with a particularly strong impact in southern Poland, where the coal-based economy is heavily concentrated (Fig. 10.15).[5] Thus, making a strong effort to reduce CO_2 emission would also have a major beneficial impact on health and healthy life expectancy. This would also be an important way to help transform the rapid economic convergence of Poland into a faster improvement in quality of life.

[5] This is part of the legacy of Soviet-type central planning. Ürge-Vorsatz et al. (2006) refer to this area as the "Black Triangle", comprising of regions of heavy industry and coal mining in Poland, (then) Czechoslovakia and (then) East Germany. The phasing out of coal-fired energy plants progressed at different speeds in the countries concerned. Moreover, in Poland, the rapid development of large and densely populated metropolitan areas also added to the pressure on air (and CO_2) pollution.

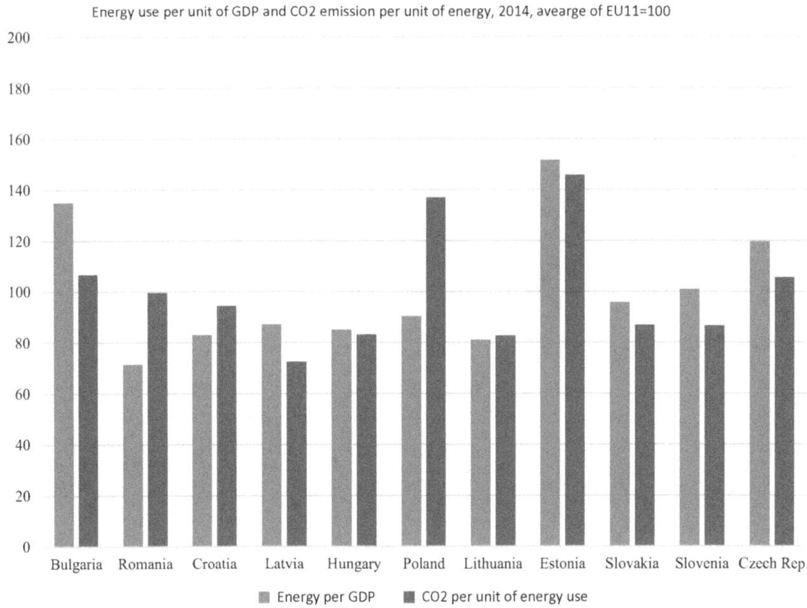

Fig. 10.11 Decomposition of carbon intensity of EU 11 countries, 2014. (Sources: International Energy Agency and World Bank)

Overall, there was a convergence within the EU in the past decade (2007–2017) regarding carbon intensity, with some outliers albeit none of them from among EU11 (Fig. 10.16). Countries with higher initial levels tended to reduce their carbon intensity faster.

10.3 The European Green Deal

The new European Green Deal suggested by the European Commission (2019) sets out a highly ambitious target of turning the EU into a carbon-neutral economy by 2050. As an intermediate target for 2030, it suggests a 50–55% reduction in the level of CO_2 emission relative to the level in 1990. This is well above the previously set target of a 40% reduction, which already would have required a major acceleration in the pace of emission reduction. To achieve this new target requires an annual rate of reduction in the CO_2 intensity of the EU economy (CO_2 emission per unit

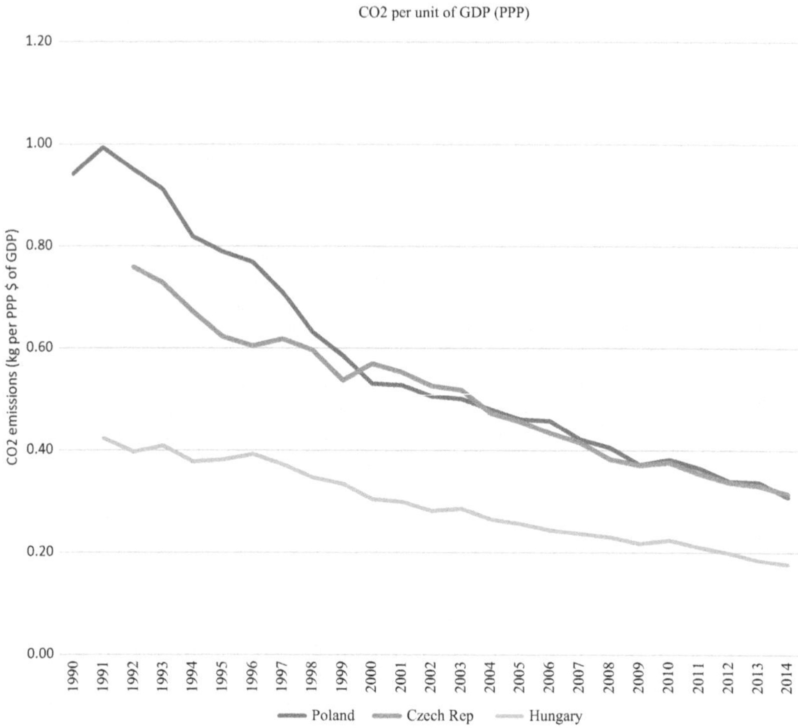

Fig. 10.12 Carbon intensity of selected EU 12 economies, 1990–2014. (Sources: International Energy Agency and World Bank)

of real GDP) by some 5.5%, more than double the rate achieved in 2007–17 (Fig. 10.17).

As Fig. 10.17 shows, EU11 are concentrated in the central cluster, that is, the levels of the carbon intensity of their economies, as well as the rate of change in this in the past decade are rather close to the EU averages. Romania registered an average rate of reduction in the past decade that was faster than the required rate for the EU as a whole to achieve this new target. As Fig. 10.6 shows, EU11 countries followed a rather similar trend to the rest of the EU regarding their carbon intensity in the past decade or so. Thus, if the individual country targets are agreed based on the expectation of roughly similar efforts (rate of reduction), the challenge involved in meeting this new target will not be bigger for EU11 countries than for

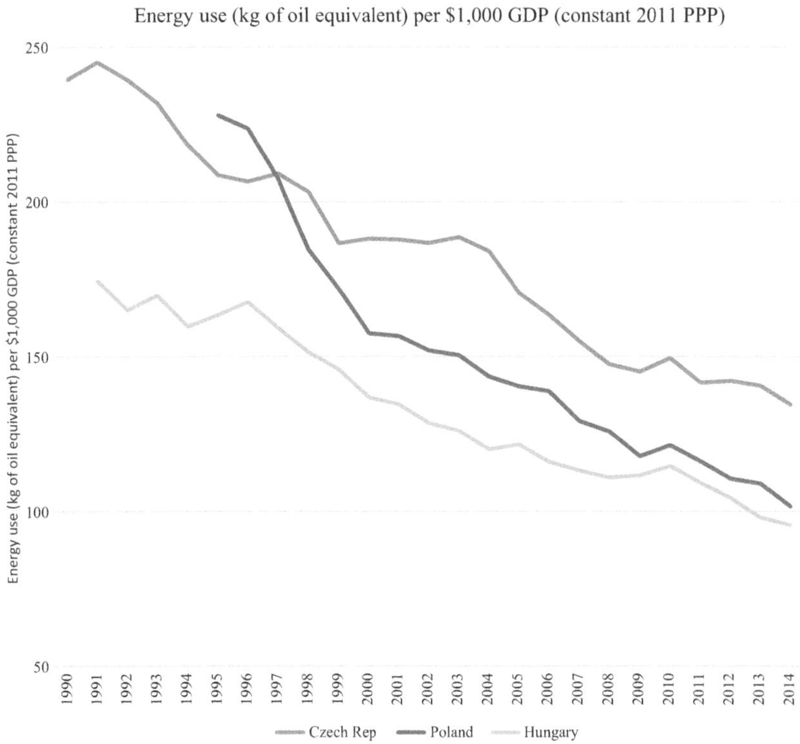

Fig. 10.13 Energy intensity. (Sources: International Energy Agency and World Bank)

the rest. However, if the expectation was that countries that have significantly more carbon-intensive economies should make bigger effort, some of the EU11 countries would face major challenges, as the overall target for the EU is already a very ambitious one.

Within this group, Poland stands out, as it is the fifth biggest CO_2 emitters in the EU accounting for almost 10% of the total emission by the EU. As we mentioned before, Poland's problem is with its energy mix, as the energy intensity of its economy is at around the average of EU11 economies. Albeit it has continuously reduced its heavy reliance on coal, still almost half of its total primary energy supply (TPES) is based on coal (down from about three-fourth in 1990).

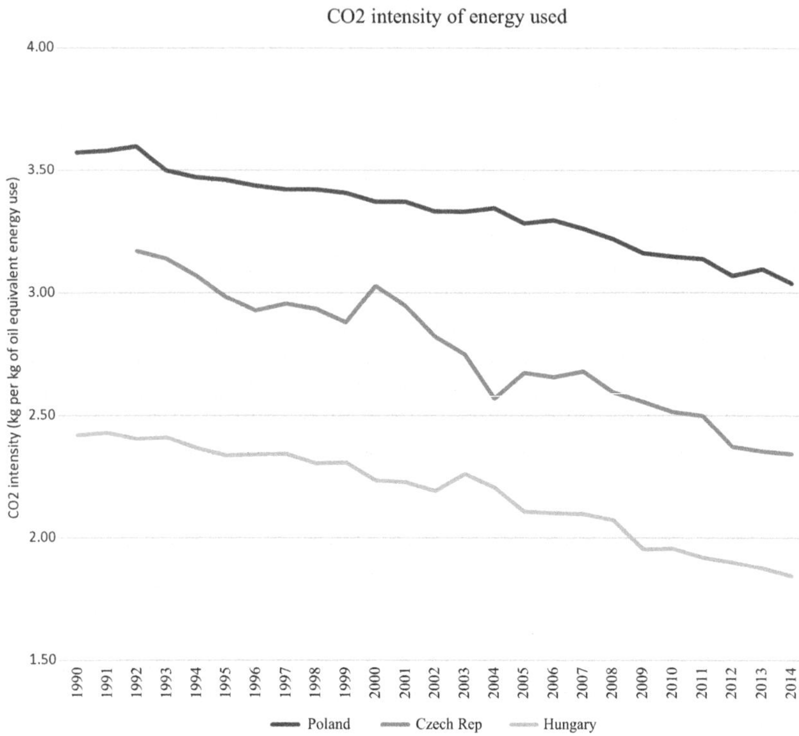

Fig. 10.14 Carbon intensity of energy use. (Sources: International Energy Agency and World Bank)

Besides financial support through its existing instruments, such as the European Regional Development Fund and the European Social Fund Plus, the EU plans to dedicate at least 30% of the InvestEU fund to facilitate the investments necessary to implement the European Green Deal. Moreover, it plans to set up a Just Transition Mechanism, including a Just Transition Fund to support regions and sectors most affected by the transition (European Commission 2019). As the convergence experience of EU11 shows, it is essential to maintain social cohesion during a major transformation of an economy, because a failure on this front creates a fertile ground for policy (reform) reversals (Székely and Ward-Warmedinger 2018).

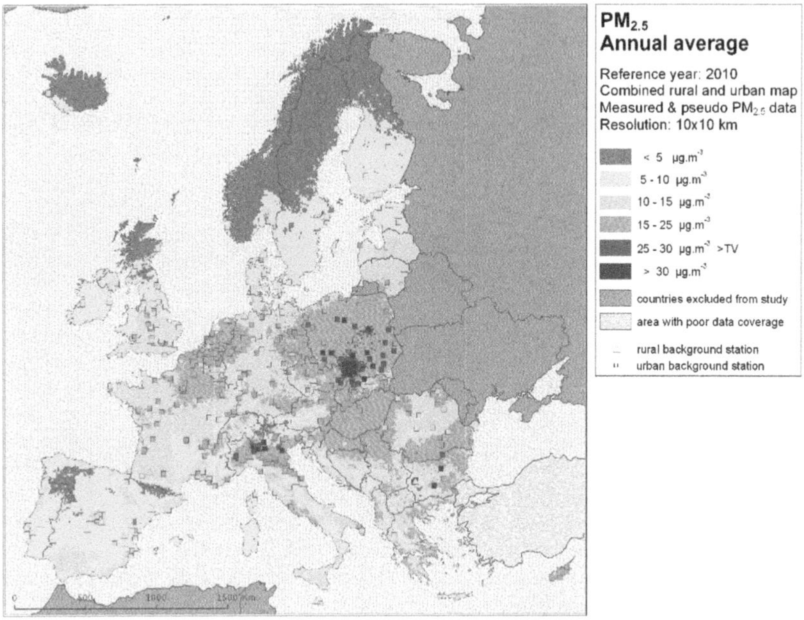

Fig. 10.15 Air pollution in Europe. (Source: 25 1994-2019 European Environment Agency)

10.4 Conclusions

EU11 countries started their transition in the early 1990s with highly carbon- (and energy-)intensive economies. The collapse of heavy industry early in the transition reduced excessive energy intensity rapidly. This was followed by a more gradual restructuring of the rest of the economy, which put the carbon intensity of these economies on a declining path. The prospect of EU membership and later EU membership boosted foreign trade and FDI, leading to a rapid re-industrialization of EU11 and making them the fastest converging group of upper-middle-income countries in the world. Nevertheless, EU11 economies maintained the previously established trend decline in carbon intensity. This suggests that there was no significant carbon leaking involved in their trade integration. The convergence path of EU11 was unique among converging upper-middle-income countries in this regard; only other non-EU countries followed similar trends albeit combined with a much slower convergence process.

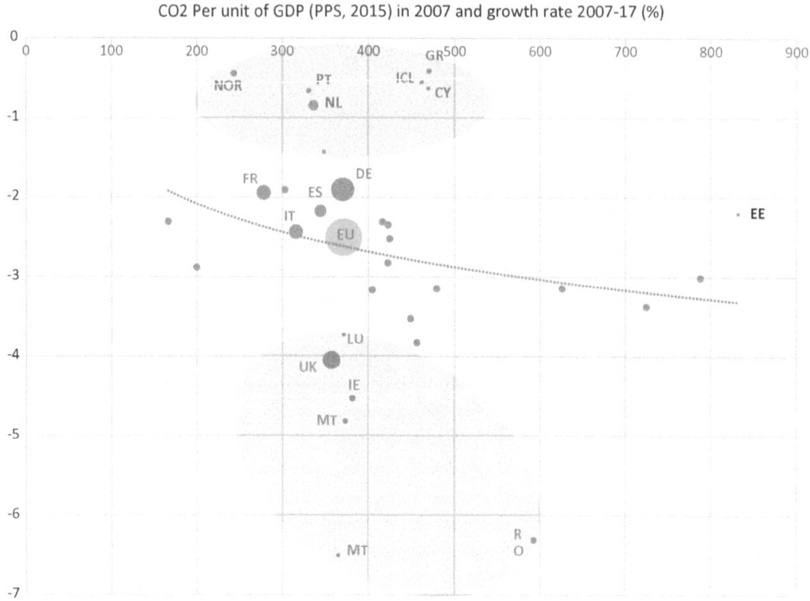

Fig. 10.16 Convergence in carbon intensity, level in 2007 versus growth in 2007–17. (Sources: Eurostat for CO_2 per unit of GDP, author's own calculations for the rate of change. Note: This a scatter plot of CO_2 emission per unit of GDP (in 2015 PPS, horizontal) and the annual rate of change in this indicator in 2007–17 (vertical))

In other parts of the world, convergence was coupled with increasing carbon intensity.

The role of EU membership in bringing about this unique trend is well identifiable. On the legal-institutional side, the adoption of the acquis and the EU institutions, the environmental norms and the shared decision to reduce CO_2 emission (to achieve the EU goals for 2020) required also EU11 countries to reduce their CO_2 emission. The EU not only set requirements, but also provided significant financial support through several channels to EU11 to help achieve these targets and to mitigate the social consequences of the measures involved. Moreover, it provided financial support to improve the connectivity of the energy systems of EU11 countries, thus allowing them to phase out faster the most polluting parts of their energy sectors.

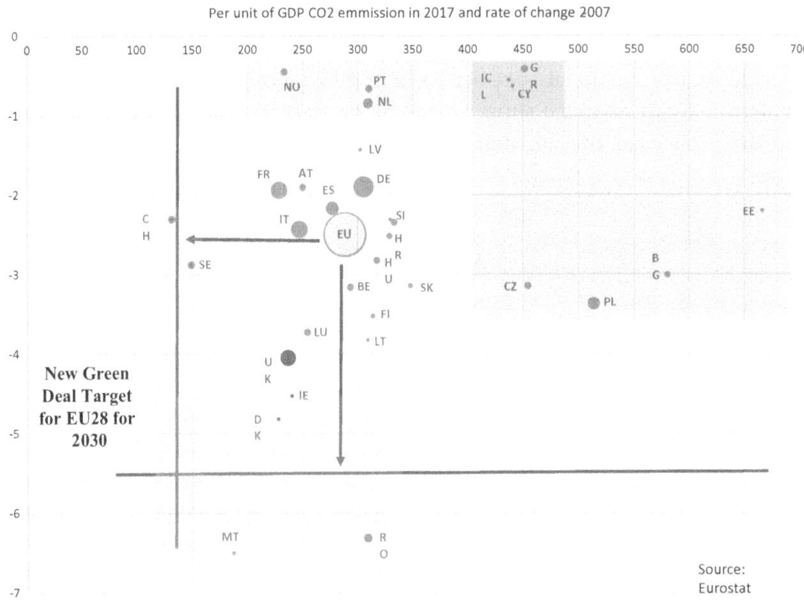

Fig. 10.17 Carbon intensity of EU economies in 2017 and its rate of change in 2007–17. (Sources: Eurostat for CO_2 per unit of GDP, author's own calculations for the rate of change. Note: This a scatter plot of CO_2 emission per unit of GDP (in 2015 PPS, horizontal) and the annual rate of change in this indicator in 2007–17 (vertical))

In general, the institutional channel remained rather weak in the EU (Székely and Kuenzel 2020). That is, EU membership did not bring about a faster improvement in the quality of institutions in EU11 than in other upper-middle-income countries. Slow improvement of institutions also reduced the capacity of EU11 countries to transform rapid economic convergence into concomitant social convergence. However, EU membership helped EU11 countries to achieve a unique convergence path regarding carbon intensity of their economies.

Nevertheless, more needs to be done in the EU and at the global level to tackle climate change. The EU has decided to take a leading role in this area. The European Green Deal sets out ambitious targets for the EU, most importantly it aims to achieve carbon neutrality by 2050. This will pose a major challenge for most EU countries, particularly for EU11 countries, as they will have to increase their efforts to reduce carbon intensity significantly relative to past trends. The European Green Deal plans to provide sizable financial support to help EU member states to meet this challenge. Such financial support will be particularly important for EU11 countries to ease the burden of a rapid restructuring of their energy sectors.

References

Carter, F., & Turnock, D. (2001). *Environmental Problems in East-Central Europe.* New York: Routledge.

Chandler, W. (2018). *Energy and Environment in the Transition Economies. Between Cold War and Global Warming.* New York: Routledge. (first published by Westview Press in 2000).

European Commission. (2019). *Communication from the Commission to the European Parliament, the European Council, the Council, the European Economic and Social Committee and the Committee of the Regions.* The European Green Deal. Brussels, 11.12.2019 COM(2019) 640 final.

Jorgenson, A. K., Clark, B., & Giedraitis, V. R. (2012). The Temporal (In)Stability of the Carbon Dioxide Emissions/Economic Development Relationship in Central and Eastern European Nations. *Society & Natural Resources, 25*(11), 1182–1192.

Jorgenson, A., Longhofer, W., Grant, D., Sie, A., & Giedraitis, V. (2017). The Effects of Economic and Political Integration on Power Plants' Carbon Emissions in the Post-Soviet Transition Nations. *Environmental Research Letters, 12*(4), 044009.

Székely, I. P., & Kuenzel, R. (2020). Convergence of the EU Member States in Central-Eastern and South Eastern Europe to the Frontier: A Framework for Convergence Inside a Close Regional Cooperation. In M. Landesmann & I. P. Székely (Eds.), *Does EU Membership Facilitate Convergence? The Experience of the EU's Eastern Enlargement.* forthcoming: Palgrave Macmillan.

Székely, I. P., & Ward-Warmedinger, M. (2018). Reform Reversals: Areas, Circumstances and Motivations. *Comparative Economic Studies, 60*(4), 559–582.

Ürge-Vorsatz, D., Miladinova, G., & Paizs, L. (2006). Energy in Transition: From the Iron Curtain to the European Union. *Energy Policy, 34*(2006), 2279–2297.

Vlčková, J., Nosek, V., Novotný, J., & Lupíšek, A. (2015). *Carbon Dioxide Emissions Embodied in International Trade in Central Europe Between 1995 and 2008.* Moravian Geographical Reports.

York, R. (2008). De-carbonization in Former Soviet Republics, 1992–2000: The Ecological Consequences of De-modernization. *Social Problems, 55*, 370–390.

CHAPTER 11

The Impact of the EU on National Fiscal Governance Systems

László Jankovics, Leire Ormaetxea Igarzabal, and Ştefan Ciobanu

11.1 Introduction

National fiscal frameworks (NFFs) represent a set of domestic arrangements (i.e. numerical rules, medium-term planning, forecasting, independent fiscal institutions (IFIs), budgetary coordination mechanisms, etc.). The rationale for having NFFs in place is that they enhance the predictability and transparency of domestic budgetary planning by establishing

The views expressed are solely those of the authors and do not necessarily represent the official views of the European Commission. The information used in this chapter and the related analyses have been prepared with a reference date of end-2019.

L. Jankovics (✉) • L. O. Igarzabal • Ş. Ciobanu
DG ECFIN, European Commission, Brussels, Belgium
e-mail: Laszlo.JANKOVICS@ec.europa.eu; Leire.ORMAETXEA-IGARZABAL@ec.europa.eu; Stefan.CIOBANU@ec.europa.eu

M. Landesmann, I. P. Székely (eds.), *Does EU Membership Facilitate Convergence? The Experience of the EU's Eastern Enlargement - Volume II*, Studies in Economic Transition,
https://doi.org/10.1007/978-3-030-57702-5_11

incentives for budgetary discipline and constraints on policy discretion. As the EU fiscal framework does not operate in a vacuum, effective NFFs facilitate the respect of the Member States' European commitments as per the Stability and Growth Pact (SGP).

This chapter will look into a specific aspect of institutional convergence: the development of NFFs. It is worth recalling that at the time of the Eastern accession waves, there were no specific common requirements defined in this policy domain. It implied that up until the eruption of the Great Recession and the launch of the economic governance revamp process, there was only moderate progress in budgetary planning and reporting in the EU-11 countries, triggered chiefly by the annual requirement of preparing Stability and Convergence Programmes and submitting the bi-annual fiscal notifications. Thereafter, a clear reform acceleration ensued in the region, most notably as regards the (re-)design of domestic numerical rules, the guiding role of medium-term plans and the establishment of national IFIs. It has led by now, in many aspects, to a similar state of advancement compared to the 'old' Member States (which, by the way, also made significant improvements in the meantime). The assumption of this general catching-up is broadly corroborated by various indicators, notably the strength indices calculated by the Commission on the basis of its Fiscal Governance Database (see details in the following sections).

The remainder of this chapter is structured as follows. Section 11.2 will provide a brief account of the theoretical and empirical literature on the rationale and potential benefits of sound fiscal governance arrangements and the relevant EU legal provisions which were prominently inspired by these insights. Subsequently, there will be stylised overviews on the main pillars of NFFs in the EU-11 countries, namely numerical rules, medium-term budgetary frameworks and IFIs. The next section will zoom in on the issue of IFIs by discussing the observable patterns of their main functions in a region where the starting point was very rudimentary—only one IFI (Slovenia's Institute of Macroeconomic Analysis and Development (IMAD)) predated the EU accession—and the diversity of national arrangements could probably be best captured. Finally, Sect. 11.5 will conclude.

11.2 Literature Review and EU Legal Requirements

Discretionary fiscal policy has been consensually identified in the economic literature as suffering from two interrelated shortcomings: deficit bias (i.e. the tendency for government to run budget deficits above what is permissible) and pro-cyclicality. The persistent deviation from an optimal policy path, resulting in sustained debt accumulation, has primarily been explained by political economy considerations,[1] ranging from fiscal illusions by an ill-informed electorate to the time inconsistency phenomenon, and more recently including models on indebtedness as a strategic tool by incumbents to limit the fiscal space of a successor government. Partly linked to this, the convincingly documented pro-cyclicality of fiscal policy, especially during good economic times,[2] entails two important drawbacks. First, pro-cyclical policies tend to exacerbate the volatility of output and employment, thereby depressing the accumulation of capital via increased uncertainty. Second, they lead to insufficient elbowroom in cyclical downturns, essentially undermining the stabilisation function of fiscal policy.

Rule-based fiscal policy as embodied by numerical rules was first typically deployed in order to address the above deficiencies. In terms of empirical evidence, based on an EU dataset over the period 1990–2005, Debrun et al. (2008) found statistically significant and economically large impacts of fiscal rules on budgetary aggregates, controlling for other factors. In their baseline specification, when fiscal outcomes were measured by the cyclically adjusted primary balance (CAPB) and the design of fiscal rules by the European Commission's Fiscal Rule Index (FRI),[3] a 0.4% of GDP improvement in the CAPB was found for every standard-deviation increase in the FRI in the short term. Nerlich and Reuter (2013) found strong evidence on the positive impact of national fiscal rules in the EU, too: over the period 1990–2012, the CAPB improved by 0.55% of GDP in countries with at least one fiscal rule in place compared with those with no rules.

[1] For a recent survey of the related political economy models, see Alesina and Passalacqua (2015).

[2] See, for example Turrini (2008) for the euro area evidence.

[3] See the detailed explanation of the FRI and its evolution for the regional countries in the next section.

However, a growing awareness of disappointing outcomes in terms of fiscal rule enforcement put the spotlight on the other components of domestic fiscal frameworks as additional features (i.e. not as substitute for fiscal rules). There are an increasing number of studies analysing the effects of specific fiscal characteristics on budgetary performance. Most notably, effective medium-term budgetary planning appears instrumental in sticking to budgetary plans (European Commission 2007), while the quality of domestic budgetary procedures was also shown to contribute to better budgetary performance (Fabrizio and Mody 2006). Finally, national IFIs have also recently emerged as complementary pillars in a comprehensive fiscal framework. In fact, also through their continuous monitoring of public finance developments, IFIs are expected to promote transparency and accountability, thereby reducing information asymmetries and raising the quality of fiscal policy debates.

In terms of empirical evidence for the impact of IFIs, a recent IMF (2017) paper showed that fiscal rules equipped with independent monitoring arrangements were associated with lower sovereign debt financing costs. This result held even for countries with a mixed track record of fiscal responsibility. Furthermore, based on the IMF Fiscal Council Dataset, Debrun and Kinda (2014) empirically investigated whether the observable design of independent bodies possesses a discipline-enhancing power. Overall, they conclude that only well-designed IFIs are associated with better fiscal outcomes and less biased forecasts, so the mere existence of IFIs is not by itself conducive to sound public finances.[4] Specifically, the identified key characteristics for an effective operation are the following ones: (i) independent functioning; (ii) a visible presence in the public debate; (iii) mandate to monitor numerical rules; and (iv) mandate to assess/produce the official macro-fiscal forecasts.

In the context of successive economic governance reform waves and with a view to the benefits outlined in the literature, a number of legislative initiatives at the EU level between 2010 and 2013 provided a significant impetus for the development of national fiscal frameworks (see below). It should be stressed that Member States have retained a significant degree of freedom in terms of designing their own national frameworks (most

[4] The authors stress that even significantly positive correlations should not be interpreted as a causal relation as these may simply reflect deeper, often unobservable factors. Moreover, the limited time span for many of the IFIs in the database may also affect the empirical results.

notably, domestic rules, annual and medium-term planning procedures, and IFIs). Given that existence of some key governance elements in most of the Member States predated the supranational legislation, and also as a recognition of the diversity of national fiscal and administrative settings, there was no attempt to impose a one-size-fits-all model in the EU legislation.

- First, one component of the 'Six-Pack', the Budgetary Frameworks Directive[5] set minimum standards for domestic fiscal governance arrangements in 2011, in an attempt to foster budgetary discipline and to increase national ownership of the EU fiscal rulebook. Specifically, it established essential requirements in the following areas: (i) public accounting and fiscal statistics; (ii) forecasts; (iii) numerical fiscal rules; (iv) medium-term planning; (v) transparency and comprehensive scope of budgetary frameworks. It also introduced a reference to the need for involving IFIs or 'bodies endowed with functional autonomy' in the monitoring of compliance with national fiscal rules.
- Second, the intergovernmental Fiscal Compact[6] was signed in 2012 (it currently binds 22 signatory Member States). It obliges the contracting parties to establish a structural balanced-budget rule, preferably at constitutional level, with a general lower limit of the structural deficit set at 0.5% of GDP. The rule must include an automatic correction mechanism in case of deviation from the deficit target or the adjustment path towards it. It should also be equipped with monitoring arrangements involving designated domestic IFIs. The accompanying common principles proposed by the Commission[7] set minimum independence standards for IFIs in terms of, inter alia,

[5] Council Directive 2011/85/EU of 8 November 2011 on requirements for budgetary frameworks of the Member States – OJ of 23.11.2011, L306/41.

[6] The Fiscal Compact is Title III of the intergovernmental Treaty on Stability, Coordination and Governance in the Economic and Monetary Union, signed in March 2012. It requires euro area countries to introduce in the national legislation a balanced budget rule in structural terms, an automatic correction mechanism and an independent fiscal institution to monitor the rule. Bulgaria, Denmark and Romania are also bound by the same requirements on a voluntary basis.

[7] Communication from the Commission: Common principles on national fiscal correction mechanisms (COM/2012/0342 final). Web: https://eur-lex.europa.eu/legal-content/EN/TXT/HTML/?uri=CELEX:52012DC0342&from=EN

legal underpinnings for the set-up, nomination procedures for members, access to information and availability of resources.
- Finally, in 2013, one of the 'Two-Pack' Regulations for euro area Member States[8] introduced, among others, the requirement for national medium-term fiscal plans and draft budgets to be based on independently produced or endorsed macroeconomic forecasts. It also extended the requirement of monitoring by independent bodies to all domestic numerical rules in force.

11.3 The Main Fiscal Governance Pillars in the EU-11 Countries

11.3.1 Numerical Fiscal Rules

Numerical fiscal rules consist in permanent constraints on fiscal policy, typically expressed in terms of a summary indicator of fiscal performance[9] like budget balance or debt-to-GDP ratio, to mention some common examples. They are intended to make policy-makers commit to a disciplined fiscal behaviour, thereby improving fiscal sustainability and transparency.

According to the information reflected in the latest vintage (2017) of the Fiscal Governance Database[10] maintained by the European Commission, there was a total of 42 fiscal rules in force in the EU-11 countries in 2017, whereas only 15 had been in place back in 2003. Against the backdrop of a steep rise in the number of rules for the EU as a whole in this period, the increase for the EU-11 subgroup was even more substantial, suggesting that EU membership has brought about significant reforms to the frameworks in these new Member States.

Back in 2003, debt rules were dominant in the EU-11 countries (10 rules, two thirds of the total), followed by budget balance rules (four rules, or under one third) and expenditure rules (just one rule). Data also show that, before the EU membership, the focus of fiscal rules used to be

[8] Regulation (EU) No 473/2013 of the European Parliament and of the Council of 21 May 2013 on common provisions for monitoring and assessing draft budgetary plans and ensuring the correction of excessive deficit of the Member States in the euro area – OJ L 140, 27.5.2013.

[9] See Kopits and Symansky (1998).

[10] Fiscal Governance in the EU Member States: Numerical Fiscal Rules. Web: https://ec.europa.eu/info/business-economy-euro/indicators-statistics/economic-databases/fiscal-governance-eu-member-states/numerical-fiscal-rules-eu-member-countries_en

on controlling public finances at the local level, as rules targeting the local level constituted more than a half of the rules. Overall, there seemed to be a general approach to use fiscal rules as a constraining device of local governments' debt levels. Only four (20%) of the rules targeted the general government as a whole.

The picture changed markedly in the following years, primarily due to the crisis-prompted requirements set in law at the EU level, such as the 2011 Six-Pack, the 2013 Two-Pack or the intergovernmental Fiscal Compact, but also in relation to some of the EU-11 countries becoming members of the Euro area. The new Member States are bound not only by the Treaty reference values of 3% headline deficit and 60% government debt, but also—as mandated by the EU fiscal framework—by the required adjustment towards their respective medium-term budgetary objective (MTO) and by the debt reduction benchmark, among others.[11] This reality is clearly reflected in the national rules that were adopted in the last decade, some of which mimic these European requirements.

Over 2003–2017, budget balance rules became the most widely used in the EU-11 countries (18 rules, almost half of the total). Importantly, half of those rules were defined in structural terms, which reflect the shift towards an approach to fiscal rules more in line with the revised SGP, largely achieved through the national implementation of Fiscal Compact obligations.[12] The total number of debt rules also went up, resulting from the replacement over the years of some rules at the local level by rules targeting the whole general government, a more encompassing type of debt rule, which is also more in line with the SGP. Overall, by 2017, rules targeting the whole general government, which facilitate a coordinated approach to the management of public finances in a country, came to account for almost 60% of the rules.

Beyond the sheer number of fiscal rules in place, the quality of those rules is equally or even more essential when analysing the strength of the fiscal framework of a country. The European Commission uses its own Fiscal Rules Index (FRI) as a proxy of the quality of a rule, which is then aggregated to produce a country index. The FRI is based on qualitative information on five key dimensions, namely: the legal base of the rule, the extent to which the target is binding, the institution which monitors and

[11] See European Commission (2019) for a detailed explanation on the SGP requirements.

[12] Communication from the Commission: The Fiscal Compact: Taking Stock (C(2017) 1200 final). Web: https://ec.europa.eu/info/sites/info/files/1_en_act_part1_v3_0.pdf

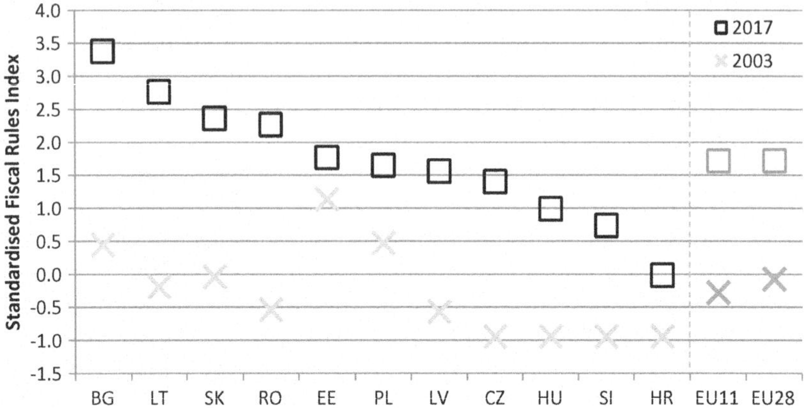

Fig. 11.1 The Fiscal Rules Index for EU-11 in 2017 as compared to 2003. (Source: European Commission's Fiscal Governance Database)

enforces the rule, the forecasting institution, the corrective measures triggered in case of non-compliance and the extent to which the rule is resilient to economic shocks.

Figure 11.1 illustrates how the FRI improved in all EU-11 Member States between 2003 and 2017. In most cases, the improvement is substantial, with only Estonia and Poland showing smaller increases in their indices. The set of fiscal rules in Bulgaria and Lithuania rank the highest in this hierarchy, which admittedly is partly due to the higher number of rules in force, whereas Croatia, Slovenia and Hungary are at the other end of the spectrum. When compared to the EU-28 average FRI, the EU-11 average FRI was lower in 2003, whereas by 2017 the two indices became almost identical, as an indication of the upwards convergence achieved by the EU-11 in terms of fiscal rule strength.

Overall, more and better-designed fiscal rules are now in place in the EU-11 countries than before their accession to the EU. The current rules cover well the scope of general government, are more robust and provide for more detailed corrective action in case they are not complied with while allowing for flexibility in difficult economic times. Not least, the vast majority of rules are monitored by independent fiscal councils, which increases the reputational cost of non-compliance (see also next subsection). All this contributes to a more responsible and predictable approach to fiscal policy for which delivers better in terms of both macroeconomic stabilisation and sustainability of public finances. Undoubtedly, EU membership has been decisive in the development of these features in the newer Member States.

11.3.2 Medium-Term Budgetary Frameworks

Because the effects and implications of discretionary fiscal measures usually extend over multiple years, policy-makers require a medium-term perspective in order to design a sound strategy for the fiscal plans of their respective countries. Medium-term budgetary frameworks (MTBF) constitute institutional policy instruments that allow this extension of the horizon for fiscal policy-making beyond the annual budgetary calendar.[13]

EU requirements attach great importance to having a credible and realistic medium-term planning across the Member States. Going beyond the long-established submission of Stability or Convergence Programmes, more recently provisions conducive to adopting a medium-term approach in every Member State were enshrined in EU law via the Budgetary Frameworks Directive and the Two-Pack. The relevant EU legislation still leaves substantial room for Member States to transpose the measures into their national legal and institutional settings and, consequently, a wide array of MTBF arrangements is now in place across the EU, including within the EU-11 group.

The development of MTBFs in the Member States is reflected as well in the European Commission's Fiscal Governance Database.[14] A dedicated module of the database covers in detail the design of the national MTBFs as of 2006, notably as regards the following aspects: coverage, the extent to which the medium-term plan is binding, the involvement of national parliament, the involvement of IFIs and the level of detail in those medium-term plans (e.g. whether revenue and expenditure projections are broken down by categories, whether alternative macroeconomic scenarios are being taken into account).

In general terms, a similar trend as for the Member States' numerical fiscal rules is observed for MTBFs, that is, an improvement in design across the board, as illustrated by the graph in Fig. 11.2. There was a

[13] See Sherwood (2015) for a detailed overview in EU Member States.

[14] Fiscal Governance in the EU Member States: Medium-term budgetary frameworks. Web: https://ec.europa.eu/info/business-economy-euro/indicators-statistics/economic-databases/fiscal-governance-eu-member-states/medium-term-budgetary-framework_en

notable increase in the MTBF index (calculated by the Commission based on the information in the Fiscal Governance Database) between 2006 and 2017 for all EU-11 Member States with the exception of Czechia (where a marginal decrease of 0.05 points was recorded). Back in 2006, Bulgaria, Romania, Croatia and Hungary still did not have a medium-term plan in place, but adopted one shortly afterwards. Overall, the situation in this subgroup of countries has remarkably improved so that by 2017 a large number of the EU-11 countries were at the EU-28 average or above it (namely, Latvia, Slovakia, Bulgaria, Lithuania, Estonia, Romania and Slovenia). However, in spite of the good progress made, in 2017 the EU-11 index average still remained at a slightly lower level than the overall EU-28.

Having detailed MTBFs that can be actively used as fiscal policy instruments has been another concrete consequence of EU membership that benefitted the EU-11 Member States. As fiscal policy choices usually have effects that extend over various budgetary exercises, the emphasis on medium-term approach creates better pre-requisites for prudent policy-making.

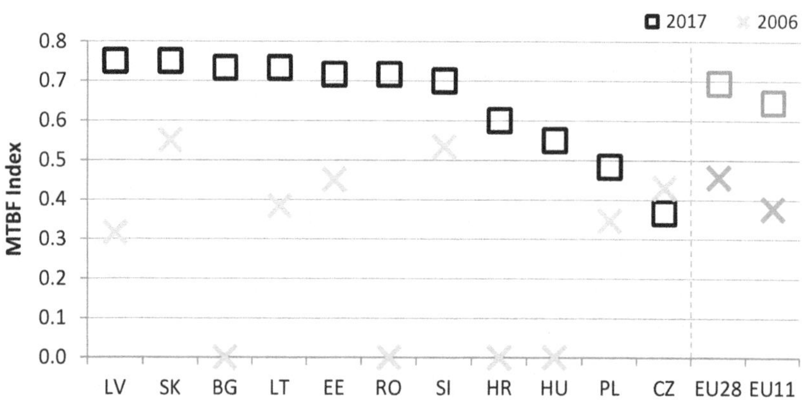

Fig. 11.2 The MTBF Index for EU-11 in 2017 as compared to 2006. (Source: European Commission's Fiscal Governance Database)

11.3.3 Independent Fiscal Institutions

The previously mentioned EU-level legislative initiatives in the area of fiscal governance provided, among others, a significant impetus for IFI development. The number of IFIs has exponentially increased in the recent past: out of the 12 IFIs that were present in the EU-11 at the end of 2018, only the Slovenian IMAD had been active before the global crisis (see Table 11.1).[15] The latest arrivals on the scene are the Slovenian Fiscal Council, which became operational in late spring 2017, and the Czech Fiscal Council, whose members were nominated in January 2018. It should be stressed that while there are considerably more stringent EU legal requirements for euro area Member States in this domain, even this group of countries has retained a significant degree of freedom in terms of designing their own independent bodies.

In terms of independence safeguards, all regional IFIs rely on a statutory base grounded in ordinary legislative provisions or those of higher legal standing (in Estonia, Hungary, Lithuania and Slovakia, IFIs were established through constitutional norms or laws with qualified majority quorums). Requirements for IFI decision-making members typically include qualification criteria as well as provisions aimed at avoiding conflicts of interest with other public or private entities. Most IFIs function as a detached body (i.e. operating on a standalone basis) while the remaining ones are either attached to or embedded[16] in other existing domestic institutions (typically national parliaments, central banks or courts of auditors). The main rationale for attachment is that it facilitates access to resources (offices, IT equipment, etc.) and enables a smooth start-up.

IFIs exhibit a large variance in allocated budgets and human resources, partly reflecting the differences in their mandate. There are a number of

[15] It is instructive to take stock of the IFIs in the candidate and potential candidate countries in the Western Balkans (Albania, Montenegro, Serbia, the Republic of North Macedonia, Bosnia and Herzegovina and Kosovo): as of mid-2019, one IFI was in place (the Serbian Fiscal Council established in 2011) and there was also a plan to found one in the Republic of North Macedonia.

[16] 'Attached' means that the IFI has financial and organisational links with the host institution (e.g. the Romanian Fiscal Council is attached to the National Academy), whereas 'embedded' signifies that the IFI is a section of the host institution (e.g. the Lithuanian Budget Policy Monitoring Department is embedded in the National Audit Office). It should be noted that some of the standalone institutions (e.g. the Bulgarian and the Hungarian Fiscal Councils) also receive administrative support from existing public bodies.

Table 11.1 Main structural characteristics of EU-11 IFIs

	Name	*Est. (1)*	*Legal base*	*Terms of office (2)*	*Set-up*	*Staff size (3)*
BG	Fiscal Council	2015	Law	6 years	Standalone**	3
CZ	Fiscal Council	2017	Law	6 years	Standalone	12
EE	Fiscal Council	2014	Constitutional Law	5 years	Attached to NCB	2
HR	Fiscal Policy Committee	2018*	Law	5 years	Standalone	Under reorganisation
HU	Fiscal Council	2011*	Constitutional Law	6 years	Standalone**	5
LT	Budget Policy Monitoring Department	2014*	Constitutional Law	n.a.	Embedded in NAO	7
LV	Fiscal Discipline Council	2013	Law	6 years	Standalone	4
RO	Fiscal Council	2010	Law	9 years	Attached to Romanian Academy	8
SI	Fiscal Council	2015	Law	5 years	Standalone	5
	Institute of Macroeconomic Analysis and Development	1991	Decree	5 years	Standalone	18
SK	Council for Budget Responsibility	2012	Constitutional Law	7 years	Standalone	15
	Macroeconomic Forecasting Committee	2012	Constitutional Law	n.a.	Standalone	Not applicable

Notes: (1) Date of establishment, year may differ from date of effective start; (*) date of reorganisation; (2) for leadership of institution (in case of different terms, for the President); (**) in administrative terms, attached to Parliament; (3) number of full-time technical staff, including administrative assistants

NAO National Audit Office, *NCB* National Central Bank

Source: European Commission's Fiscal Governance Database; IFI webpages

regional bodies with solid analytical capacities with a staff of 10 or more people: the Slovenian Institute of Macroeconomic Analysis ('forecasting institutions' are traditionally the most sizeable in the EU) and the Czech and Slovak fiscal councils. This being said, most EU-11 institutions employ less than 10-strong support staff, which is consistent with the endowment of IFIs in the 'old' Member States: on average, four economists and/or statisticians are working in non-forecasting EU IFIs.[17] Funding for standalone IFIs is typically included in the central budget; other examples involve the central bank's budget (e.g. Slovak Council for Budget Responsibility) or the parliament's budget (e.g. Bulgarian Fiscal Council). In the case of attached/embedded IFIs, funding is generally provided via an earmarked appropriation within the budget of the host institution.

11.4 Zooming in on the Activities of Regional IFIs

EU-11 IFIs' mandates differ significantly in scope, and in addition, some of them perform tasks based on their own initiative, for example beyond those explicitly laid down in their statutory provisions (legislation or statutes). The remits typically consist of a subset of the following activities: (1) macroeconomic and/or budgetary forecasting (endorsement/assessment of the government's forecasts or, less frequently, autonomous production of forecasts for fiscal planning); (2) assessment of compliance with fiscal rules; (3) quantitative policy costing; (4) analysis of the long-run sustainability of public finances; (5) promotion of fiscal transparency; (6) recommendations on fiscal policy (e.g. on the fiscal stance, the composition of fiscal measures or the consequences of alternative policies). It is worth recalling that European legal requirements concern only the first two items, and naturally these are laid down as compulsory tasks for most of the IFIs. The remaining elements are typically carried out on the own initiative of the councils (legally sometimes underpinned by a broad optional reference in the mandate, such as the body 'may' prepare a report on any issues deemed to be relevant for public finances).

[17] IMF (2013: 35–36) outlines some broad principles for determining the size of the support staff: it argues that a mandate consisting of macro-fiscal assessments could properly be carried out with a staff of less than 10 analysts, the production of a fully fledged independent forecasts would necessitate a staff of at least 20, while the preparation of regular policy costings would demand the work of another 20 professionals.

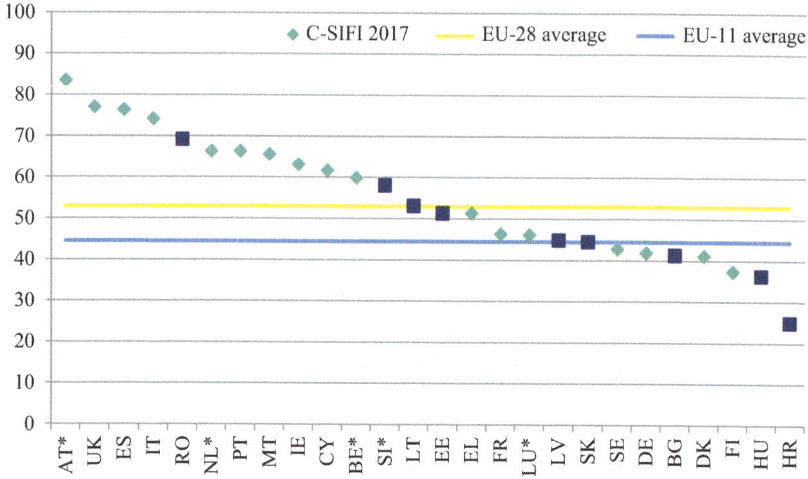

Fig. 11.3 The country-specific Scope Index of Fiscal Institutions in the EU (2017). (Note: * There are two IFIs in place in the country. Source: European Commission's Fiscal Governance Database)

Based on its Fiscal Governance Database, the Commission has recently started calculating a Scope Index of Fiscal Institutions (SIFI) that aims to measure the breadth of tasks discharged by IFIs. The index covers the above-mentioned six dimensions of IFIs' activities. The relevant scores in each category are adjusted with a 'legal force coefficient' in order to capture the elements of the official mandates. The scores are then weighted so that tasks stemming from the EU legislation carry greater importance. To better capture the breadth of IFI tasks in countries with more than one IFI (Slovenia is the only country concerned in this chapter, but in the EU, there are four more similar country cases), a country-specific index (C-SIFI) is shown in the graph in Fig. 11.3 for all MSs, which builds on the institution-level SIFI index. It appears that EU-11 IFIs generally have lower scores than their counterparts in Western European MSs, which may partly reflect that the latter are typically older institutions, out of which a higher share operate in the euro area with more encompassing EU requirements. An important caveat is that the results simply reflect the extent of the mandate, hence they should not by any means be interpreted as a proxy for the effectiveness of the respective IFIs. It is also worth highlighting that Czechia is not depicted in the graph reflecting the state-of-play in 2017 as its Fiscal Council started to operate only in 2018 (Poland is not covered either as it is the only country in the EU without a full-fledged IFI). Moreover, the score for Croatia is set to improve in the near future, as the new Fiscal Responsibility Law adopted in December 2018 reformed the Fiscal Policy Commission, also by broadening its mandate.

The remainder of this subchapter will focus on the above-listed six activities that are considered to constitute the mains tasks of the IFIs and which are executed either by all or by a subgroup of these institutions. There will naturally be a more detailed discussion on producing/endorsing/assessing official macroeconomic forecasts and monitoring compliance with fiscal rules, as these are stipulated by EU legal norms.

11.4.1 Forecasts

As mentioned above, there are more stringent requirements for euro area countries in this domain, as the Two-Pack Regulation introduced the obligation for the macroeconomic forecast underlying both annual budgets and medium-term national fiscal plans to be either produced or endorsed by independent bodies. On the other hand, it (only) obliges Member States to flag when the budgetary forecasts have been produced or endorsed by an independent institution. While appropriate arrangements are in place as regards the macroeconomic forecasts for all concerned euro area regional IFIs, none of them has so far received any formal role in the production/endorsement of the official expenditure and revenue forecasts (in the entire euro area, this was granted only to the Maltese Fiscal Council).

Out of the five euro area Member States among the EU-11, Slovenia chose to continue relying on macroeconomic forecasts produced by its independent forecaster when the Two-Pack entered into force in 2013. It seemed to be a natural choice as the Institute of Macroeconomic Analysis and Development enjoys a long-standing reputation for producing accurate forecasts. Outsourcing macroeconomic forecasts to an independent institution tends to contribute to their greater objectivity and helps to avoid problems involved in the IFI forecast endorsement process, described here below. In the remaining four regional euro area economies (Estonia, Latvia, Lithuania, Slovakia), ministries of finance have retained the task of producing the official macroeconomic forecasts which are then endorsed by independent bodies. Slovakia is a peculiar case, as the endorsement competence was conferred not to the fiscal council, but to a specialised entity, the Macroeconomic Forecasting Committee. In practice, the Ministry's forecasts are considered to be endorsed provided that a majority of the Committee members—representing independent institutions (commercial banks, the Slovak Academy of Sciences and the central bank) —deem the official forecast to be either 'conservative' or 'realistic'.

Forecast-endorsing euro area IFIs base their assessment of the government's macroeconomic forecasts on comparisons with forecasts of other institutions, without producing their own. These reference forecasts are usually those published by international institutions (European Commission, IMF, OECD) as well as national ones (central banks, think-tanks, economic research institutes, universities, commercial/investment banks). The reports accompanying endorsements typically provide a comparison to other forecasts organised by GDP components. A majority of these IFIs reports include an extensive discussion of risks involved in the government forecasts. In terms of effectiveness, the provisional calculations presented in a recent Directorate General for Economic and Financial Affairs (ECFIN) Discussion Paper (Jankovics and Sherwood 2017) appear to show some improvement in the accuracy of macroeconomic forecasting since 2014, the year in which IFIs took up the duty of official endorsers. These results, however, are based on a small sample of countries and a relatively short period of time.

Outside the euro area, regional IFIs provide at best a real-time assessment of the official forecasts. In Romania, the macroeconomic forecast underpinning budgetary planning is produced by the National Commission for Strategy and Forecasting (a body subordinated to the General Secretariat of the Government) and subsequently assessed by the Fiscal Council, without any institutional consequences in case of a critical opinion. IFIs also pronounce on the realism of official macro-fiscal forecasts in Bulgaria and Hungary. In Croatia, the Fiscal Policy Commission does not publish separate reports on the government's macroeconomic forecasts and limits itself to comparing, in the reports on compliance with fiscal rules, the government's real GDP growth forecast to the one published by the European Commission. Czechia has recently established an analogous system to the Slovak case. Specifically, in parallel to the establishment of the Fiscal Council, the Committee on Budgetary Forecasts was formed in early 2018 and tasked with assessing the plausibility of the macroeconomic and budgetary forecasts prepared by the Ministry of Finance. The (at least seven) experts are appointed for a three-year term by the government on a proposal from the Fiscal Council and work on an honorary basis.

11.4.2 Assessment of Compliance with Fiscal Rules

As documented in the literature survey above, there are clear synergies between IFIs and fiscal rules. Specifically, only well-designed fiscal rules, that is those accompanied by independent monitoring mechanisms, were found to have positive impacts on fiscal policy (e.g. improved budgetary outcomes, lowered borrowing costs). Also inspired by this empirical evidence, the notion that an independent assessor is an essential ingredient in the design of an effective numerical rule has been assimilated by many national fiscal governance frameworks.

In the EU-11, all fiscal council-type IFIs are charged with verifying compliance with general or central government rules. However, extending the monitoring to other specific sectors of the general government (such as social security) or to the subnational level is much less common. A peculiar case in point is Bulgaria, where the Fiscal Council is charged with assessing both ex ante and ex post compliance with the numerical rules laid down for the national social insurance funds. Most of the IFIs are undertaking both forward-looking and backward-looking compliance assessments.

As to the frequency of ex ante monitoring reports, a relatively popular pattern is that IFIs release two main reports annually. In such cases, typically, the spring edition analyses the country's medium-term budgetary plans (linked to the submission date of Stability/Convergence Programmes), and the autumn one deals with the planned (or adopted) budget. These reports encompass many aspects of fiscal policy, with the monitoring part usually being a dedicated subchapter of the document. These ex ante opinions are sometimes complemented by dedicated ex post compliance reports on the achievement of rules (c.f. Estonia, Slovenia or the recently started practice in Hungary). There is an evolving pattern that IFIs establish a regular schedule (either for a stand-alone publication or a dedicated subchapter in a broader document), which concludes on compliance with the domestic numerical rules for the previous year.

A genuine dialogue between the fiscal authorities and IFIs on the findings and recommendations contained in the monitoring reports benefits greatly the transparency of public finances. For the seven Member

States which are bound by the Fiscal Compact in the region,[18] such a dialogue is facilitated by the so-called comply-or-explain provisions (i.e. governments 'shall be obliged to comply with, or alternatively explain publicly why they are not following the assessment of [the IFI]', under a principle which is typically enshrined in law in the concerned countries).[19] However, this requirement covers only a number of targeted cases linked to the structural budget balance rule (namely, activation of the correction mechanism, monitoring the correction process, and triggering, extending and exiting escape clauses). Moreover, as documented in Horvath (2018), in some cases the official responses to IFI opinions are neither systematic nor always pertinent to the issues raised.

The visibility of fiscal policy debates could be greatly enhanced by a publication approach which facilitates extensive coverage of government reactions by the media. For instance, the Hungarian authorities have regularly included a written response to the Fiscal Council's remarks on the preliminary draft in the explanatory annexes of the budget bill over the recent years. However, this commendable practice could not gain any meaningful traction in the media, not even in specialised outlets, as these responses were part of a bulky set of legal texts and the related budgetary documentation of sometimes more than 1000 pages.

11.4.3 Policy Costing

Policy costing consists in providing—at various stages of the budgetary cycle—estimates of the budgetary impact of new measures envisaged by fiscal authorities. Independent estimates could be essential to ensure an informed public debate and parliamentary deliberation, in particular if the government does not release its budgetary impact assessments in a consistent and timely manner. However, there are a number of important dimensions for the costing's analytical framework, which increases the resource intensity of this exercise. On the revenue side, accurate costing requires first-hand knowledge of the often-complex tax legislation and access to generally non-public databases. On the expenditure side, it often

[18] In the concerned region, the Fiscal Compact currently binds five euro area countries (Estonia, Latvia, Lithuania, Slovakia, Slovenia) and, on a voluntary basis, Bulgaria and Romania (c.f. footnote 4).

[19] See a systematic overview in the report of the European Commission (2017) assessing compliance of national legal provisions with the Fiscal Compact.

relies on detailed data which only relevant line ministries responsible for spending programmes can provide. As regards methodological options, it is increasingly acknowledged that, in many cases, it is not adequate to capture only the static impacts, but also to extend the analysis to macroeconomic feedbacks (or second-round effects). In the event of a wide-ranging tax-benefit reform package, it is justified to try to incorporate the full spectrum of dynamic effects, which would imply a further extension to behavioural changes as well. Finally, estimates should ideally be compared with a well-defined macro-fiscal baseline (i.e. technical projections prepared under the assumption of unchanged legislation or unchanged policies).

These challenges coupled with the inevitable human resource needs for undertaking rigorous computations result in that only a handful of the regional IFIs are active in this field[20] (for the entire EU, the respective share is slightly over half). In addition, none of concerned IFIs do costing over the full spectrum of new measures, but pursue a selective approach based on their own initiative. An important observation is that this group is further split between those institutions who prepare stand-alone cost estimates and others who provide only plausibility assessment of official budgetary estimates for new measures as part of their opinion on the feasibility of fiscal plans. An enlightening example for the former is the Slovak Council for Budget Responsibility, which is capable of applying both macro feedbacks and micro simulations in its quantitative work, which occasionally gets published in a separate publication ('Commentary'). Another case in point is the Romanian Fiscal Council, which works with simple analytical tools and strives to capture the static effects of measures (the related findings are used in broader fiscal assessment reports).

A costing initiative to provide clarity on the budgetary implications of party manifestos was undertaken for the first time by the Latvian Fiscal Discipline Council in the run-up to the autumn 2018 Parliamentary elections. The Council organised a survey among political parties, and as

[20] It is worth recalling that the first incarnation of the Hungarian Fiscal Council (2009–2010) was tasked with an extensive mandate in policy costing: equipped with its own staff of around 30 analysts, it was obliged to prepare budgetary impact assessments for all planned changes in the tax code and in the social benefit system (besides, it had an optional mandate for costing all other legislative initiatives). The Council's set-up was fundamentally revised in late 2010 in a controversial way, and became essentially an advisory panel with a much narrower analytical remit focusing on the annual budget bill and supported by a small secretariat.

a result published a synthetised and comparable summary about the fiscal costs of the main electoral promises. Although the Council was not in a position to certify the calculations of the political parties, it was considered a successful exercise in shifting the focus towards the appropriate financing needs for various political ideas, or more broadly towards the issues of fiscal sustainability (Kalsone and Platais 2018).

11.4.4 *Analysis on Long-Term Sustainability of Public Finances*

It should be recalled that there is no legal requirement in the EU acquis either for governments or for IFIs to regularly undertake long-term sustainability assessments. This being said, there are many potential uses for these analyses in fiscal policy-making: (i) underpin the design of the fiscal policy strategy (e.g. medium-term plans); (ii) influence the specification of fiscal targets both at the EU and ideally at the national level; (iii) identify policy areas (e.g. pensions, health care and long-term care) where reforms/adjustments are needed in the short to medium term.

Over the recent years, a number of regional IFIs have started to publish such assessment. Specifically, from the regional IFIs, four entities (the Czech Fiscal Council, the Latvian Fiscal Discipline Council, the Lithuanian Budget Policy Monitoring Department and the Slovak Council for Budget Responsibility) have published a dedicated report on long-term sustainability. In the case of Czechia and Slovakia, the regular production of such analysis is part of the core mandate of the respective national IFIs. The Slovak institution has an annual spring publication schedule since 2012, thus one can closely monitor the yearly evolution of long-term sustainability indicators. In the case of Lithuania, the first release (2015) of its long-term sustainability assessment, with the main conclusion that age-related spending was set to explode on a no-policy change basis, might have contributed to the drive for parametric pension reforms enacted in the subsequent year by the government.

11.4.5 *Promotion of Fiscal Transparency*

There are only a few EU-11 countries where there is an explicit mention about transparency as a self-standing objective or activity for IFIs. This may be explained by the fact that fostering transparency may be indirectly fulfilled by discharging other tasks (e.g. assessment of the official macro-fiscal plans and review of the government's budgetary impact studies). It is therefore rather exceptional that the Slovak Council for Budget Responsibility is explicitly tasked by the Fiscal Responsibility Act to prepare annually an evaluation report on budget transparency rules, including an assessment on the quality and availability of important information and data on public finances. Moreover, the Council recently launched "SIMTASK", a publicly available user-friendly microsimulation model of the Slovak tax and transfer system.[21] This web-based application allows for evaluating not only the static budgetary effects of parametric legislative changes in taxes and social benefits, but also the impact on disposable incomes and inequalities both at the level of individuals and households.

Furthermore, some IFIs have dedicated activities to improve the transparency of public finances, thereby contributing to a more informed debate on fiscal policy. Indeed, as users of budgetary accounts, statistics and documentation, IFIs are well placed to assess the quality and timeliness of information on budgetary matters. An example of an IFI active in the field is the Romanian Fiscal Council, with a regular chapter on fiscal transparency issues in its Annual Report.

11.4.6 Normative Recommendations

Some IFIs have the remit to top up their compliance assessments with recommendations on the fiscal stance, on the consequences of alternative policies or on more broadly defined fiscal governance issues. It is worth highlighting that issuing recommendations involves difficult trade-offs and requires a well-established reputation. From a media perspective, it raises the profile of the institution beyond a technical body, with the consequence of becoming an actor itself accountable for the relevance of its policy advice. There are a handful of regional IFIs whose legal mandate includes normative recommendations: the Czech Fiscal Council, the Croatian Fiscal Policy Commission and the Romanian Fiscal Council.

Moreover, on its own initiative the Slovenian Fiscal Council has been continuously agile in this domain as of its operationalisation in spring 2017. It has issued policy advice ranging from the stance of fiscal policy to policies to tackle demographic challenges, but also including the desirable features of the national fiscal governance legislation, in particular the

[21] Available at (English version): http://simtask.rozpoctovarada.sk/

provisions on the MTBF. More prominently, the Council formulated its policy advice to the newly formed government in autumn 2018 arguing against the full implementation of the unfunded spending promises, which would have resulted in a significant deviation from the numerical fiscal rules (the recommendations were based on an own-initiative assessment of the fiscal and macroeconomic implications of the Slovenian coalition agreement).

11.5 Conclusions

In the wake of the crisis, a number of basic requirements for the Member States' NFFs were introduced at the EU level, with a primary objective of promoting compliance with EU fiscal rules by strengthening domestic budgetary arrangements as well as by enhancing national ownership. Strong budgetary frameworks are expected to support sound fiscal policy, in particular by making use of well-designed numerical fiscal rules, promoting multiannual fiscal planning, and also through the existence of independent entities, improving the reliability of forecasting and enhancing fiscal transparency. When designing this common set of European requirements, the need for the NFFs to reflect the specificities of the Member States' legal and institutional frameworks was an important factor taken into account.

Since the adoption of the supranational NFF provisions, EU-11 domestic budgetary frameworks have registered a particularly impressive development, as illustrated by the evolution of the various indices from the Commission's Fiscal Governance Database. In turn, the progress has been even more pronounced in Central and Eastern European countries than in the 'old' Member States, since they had typically only rudimentary domestic systems before the global financial crisis, and therefore the EU requirements provided the very basis for building their national frameworks. In particular, the number and strength of domestic numerical fiscal rules have clearly been on the rise and they are now a central part of the NFFs of the 'new' Member States. The scope and transparency of medium-term fiscal planning have also been upgraded. Finally, the watchdog role of recently established IFIs has generally increased the transparency of public finances and has strengthened the public scrutiny over fiscal policy-making.

Indeed, IFIs have recently spread across the region, and by today, virtually all EU-11 Member States have at least one institution providing independent advice and input to fiscal policy-making. Given the relatively short period of time since most of the IFIs took up their duty, it is difficult to assess (both quantitatively and qualitatively) the impact of IFIs on budgetary outcomes and on the quality of fiscal policy. Nonetheless, early (primarily anecdotal) evidence suggests that these institutions do play a useful role in budgetary processes, as they exert a positive influence through the flagship six IFI functions discussed in this chapter. Several episodes were recalled in the above sections when IFIs in the region have already been successful in engaging national governments in a debate on fiscal execution and planning, thereby enhancing the public's awareness of fiscal issues. It is important to highlight that some of these activities were carried out by EU-11 IFIs without any EU legal requirements to do so and often on their own initiative, suggesting that the spread of good practices or demonstration effects across the EU have also been at play during the institution-building phase.

This being said, further efforts could be made (by legislation and/or in practice) so that IFIs in all EU-11 countries publish both forward-looking as well as backward-looking compliance assessments in a timely manner and covering most, if not all, of the domestic fiscal rules in force. In a similar vein, they could increasingly play a stronger role in the production or endorsement of official macro-fiscal forecasts, moving towards the budgetary forecasts as well. In addition, based on the existing experiences, domestic fiscal policies may benefit from a potential gradual extension of the mandate of IFIs to include those responsibilities where currently only subgroups of EU-11 IFIs are active (policy costing, long-term sustainability assessment and the promotion of fiscal transparency). Since some of these activities might require significantly more resources, such considerations should be accompanied by a reflection on appropriate resource endowment for IFIs.

References

Alesina, A., & Passalacqua, A. (2015). *The Political Economy of Government Debt* (NBER Working Paper, No. 21821).

Debrun, X., & Kinda, T. (2014). *Strengthening Post-Crisis Fiscal Credibility: Fiscal Councils on the Rise – A New Dataset* (IMF Working Paper, No. 14/58).

Debrun, X., Moulin, L., Turrini, A., Ayuso-i-Casals, J., & Kumar Manmohan, S. (2008). Tied to the Mast? National Fiscal Rules in the European Union. *Economic Policy, 23*(4), 297–362.

European Commission. (2007). "How to Stick to Medium-Term Budgetary Plans", in "Public Finances in EMU". In *Public Finances in EMU – 2007* (European Economy No. 3) (pp. 147–192). Brussels: European Commission.

European Commission. (2017). Report from the Commission Presented Under Article 8 of the Treaty on Stability, Coordination and Governance in the Economic and Monetary Union – C(2017)1201, Brussels.

European Commission. (2019). *Vade Mecum on the Stability and Growth Pact* (European Economy, No. 101), European Commission, Brussels.

Fabrizio, S., & Mody, A. (2006). Can Budget Institutions Counteract Political Indiscipline? *Economic Policy, 21*(48), 689–739.

Horvath, M. (2018). EU Independent Fiscal Institutions: An Assessment of Potential Effectiveness. *Journal of Common Market Studies, 56*(3), 504–519.

IMF. (2013). *The Functions and Impact of Fiscal Councils* (IMF Policy Paper). Washington, DC: International Monetary Fund.

IMF. (2017). A Greater Role for Fiscal Policy. In *Fiscal Monitor – April*. Washington, DC: International Monetary Fund.

Jankovics, L., & Sherwood, M. (2017). *Independent Fiscal Institutions in the EU Member States: The Early Years* (European Economy Discussion Papers No. 67), Brussels: European Commission.

Kalsone, D., & Platais, J. (2018). *Report on Political Parties Survey on Fiscal Discipline Issues in 2018* (Latvian Fiscal Discipline Council, Research Papers, No. 3).

Kopits, G., & Symansky, S. (1998). *Fiscal Policy Rules* (IMF Occasional Paper, No. 162). Washington, DC: International Monetary Fund.

Nerlich, C., & Reuter, W. H. (2013). *The Design of National Fiscal Frameworks and Their Budgetary Impact* (ECB Working Paper Series, No. 1588). Frankfurt: European Central Bank.

Sherwood, M. (2015). *Medium-Term Budgetary Frameworks in the EU Member States* (European Economy, No. 21). Brussels: European Commission.

Turrini, A. (2008). *Fiscal Policy and the Cycle in the Euro Area: The Role of Government Revenue and Expenditure* (Economic Papers, No. 323). Brussels: European Commission.

CHAPTER 12

Towards Sustainable and Adequate Pension Systems: Old-Age Pension Reforms After Economic Transition and EU Accession in Central-Eastern and South-Eastern Europe

Agnieszka Chłoń-Domińczak

12.1 Introduction

Europe's welfare states are facing a context of permanent austerity, caused by changes in the global economy, a slowdown in economic growth, the maturation of governmental commitments related to social protection systems and population ageing. All these factors contribute to a fiscal stress that is unlikely to diminish in the next few decades. This applies not only to the more developed and affluent European countries, but also to those in Central, Eastern and South-Eastern Europe (CESE), which are becoming "demographically old before being economically rich".

The CESE countries have gone through remarkable social, political and economic changes over the last three decades. Their transformation from

A. Chłoń-Domińczak (✉)
SGH Warsaw School of Economics, Warsaw, Poland

M. Landesmann, I. P. Székely (eds.), *Does EU Membership Facilitate Convergence? The Experience of the EU's Eastern Enlargement - Volume II*, Studies in Economic Transition,
https://doi.org/10.1007/978-3-030-57702-5_12

centrally planned to market economies, the shift in their political systems from communism to democracy, as well as societal and cultural changes have reshaped these countries in a formidable way. Changes to pension systems have been an integral part of these changes over this period.

Ensuring the long-term stability and adequacy of pension systems was one of the most important challenges that these countries faced following economic transition. The pension systems struggled with reduced societal trust as well as many weaknesses, including a lack of targeting, weak administration, as well as adverse incentives, which led to ineffective cost containment (Barr 1994). Parametric reforms, the typical approach in Western countries, were met with fierce resistance and were even blocked by constitutional courts (in some countries) (Müller 2003). This induced policy makers to move towards a different public-private mix. The reforms that were introduced starting from the late 1990s and which truly initiated the transformation process of the pension systems were in many cases an attempt to break with the path dependency embedded in the old systems. They also initiated a shift towards multi-pillar financing, which was not a typical feature of European welfare states at the time. As underlined by Pierson (2001): 416), once pay-as-you-go systems are in place for a long time, they are highly resistant to radical reform. Shifting to private, funded arrangements would place an unbearable burden on current workers, requiring them to finance the previous generation's retirement while simultaneously saving for their own. However, given the specific conditions present during the economic transition period, reformers in the CESE countries believed they could finance the transition to multi-pillar systems. Additional resources could be found from privatisation revenues, for example, while cost containment measures, such as a scaling back of early retirement possibilities, could also be found.

The break with path dependency was initiated at a specific time of economic transition. Many institutions and systems were being radically reformed to meet the needs of the changing economy and society and the attempted retrenchment went far beyond what would be considered viable in more affluent countries (Pierson 2001).

In reality, the pension reform processes in CESE countries have been through many twists and turns since their beginning three decades ago. As argued by Grech (2018), pension system reform has resembled a cycle in which waves of reforms to improve sustainability are followed by changes in subsequent moves in the opposite direction, as there is an unbalanced trade-off between the achievement of the pension system's goals and the pressures exerted by the constraints.

The development of pension systems in CESE countries has also followed just such cycle. According to Cerami (2010) the Central and Eastern European countries have developed around a new welfare logic, which combines, in a path-dependent and innovative way, aspects of Bismarckian social insurance, communist egalitarism and liberal market orientation. As a result, they include elements of each of the three 'welfare worlds' described by Esping-Andersen (1990). Cerami (2010) argues that in their pension reforms, the CESE countries have followed a path of development with several phases of economic, political and social transformation, including (i) compensating for the transition, (ii) introduction of multi-pillar and partial funding and (iii) rebalancing and the return to Bismarck.

Each of the phases of pension system reform needs to be seen in a wider context, including not only the national actors and politics, but also the international actors who were providing policy advice, expertise and policy coordination. The first two phases of reform took place between the economic transition of the early 1990s and the time of EU enlargement in 2004. In this period, the CESE countries embarked on a series of systemic changes that were supported by international institutions providing advisory and financial support. This can be seen as institutional convergence towards market economies. The third phase of the rebalancing took place with the EU accession, the economic and financial crisis and post-crisis developments. Upon accession to the EU, pension policies were also driven by the tools of EU coordination in social and financial policy areas.

In this chapter, the three phases of pension reform in CESE countries are discussed in the context of international convergence. The first two phases, before the EU enlargement, that is the period of compensation for market-driven economic reforms combined with the retrenchment of the pension systems through privatisation are discussed in the first section. It focuses on the main issues related to designing and implementing radical pension reforms seen as a step towards convergence towards a liberal market orientation. The second section focuses on the third phase of rebalancing that followed EU accession and convergence towards European social and financial policies. In the third section the main challenges ahead of pension systems are discussed, followed by concluding remarks.

12.2 From Transition to Enlargement: Transformation to Market Economies Supported by International Institutions

Pension systems in CESE countries were transformed significantly in the period between the early 1990s and EU accession. In the early 1990s, they were seen as an instrument to alleviate problems in the labour market and problems caused by market-oriented reforms. Many policy makers followed the "lump of labour market" fallacy, believing that the retirement of older workers with outdated skills would create jobs for young people. This phase of "compensating for the transition" led to an increase in spending on pension systems and the loss of their financial sustainability in the long run. This was followed, in turn, by a phase of systemic pension reforms with multi-pillar architecture. The main goal of these reforms was to regain the long-term sustainability of pension systems, but also to make them less reliant on labour market developments, stimulate long-term savings and the development of financial markets.

12.2.1 Compensating for the Transition

At the beginning of 1990s, the pension systems played an important role in the social and economic transition of the countries in Central, Eastern and South-Eastern Europe. Labour market restructuring led to a rapid change in the demand skills and massive unemployment. Governments widened access to pensions, including early retirement, to many of the laid-off workers, who otherwise would not have had any source of income. The retirement system was used as a substitute for welfare and unemployment benefits (Müller 2003). These arrangements, which were caused by labour market shortages, led to high costs. The normal pensionable age in CESE countries was low by Western standards (55 for women, 60 for men) and many groups could retire even earlier. As a result, a significant share of pensioners received their benefits below the pensionable age.

A comparison of selected pension indicators in the CESE countries in the mid-1990s is presented in Table 12.1. Broad access to early retirement led to very high system dependency levels. In all countries, the number of pensioners was more than half of the number of contributors. In Bulgaria and Hungary, this ratio reached 4–5, and the share of pensioners in the total population exceeded one-fourth, as they did in Estonia and Latvia as well. At the same time, labour market developments, including high unemployment, led to low coverage in many countries.

In Poland, between 1989 and 1996, the number of beneficiaries increased by 34.8%, while the number of contributors declined by 14.4%. In the same period in Hungary, these statistics were 22.4% and 25.0% respectively (Müller 1999). Pension expenditure reached 14.4% of GDP in Poland and 9.7% of GDP in Hungary, with the budgetary subsidies equal to 1.9% and 0.4% of GDP respectively. The generosity of pension systems varied significantly between countries (Table 12.1), which reflected the way pension systems adjusted to changes in wages and prices. As summarised by Barr (1994), pension systems paid too little to too many at too high a cost. An example of pension system developments in the 1990s in Poland is presented in Box 1.

Box 1. Pension System Changes in Poland in the 1990s

During the economic transition, the early retirement policy in Poland was one of the main policy instruments to absorb the excess labour force. All workers who lost their jobs due to the bankruptcy or restructuring in their companies could claim early retirement. Those, who did not qualify for early retirement could also apply for disability pensions, and disability assessment rules were relaxed. As a result, between 1990 and 1992 as many as 1.8 million people claimed old-age or disability pensions, with the peak in 1991.

Furthermore, in order to compensate for high inflation, in 1991–1992, all pensions in payment were re-calculated and regular indexation of benefits was introduced. The increase in the number of pensioners combined with the increase in benefits led to a sharp increase in pension spending. This led to further increases in pension spending: between 1990 and 1992, pension expenditure relative to GDP increased from 7% to 12.3%.

In the mid-1990s, it became evident that the demographic situation would change dramatically in the future. A rapid decline in fertility was observed after the collapse of the centrally planned economies and communist regimes. It was caused by the rapid transition of patterns of family formation, birth control and postponement of childbearing decisions (Sobotka 2003). The low fertility rates and rising life expectancies in

Table 12.1 Selected pension system indicators, mid-1990s

	System dependency rate (pensioners per 100 contributors)	*Old-age dependency rate (60+ per 100 20–59 years old)*	*Pensioners (% of population)*	*Coverage rate (contributors as % of labour force)*	*Benefit ratio (average pension as % of average wage)*	*Pension spending (% of GDP)*
Bulgaria	81.0	38.5	27.5	64.0	30.0	7.3
Croatia	61.7	37.6	19.0	66.0	46.1	11.6
Czechia	53.0	31.3	24.2	85.0	41.5	9.8
Estonia	60.0	33.3	25.0	76.0	31.6	7.0
Hungary	78.1	35.7	27.5	77.0	39.1	9.7
Latvia	65.9	34.5	25.0	60.5	62.8	10.2
Lithuania	69.2	32.3	22.5	74.3	30.8	7.3
Poland	53.7	29.4	18.2	68.0	63.5	14.4
Romania	58.3	32.3	15.1	55.0	23.9	5.1
Slovakia	57.0	27.8	22.0	73.0	41.0	9.1
Slovenia	58.9	31.3	22.2	86.0	68.7	13.6

Source: Müller (2003: 66)

Central-Eastern and South-Eastern Europe mean that populations in the region are ageing more quickly than in Western or Northern Europe. Changes in the population structure and the growing number of people above the age of 65 will put significant pressure on the stability of pension systems in the long run.

The pension systems also faced many weaknesses (Barr 1994). These included ineffective cost containment, as benefits were easy to obtain and (in some cases) were too high. The systems also created adverse incentives, particularly with respect to work effort. Contributions were also high which depressed the demand for labour. At the same time, everyone thought that benefits were paid by "someone else" and there were pressures to increase the generosity of pension systems. The high burden placed on employers to contribute to the system led to a low degree of compliance, which could not be enforced by the weak administration responsible for collection. A large portion of contribution arrears was also attributable to large firms with close ties to the state (Fultz and Stanovnik 2004).

12.2.2 Towards Multi-pillar Systems

12.2.2.1 The Need for Pension Reform in CESE Countries

The weaknesses of pension systems combined with the looming long-term outlook led to a rising discussion on the need for systemic pension reforms. The reform goals included, among other priorities, cost containment measures through tightening eligibility to disability pensions as well as removing artificial incentives to early retirement and improving the equity of the system between different groups of workers. Secondly, the policy recommendations focused on improving incentives by reducing payroll contributions and sharing them between workers and employers. Incentives to postpone retirement decisions by changes in the pension formulae were also proposed.

However, the most important reform directions included the diversification of pension financing by introducing a mandatory funded component. There were several advantages of such reforms presented in the literature (Barr 1994). First, the introduction of funding (taking over from state pensions) reduces public spending in the long run. Second, they can support increased savings and hence higher economic growth that would help the sustainability of pension systems, but also stimulate development of financial markets and assist privatisation. Last but not least, it was believed that it would help to protect the system from political pressures as future increases in pensions would be possible only if contributions increased in the present.

At the same time, there were also important arguments about the risks related to introducing funding. First, although private schemes can cope with inflation during the accumulation phase, it is more difficult for them during the payout phase. Furthermore, a significant move to funding increases public spending at the beginning of reform introduction, due to the transition costs—pensions of the elderly need to be paid out, and additional contributions are needed to build the fund. The reforms required key policy decisions regarding redistribution in the pension system, distribution of risk in the private system, the scope of individual choices with regard to the pension portfolio, asset management principles, the level of risk in the asset portfolio, monitoring compliance and state guarantees. To implement the reforms, both institutional and political capacity needed to be developed.

Nevertheless, the advantages associated with funding were perceived by policy makers as important enough and the introduction of funding was not seen only as a solution to pay-as-you-go system problems, but also as a way of enhancing the economic and social efficiency of pension systems.

12.2.2.2 The Process of Pension Reform Development: National and Transnational Actors

The shaping of the pension systems in CESE countries involved different actors: national stakeholders (governments, social partners, experts) as well as transnational institutions active in the area of policy support and advice. These included, among others, the World Bank, the International Monetary Fund, the International Labour Office, the OECD and multiple international and national donor agencies (most notably USAID). The transnational institutions were frequently competing in the area of policy advice in social protection as well as policy entrepreneurs (Heneghan and Orenstein 2019). The countries were also learning from each other both on the design and on the implementation of reforms. The learning process was also supported by transnational institutions, which organised regional conferences and seminars where national experiences and common issues were discussed. The exchange of policy thinking between countries also meant that the governments perceived the multi-pillar reforms as “trendy” and they followed this direction.

The timing of the pension reform thinking in the CESE countries coincided with the publication of the World Bank book *Averting the Old-Age Crisis* (World Bank 1994). The publication of this book was followed by active advocacy for structural reforms, including the introduction of voluntary or mandatory individual private accounts. Most of the countries that implemented reforms of this kind in the CESE region did so with World Bank advice. As underlined by Orenstein (2008) *Averting* represented a turning point in the global pension reform effort. It represented major advancement in pension reform thinking and the process of writing and disseminating the work helped to establish a large group of pension privatisation experts and broad consensus within the Bank on pension privatisation methods.

The idea of multi-pillar systems seemed to be particularly attractive for decision makers, who saw the opportunity to develop national financial market, including stable national financial investors (pension funds) as well as creating conditions for the development of the national stock exchanges and equity markets. This process was also stimulated by international financial companies, who sought opportunities to expand their markets and activities. Interactions with international institutions were a part of the convergence towards a common thinking on pension reform in the CESE countries. Orenstein (2008) following the typology proposed by Jacoby (2008) assessed that in the pension policy area, policy transfer has been achieved through a combination of "inspiration" (i.e. transnational actors influencing state bodies with the development and promotion of ideas), "subsidy" (i.e. external actors offering support conditional on the enactment of reforms) and "partnership" (i.e. an external actor supporting the domestic political allies), with various modes and mechanisms of influencing pension policies at different stages, as presented in Table 12.2. The modes and mechanisms of influence covered mainly the stages of policy development and policy transfer, with limited involvement in implementation, focusing on building capacity in the areas of regulation and supervision of funded pillars. Regulatory capacity was also supported by the OECD through the establishment of the International Network of Pension Regulators and Supervisors in 2001 and International Organisation of Pension Supervisors (IOPS) in 2004. During and after EU accession, the influence of the organisations involved in supporting policy development declined.

Table 12.2 Modes and mechanisms of influence of transnational institutions at different policy stages of pension reforms

Stage	*Policy development*	*Policy transfer*	*Implementation*
Modes of influence	Norms creation	Norms teaching Coercion	Norms teaching Coercion
Mechanisms	Publications Working groups Conferences	Training seminars Reform team funds Technical assistance Loans	Agency funds Employee training Public relations
Organisations (pension privatisation)	World Bank Policy entrepreneurs	World Bank USAID Policy entrepreneurs	World Bank USAID

Source: Orenstein (2008: 64)

12.2.2.3 Introducing Multi-pillar Systems in CESE Countries

Between 1999 and 2008, 9 out of 11 new member states from Central, Eastern and South-Eastern Europe decided to introduce pension reforms that included a mandatory funded component. As pointed out by Cerami (2010) this policy seemed the best way to cut expenditures, while, at the same time, ensuring a market orientation. The main features of the pension system designs are presented in Table 12.3.[1]

With regard to the design of pension systems, there is convergence on models with a funded component. This part of the pension system was based on individual choice and defined contributions, which meant that there was a close link between contribution payments and future pension benefits. Another similar feature is the transition to funded systems, which was made mandatory only for younger workers, while in the majority of the countries, those who were already participating in social insurance for some time (though with some different age limits between countries) had a choice on whether to join the funded component or not. Only in Lithuania was the option to join the funded scheme voluntary for all workers. The CESE countries also commonly adopted a solution, that the contributions for the funded component are deducted from mandatory social insurance contribution. As a result, loss in the contribution income in the non-financial (PAYG) pension system needed to be compensated from other sources. This resulted in transition cost that appeared in all countries. Only in Estonia, those who decided to join the funded component needed to agree on the additional contribution co-payment, equal to 2% of wage, which reduced the necessity to subsidise the pension payments.

However, the size of contributions assigned to the funded pillars ranged from 2% to 9% of wages, which shows rising consideration of the transition costs. Countries that initiated the shift towards multi-pillar frameworks (Hungary, Poland, Latvia) decided to have higher contributions in the funded pillar, compared to those countries which followed later (with the exception of Slovakia).

The changes to pension systems also included the design of the PAYG part. Countries needed to adjust the accrual of pension rights to the reduced contributions paid to this part of the pension system. Many countries also decided to increase the link between lifetime wages (or contributions) and pension benefits. Latvia and Poland implemented the

[1] A statutory funded pension scheme (defined contribution (DC), fully funded) was also introduced in Czechia from the beginning of 2013 (as a voluntary partial opt-out from the first pillar), but it closed at the end of 2015.

Table 12.3 Main features of pension schemes in eight CESE countries at the time when reform was introduced

	Public pension scheme (PAYG)	*Retirement age*	*Mandatory Funded Scheme (FDC)*		
			Initial contributions (%)	*Enactment date*	*Who participates*
Hungary	DB	60/55 to 62/62	6–8	1998	Mandatory for new entrants, voluntary for all employed
Poland	NDC	65/60 with removal of early retirement	7.3	1999	Mandatory for new and workers <30, voluntary for 30–50
Latvia	NDC (from 1998)	60/55 to 62/62	2–8	2001	Mandatory for entrants and workers <30, voluntary for 30–50
Bulgaria	DB	60/55 to 63/60	2–5	2002	Mandatory for all workers <42, no cohorts with choice option
Croatia	Points	60/55 to 65/60	5	2002	Mandatory for entrants and workers <40, voluntary for 40–50
Estonia	DB	60/55 to 63/63	6 (4 +2)	2002	Mandatory for new entrants, voluntary for 19–60 in the year of reform
Lithuania	DB	60/55 to 62.5/60	2.5–5.5	2004	Voluntary for current and new workers but no opt-out
Slovakia	Points	60/53–57 to 62/62	9	2005	Mandatory for born after 1983, voluntary for all being in the social insurance before 2005
Romania	DB	62/57 to 65/60	2–3	2008	Mandatory for new and workers <35, voluntary for 36–45

Source: Bielawska et al. (2018) based on Schwarz and Arias (2014) with author's update

non-financial defined contribution (NDC systems), Croatia and Slovakia introduced the point systems, however, in Croatia, a minimum pension plays an important role in providing income redistribution for those with low wages. Income redistribution was also limited in pension systems in Hungary, Bulgaria, Romania and to some extent Estonia and Slovenia, as presented later in this chapter. Lithuania and the Czech Republic maintained income redistribution elements. At the same time, the projected replacement rates indicate differences in the generosity of pension systems.

Another element of convergence among the CESE countries is linked to changes in the retirement age. At the initial stage of reforms, all countries either increased pensionable age limits or reduced access to early retirement. Equal retirement age for men and women was introduced in 4 out of 11 countries. As discussed by Guardiancich (2009) in several countries (i.e. Hungary, Poland) equal retirement age was initially proposed, but then following the political compromise the difference between the retirement ages for men and women was continued.

The long-term projections of pension system sustainability were produced, focusing on the long-term goal of balancing pension system finances. The projections took into account the path of implementation, which included, among other things, following the initial path of retirement age increases as well as benefit indexation rules that were close to price indexation.

Last but not least, there were also some similarities in the design of the institutions in the funded part of the pension systems. New legislation on the functioning of pension funds followed a similar blueprint. The initial Polish law served as a blueprint for legislation development in Bulgaria, Romania and Croatia. The institutional design in Hungary was different, with pension funds functioning as mutual companies, which led to reduced transparency, particularly in relation to the fees and costs of the pension funds. Although their frameworks were relatively similar, there were significant differences among CESE in terms of the level of administrative costs, investment regulations as well as assumptions on the available investment portfolios, which are discussed below.

12.2.2.4 Implementing Multi-pillar Systems in CESE Countries

The early years of implementation focused mainly on the introduction of funded pillars as well as individual insurance accounts, particularly in those countries that did not have information on individual insurance records. As discussed earlier, this stage of the implementation was also supported by transnational institutions, mainly related to capacity building in the area of pension fund regulation and supervision.

Initially, workers were making their choices related to participation in this part of the pension system. Due to differences in expectations, when presented with a choice, younger workers were more likely to choose pension funds, while older ones tended to remain only in the PAYG component (Palacios and Whitehouse 1998). The pension fund management companies were very active in advertising the choices, frequently with excessive promises related to the expected value of future pensions (see, e.g. Chłoń 2000). Overall, more than half of those that had a choice joined funded schemes.

The relatively broad access to pension funds was not accompanied by efforts to develop the necessary level of financial literacy. After public information campaigns that followed the introduction of reforms, no broader government activity related to developing basic knowledge about long-term pension savings followed. As a result, many workers were not adequately informed about issues such as exposure to risk, or the costs and returns related to pension funds.

Most pension funds followed a very conservative investment strategy. Until 2005, the percentage of public and private bonds in their portfolios was substantial, ranging from 45–50% (Estonia in 2001 and Slovakia in 2001–2003) to 60–75% in other countries (Bielawska et al. 2017). At the same time, investment in equity represented less than 10% pension fund portfolios in most of the cases. Only in Poland, around 30% of assets were invested in equity. This also meant that the hope that pension funds would contribute to the development of domestic financial markets failed to materialise in most countries. Among the CESE countries, in Croatia, Estonia, Latvia, Lithuania and Hungary, participants could choose between three or four types of portfolio (i.e. aggressive, stable, conservative), with some constraints related to age. In Bulgaria, Poland and Romania only one type of portfolio was available (ibid.). The real returns of pension funds also varied, and at the end of 2012 in most of the countries, the average annual real rates of return were negative or close to zero in Bulgaria, Estonia, Lithuania and Slovakia. In Hungary, Poland and Romania, the real returns were positive, and in the latter two countries the real average annual rate of return exceeded 5% (ibid.).

Another important aspect was the fees and charges related to the management of pension funds. The fee structure in the CESE countries was quite complex, including fees and charges levied on contributions, assets and investment returns (shown in Table 12.4). Upon introduction of the

Table 12.4 Types of costs and fees charged in selected CESE countries

Country	*Plan/scheme administration fees*	*Investment management fees, for*		*Custodian fees*	*Investment transaction costs*	*Guarantee fees*	*Other*
		primary funds only	*Underlying funds*				
Bulgaria	x	x	x				X
Romania	x	x		x	x	x	
Hungary	x	x		x		x	x
Croatia	x	x			x		x
Poland	x	x					x

Source: Han and Stańko (2018), Ionescu and Robles (2014)

multi-pillar systems, fees were perceived as one of the elements of competition between fund providers. However, fees were initially relatively high. In response to these developments, the regulators in some countries (i.e. Croatia, Hungary, Poland, Romania) decided to introduce caps on the fees (Ionescu and Robles 2014; Han and Stańko 2018). In the first years, the fees-to-assets ratio was high, both due to high fees and due to the low level of assets. For example, in Hungary in 2000, the fees were around 3.5% of assets of pension funds and by 2010 this ratio dropped to around 1%. In Poland in 2004, total fees exceeded 1.6% of assets and by 2011 it dropped to below 0.8% (ibid.).

According to the IOPS estimates (Ionescu and Robles 2014; Han and Stańko 2018) the impact of fees on total pension savings varies significantly between countries, as shown in Table 12.5. It presents the estimated charge ratio for 40 years of savings, which measures the impact that any type of charge can have on the final balance of an individual retirement account compared to the hypothetical balance that could be obtained if no fees were charged. In 2008, prior to the financial crisis, the charge ratio ranged from 18.74% in Poland to 26.51% in Bulgaria. The later estimates that included also Baltic countries and Romania indicate that the fees are quite high in Latvia and Estonia. The complicated fee structures also impede the ability of pension fund members to compare the costs of pension funds and were one of the reasons for the loss of trust in funded schemes, particularly during the financial crisis. As noted by Han and Stańko (2018), between 2014 and 2017 there was a tendency to decrease the average fees, including legal limits in Bulgaria, Lithuania, Poland and the Slovak Republic, while Romania did not change the fee levels.

Summing up, the first years after the introduction of mandatory pension funds saw the development of the pension funds market and the adjustment of regulatory regimes, which was particularly visible in the area of fees. After initial activities related to supporting workers' choices, CESE countries usually did not pursue wider policies to build financial literacy among pension fund members.

12.2.2.5 Transition Costs and the Situation of Public Finances

The introduction of the mandatory funded component is associated with transition costs, which are related to the part of the contribution diverted to pension funds, while at the same time financing the pay-as-you-go pensions paid to the old-age pensioners. The size of the transition costs depended on the contribution rate for the funded component and its

Table 12.5 Charge ratio for 40 years for average fees in CESE countries, percentage of accumulated assets

	2008	*2012/2013*	*2018*
Bulgaria	26.51%	26.51%	21.5%
Croatia	22.21%	11.74%	n.a
Estonia	n.a.	31.56%	n.a
Hungary	22.57%	5.93%	n.a
Latvia	n.a.	39.59%	n.a
Lithuania	n.a.	22.72%	n.a
Poland	18.74%	14.35%	13.8%
Romania	n.a.	16.10%	n.a.
Slovakia	19.03%	19.17%	19.0%

Source: Han and Stańko (2018), Ionescu and Robles (2014)

Table 12.6 Transition costs to the multi-pillar system, 2000–2008 (percentage of GDP)

	2000	*2001*	*2002*	*2003*	*2004*	*2005*	*2006*	*2007*	*2008*
HU	0.5	0.5	0.5	0.7	0.8	1.0	1.0	1.2	1.2
PL	1.0	1.1	1.2	1.2	1.1	1.3	1.4	1.4	1.6
LV		0.1	0.2	0.4	0.4	0.6	0.7	1.0	1.1
HR			0.9	1.1	1.1	1.2	1.2	1.2	1.3
BG			0.6	0.5	0.6	0.7	0.8	1.1	1.1
EE			0.0	0.4	0.6	0.7	0.7	0.8	0.5
LT					0.3	0.4	0.6	0.9	1.1
SK						0.6	1.1	1.2	1.2
RO									0.2

Source: Bielawska et al. (2018) with author's update

coverage. In countries with a higher contribution rate and higher participation, the costs were obviously higher. As shown in Table 12.6, the transition costs increased over time, as more people joined the pension funds and contribution rates increased in those countries that adopted the strategy of rising contributions (Hungary, Latvia, Lithuania, Bulgaria). Around the time of EU accession (2004) the transition costs varied between countries. In the post-accession years (until the financial crisis), the costs increased further, exceeding 1% of GDP in almost every country.

Initially, all CESE countries planned to use savings in the PAYG component and higher government sector revenues to finance the transition.

In Poland and Lithuania, privatisation revenues were also earmarked (Bielawska et al. 2018).

However, in the years following the introduction of the multi-pillar pensions, many of the countries did not follow the plan to reduce pension spending. In Hungary, the initially planned increase in contribution rates to the mandatory funded pillar was postponed. More generous indexation in Croatia, Hungary, Latvia and Poland, as well as the introduction of the additional pension payment (a so-called 13th monthly pension) for three years in Hungary, led to further increases in pension spending (Guardiancich 2009; Chłoń-Domińczak et al. 2012). In Poland, the initial plans of withdrawing early retirement were postponed by two years. In Latvia, pensions were increased at a higher rate in the late 1990s. As a result, pension expenditure increased or remained unchanged.[2]

The ability of CESE countries to finance the transition costs was also linked to their overall fiscal situation. As shown in Tables 12.7 and 12.8, the CESE countries prior to accession and before the crisis faced relatively mild fiscal pressures, as many had either budget surpluses (in Bulgaria and Estonia) or relatively low deficits. Their debt levels (with the exception of Hungary and Poland, which struggled with already high government debt in the 1990s and before) were also below 40% of GDP.

Table 12.7 General government net lending (+)/net borrowing (-) in CESE countries, 2000–2008 (percentage of GDP)

	2000	*2001*	*2002*	*2003*	*2004*	*2005*	*2006*	*2007*	*2008*
Bulgaria	-0.5	1.1	-1.2	-0.4	1.8	1.0	1.8	1.1	1.6
Estonia	-0.1	0.2	0.4	1.8	2.4	1.1	2.9	2.7	-2.7
Croatia	n.a.	-2.2	-3.5	-4.7	-5.2	-3.9	-3.4	-2.4	-2.8
Latvia	-2.7	-1.9	-2.3	-1.5	-0.9	-0.4	-0.5	-0.5	-4.2
Lithuania	-3.2	-3.5	-1.9	-1.3	-1.4	-0.3	-0.3	-0.8	-3.1
Hungary	-3.0	-4.1	-8.8	-7.1	-6.5	-7.8	-9.3	-5.0	-3.7
Poland	-3.0	-4.8	-4.8	-6.1	-5.0	-4.0	-3.6	-1.9	-3.6
Romania	-4.6	-3.4	-1.9	-1.4	-1.1	-0.8	-2.1	-2.7	-5.4
Slovenia	-3.6	-3.9	-2.4	-2.6	-2.0	-1.3	-1.2	-0.1	-1.4
Slovakia	-12.0	-6.4	-8.1	-2.7	-2.3	-2.9	-3.6	-1.9	-2.4

Source: Eurostat [gov_10dd_edpt1]

[2] See Sect. 12.3 for details.

Table 12.8 General government consolidated gross debt in CESE countries, 2000–2008 (percentage of GDP)

	2000	*2001*	*2002*	*2003*	*2004*	*2005*	*2006*	*2007*	*2008*
Bulgaria	71.2	65.0	51.4	43.7	36.0	26.8	21.0	16.3	13.0
Estonia	5.1	4.8	5.7	5.6	5.1	4.5	4.4	3.7	4.5
Croatia	35.5	36.5	36.6	38.1	40.3	41.2	38.6	37.2	39.0
Latvia	12.1	13.8	13.0	13.7	14.0	11.4	9.6	8.0	18.2
Lithuania	23.5	22.9	22.1	20.4	18.7	17.6	17.2	15.9	14.6
Hungary	55.3	51.9	55.3	57.9	58.7	60.5	64.5	65.5	71.6
Poland	36.5	37.3	41.8	46.6	45.0	46.4	46.9	44.2	46.3
Romania	22.4	25.7	24.8	21.3	18.6	15.7	12.3	11.9	12.4
Slovenia	25.9	26.1	27.3	26.7	26.8	26.3	26.0	22.8	21.8
Slovakia	49.6	48.3	42.9	41.6	40.6	34.1	31.0	30.1	28.5

Source: Eurostat [gov_10dd_edpt1]

Developments in the pension systems and public finances after the implementation of pension reforms meant that savings in the old-age pension systems made only a small contribution to financing the transition costs, except in Latvia where the expenditure on pension systems declined following the implementation of the NDC system. A decomposition of the financing of the transition costs between 2000 (or from the date that reforms were implemented) and 2008 is presented in Fig. 12.1.

In Bulgaria, Lithuania and Slovakia, the transition was financed mainly by taxes. In Hungary and Poland, the transition costs were mainly financed by an increase in the public debt. In Croatia and Estonia, the financing was divided between taxes and government debt financing. These outcomes differed from the initial plans. The financing of the transition to multi-pillar systems using government debt became an important issue in the discussions on pension system policy after EU accession.

The long-term financial cost of the transition to multi-pillar systems was not fully recognised by many governments, which believed that they would not require significant fiscal effort. This proved more challenging than expected, particularly during the crisis. Furthermore, the expected benefits of the reforms, particularly increased savings, turned out to be smaller than expected.

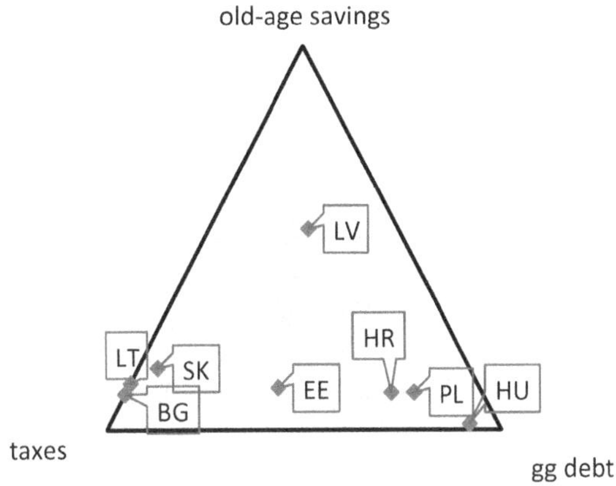

Fig. 12.1 Decomposition of sources of financing transition costs in CESE countries, 2000–2008. Note: Romania is excluded, as the multi-pillar reform was introduced in 2008. (Source: Bielawska et al. (2018) with author's update)

12.3 EU Accession and Post-accession: Rebalancing the Pension Systems and the Return to Bismarck?

Upon EU accession, countries in the region shifted their focus towards EU policy coordination, including fiscal, financial and pension policies. While pension legislation and organisation of pension systems, according to the subsidiarity principle, are the responsibility of national governments, there is some degree of coordination for pension policies at the EU level through instruments such as the so-called open method of coordination in pensions (pensions OMC), and the joint work of the EU member states and the European Commission on fiscal policies, including the long-term sustainability. This interplay between the European and national policies leads to the Europeanisation of social protection, understood as a two-way process which shapes both the EU and national policies. At the time of enlargement, the EU concepts and policies that related to pension systems included the Social Policy Agenda; the streamlining of social protection under the open method of coordination, reflected in the national reports of strategies on social protection and social inclusion; as well as demographic changes reflected in the communication on demographic change (Kvist and Saari 2007).

The logic of pension reforms differed significantly between the CESE countries and the older EU member states. Beblavý (2011) underlines that in the latter countries, paradigmatic change in pension systems has not happened, and instead, parametric reforms (some of them far-reaching) have been the preferred way forward. In contrast, the new EU member states have served as a veritable laboratory of social and economic change, including orientation towards neoliberal, market-driven policies, including compulsory pension savings based on individual choices. This means that the design of the (multi-pillar) pension systems was different in the majority of the new member states compared to the traditional pension system in the older EU countries. These differences are particularly visible when looking at the actual and projected contributions and expenditure in occupational, private mandatory and non-mandatory pensions in the 2009 Ageing Report (European Commission DG ECFIN 2009). The eight new member states (BG, LT, SK, PL, HU, EE, RO, LV) and only one old member state (SE) at that time had private mandatory pensions that were expected to finance some of the pension expenditure by 2060.

The new member states adopted the common goals of the pensions OMC, including adequacy of benefits and financial sustainability. The national strategy reports on adequate and sustainable pensions, presented in 2005, identified the challenges that their pension systems faced. However, as underlined by Wóycicka and Grabowski (2007) in the case of Poland, projections of a high probability of low-adequacy pension benefits were largely ignored. At the same time, an important controversy between the Commission and the new member states was the definition of the contributions transferred to mandatory funded scheme. The new member states assumed that the contributions diverted to these schemes and the accumulated assets would be treated as a part of public finances. However, Eurostat and the European Commission disagreed and, from 2007, after the initial transition period, the transition costs were fully accounted for in general government deficit and debt figures (ibid.). This led to a substantial increase in the public deficit and debt figures for the new member states in the light of the Maastricht criteria and excessive deficit rules. This process changed the locus of attention in pension policy. During the first years after EU accession, as presented in the previous section, the new member states faced limited fiscal pressure. Countries enjoyed relatively high economic growth. The first country among the new member states that joined the euro area was Slovakia, in 2009, which happened before the consequences of the fiscal crisis affected the public finance system.

12.3.1 *Reversal of Multi-pillar Pension Reforms*

When the crisis hit the CESE region, their fiscal positions worsened. Estonia was the only country that avoided an excessive deficit procedure (EDP) in 2009 and 2010. The Estonian government conducted fiscal consolidation, achieving a near balance or surplus in 2010 and the following years, a policy motivated by the country's intention to join the euro area, which it did in 2011 (Staehr, 2016). The same mechanism of strong fiscal consolidation worked in Bulgaria, the second country (after Estonia) with very tight national fiscal rules aimed at achieving a budgetary medium-term objective. Latvia joined the euro area in 2014 and Lithuania in 2015.

In other countries, general government deficits soared to 7–9% of GDP during 2009 and 2010, as indicated in Table 12.9 (Bielawska et al. 2018). Some countries also faced increasing public debt (Table 12.10). In Hungary, Croatia and Slovenia, debt levels exceeded the 60% of GDP threshold in the years following the fiscal crisis. In Hungary and Poland, despite the transfer of assets from pension funds back to public finances, government debts remained high.

The advent of the global financial and economic crisis changed the political calculus. The extreme fiscal stress created a new reality for the new member states, who decided to rebalance their pension systems and downsize their mandatory funded pension schemes (Beblavý 2011). Such changes were implemented in seven new member states, which is shown in Table 12.11.

Table 12.9 General government net lending (+)/net borrowing (-) in CESE countries, 2000–2008 (percentage of GDP)

	2009	*2010*	*2011*	*2012*	*2013*	*2014*	*2015*	*2016*	*2017*
Bulgaria	-4.1	-3.1	-2.0	-0.3	-0.4	-5.4	-1.7	0.2	1.1
Estonia	-2.2	0.2	1.2	-0.3	-0.2	0.7	0.1	-0.3	-0.4
Croatia	-6.0	-6.3	-7.9	-5.3	-5.3	-5.1	-3.4	-0.9	0.9
Latvia	-9.1	-8.7	-4.3	-1.2	-1.2	-1.5	-1.4	0.1	-0.6
Lithuania	-9.1	-6.9	-8.9	-3.1	-2.6	-0.6	-0.3	0.3	0.5
Hungary	-4.5	-4.5	-5.4	-2.4	-2.6	-2.6	-1.9	-1.6	-2.2
Poland	-7.3	-7.3	-4.8	-3.7	-4.1	-3.7	-2.7	-2.2	-1.4
Romania	-9.1	-6.9	-5.4	-3.7	-2.2	-1.3	-0.7	-2.9	-2.9
Slovenia	-5.8	-5.6	-6.7	-4.0	-14.7	-5.5	-2.8	-1.9	0.1
Slovakia	-7.8	-7.5	-4.3	-4.3	-2.7	-2.7	-2.6	-2.2	-0.8

Source: Eurostat [gov_10dd_edpt1]

Table 12.10 General government consolidated gross debt in CESE countries, 2000–2008 (percentage of GDP)

	2009	*2010*	*2011*	*2012*	*2013*	*2014*	*2015*	*2016*	*2017*
Bulgaria	13.7	15.3	15.2	16.7	17.1	27.1	26.2	29.6	25.6
Estonia	7.0	6.6	6.1	9.7	10.2	10.5	9.9	9.2	8.7
Croatia	48.3	57.3	63.8	69.4	80.4	84.0	83.7	80.2	77.5
Latvia	35.8	46.8	42.7	41.2	39.0	40.9	36.8	40.3	40.0
Lithuania	28.0	36.2	37.2	39.8	38.8	40.5	42.6	39.9	39.4
Hungary	77.8	80.2	80.5	78.4	77.1	76.6	76.6	75.9	73.3
Poland	49.4	53.1	54.1	53.7	55.7	50.4	51.3	54.2	50.6
Romania	22.1	29.7	34.0	36.9	37.6	39.2	37.8	37.3	35.1
Slovenia	34.6	38.4	46.6	53.8	70.4	80.4	82.6	78.7	74.1
Slovakia	36.3	41.2	43.7	52.2	54.7	53.5	52.2	51.8	50.9

Source: Eurostat [gov_10dd_edpt1]

Additionally, Romania's finance and pensions sector faced the ongoing discussion related to the government requirements made for the pension fund managers. At the end of 2018, the government proposed to introduce a minimum capital requirement of up to 10% of annual pension contributions, with which no provider would be able to comply. It would effectively force second pillar providers out of business, as it would lead to an 11-fold increase of the minimum capital. After discussions with the representatives of the industry, but also with the European Commission and the IMF, the required increase of the minimum capital was reduced to EUR 80 million (that is ten times less than the original proposal). This means that the minimum capital is to be increased by 12% compared to its current value.

In Hungary and Poland, all or part of the assets already accumulated were diverted back to the PAYG schemes. The Hungarian government was explicit about its objectives of reversing the funded scheme, declaring: "the key objectives of the proposed measures is to improve the budget balance that has been gradually deteriorated year after year since the implementation of the multi-pillar system, [...] and to cut explicit public debt relative to GDP in order to minimise the country's exposure to external shocks"—announcement of the Hungarian Ministry for the National Economy (Datz and Dancsi 2013). The Polish prime minister and the Minister of Finance advocated that the main reason for the reversal was the excessively high administrative costs and insufficient investment in the

Table 12.11 Reversals of funded components of pension systems in CEE countries

Country	*Short description of the change to contributions, assets, membership*
Estonia	**Temporary reduction with off-set** 6% contribution rate cut to 0% between June 2009 and January 2011 and shifted to PAYG. Gradual increase from 2011. Rate set at 3% in January 2011 and 6% in January 2012. In 2014–2017 at 8% to offset missed contributions
Latvia	**Partial reduction** 8% contribution rate reduced to 2% in May 2009. Rates increased to 4% from 2013
Lithuania	**Partial reduction** 5.5% contribution rate reduced to 2% in July 2009. Rates further lowered to 1.5% in January 2012 and 2.5% in 2013. Change to 3% (2%+ 1%) January 2014, voluntary participation. Additional contribution at 2% in 2016–2019
Hungary	**Permanent reversal** Contribution rate reduced to 0% in January 2011 assets transferred to the mandatory PAYG system
Poland	**Permanent reduction and partial reversal** Contribution rate reduced to 2.3% in May 2011. From February 2014 contribution at 2.92%, in February 2014 assets invested in government bonds transferred to PAYG scheme and redeemed. In 2014 system made opt-out and opt-in in specified time slots. Assets from pension funds transferred gradually to PAYG ten years prior to retirement. In 2019 the government announced that the funded pillar will be eliminated and accumulated assets will be either transferred to individual retirement accounts (with 15% transaction fee) or to NDC accounts
Romania	**Temporary reduction** Reduction in planned growth path of contribution rate from 2% to 6%. Rate froze at 2%, started to increase from 2010 at annual rate of 0.5 pp. up to 5% in 2015. In 2016 contribution rate 5.1% instead of 6%
Slovakia	**Permanent reduction** 9% contribution reduced to 4% in 2013; since 2017 increase in contribution rate by 0.25 pp. up to 6% in 2024. Funded scheme opt-out and opt-in system; since 2008 with reopening every two years (from 2009). New entrants are by default enrolled only to PAYG part but may apply for membership in the funded component up to age 35

Source: Schwarz and Arias (2014) updated by Bielawska et al. (2018)

real economy due to the high share of assets invested in Polish treasury bonds (Bielawska et al. 2018). The reversal decisions led, among others, to the elimination of transition costs (in Hungary) or their reduction in the other countries (Table 12.12).

Table 12.12 Transition costs to the multi-pillar system, 2009–2016 (percentage of GDP)

	2009	*2010*	*2011*	*2012*	*2013*	*2014*	*2015*	*2016*
BG	1.1	1.0	0.9	0.9	1.3	1.1	1.3	1.3
EE	1.1	0.1	0.4	0.9	1.4	1.8	1.9	2.0
LV	0.1	0.1	0.1	0.1	0.5	0.5	0.8	1.1
LT	0.6	0.3	0.4	0.4	0.4	0.5	0.5	0.8
HU	1.4	1.1	–	–	–	–	–	–
PL	1.6	1.6	1.0	0.5	0.7	0.5	0.2	0.2
RO	0.3	0.3	0.4	0.5	0.7	1.0	1.2	1.3
SK	1.2	1.2	1.2	1.1	0.6	0.6	0.6	0.7
HR	1.4	1.4	1.4	1.5	1.5	1.5	1.5	1.5

Source: Bielawska et al. (2018) with author's update

The reduction is due to a lower level of contributions but also the opt-out possibilities, noticeable in Poland and Slovakia. In the latter, the opt-out wave was particularly high in 2015, due to the reaction to the low level of actual benefits paid out by the pension funds. The worsening fiscal situation led to a change in the sources of financing for the transition costs, as shown in Fig. 12.2, with higher reliance on public debt and less reliance on taxes in almost all countries.

Recalibration of pension systems also affected the assets and investments of pension funds (Fig. 12.3). Pension fund assets in Poland and Hungary experienced severe drops as a result of the shift in assets back to the public sector. As a result, the growth of funded systems' assets in CEE countries has been smaller in the second decade of the century and in turn, financing of future pensions will rely mainly on PAYG pension schemes. As summarized by Beblavý (2011), even if the much smaller, private pillar survives, it can no long serve as an equal or significant addition to the public system. It becomes a small supplement, and the countries effectively return to the Bismarckian character of their pension systems, that is: primarily financed by social insurance contributions, earnings-related and granted on the basis of work record, which indicate a convergence towards the character of pension systems in Western European countries. This is also confirmed by the projections in the 2018 Ageing Report (European Commission DG ECFIN 2018).

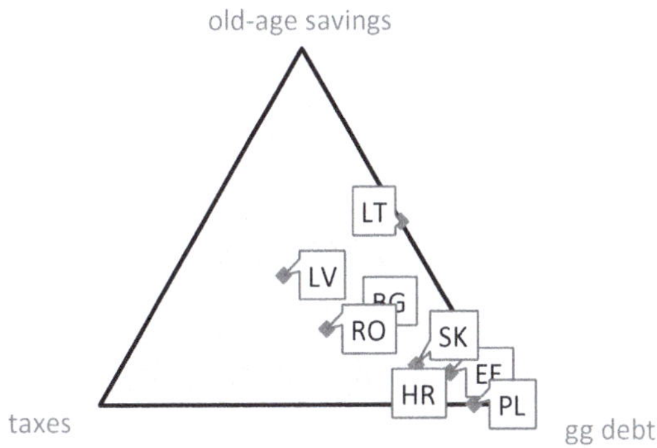

Fig. 12.2 Decomposition of sources of financing transition costs in CESE countries, 2009–2016. Note: Romania is excluded, as the multi-pillar reform was introduced in 2008. (Source: Bielawska et al. (2018) with author's update)

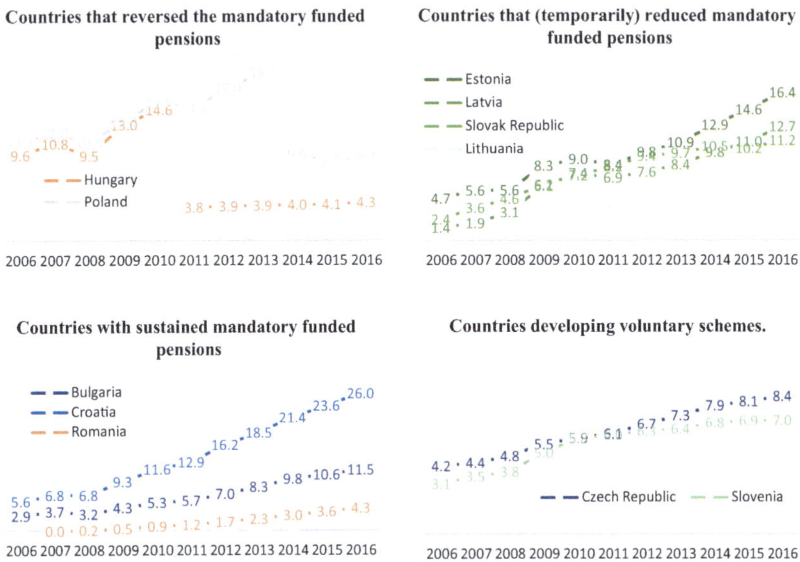

Fig. 12.3 Total investment of providers of funded and private pension arrangements in CESE countries, as a percentage of GDP, 2006–2016. Notes: The drop in investments in Hungary. 2011 comes from a pension reform which suspended payments to the mandatory individual schemes and redirected all the contributions to pay-as-you-go public pension schemes, unless workers chose to keep these individual schemes by the end of January 2011. The drop in investments in 2014 in Poland comes from the reversal of the mandatory private pension system that led to a transfer of domestic sovereign bonds held by open pension funds into the social security system. (Source: OECD Global Pension Statistics)

12.3.2 Automatic Balancing, Demographic Factors and Retirement Ages

Changes in the financing of pension systems were accompanied by other modifications that were also promoted by the EU policies. These included introducing automatic balancing mechanisms or sustainability factors as well as linking pensionable ages to life expectancy. Implementation of Non-financial Defined Contribution (NDC) systems in Latvia in Poland in 1998 and 1999 respectively means that such sustainability factors already existed in these two countries (Chłoń-Domińczak et al. 2012). Lithuania introduced an automatic balancing mechanism and Slovakia decided to introduce a system of a continuous automatic increase of the legal retirement age in line with life expectancy.

Another important sign of convergence in pension policies is the evolution of retirement ages in CESE countries, which is shown in Table 12.13.

By 2050, the retirement ages in CESE countries will reach 65 or even 67 or more (in Bulgaria, Croatia and Slovakia). While during the initial reforms, the legal retirement ages were still below the European average, the situation changed significantly after EU accession. In almost all new member states, the retirement age was also equalised for men and women. This change can be clearly attributed to the influence of the European

Table 12.13 Statutory retirement ages in CESE countries

	Male			*Female*		
	2016	*2030*	*2050*	*2016*	*2030*	*2050*
Bulgaria	65	67	67	65	67	67
Czechia	63.1	65	65	60.5	64.7	65
Estonia	63	65	65	63	65	65
Croatia	65	65	67	61.5	65	67
Latvia	62.8	65	65	62.8	65	65
Lithuania	63.3	65	65	61.7	65	65
Hungary	63.1	65	65	63.1	65	65
Poland	65	65	65	60	60	60
Romania	64.8	65	65	60.4	63	63
Slovenia	65	65	65	63	65	65
Slovakia	62	64.2	67.3	60.2	64.2	66.8

Note: Further increases in Slovakia and Estonia are expected due to the link of the retirement age with life expectancy changes

Source: European Commission DG ECFIN (2018)

policies related to achieving sustainability and adequacy of pension systems, as well as pursuing gender-equal policies. The only exceptions are Romania (where the equalisation of retirement age is being considered) and Poland. In the latter, the equalisation of retirement age to 67, adopted in 2012, was reversed in 2017 (Chłoń-Domińczak 2016).

12.4 Adequacy and Sustainability of Pension Systems in CESE Countries: Are There Commonalities?

12.4.1 Social Protection Systems and Adequacy of Old-Age Income in CESE Countries: Current Situation

The evolution of pension policies is a part of the overall development of social protection systems in CESE countries. Social protection spending[3] in CESE countries, relative to GDP, remains significantly below the EU average. In Romania, Estonia, Latvia and Lithuania it is slightly more than half of the EU figure; while in Slovenia, Croatia and Poland the difference is smaller. The gap with the EU average between 2005 and 2016 declined in Bulgaria, Estonia, Croatia, Latvia and Slovakia, while in the other countries the growth of social protection expenditure relative to GDP was below the EU average and in Hungary it was even reduced (Table 12.14).

Lower social protection spending relative to GDP is associated with lower levels of economic development, which affects the overall capacity of welfare states. However, in constant 2005 prices, the expansion of social protection expenditure in 8 out of 11 CESE countries was higher than in the EU. This growth was particularly high in Bulgaria, Romania, Estonia, Poland and Latvia (Table 12.15). These developments indicate that CESE countries are making an effort to sustain and develop their social protection systems, which in many cases grow in line with (higher than EU) economic growth.

Another "Bismarckian" feature of the social protection systems in the CESE countries is their reliance on social contributions financing. In all

[3] According to the ESSPROSS definition this includes coverage of risks and needs associated with sickness/healthcare and invalidism, disability, old-age, parental responsibilities, the loss of a spouse or parent, unemployment, housing and social exclusion. Further information is available at: https://ec.europa.eu/eurostat/statistics-explained/index.php?title=Social_protection_statistics_-_background

Table 12.14 Share of gross expenditure on social protection in total GDP in CESE countries, 2005–2016

	Percentage of GDP	*Percentage point change*						
	2005	*2008*	*2010*	*2016*	*2005–2008*	*2008–2010*	*2010–2016*	*2005–2016*
EU28	26.0	25.9	28.6	28.2	-0.1	2.7	-0.4	2.2
BG	14.7	14.7	17.0	17.5	0.0	2.3	0.5	2.8
CZ	18.0	17.9	20.0	18.9	-0.1	2.1	-1.1	0.9
EE	12.5	14.7	17.6	16.6	2.2	2.9	-1.0	4.1
HR	n.a.	18.8	21.3	21.3	n.a.	2.5	0.0	2.5
LV	12.2	12.1	18.3	15.2	-0.1	6.2	-3.1	3.0
LT	13.2	15.9	19.1	15.4	2.7	3.2	-3.7	2.2
HU	21.4	22.3	22.5	19.2	0.9	0.2	-3.3	-2.2
PL	20.0	19.3	19.7	20.3	-0.7	0.4	0.6	0.3
RO	13.4	13.7	17.4	14.6	0.3	3.7	-2.8	1.2
SI	22.6	21.0	24.4	23.3	-1.6	3.4	-1.1	0.7
SK	16.1	15.7	18.2	18.4	-0.4	2.5	0.2	2.3

Source: Eurostat, ESSPROS tables

Table 12.15 Gross expenditure on social protection in real terms (i.e. at constant 2005 prices) in CESE countries, 2005–2016

	Index, 2005 = 100			*Annual average change (%)*				
	2005	*2008*	*2010*	*2016*	*2005–2008*	*2008–2010*	*2010–2016*	*2005–2016*
EU28	100.0	106.5	115.1	122.6	2.1	4.0	1.0	1.9
BG	100.0	130.8	148.9	180.2	9.4	6.7	3.2	5.5
CZ	100.0	111.0	120.3	127.3	3.5	4.1	0.9	2.2
EE	100.0	137.4	143.4	169.3	11.2	2.1	2.8	4.9
HR		100.0	102.4	104.3		1.2	0.3	0.5
LV	100.0	122.2	147.8	152.3	6,9	9.9	0.5	3.9
LT	100.0	148.5	145.8	148.1	14.1	-0.9	0.3	3.6
HU	100.0	108.5	102.5	100.1	2.8	-2.8	-0.4	0.0
PL	100.0	115.0	124.6	153.8	4.8	4.1	3.6	4.0
RO	100.0	148.5	170.9	176.7	14.1	7.3	0.6	5.3
SI	100.0	106.6	115.1	117.6	2.2	3.9	0.4	1.5
SK	100.0	117.4	132.4	147.4	5.5	6.2	1.8	3.6

Source: Eurostat, ESSPROS tables

CESE countries, with the exception of Bulgaria, the share of social protection expenditure financed from contributions is higher than the EU average. Moreover, the reliance on social contributions increased between 2005 and 2016 in Romania, Lithuania, Hungary, Poland and Slovenia, while on average in the EU, the share of general government contributions in financing social protection increased (Fig. 12.4).

The share of pension expenditure in total social protection expenditure in the CESE countries is higher than the EU average; only in Slovenia it is at the EU average (Fig. 12.5). This indicates the existing path dependency, particularly linked to the role of pension systems in compensating the consequences of economic transition. Between 2008 and 2016 the old-age pension expenditure relative to GDP increased in ten CESE countries, with the exception of Lithuania. Yet, similarly to overall social protection expenditure, the old-age pension expenditure in relation to GDP in CESE countries remains below the EU average. In countries that were significantly affected by the crisis, pension expenditure relative to GDP experienced an increase, particularly in 2009, as their GDP levels fell.

The CESE countries also differ in terms of the ability of their pension systems to protect older people against poverty. The relative monetary poverty[4] of people 65+ is lower than the EU average in Slovakia, Hungary,

Sources of financing in 2016

	Social contributions	General government contributions	Other receipts
EU28	54.5	40.4	5.1
RO	69.8	29.3	0.8
LT	75.6	23.6	0.8
HU	69.5	30.5	0.0
PL	67.2	18.9	13.9
SI	68.2	30.6	1.2
SK	68.2	28.9	2.9
EE	78.9	21.0	0.1
CZ	73.9	24.7	1.4
LV	57.3	42.1	0.6
HR	58.7	38.5	2.8
BG	52.1	46.3	1.6

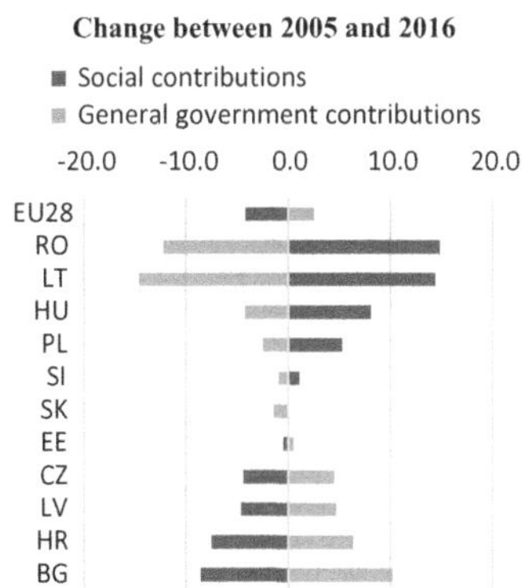

Fig. 12.4 Sources of social protection financing in 2016 and the change between 2005 and 2016 in CESE countries. (Source: Eurostat, ESSPROS tables)

[4] According to Eurostat people are considered at risk of monetary poverty when their equivalised disposable income (after social transfers) is below the at-risk-of-poverty threshold. This is set at 60% of the national median equivalised disposable income after social transfers.

Share of pension expenditure in total social protection expenditure in 2016

	2005	2008	2010	2016
EU28	38.6	39.4	39.1	40.1
BG	46.5	45.0	46.6	44.5
CZ	37.3	40.3	41.8	43.7
EE	43.1	42.3	43.6	41.5
HR		31.1	30.8	34.2
LV	45.6	43.0	51.3	47.8
LT	42.2	41.0	40.4	43.0
HU	36.5	39.4	40.3	44.5
PL	47.6	47.3	47.6	46.4
RO	39.9	46.2	46.3	50.3
SI	42.4	38.5	39.5	41.9
SK	39.1	37.1	37.5	40.1

Fig. 12.5 Old-age pension expenditure and share of pension expenditure in total social protection expenditure in CESE countries. (Source: Eurostat, ESSPROS tables)

Czechia and Poland, while it is higher in the rest of the countries, particularly Bulgaria and the Baltic states (exceeding 30%), where it is twice as high as the EU average (15%). This indicates that ensuring the adequacy of old-age income is already an important challenge for many of the new member states.

The high (and increasing) reliance on social contributions and the high share of pension expenditure in total social protection expenditure, typical for CESE countries, require further attention from policy makers, particularly in the light of increasing demographic dependency.

12.5 Outlook for the Adequacy and Sustainability of Pensions

According to Eurostat population projections from 2013, the old-age dependency ratio (number of people aged 65 and over per 100 people aged 15–64) will rise in 9 out of 11 countries in this region more than the EU average (22.4 points). In Poland and Slovakia, the dependency rate will rise by 38.5 and 35.8 points respectively (European Commission DG ECFIN 2018). By 2070, the old-age dependency ratio will exceed 60 in Poland and 55 in Slovakia, Croatia and Bulgaria (Fig. 12.6). Such population ageing will create significant pressure on the financing of old-age pensions, as well as on sustaining adequate pension benefits.

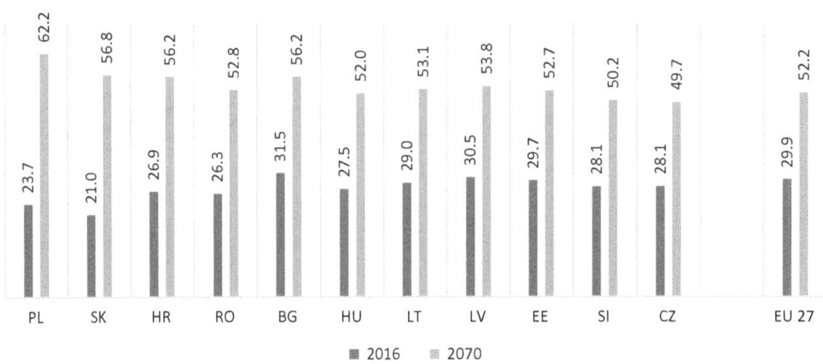

Fig. 12.6 Old age dependency ratio in CESE countries, 2016 and 2070. (Source: European Commission DG ECFIN 2018)

According to the 2018 Pension Adequacy Report (European Commission 2018), the design of pension systems in CESE countries varies, as was indicated earlier. These can be divided into two broad groups (Fig. 12.7). First, countries with limited income redistribution, where replacement rates of low wage earners are equal to those of average wage earners: Hungary, Latvia, Poland, Bulgaria and Romania. Second, countries with income redistribution, with higher relative benefits for low wage earners: Czechia, Estonia, Lithuania, Slovakia, Slovenia and Croatia. There are also differences in the theoretical replacement rates (TRRs) within those groups of countries. For the low-income earners (66% of average wage), the TRRs exceed 50% in Bulgaria, Hungary, Slovenia, Czechia and Estonia. They are below 40% in Romania, Poland, Latvia and Croatia.

The 2018 Ageing Report results show that the following CESE countries between 2007 and 2016 introduced measures to reduce the growth of pension spending in the future: Bulgaria, Czechia, Latvia, Lithuania, Hungary, Romania, Slovenia and Slovakia. Compared to the 2016 level of pension expenditure, old-age spending relative to GDP is expected to decline in Estonia, Croatia, Latvia and Poland. Sustainability of pension systems in the context of population ageing can be achieved through various measures, including raising retirement ages, increasing labour market participation or reducing benefits relative to wages. The decomposition of future old-age spending presented in Ageing Reports makes it possible to identify which of these policies contribute the most to offsetting the ageing effects (Fig. 12.8).

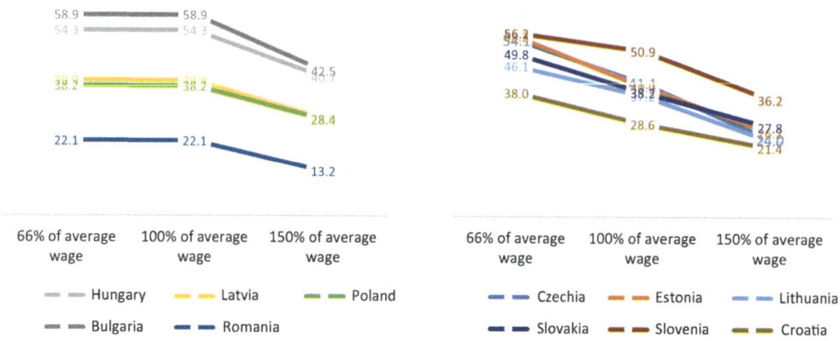

Fig. 12.7 Gross theoretical replacement rates in 2056 by wage level. (Source: European Commission 2018)

	Ageing Report edition	2007 level 2016 level	Dependency ratio contribution	Coverage ratio contribution	Labour market effect contribution	Benefit ratio contribution	Interation effect	2060 level 2070 level	Change	
BG	2009	8.3	9.1	-3.0	0.5	.9	-0.8	11.3	3.0	2007-2060
	2018	9.6	6.0	-3.0	0.2	.1	-0.3	10.9	1.3	2016-2070
CZ	2009	7.8	9.5	-3.5	0.5	.2	-1.1	11.0	3.2	2007-2060
	2018	8.2	5.4	1.9	0.0	-0.5	-0.3	10.9	2.7	2016-2070
EE	2009	5.6	4.6	1.6	0.2	.1	-0.4	4.9	-0.7	2007-2060
	2018	8.1	4.6	-3.0	0.2	.0	-0.7	6.4	-1.7	2016-2070
HR	2009									2007-2060
	2018	10.6	6.3	-3.3	1.5	.9	-0.4	6.8	-3.8	2016-2070
LV	2009	5.4	5.7	1.6	0.2	.9	-0.4	5.1	-0.3	2007-2060
	2018	7.4	4.4	.4	0.5	.7	-0.5	4.7	-2.7	2016-2070
LT	2009	6.8	9.6	-2.4	0.0	.8	-0.8	11.4	4.6	2007-2060
	2018	6.9	5.0	1.8	0.3	.0	-0.6	5.2	-1.7	2016-2070
HU	2009	10.9	1.3	-5.4	0.7	.1	-1.0	13.8	2.9	2007-2060
	2018	9.7	6.4	1.8	1.1	.6	-0.3	11.2	1.5	2016-2070
PL	2009	11.6		-6.3	1.0	.1	-1.8	8.8	-2.8	2007-2060
	2018	11.2	.7	-3.0	0.4	.1	-1.2	10.2	-1.0	2016-2070
RO	2009	6.6		-4.9	0.3	.7	-1.5	15.8	9.2	2007-2060
	2018	8.0	5.6	1.7	0.1	.6	-0.5	8.7	0.7	2016-2070
SI	2009	9.9		-3.5	0.1	-0.7	-0.7	18.6	8.7	2007-2060
	2018	10.9	7.5	-2.1	0.7	-0.3	-0.5	14.9	4.0	2016-2070
SK	2009	6.8	.7	-3.9	0.6	.4	-1.4	10.2	3.4	2007-2060
	2018	8.6	8.8	-4.1	1.2	.5	-0.2	13.9	5.3	2016-2070

Fig. 12.8 Decomposition of changes in old-age pension expenditure in 2009 and 2018 Ageing Reports. (Source: Author's analysis based on European Commission DG ECFIN (2018) and European Commission DG ECFIN (2009)

The decomposition of the changes in the old-age pension expenditure indicates that in the majority of countries, the main policy measure to maintain the sustainability of pension systems is the raising of the retirement age (measured by the contribution of the coverage ratio). Hungary, Poland, Slovenia and Slovakia also aim to introduce labour market reforms enhancing the labour market participation of those of working age, particularly women. The benefit ratio contribution, indicating reduced adequacy of future pensions, is noticeable in Poland (which predominantly reflects the lower retirement age of women), but also Latvia and Lithuania, which is consistent with the projections of theoretical replacement ratios.

Summarising, population ageing is an important context for the future sustainability and adequacy of pension systems in CESE countries. After the rebalancing of multi-pillar pension systems, the public pay-as-you-go pension systems will be the main source of income for future pensioners. The design of pension systems, current and future expenditure as well as benefits differ between the countries, which show the diversity of pension system designs in the CESE countries and different approaches to maintaining their sustainability and adequacy in the future.

12.6 Conclusions

The process of pension system reforms in the countries in Central, Eastern and Southern Europe is embedded in broader economic, social and political changes that these countries faced over the past three decades. During the economic transition, pension systems were used to compensate workers caught up in the transformation of the labour market, mainly through broad access to early retirement. This led to a rapid growth in pension expenditure, despite the relative youth of populations in these countries, compared to Western Europe.

The wave of pension reforms in the late 1990s and the beginning of the century aimed to break with the path dependency and introduce multi-pillar pension systems, with the support of transnational institutions, advocating for market-oriented pension reforms. These reforms required a long-term commitment to meet the transition costs of accumulating pension savings, while at the same time paying pensions to current pensioners. The implementation of these reforms continued during the period of the EU accession. The new member states embraced the goals of the social open method of coordination, with a distinct model for financing future pensions.

The need to meet EU fiscal conditions, particularly during the economic and financial crisis, placed a significant challenge on the multi-pillar pension models. Many of the CESE countries decided to scale down or modify their reforms and return to the dominant pay-as-you-go financing of future pensions, typical of Bismarckian pension systems. However, these were not reversals to the pension systems as they were before, but rather to the more modern PAYG-financed schemes with modified rules (raised retirement ages and often, closer links between contributions and benefits, such as in NDC schemes in Poland and Latvia, or point systems, as in Slovakia).

The fiscal situation was one of the strongest drivers behind decisions to step back from the initial design of the multi-pillar schemes. A weak political consensus on reform priorities and a lack of strong national fiscal rules diluted the initial concept of financing the transition cost. As a result, rising fiscal pressures led to decisions to scale down or effectively eliminate the funded components and return to pension financing based fully or predominantly on a PAYG basis. Another important trigger for these decisions was compliance with the Stability and Growth Pact rules after EU accession, particularly after 2008, when the financial and fiscal crisis hit. This, combined with the end of the transition treatment of pension funds' assets as a part of the public system, provided further arguments for the opponents of multi-pillar systems to reduce or close down the mandatory funded components.

At the same time, exposure to European social policies led to significant progress in setting retirement ages. An increase in the retirement age and its equalisation for men and women was one of the key veto points during the initial reform discussions. Exposure to European discussions led to convergence with EU policies—retirement ages are gradually equalising and increasing in all countries, with the exception of Poland and Romania.

Analysis of current and future pension expenditure trends and benefit levels shows that the pension systems in the CESE countries are contribution based, linked to earnings and employment history. However, there are significant differences in pension expenditure and benefit ratios. This means that the design of pension systems in CESE countries today remain quite different.

The latest projections of benefit adequacy (measured by TRR) and financial sustainability indicate that most of the CESE countries still struggle with challenges. In six countries, the projected TRRs fall below 40% for average earners and, at the same time, in two of them (Poland and Slovakia), pension expenditure by 2070 is forecast to be over 10% of GDP. In four countries the benefits are expected to be higher, but at the same time, pension spending is also forecast to remain at a high level of more than 10% of GDP. Only in Estonia is pension spending forecast to remain below 10%, with a projected TRR of over 40% (Table 12.16).

Table 12.16 Adequacy and sustainability of pension systems in CEE countries

	TRR (average earner) below 40%	*TRR (average earner) above 40%*
Pension spending in 2070 above 10% of GDP	**PL, SK**	BG, CZ, HU, SI
Pension spending in 2070 below 10% of GDP	HR, LV, LT, RO	EE

Source: Own analysis based on Figs. 12.7 and 12.8

This means that the history of pension reforms in the region is far from over and that further efforts will be needed to maintain sustainability and adequacy. Achieving such goals will require not only policy developments in the area of pensions, but also a life course perspective, including education policies stimulating development of high-quality human capital, as well as labour markets that fully utilise the potential of workers and lead to high employment rates. Policy debates at the EU level are likely to continue to exert a significant influence on national developments.

Acknowledgements I would like to thank István P. Székely from DG ECFIN and Michał Rutkowski, Robert Palacios and Melis Gvuen from World Bank for their comments to the earlier version of this chapter.

References

Barr, N. (1994). *Labour Markets and Social Policy in Central and Eastern Europe. The Transition and Beyond.* London: Oxford University Press.

Beblavý, M. (2011). *Why Has the Crisis Been Bad for Private Pensions, But Good for the Flat Tax? The Sustainability of 'Neoliberal' Reforms in the New EU Member States* (CEPS Working Document).

Bielawska, K., Chłoń-Domińczak, A., & Stańko, D. (2017). *Retreat from Mandatory Pension Funds in Countries of the Eastern and Central Europe in Result of Financial and Fiscal Crisis: Causes, Effects and Recommendations for Fiscal Rules.* Instytut Zarządzania Ryzykiem Społecznym.

Bielawska, K., Chłoń-Domińczak, A., & Stańko, D. (2018). *Retreat from Mandatory Pension Funds in Countries of the Eastern and Central Europe in Result of Financial and Fiscal Crisis: Causes and Effects.* Paper Presented at 2018 ASSA Meeting in Philadelphia.

Cerami, A. (2010). The Politics of Social Security Reforms in the Czech Republic, Hungary, Poland and Slovakia. In B. Palier (Ed.), *A Long Goodbye to Bismarck?*

The Politics of Welfare Reform in Continental Europe (pp. 233–253). Amsterdam University Press. Retrieved from http://dare.uva.nl/cgi/arno/show.cgi?fid=183117.

Chłoń, A. (2000). *Pension Reform and Public Information in Poland* (World Bank SP Discussion Paper).

Chłoń-Domińczak, A. (2016). *Reversing the 2013 Retirement Age Reform in Poland*. ESPN Flash Report.

Chłoń-Domińczak, A., Franco, D., & Palmer, E. (2012). The First Wave of NDC Reforms: The Experiences of Italy, Latvia, Poland, and Sweden. In R. Holzmann & E. Palmer (Eds.), *Nonfinancial Defined Contribution Pension Schemes in a Changing Pension World* (pp. 31–84). The World Bank. https://doi.org/10.1596/9780821388488_CH02.

Datz, G., & Dancsi, K. (2013). The Politics of Pension Reform Reversal: A Comparative Analysis of Hungary and Argentina. *East European Politics*. https://doi.org/10.1080/21599165.2012.759940.

Esping-Andersen, G. (1990). *The Three Worlds of Welfare Capitalism*. Princeton: Princeton University Press.

European Commission. (2018). *Pension Adequacy Report 2018: Current and Future Income Adequacy in Old Age in the EU* (Volume 2 – Country Profiles (Vol. II)). Luxembourg: Publications Office of the European Union. https://doi.org/10.2767/1907.

European Commission DG ECFIN. (2009). The 2009 Ageing Report: Economic and Budgetary Projections for the EU-27 Member States (2008–2060). *European Economy, 2*, 27. https://doi.org/10.2765/80301.

European Commission DG ECFIN. (2018). *The 2018 Ageing Report. Economic & Budgetary Projections for the 28 EU Member States (2016–2070)* (European Economy Institutional Paper No. 079). https://doi.org/10.2765/615631.

Fultz, E., & Stanovnik, T. (2004). *Collection of Pension Contributions: Trends, Issues and Problems in Central and Eastern Europe*. Budapest: International Labour Office Subregional Office for Central and Eastern Europe.

Grech, A. G. (2018). What Makes Pension Reforms Sustainable. *Sustainability (Switzerland), 10*(8). https://doi.org/10.3390/su10082891.

Guardiancich, I. (2009). *Pension Reforms in Central, Eastern and Southeastern Europe: Legislation, Implementation and Sustainability*. Doctoral thesis, European University Institute. https://doi.org/10.2870/1700.

Han, T., & Stańko, D. (2018). *2018 Update One IOPS Work on Fees and Charges* (IOPS Working Papers on Effective Pension Supervision No. 32 OECD). Paris.

Heneghan, M., & Orenstein, M. A. (2019). Organizing for Impact: International Organizations and Global Pension Policy. *Global Social Policy*, 146801811983473. https://doi.org/10.1177/1468018119834730.

Ionescu, L., & Robles, E. A. (2014). *Update of IOPS Work on Fees and Charges* (20).

Jacoby, W. (2008). Minority Traditions and Post-Communist Politics: How Do IGOs Matter? In M. A. Orenstein, S. Bloom, & N. Lindstrom (Eds.), *Transnational Actors in Central and East European Transitions*. Pittsburgh: University of Pittsburgh Press.

Kvist, J., & Saari, J. (Eds.). (2007). *The Europeanisation of Social Protection*. Bristol: Bristol University Press. https://doi.org/10.2307/j.ctt9qgx97.

Müller, K. (1999). *The Political Economy of Pension Reform in Central-Eastern Europe*. Cheltenham: Edward Elgar Publishing Limited.

Müller, K. (2003). *Privatising Old-Age Security: Latin America and Eastern Europe Compared*. Aldershot: Edward Elgar Publishing Limited.

Orenstein, M. A. (2008). *Privatising Pensions: The Transnational Campaign for Social Security Reform*. Princeton: Princeton University Press.

Palacios, R., & Whitehouse, E. (1998). *The Role of Choice in the Transition to a Funded Pension System* (Social Protection Discussion Paper Series No. 9812), pp.1–8. https://doi.org/10.5897/JAERD12.088.

Pierson, P. (2001). Austerity: Coping with Permanent in Affluent Welfare State Restructuring Democracies. *The New Politics of the Welfare State*, 410–457. https://doi.org/10.1093/0198297564.003.0014.

Schwarz, A., & Arias, O. (2014). *The Inverting Pyramid. Pension Systems Facing Demographic Challenges in Europe and Central Asia*. Washington, DC: World Bank.

Sobotka, T. (2003). Re-Emerging Diversity: Rapid Fertility Changes in Central and Eastern Europe After the Collapse of the Communist Regimes. *Population (English Edition), 58*(4–5), 451–486. https://doi.org/10.2307/3246652.

World Bank. (1994). *Averting the Old Age Crisis: Policies to Protect the Old and Promote Growth*. Washington, DC: World Bank. Retrieved from http://documents.worldbank.org/curated/en/973571468174557899/Averting-the-old-age-crisis-policies-to-protect-the-old-and-promote-growth.

Wóycicka, I., & Grabowski, M. (2007). Poland – Redefining Social Policies. In J. Kvist & J. Saari (Eds.), *The Europeanisation of Social Protection*. Bristol: Bristol University Press. https://doi.org/10.2307/j.ctt9qgx97.

Index[1]

[1] Note: Page numbers followed by 'n' refer to notes.

M. Landesmann, I. P. Székely (eds.), *Does EU Membership Facilitate Convergence? The Experience of the EU's Eastern Enlargement - Volume II*, Studies in Economic Transition, https://doi.org/10.1007/978-3-030-57702-5

The manufacturer's authorised representative in the EU is Springer Nature Customer Service Centre GmbH, Europaplatz 3, 69115 Heidelberg, Germany. If you have any concerns regarding our products, please contact ProductSafety@springernature.com

Printed and bound by CPI Group (UK) Ltd, Croydon, CR0 4YY
22/09/2026
02221062-0002